*SEARCHES & SEIZURES,*

*ARRESTS AND CONFESSIONS*

# *SEARCHES & SEIZURES, ARRESTS AND CONFESSIONS*

*by*

*WILLIAM E. RINGEL*



Clark Boardman Company, Ltd.
New York, New York
1972

Library of Congress Catalog Number: 70–186243
ISBN: 87632–079–5

Fourth Printing, April 1977

*TO MY WIFE, IRMA*

# FOREWORD

This book is the culmination of many years of research and work by the author. It is a revised and expanded edition of an earlier work by Judge Ringel published in pamphlet form. While the focus of this book is on the law of search and seizure, other areas which have been affected and are closely related are also treated.

It is hoped, and believed, that this book will be of assistance to the legal profession.

Recognizing the fact that this field is ever changing, the author and the publisher plan to keep this work up-to-date with annual supplementations.

The author, Judge William E. Ringel, retired at the end of 1971 as a Judge of the Criminal Court of the City of New York after 32 years.

During his extensive service as a Judge, he has presided in every Criminal Court of the State of New York including the Magistrate's Court, Court of Special Sessions, Court of General Sessions, County Court and Supreme Court.

He has written and lectured extensively on criminal law and is regarded as an authority in this field. As *The New York Times* (Aug. 4, 1971) said of him, "Criminal Court Judge William E. Ringel, author of legal textbooks [is] regarded by lawyers and fellow judges alike as a sharp spoken and able magistrate."

Among Judge Ringel's previous publications are *Legal and Illegal Searches; Arrests, Searches and Confessions, Obscenity Law Today; Identification and Police Lineups,* in addition to numerous articles for various legal publications.

JUSTIN D. FRANKLIN, JR.
*Editor,*
Clark Boardman Company, Ltd.

New York, New York
February, 1972

# CONTENTS

## INTRODUCTION

The Fourth Amendment to the United States Constitution protects the people against unreasonable searches and seizures. The Amendment is not self-enforcing and it was not until 1914 that teeth were put into it when the Supreme Court promulgated its exclusionary rule barring from use as evidence in federal prosecutions evidence obtained in violation of the Amendment's provisions.

Nearly half a century later, in 1961, the same rule was made applicable to the states by virtue of the Fifth Amendment and the Due Process Clause of the Fourteenth Amendment.

The rationale behind these decisions is based on the doctrine of basic legal fairness and not on any procedural violations implicitly interdicted by the provisions of the other amendments contained in the Bill of Rights.

The scope of the application of the Fourth Amendment has always been the subject of much debate in which the Supreme Court itself has been involved. As a result, that learned Court has discarded, then reaffirmed previously held concepts in this controversial field. Therefore, the need for a definitive work on searches and seizures is indicated.

I have set forth in Chapter 1 a review of the judicial history of the Fourth Amendment. This should enable the student to obtain a true perspective of the development and present interpretation of its provisions.

As will be noted, the waves caused by the 1961 Supreme Court decision in *Mapp v. Ohio* have washed up onto other shores. Thus, we find the law of confessions and admissions, self-incrimination, identification, stop and frisk, etc., also affected. For example, admissions obtained as a result of a police trespass are excludable. Accordingly, several chapters of this book are devoted to these affected areas.

The *Mapp* decision created considerable furor. Those who preach "law and order" decry it. The civil libertarians praise it. The former cite the late Mr. Justice Cardoza who would not free a defendant because the "constable erred." The latter insist that the constable obey the law of the land. No matter

—the courts are caught in the middle or muddle, depending on one's point of view.

The resolution of the "middle-muddle" problem is not aided by the seemingly ambivalent nature of certain Supreme Court decisions as to the application and scope of permissible reasonable searches. Thus, the area of the permissible reasonable search conducted as incident to a lawful arrest has been severely restricted. Previously the Supreme Court had held that such an incident search could lawfully include one's apartment or office. Now such search is restricted to the suspect's person and the area within his easy reach—the arm's length rule.

So, too, a search for "mere evidence," long condemned, has now been approved by the Supreme Court in a case of close pursuit. Likewise the right to stop and frisk suspects in non-sumptuary offenses has also received the imprimatur of approval by the same Court.

Evidence obtained by eavesdropping without trespass, previously held admissible, has now been condemned on the theory that the Fourth Amendment protects people, not places.

The sanctity previously accorded the curtilage area has also been modified by the "probable cause" theory in search and seizure cases and in cases involving apartment houses.

The authority of local governments to inspect residential and business structures without a search warrant under their police powers for the protection of health and safety has been abrogated. Now warrants are required, absent special circumstances.

Similarly, the right of customs inspectors to conduct border searches of the person of suspects has been modified. But the seizure of blood from a suspect in a drunken driving case is approved.

So, too, the authority to seize obscene material, without a warrant and without prior judicial scrutiny and absent a prior adversary proceeding as to motion pictures, has been curtailed even though that material is contraband. Seizure of obscene pictures kept in the privacy of one's home has likewise been proscribed as violative of the First Amendment.

The right to the presence of counsel at police lineup and

identification proceedings has been approved since they are deemed to be critical stages of a criminal proceeding.

The Fourth Amendment was originally interpreted as barring all searches without a search warrant. Subsequently, the Supreme Court held that the search warrant was not a sine qua non to a lawful search. However, in 1967, that Court came full circle in holding that all searches without a warrant were unlawful with certain exceptions.

A study of Supreme Court decisions on constitutional law raises many questions. How fixed is the law? Does it depend on the mortality tables of the Supreme Court? Whatever the answers to these questions may be, there is no gainsaying the fact that the Fourth Amendment tops the list of litigated problems that have been before the Supreme Court in the last decade. Students of the Court do not anticipate the same situation will occur during the life of the present Burger Court as existed in its predecessor, the Warren Court. Time will tell.

It would be helpful to the Bench and the Bar if the Supreme Court announced in advance what radical changes in practice and theory it would condemn—a practice utilized in England. This practice would avoid catching litigants flat-footed because they relied on the "old" law and would avoid the necessity of retrials.

However, it is not the purpose of this book to examine the philosophy of the changes of constitutional concepts as enunciated by our courts. Rather, its purpose is to set forth the law as presently interpreted by the courts.

I wish to express my thanks to Elliott L. Biskind, Esq., for his many valuable suggestions. I also wish to thank Justin D. Franklin, Jr., Esq., editor for my publisher, for his assistance in preparing this manuscript and for his helpful suggestions.

My thanks also to Philip Parker, Esq., for his valued assistance in checking many of my citations.

Last, but not least, my thanks to my dear wife, Irma, for the careful task of proofreading on which she spent so many arduous hours.

William E. Ringel

New York, New York
January, 1972

# CONTENTS OF CHAPTERS

## Chapter 1

## THE JUDICIAL HISTORY OF THE FOURTH AMENDMENT



## Chapter 2

## THE EXCLUSIONARY RULE



## Chapter 3

## SELF-INCRIMINATION

## Chapter 4

## ESCOBEDO AND MIRANDA: POISONED OR TAINTED EVIDENCE—RIGHT TO COUNSEL

## Chapter 5

## POLICE LINEUPS AND IDENTIFICATION

## Chapter 6

## JOINT TRIALS



## Chapter 7

## VOLUNTARY CONFESSIONS AND ADMISSIONS

## Chapter 8

## DISCOVERY AND INSPECTION

## Chapter 9

## DISTINCTION BETWEEN SEARCH AND SEIZURE



## Chapter 10

## REASONABLE SEARCH AND SEIZURE



## Chapter 11

## PROBABLE CAUSE

## Chapter 12

## SEARCH AND ARREST WARRANTS



## Chapter 13

## ARREST WITHOUT A WARRANT

## Chapter 14

## SEARCH INCIDENT TO LAWFUL ARREST



## Chapter 15

## SEARCH ON CONSENT



## Chapter 16

## SEARCH BY GOVERNMENT OFFICERS AND AGENTS

## Chapter 17

## ABANDONED PROPERTY AND OPEN FIELDS



## Chapter 18

## EXIGENT CIRCUMSTANCES AND HOT PURSUIT



## Chapter 19

## STOP AND FRISK



## Chapter 20

## CURTILAGE

## Chapter 21

## SEARCH OF MOTOR VEHICLES



## Chapter 22

## SEARCH AND SEIZURE OF OBSCENE MATERIAL

## CONTENTS OF CHAPTERS

### Chapter 23

### EAVESDROPPING



### Chapter 24

### THE INFORMER



### Chapter 25

### THE MOTION TO SUPPRESS

# *SEARCHES & SEIZURES, ARRESTS AND CONFESSIONS*

# Chapter 1

## THE JUDICIAL HISTORY OF THE FOURTH AMENDMENT



---

**§ 1. Introduction to Judicial History of Fourth Amendment.** The landmark decision of *Mapp v. Ohio* (1961), 367 US 643, reinforced by *Ker v. California* (1963), 374 US 23, was followed by an avalanche of Supreme Court decisions, which gave new, and what seemed to many, radical interpretations of the various Amendments contained in the Bill of Rights. Most of these cases centered around the Fourth Amendment.

The importance of the Fourth Amendment is exemplified by the fact that hardly a term of the Supreme Court passes today without resulting in some decision in the area of search and seizure.

The Fourth Amendment reads:

> "The right of the people to be secure in their person, houses, papers, and effects, against unreasonable searches and seizures, shall not be violated, and no Warrants shall issue, but upon probable cause, supported by Oath, or affirmation, and particularly describing the place to be searched and the persons or things to be seized."

No real understanding of this Amendment and its development through judicial interpretation is possible without a review of its historical background. This will be found in

English as well as American history, with particular emphasis on its English precedents. In fact, many Supreme Court decisions were based on the court's interpretation of the historical events which led to the adoption of the Fourth Amendment, highlighted in Mr. Justice Frankfurter's opinions. The adoption of this Amendment, it was held, was inspired by the desire of the Founding Fathers and their constituents to establish real safeguards against a recurrence of the arbitrary searches and seizures that occurred in the Colonies prior to the Revolution and which even continued in England after that time. The concept of a man's home being his castle prompted the drafters of the Constitution to try to keep it that way.

"We have examined on many occasions the history and purposes of the [Fourth] Amendment." *Warden v. Hayden* (1967), 387 US 294. *See: Stanford v. Texas* (1965), 379 US 476, 481–485; *Marcus v. Search Warrant* (1961), 367 US 717, 724–729; *Frank v. Maryland,* (1959), 359 US 360, 363–365; Lasson, *The History and Development of the Fourth Amendment* (1937); Landynski, *Search and Seizure and the Supreme Court* (1966).

"It [the Fourth Amendment] was a reaction to the evils of the use of the general warrant in England and the writs of assistance in the Colonies, and was intended to protect against invasions of 'the sanctity of a man's home and the privacies of life,' *Boyd v. United States,* 116 US 616, 630, from searches under indiscriminate general authority. Protection of these interests was assured by prohibiting all 'unreasonable' searches and seizures, and by requiring the use of warrants, which particularly describe 'the place to be searched, and the persons or things to be seized'." *Warden v. Hayden* (1967), 387 US 294, 301.

**§ 2. The Stationers Company and Writs of Assistance.** In both the Colonies and in England judicially unsupervised searches were rampant. These searches started in England during the reign of the Tudors under a system of state licensing of printers ostensibly to control "undesirable" publications. The enforcement of this licensing provision was given to the Stationers Company, a private printing guild, with broad powers "to make search whenever it shall please them in any place * * * within our kingdom of England * * * and to seize, take hold, burn * * * those books and things which are or shall be printed contrary to the form of any statute, act or proclamation." Landynski, *Search and Seizure and the Supreme Court,* p. 21; Arber, *A Transcript of the Registers of the Company of Registers of London* (London 1875, Vol. I, p. xxxi). The notorious Star Chamber was one of the tribunals selected for handling these matters.

Later, probably during the reign of James I, Writs of Assistance came into being.

These writs were nothing more than general search warrants and were aimed at discovering and seizing smuggled goods. The name was derived from the language which directed all the King's officers to assist in their execution.

In spite of landmark decisions in England such as *Entick v. Carrington* (1765), 19 Howells State Trials 1029, Writs of Assistance were used rather extensively in the Colonies by customs officials to ferret out and prevent smuggling. They were in effect, permanent search warrants, which could be executed at the discretion of the officer during the life of the Sovereign. *(Quincey's* [*Gray*] *Massachusetts Reports,* 1761–1772, App 1, pp. 395–540.) The Colonists' opposition to their use continued right up to the Revolutionary War.

It is not surprising, therefore, that several of the Colonies adopted provisions in their constitutions proscribing such general warrants and general searches and seizures (*see, e.g.,* Art. XIV, Massachusetts Declaration of Rights [1780] ).

With the adoption of the United States Constitution, the Fourth Amendment became enshrined in our Bill of Rights (1791).

The Amendment guarantees freedom from "unreasonable" searches and specifies the conditions under which a lawful search warrant may be issued. However, it is to be noted that nowhere does the Amendment contain a definition of the term "unreasonable."

Nor does the Amendment or any other provision of the Constitution or Bill of Rights mention anything with respect to the interplay of the Fourth Amendment with any other Amendment (*e.g.,* the First, Fifth, Sixth and Fourteenth

Amendments). The existence of such interplay is a result of judicial interpretation.

Nor does the Fourth Amendment contain any exceptions to the search without a warrant. Such exceptions as we have today also were evolved by judicial interpretation, *e.g.*, moving vehicles, (*Carroll v. U.S.* (1925), 267 US 132), and search incident to a lawful arrest, (*Cooper v. California* (1967), 386 US 58; *Abel v. U.S.* (1960), 362 US 217).

It is also clear from the history of the Amendment and its adoption that its proscriptions were aimed at wrongful acts of the government and its officers acting in their official capacities, and not against a private person not acting on or in behalf of any governmental agency or officer. It was only official lawlessness that the Amendment sought to guard against. *Burdeau v. McDowell* (1921), 256 US 465.

As originally interpreted, the Amendment did not apply to the several states. *Wolf v. Colorado* (1948), 338 US 25; *Mapp v. Ohio* (1961), 367 US 643.

However, it was intended to apply and protect against arbitrary arrests. *Ex parte Burford* (1806), 3 Cranch 448; *Giordenello v. U.S.* (1958), 357 US 480, 485–486.

As to searches, not all searches are invalid—only the "unreasonable" ones.

## § 3. Judicial Development.

**§ 3.01. The Fourth Amendment Defined: Interplay with Fifth Amendment.** *Boyd v. U.S.* (1886), 116 US 616, was the first case of any importance involving the Fourth Amendment. It started the chain of definitive interpretations of the Fourth Amendment by the United States Supreme Court, a process still in evolution. Though *Boyd* has been somewhat modified, it is still regarded as a landmark decision and "the leading case on the subject of search and seizure." *Carroll v. U.S.* (1925), 267 US 132.

Briefly stated, *Boyd* was a civil action brought by the government to declare forfeit 35 cases of plate glass alleged to have been imported by the Boyd brothers in violation of the customs laws. The district court judge issued a subpoena directing the Boyds to produce an invoice covering a prior shipment of glass. Use of this invoice in the trial was essential to prove the government's case. The Boyds complied with the subpoena under protest. A verdict in favor of the government was rendered and the 35 cases of plate glass were forfeited. The United States Supreme Court reversed. Relying to a large extent on *Entick v. Carrington* (1765), 19 Howells State Trials 1029, the Court made the following pronouncements:

1. A forfeiture proceeding comes within the ambit of the Fourth Amendment and is equated with a criminal or penal proceeding. This is true even though the action is civil in form and the rule applies whether the action is *in rem* or *in personam.*

2. The unlawful seizure or compulsory production of a man's private books or papers to be used in evidence against him is equivalent to compelling him to be a witness against himself, and whether it be a prosecution for a crime, penalty or forfeiture, it is violative of the Fifth Amendment.

3. Compulsory production of a party's private books and papers to be used against himself or his property, in a criminal or penal proceeding, or for a forfeiture, constitutes an unreasonable search and seizure, within the meaning and spirit of the Fourth Amendment. Unreasonable searches and seizures are not limited to actual entry upon constitutionally protected areas.

4. Both the Fourth and Fifth Amendments should be liberally construed. Both amendments relate to the personal security of the citizen. They nearly run into each other.

> "They throw great light on each other. For the 'unreasonable searches and seizures' condemned in the Fourth Amendment are almost always made for the purpose of compelling a man to give evidence against himself, which in criminal cases is condemned in the Fifth Amendment; and compelling a man 'in a criminal case to be a witness against himself,' which is condemned in the Fifth Amendment, throws light on the question as to what is an 'unreasonable search and seizure' within the meaning of the Fourth Amendment. And we have been unable to perceive that the seizure of a man's private books and papers to be used in evidence against him is substantially differ-

> ent from compelling him to be a witness against himself. We think it is within the clear intent and meaning of those terms." *Boyd,* 116 US at 633.

**§ 3.02. The Federal Exclusionary Rule.** The Supreme Court reaffirmed its holding in *Boyd* in the case of *Weeks v. U.S.* (1914), 232 US 383, and put teeth into the Fourth Amendment's prohibitions.

*Weeks* involved the unlawful seizure of certain items from Weeks' apartment without a warrant by a United States Marshal. Some of the items seized were returned to him. Before trial, Weeks moved for a return of the remainder. The court directed the prosecution to return only those items not required for the trial. Obviously, the items retained were the fruits of an unlawful search and seizure. Weeks was thereafter convicted and jailed for the illegal transmission of lottery tickets through the mails.

In reversing the conviction, the Court said:

> "This protection [of the Fourth Amendment] reaches all alike, whether accused of crime or not, and the duty of giving to it force and effect is obligatory upon all entrusted under our Federal system with the enforcement of the laws." *Weeks,* 232 US 383, 392.

Thus, where timely application, *i.e.,* before trial, is made for a return of items seized unlawfully, the application will be granted and the items seized will be excluded from evidence in a federal criminal prosecution.

The Court held further that it is the duty of the court to inquire and determine the source of proffered evidence.

If the evidence was obtained unlawfully by federal officers, it will be excluded from evidence in a federal prosecution.

The Fourth Amendment is not directed to the individual misconduct of state officers. Its limitations reach the federal government and its agencies.

Thus did the "Weeks Exclusionary Rule" implement the Fourth Amendment. *Cf. Adams v. New York* (1904), 192 US 585.

In *Silverthorne Lumber Company v. U.S.* (1920), 251 US

385, the Supreme Court amplified the *Weeks* doctrine. Silverthorne and his son were indicted by a federal grand jury and while in detention, federal officers ransacked their office, "without a shadow of authority" and "made a clean sweep of all the books, papers and documents found there." The government made copies and photographs of these seized documents and a new indictment was obtained based thereon. A motion for the return of the original documents was granted but the government was permitted to retain the copies. The Silverthornes refused to obey a subpoena calling for production of the originals. The son was imprisoned for contempt and the company was fined.

In reversing, the Supreme Court ruled that the government may not exploit its own illegal act. The original seizure of petitioner's papers, being unlawful under a void writ, precluded the government's use of copies. "The essence of a provision forbidding the acquisition of evidence in a certain way is that not merely evidence so acquired shall not be used before the Court but that it shall not be used at all." 251 US at 392.

*See also: Wong Sun v. U.S.* (1963), 371 US 471; *People v. Rodriguez,* 11 NY2d 279, 183 NE2d 651.

Further, the Court held that a corporation also comes within the protection of the Fourth Amendment, but this protection, however, does not extend to the Fifth Amendment. *U.S. v. Kordel* (1970), 397 US 1, 90 SC 763, 25 L Ed2d 1. It reiterated one of the rules laid down in *Weeks,* to wit, that the defense of a Fourth Amendment violation must be raised before trial.

However, in *Gouled v. U.S.,* 255 US 298, the Court modified *Weeks* and *Silverthorne* by authorizing a motion for a Fourth Amendment violation to be made during trial, where the violation was not discovered by the defendant until the trial itself. In *Gouled,* a friend of his surreptitiously removed certain incriminating documents from his apartment, at the behest of the government, during the course of an ostensible social call. It was not until the trial itself was under way that Gouled learned of the theft. The rule requiring exclusion motions to be made before trial was to prevent excursions into collateral matters by the trial court. The Court in *Gouled* held, however, that such motions would be entertained during trial where justice and necessity demand it. "A rule of practice must not be allowed for any technical reason to prevail over a constitutional right." 255 US at 313.

The *Gouled* rule was subsequently adopted by the Federal Courts. Fed R Crim P 41[e]. New York has a similar statute. CPL art. 710. *See also: Amos v. U.S.* (1921), 255 US 313, in which the motion was held to be timely when made immediately after the jury had been sworn, but before any testimony had been taken. *Cf. Segurola v. U.S.* (1927), 275 US 106.

*Gouled* also held that entry into the apartment "obtained by stealth instead of by force or coercion," absent consent by the aggrieved party, constituted an unconstitutional search.

In *Amos* (1921), 255 US 313, petitioner's wife allowed government agents to enter his home without a warrant upon their demand for admission for the purpose of making a search. They found some contraband liquor in his bed. The wife's act in permitting the entrance is not deemed a waiver of his constitutional privilege against unreasonable searches and seizures, even assuming that a wife may waive her husband's rights under the Fourth Amendment. The search and seizure were found to be unconstitutional as violative of both the Fourth and Fifth Amendments.

However, the *Weeks* exclusionary rule does not apply where an unlawful search and seizure has been committed by a private person and where neither the federal government nor its agents have participated in the violation. *Burdeau v. McDowell* (1921), 256 US 465. Excluding evidence unlawfully seized by federal officers from a federal prosecution was aimed at deterring federal officers from violating the rights of individuals under the Fourth Amendment.

In *Burdeau,* the defendant's private safe was blown open and certain incriminating letters and papers were taken from it and from his desk. One of these letters was turned over to the federal authorities for prosecution on a mail fraud charge. McDowell was an officer in a private company and had been discharged for fraud. The search and seizure complained of was perpetrated by his successor.

McDowell, fearing an indictment based on the purloined papers, obtained an injunction from the district court against their use before the grand jury. However, the injunction was set aside on the ground that the Fourth Amendment is a restraint on the unlawful acts of the Government and is inapplicable to private persons, (Justice Holmes and Brandeis dissented in *Burdeau*).

**§ 4. The Silver Platter Doctrine.** As indicated in *Weeks* and *Burdeau,* the exclusionary rule was applicable to those federal prosecutions where evidence was illegally obtained by federal officers. The rule was not applicable where private persons or state officers committed the unlawful seizures.

"The right of the federal government to avail itself of evidence improperly seized by state officers operating upon their own account" has been deemed proper. *Byars v. U.S.* (1927), 273 US 28. The Fourth Amendment, as originally conceived, was not intended to govern the acts of the officers of the several states (*Barron v. Baltimore* (1833), 7 Peters 242; *Smith v. Maryland* (1855), 18 Howard 71), nor was it aimed at the unlawful acts of private persons (*Burdeau v. McDowell* (1921), 256 US 465).

Accordingly, it is not surprising to note that evidence seized by state officers in violation of the Fourth Amendment was often turned over to the federal authorities for prosecution in federal courts. This resulted in cases being handed over on a silver platter for federal prosecutions and was perfectly lawful even though most of the states proscribed unlawful searches and seizures. *See: Elkins v. U.S.* (1960), 364 US Appendix at p. 224.

Since *Barron* and *Smith,* the "silver platter" doctrine as this practice came to be known, has undergone great change.

The first case in this area was *Weeks v. U.S.* (1914), 232 US 383. *Weeks* promulgated the "exclusionary rules," a term which has become synonymous with *Weeks.*

As noted above, the Court held that in order to remove the temptation to ignore the constitutional restraints on search and seizure, evidence obtained in violation of the Fourth Amendment was inadmissible against the accused in federal courts. Thus, *Weeks* put teeth into the Fourth Amendment's proscriptions. But it is to be noted that *Weeks* applied only to federal prosecutions.

It seems logical to conclude that *Weeks* gave added impetus to the "silver platter" doctrine.

Although the rationale behind the exclusionary rule was not set forth by the court in its decision in *Weeks,* nevertheless the exclusionary rule having been announced and accepted, certain other pronouncements in this area were logically to be expected.

Thus, the Court subsequently ruled that evidence seized by state officers during an unlawful search and seizure would be excluded in a federal court if federal officers participated in the search. *Byars v. U.S.* (1927), 273 US 28. The same rule was enunciated where the unlawful search was a joint operation of local and federal officers.

"[A] search is a search by a Federal officer if he had a hand in it; it is not a search by a federal official if evidence secured by state authorities is turned over to federal authorities on a silver platter." *Lustig v. U.S.* (1949), 338 US 74, 78–79.

In *Lustig,* the petitioner's room was searched unlawfully by local police. A federal officer was invited to join the local police while they were examining certain items in Lustig's room. They turned over to the federal officer for his inspection and selection such items as he deemed appropriate for a federal prosecution. In holding that the evidence so obtained by the federal agent was inadmissible in a federal prosecution, the court said:

> "It surely can make no difference whether a state officer turns up the evidence and hands it over to a federal agent for his critical inspection with the view to its use in a federal prosecution, or the federal agent himself takes the articles out of a bag." *Lustig* at 78.

As long as the federal agent had a hand in the unlawful search and seizure, the fruits would be barred, even though he did not initiate it.

In another case, which preceded *Lustig, Gambino v. U.S.* (1927), 275 US 310, the Supreme Court ruled that where state officers execute an unlawful search and seizure for the benefit of the federal government, the fruits of the search would also be inadmissible in a federal court, even though the federal officers had nothing to do with the search. Gambino's automobile was unlawfully searched by New York State Police in accordance with that state's policy of cooperating with the federal government in enforcing the National Prohibition Act. Gambino was a bootlegger, and the liquor found in his car as a result of the unlawful search was turned over to the federal officers for prosecution in the federal courts. In such a situation, the unlawful acts of the state officers are equated with that of the beneficiary, the federal officers.

In any event, *Lustig* marked the beginning of the end of the "silver platter" doctrine, although the doctrine did not meet its demise until *Elkins v. U.S.* (1960), 364 US 206. *Elkins,* however, was based in part on *Wolf v. Colorado* (1949), 338 US 25. *Wolf* held that the "core" of the Fourth Amendment applied to the states by virtue of the Due Process Clause of the Fourteenth Amendment, even though the court had refused to order the exclusion in state trials of evidence unlawfully seized by state officers. It should be noted that Justice Frankfurter in *Wolf* intimated that the *Weeks* exclusionary rule was not of constitutional dimensions, but merely a judicially created rule of evidence.

Overruling *Wolf,* in part, *Elkins* made two important rulings: *one,* if evidence is obtained by state officers in violation of the Fourth Amendment, it is inadmissible in a federal court by virtue of the Due Process Clause of the Fourteenth Amendment; *two,* it is incumbent upon the federal court to make an independent inquiry to determine the lawfulness of the search and seizure of the proffered evidence, regardless of whether the state court had made such an inquiry. In other words, the lawfulness of the search is to be determined by federal constitutional standards and not by state law. This was the end of the "silver platter" doctrine.

Although there was no official doctrine of "reverse silver platter," states were permitted to use in evidence all unlawfully seized evidence whether of federal or state origin. The upshot of this was that in cases in which the evidence was inadmissible in a federal prosecution, those cases were on occasion turned over to the states for prosecution. *See: Rea v. U.S.* (1956), 350 US 214; *Rios v. U.S.* (1960), 364 US 253; *cf. Wilson v. Schnettler* (1961), 365 US 381. Whether this practice was deliberately indulged in by some federal officers or whether it was the result of happenstance, is moot. In any event, it was "a neat arrangement" that met its end in the landmark decision of *Mapp v. Ohio* (1961), 367 US 643. In that case, the Supreme Court said that both silver platter doctrines were equally tainted. Henceforth, the fruits of an unconstitutional search would be inadmissible in federal and state criminal prosecutions, by virtue of the *Due Process Clause.*

Since the lawfulness of the silver platter doctrine per se, and its reverse, had never been specifically condemned by the United States Supreme Court, but only its use in unlawful search cases under the Fourth Amendment by virtue of its interplay with the Fourteenth Amendment, it was inevitable that its extension to other fundamental constitutional rights would be urged. This extension was advocated in California in the case of *People v. Kelley* (1967), 57 Cal Rptr 363, 424 P2d 947, in all cases in which fundamental constitutional rights were placed in jeopardy.

**§ 5. Interplay Between Fourth and Fourteenth Amendments.** The *Elkins* decision was the logical precursor of a rule requiring the application of the Fourth Amendment to the several states by virtue of the Due Process Clause of the Fourteenth Amendment. *Wolf v. Colorado* stated the rule but did not implement it. *Elkins* implemented the rule as to prosecutions in federal court. *Mapp v. Ohio* (1961), 367 US 643, finalized the rule by making it applicable to state as well as federal prosecutions.

Basically, *Mapp v. Ohio* was a Fourth Amendment case. In that case, the police in Cleveland, Ohio, acting on a tip that a bomb suspect, who also had some policy paraphernalia, was in the petitioner's home, went to her apartment and demanded admission so they might question her. They did not tell her why they desired to interrogate. After speaking to her attorney by telephone, she denied entry to the police unless they had a search warrant. After a wait of three hours, other police arrived and forced their way into her apartment. Her attorney then arrived on the scene, but he was denied access to his client. Miss Mapp demanded to see a search warrant. A piece of paper was waved, purporting to be a warrant. She seized it, concealed it in her bosom from which the police forcibly removed it after a struggle. This paper, if it were indeed a warrant, was never produced. Mapp was then handcuffed and incarcerated in her bedroom. The apartment was then ransacked but neither the bomb suspect nor any gambling material was found.

Some obscene material was found in a trunk in the basement of the building. She was convicted of possession of obscene material and imprisoned, although she denied possession. The Ohio court affirmed on the common law theory of the admissibility of the evidence of obscenity even though they concurred in a finding that the search and seizure was unlawful.

In reversing, the Supreme Court ruled:

1. The Due Process Clause of the Fourteenth Amendment is coextensive with the Fourth Amendment.

2. Evidence seized in an unconstitutional search by state officers may not be used in federal prosecutions (the "silver platter" doctrine).

3. The fruits of an unconstitutional search would henceforth be inadmissible in both state and federal courts. Thus, evidence unconstitutionally obtained by federal officers would also be precluded in state prosecutions (the "reverse silver platter" doctrine).

4. *Wolf v. Colorado,* which refused to apply the federal exclusionary rule to the states, was overruled.

"Since the Fourth Amendment's right of privacy has been declared enforceable against the States through the Due Process Clause of the Fourteenth, it is enforceable against them by the same sanction of exclusion as is used against the Federal Government. Were it otherwise, then just as without the Weeks rule the assurance against unreasonable federal searches and seizures would be 'a form of words,' valueless and undeserving of mention in a perpetual charter of inestimable human liberties, so too, without that rule the freedom from state invasions of privacy would be so ephemeral and so neatly severed from its conceptual nexus with the freedom from all brutish means of coercing evidence as not to merit this Court's high regard as a freedom 'implicit in the "concept of ordered liberty".' . . . To hold otherwise is to grant the right but in reality to withhold its privilege and enjoyment." 367 US 655–656.

*Ker v. California* (1963), 374 US 23 followed *Mapp*. In *Ker*, having reason to believe that one of the petitioners was selling marijuana and had just purchased some from a person who was known to be a dealer in marijuana, California police officers, without a search warrant, used a passkey to enter the apartment occupied by petitioners (husband and wife) and arrested them on suspicion of violating the State Narcotic Law. They searched the apartment, found and seized three packages of marijuana. These packages were admitted in evidence, over objection, and the Kers were convicted. The California District Court of Appeals found that there was probable cause for the arrests, that the entry into the apartment was for the purpose of arrest and was not unlawful under California law and that the search was lawful as incident to a lawful arrest.

> "This being the first case arriving here since our opinion in *Mapp* which would afford suitable opportunity for further explication of that holding in the light of intervening experience, we granted certiorari . . . We affirm the judgment before us." *Ker* at 25.

The Supreme Court reaffirmed its holding in *Mapp* that prohibition of the Fourth Amendment against unreasonable searches and seizures is enforceable against the states through the Fourteenth Amendment.

**§ 6. The Right to Privacy Under the Fourth Amendment Defined.** The Fourth Amendment's ban against unlawful searches and seizures is aimed at the protection of the privacy of people, not places. The ban is thus applicable to conversations overheard by an electronic eavesdropping device (absent a lawful search warrant), even where the eavesdropping occurred without trespass or unlawful intrusion. It is the "uninvited ear" that the Amendment inveighs against.

"But what he seeks to preserve as private, even in an area accessible to the public [a public telephone booth], may be constitutionally protected. . . . One who occupies it, [a phone booth] shuts the door behind him, and pays the toll that permits him to place a call is surely entitled to assume that the words he utters into the mouthpiece will not be broadcast to the world." Thus the question of a physical trespass is irrelevant. *Katz v. U.S.* (1967), 389 US 347, 351, 352, 88 SC 507, 19 L Ed2d 576.

*See also: Griswold v. Connecticut* (1965), 381 US 479; *cf. Clinton v. Virginia* (1964), 377 US 158; *Silverman v. U.S.* (1961), 365 US 505.

§ 6.01. **The Incident Search.** The search of an individual without a warrant has been sustained by the court where it is incident to a lawful arrest. This is based on the theory that the search is necessary (grounded in the common law) to protect the arresting officer from harm (search for concealed weapons), to prevent the arrestee's escape (search for instruments that may aid him in escape), and to prevent the destruction of evidence of the crime.

There had been much confusion in the Supreme Court on the question of how large an area an incident search may encompass (*Harris v. U.S.* (1947), 331 US 145; *U.S. v. Rabinowitz* (1950), 339 US 56), and how intensive such a search may be (*Abel v. U.S.* (1960), 362 US 217; *Ker v. California* (1963), 374 US 23; *Kremen v. U.S.* (1957), 353 US 346).

The confusion referred to has now been largely dissipated by the decision in *Chimel v. California* (1969), 395 US 752, which overruled both *Harris,* and *Rabinowitz, supra.* In effect, *Chimel* limited the search to the "arms length" rule of the defendant, that is, the area in which the defendant could reach out to obtain a weapon, or instrument to aid in his escape or to obtain the evidence or contraband in question.

In its most recent decision in this area the court stated that an incident search was unlawful if it were not truly incident to the purpose of the arrest. Thus, where the defendant was arrested in his automobile for trafficking in narcotics, a search of his automobile was lawful. This was held to be a search for contraband narcotics in an area of his immediate control. *Cooper v. California* (1967), 386 US 58.

In contrast, the court differentitated the *Cooper* case from *Preston v. U.S.* (1964), 376 US 364. Preston was arrested on a charge of vagrancy. The search of his automobile without a warrant was not a lawful "incident search" since nothing that could be found in the automobile could in any way relate to a vagrancy charge. The automobile had been removed from the scene of the arrest to avoid blocking traffic.

*See: Search Incident to Lawful Arrest, Chapter 14, infra.*

§ **6.02. Search for Mere Evidence.** The rule that a search for "mere evidence" was exploratory and therefore in violation of the Fourth Amendment, *Gouled v. U.S.* (1932), 255 US 298; *Boyd v. U.S.* (1886), 116 US 616; *Entick v. Carrington* (1765), 19 Howell's State Trials 1029, has been modified. The items seized related to the crime that prompted the police in hot pursuit to make the search are now admissible. Thus, certain clothing allegedly worn by the defendant when he is alleged to have committed an armed robbery was seized during a search of a certain house he had entered after the robbery. The fact that this clothing was "mere evidence," as distinguished from fruits, instrumentalities and contraband, did not render them inadmissible.

This new rule does not overrule *Boyd v. U.S., supra,* which applies to self-incriminating documents under the Fifth Amendment, but it does modify *Gouled v. U.S., supra,* in this respect. *Warden v. Hayden* (1967), 387 U.S. 294.

*See also: Seizure of Mere Evidence, § 183.01, infra.*

§ **6.03. Administrative Searches.** Inspections of dwellings and places of business, conducted under the police powers of local government for the protection of life, health, and property, without a search warrant had been ruled lawful and not in violation of the Fourth Amendment. *Frank v. Maryland* (1959), 359 US 360. This case has now been overruled, so that a search warrant must first be obtained for the inspection and subsequent valid prosecution for failure to permit the inspection. The new rule applies to dwellings, *Camara v. Municipal Court* (1967), 387 US 523, as well as to commercial and factory buildings. *See v. Seattle* (1967), 387 US 541.

However, the provisions for obtaining such a search warrant have been so watered down they amount to compliance with the form but not the substance of the Fourth Amendment. *Camara v. Municipal Court, supra; See v. Seattle, supra.*

*See: Searches by Government Officers and Agents, Chapter 16, infra.*

§ 6.04. **Eavesdropping.** The sophisticated development of modern electronic devices has increased the potential for the invasion of one's privacy.

Warrants issued by courts authorizing eavesdropping (*e.g.*, wiretapping) constitute legal authority to "seize" one's conversation. Thus, this area of activity comes within the ambit of the Fourth and Fourteenth Amendments.

It is for the trial court to determine reasonableness of a search, but this determination will be respected only if it is consistent with federal constitutional guarantees.

The states are not precluded from developing working rules governing arrests, searches and seizures to meet "the practical demands of effective criminal investigation and law enforcement," provided that those rules do not violate the constitutional proscription of unreasonable searches and seizures and the concomitant command that evidence so seized is inadmissible against one who has standing to complain.

Eavesdropping warrants must be specific as to what conversations may be intercepted. They must be based upon probable cause, spelled out in a supporting affidavit. The reason for this requirement is to guard against rights protected by the Fourth Amendment, supervised under the neutral eye of a magistrate. *See: Berger v. New York* (1967), 388 US 41, in which, for defects indicated above, the court held that former New York Code of Criminal Procedure, § 813-a, was unconstitutional. *See also: Katz v. U.S.*, 389 US 347; *Olmstead v. U.S.*, 277 US 438; *Lopez v. U.S.*, 373 US 427; *cf. Silverman v. U.S.*, 365 US 505; *Clinton v. Virginia*, 377 US 158.

*See: Eavesdropping, Chapter 23, infra.*

# Chapter 2

# THE EXCLUSIONARY RULE



---

**§ 10. The Fourth Amendment.** The Fourth Amendment to the United States Constitution reads:

> "The right of the people to be secure in their persons, houses, papers, and effects, against unreasonable searches and seizures, shall not be violated, and no Warrants shall issue, but upon probable cause, supported by Oath or affirmation, and particularly describing the place to be searched and the persons or things to be seized."

The amendment has been interpreted to apply to persons, not places, *Katz v. U.S.*, 389 US 347; *Terry v. Ohio*, 392 US 1.

**§ 10.01. Applicability to State and Federal Courts.** As originally interpreted, the Fourth Amendment did not apply to the several states, (*Wolf v. Colorado*, 338 US 25; *Mapp v. Ohio*, 367 US 643; *Weeks v. U.S.*, 232 US 383), even though it was intended to protect all persons against invasions of "the sanctity of a man's home and the privacies of life" from indiscriminate searches by governmental authority. *Warden v. Hayden*, 387 US 294; *Boyd v. U.S.*, 116 US 616, 630.

*Mapp v. Ohio* made the proscriptions of the Fourth Amendment binding upon the states as well as the federal government.

It is to be noted that most state constitutions, including New York, contained a provision similar to the Fourth Amendment.

*Mapp* held that evidence obtained in violation of the Fourth

Amendment (unreasonable search and seizure) is inadmissible in both federal prosecutions (*Weeks v. U.S.,* 232 US 383) as well as in state prosecutions (*Mapp v. Ohio,* 367 US 643; *Ker v. California,* 374 US 23; *People v. Loria,* 10 NY2d 368, 179 NE2d 478; U.S. Const. Amends. IV, V, XIV; N.Y. Const. art. I, § 12), by virtue of the Fifth Amendment, and the Due Process clause of the Fourteenth Amendment.

The Fourth Amendment's ban against the use of such evidence applies equally to tangible evidence as well as to conversations or statements which are intangibles. *Katz v. U.S.,* 389 US 347; *Berger v. N.Y.,* 388 US 41; *People v. Grossman,* 45 Misc2d 557, 257 NYS2d 266, revd other grds 27 AD2d 572.

The new rule does not preclude the several states from developing workable rules governing arrests, searches and seizures to meet their own problems of law enforcement, providing that those rules do not violate the Fourth Amendment's proscriptions against unreasonable searches and seizures. *Ker v. California, supra.*

**§ 11. Retroactivity.** The *Mapp* rule is not retroactive. It does not affect cases finally decided prior to *Mapp. Linkletter v. Walker,* 381 US 618; *Angolet v. Fay,* 381 US 654.

Cases in the process of "review of pending appeals from pre-*Mapp* convictions" come within the ambit of *Mapp* since they are cases which have not been "finally decided." The term "pending appeals" refers only to those cases that are within the stream of normal appellate process. *People v. Loria, supra; People v. Eastman,* 33 Misc2d 583, affd 18 AD2d 1102, 239 NYS2d 972; *cf. People v. Muller,* 11 NY2d 154, 182 NE2d 99, cert. den. 371 US 850.

However, in pre-*Mapp* cases still in the normal appellate process, the issue of unreasonable search and seizure will not be reviewed if that issue was not raised at the trial. *People v. Friola,* 11 NY2d 157, 182 NE2d 100; *cf. People v. Loria, supra.*

**§ 12. Unreasonable and Illegal Searches Defined.** The Fourth Amendment does not make all searches invalid. It bars only those searches that are "unreasonable." Unfortunately, it does not define that term. Even though the Fourth Amendment contains two parts, one referring to "unreasonable searches" and one referring to the basis for obtaining a search warrant, the relationship between the two parts, if any, is never explained. This has been left to judicial interpretation. Thus, in some early cases, a search absent a lawful search warrant, was an "unreasonable search." *Boyd v. U.S., supra; Gouled v. U.S.,* 255 US 298.

After 1940, however, the Supreme Court has consistently held that the two parts of the Amendment were separate and that a search could be "reasonable" under the Fourth Amendment even though no search warrant had been issued, *U.S. v. Rabinowitz,* 339 US 56; *cf. Harris v. U.S.,* 331 US 145 (dissent Frankfurter J).

**§ 12.01. Unreasonable Search.** Based on the Supreme Court decisions, it is concluded that a search is "unreasonable" if it is conducted in violation of the Fourth Amendment. A search which is made in violation of one's privacy—one's home, papers, effects, office or even one's automobile—are "unreasonable" searches, absent a search warrant. *Boyd v. U.S., supra; Gouled v. U.S., supra; Taylor v. U.S.,* 286 US 1; *Carroll v. U.S.,* 267 US 132.

**§ 12.02. Illegal Search.** A search that is illegal is one conducted in violation of some statute in contradistinction to a search conducted in violation of the Fourth Amendment.

For example, in New York a search warrant may not be executed by a building inspector since he is not a peace officer. CPL § 1.20(33). A search conducted by him would be an illegal search, not an "unreasonable search." *People v. Laverne,* 14 NY2d 304, 200 NE2d 441. Unfortunately, both terms are used synonymously.

**§ 13. The Silver Platter Doctrine.** In *Weeks v. U.S.,* 232 US 383, the court held that evidence seized by federal officers in violation of the Fourth Amendment is inadmissible against a defendant in a federal prosecution over his timely objection.

Prior to *Mapp,* the *Weeks* exclusionary rule was held inapplicable to the states. *Wolf v. Colorado,* 338 US 25. Accordingly, it was not uncommon for state officers to deliver to federal officers for prosecution evidence that they, the state officers, had seized by an unlawful search. Such evidence was admissible in federal prosecutions since it was not excludable under the *Weeks* exclusionary rule. *Byars v. U.S.,* 273 US 28. In effect, the case was being handed to the federal authorities on a "silver platter," the term which was used to denote this practice. *Elkins v. U.S.,* 364 U.S. 206; *Rea v. U.S.,* 350 US 214. On occasion, the reverse situation occurred. In these cases, evidence seized by federal officers in violation of the Fourth Amendment was delivered to state officers for prosecution. *Rea v. U.S., supra; Rios v. United States,* 364 US 253; *Wilson v. Schnettler,* 365 US 381. This technique soon became known as "reverse silver platter." *Mapp* put an end to both practices as equally tainted.

**§ 14. Unlawful Searches and Seizures by Private Persons.** Technically speaking, a private person cannot commit an unlawful search and seizure in a constitutional sense, since the Fourth Amendment seeks to interdict those unlawful acts only when committed by officials of the government. The punishment for such official lawlessness is the exclusion of the fruits of such searches from evidence at the trial, *Mapp v. Ohio, supra.*

It is common knowledge that private persons invade the privacy of others and on occasion seize items which would inculpate the person whose privacy is invaded. On some occasions, the trespasser has delivered the fruits of his trespass to government officials and the latter have prosecuted.

Actually, these acts by a trespasser also result in delivering a case to the government on a "silver platter." Nevertheless, the use by the government of such evidence seized by a private person does not violate the Fourth Amendment, provided government officials did not have a part in the seizure and there has been no governmental connivance or collusion in the act. *Lustig v. U.S.,* 338 US 74, 78–79; *Burdeau v. McDonald,* 256 US 465; *U.S. v. McGuire,* 381 F2d 306; *People v. Randazzo,* 34 Cal Rptr 65; *People v. Trimarco,* 41 Misc2d 775, 245 NYS2d 795; *cf. Hoffa v. U.S.,* 385 US 293, 301.

# Chapter 3

## SELF-INCRIMINATION



---

**§ 18. In General.** The interplay of the Fourth, Fifth, Sixth and Fourteenth Amendments has been repeatedly noted by the United States Supreme Court. *See: Boyd v. U.S.*, 116 US 616; *Mapp v. Ohio,* 367 US 643; *Miranda v. Arizona,* 384 US 436; *Massiah v. U.S.,* 377 US 201.

The emphasis placed on self-incrimination and the right to counsel in the area of admissions and confessions, *Miranda v. Arizona, supra; Escobedo v. Illinois,* 378 US 478, requires an examination of these Amendments particularly in the area of compelled testimony, *e.g.,* appearances before grand juries.

The Fifth Amendment which grants immunity against self-incrimination protects "a state witness against incrimination under federal as well as state law and a federal witness against incrimination under state as well as federal law." *Murphy v. Waterfront Comm.,* 378 US 52.

The protection applies equally to a witness in a federal prosecution. The orders issued by the Subversive Activities Control Board requiring the Communist Party to register, were set aside as violative of the Fifth Amendment. The Supreme Court held such registration orders violate the privilege against self-incrimination. The whole area and the forms required to be completed are permeated with criminal statutes, immunity provision in the statute was deemed inadequate, and did not preclude use of the information required in the forms from being used as evidence or investigatory leads. *Albertson v. Subversive Activities Control Board,* 382 US 70.

Similarly, it was held that the Federal Tax Statutes (28 USC §§ 4401, *et seq.*) that require a gambler to register with the government and pay special occupational and excise taxes are unconstitutional. The records of these gamblers are publicly posted and open for inspection by local prosecuting officers. Furthermore, payment of these special taxes does not exempt the gambler from prosecution for violation of local gambling laws by local authorities. Compelling a gambler to register infringes on his constitutional privilege against self-incrimination. *Marchetti v. U.S.,* 390 US 39.

Following the same rationale, the Supreme Court also declared certain sections of the National Firearms Act unconstitutional (26 USC §§ 5841, 5848, 5851). The sections require owners of sawed-off shotguns and rifles, machine guns, mufflers and silencers to register them. These sections are aimed at taxing persons engaged in unlawful activities. Obviously, persons complying with these tax statutes are "immediately threatened by criminal prosecutions under sections 5851 and 5861. They are unmistakably persons 'inherently suspect of criminal activities.' *Albertson* v. *SACB,* 382 U.S. 70, 79." *Haynes v. U.S.,* 390 US 85, 96.

**§ 19. Compelled Testimony.** Persons under subpoena to appear and testify before various lawfully established tribunals, grand juries, boards and similar bodies, give their testimony under legal compulsion. Their testimony is legally "compelled." In the area of self-incrimination the federal and state rules differ with respect to the immunization of the witness.

**§ 19.01. Compelled Testimony in a State Court Under a Grant of Immunity.** A proper understanding of the federal and the New York rule regarding compelled testimony requires an analysis of the decisions of *Malloy v. Hogan,* 378 US 1, and of *Murphy v. Waterfront Commission,* 378 US 52. Both of these cases deal with the Fifth Amendment.

In the former, Malloy appeared as a witness in a statutory investigation concerning gambling. He had pleaded guilty to a misdemeanor gambling charge and was on probation. At the hearing he refused to answer questions relating to his arrest and conviction on the ground of possible self-incrimination. He was adjudged in contempt. This adjudication was affirmed by the Connecticut courts on the theory that since he had already been convicted, the answers he might give at the hearing could not incriminate him.

The U.S. Supreme Court reversed the adjudication of contempt, applying the federal standards as enunciated in *Hoffman v. U.S.,* 341 US 479. The rule laid down in *Hoffman* protects a witness in his right to refuse to answer questions which might furnish leads or clues to other "criminal facts" for which a witness might be prosecuted. The witness alone is the best judge of that fact. He alone, the Court reasoned, is probably the only person who can determine if the question asked might tend to incriminate or lead to some clue or link which would result in incrimination.

The Court then stated further that the Fourteenth Amendment prohibits a state from infringement on the privilege against self-incrimination just as the Fifth Amendment prevents the federal government from denying the privilege. And it makes no difference, the Court added, whether the claim is asserted in a state court or in a federal court. In applying the privilege against self-incrimination, the same standards determine whether an accused's silence is justified, whether it is a federal or state proceeding at which he is called to testify. Furthermore, the privilege against self-incrimination may be claimed by a witness in a statutory inquiry, as well as by a defendant in a criminal prosecution.

It is interesting to note that New York adopted this rule in the case of *People ex rel Taylor v. Forbes* (1894), 143 NY 219, 231, many years before *Malloy v. Hogan.* In the

Taylor case, Taylor refused to answer a question as to the purchase of a certain chemical. The court, in sustaining him, said: "But the courts have recognized the impossibility in most cases of anticipating the effect of the answer. Where it is not so perfectly evident and manifest that the answer called for cannot incriminate, as to preclude all reasonable doubt or fair argument, the privilege must be recognized and protected."

*Malloy v. Hogan* held "that the Fifth Amendment privilege against self-incrimination must be deemed fully applicable to the States through the Fourteenth Amendment." *Malloy* further held that the refusal of a witness to answer questions that he feels might incriminate him is based on the rationale enunciated in *Hoffman v. U.S., supra.*

The rationale behind the New York rule is the same as that in the federal rule.

*Murphy v. Waterfront Commission, supra,* was decided the same day as *Malloy v. Hogan, supra.* The decision in *Murphy,* however, is bottomed on *Malloy.* Murphy was subpoenaed to testify at a hearing held by the Waterfront Commission of New York Harbor. (The Commission was organized by compact between New York and New Jersey, and approved by Congress, 67 Stat. 541.) He refused to answer certain questions on the ground of possible self-incrimination. He was then granted immunity from prosecution under New York and New Jersey laws, but still refused to answer. He based this second refusal on the ground of possible self-incrimination under federal law. He was held in civil contempt, which was upheld by the New Jersey Supreme Court. Thus, the New Jersey court held "that a State may constitutionally compel a witness to give testimony which might be used in a federal prosecution against him." *Application of the Waterfront Comm. etc,* 39 NJ 436, 189 A2d 36.

The dilemma of a witness in such a position was noted in that "* * * these policies and purposes (of the Fifth Amendment) are defeated when a witness 'can be whipsawed into incriminating himself under both state and federal law even though' the constitutional privilege against self-incrimination is applicable to each." *Murphy v. Waterfront Comm., supra,* p. 55.

The court, however, recognized the necessity for a state to obtain information requisite for effective law enforcement within its own boundaries. In synthesizing the privilege of a defendant under the Fifth Amendment with the need for effective law enforcement in the several states, the court ruled that a witness, immunized under state law, may be compelled to give testimony which might incriminate him under federal law *providing* such testimony and its fruits are not used in connection with a federal prosecution against him.

"We hold that the constitutional privilege against self-incrimination protects a state witness against incrimination under federal as well as state law and a federal witness against incrimination under state as well as federal law." *Id.* at 77–78.

The testimony thus "compelled" from a state witness "and its fruits cannot be used in any manner by federal officials in connection with a criminal prosecution against him." This holding does not mean that such a witness obtains complete immunity from federal prosecution. If the federal authorities can gather enough evidence to indict the witness, independent of his compelled testimony or its fruits, they may do so. However, "the federal authorities have the burden of showing that their evidence is not tainted by establishing that they had an independent legitimate source for the disputed evidence."

*Murphy* overruled *Feldman v. U.S.*, 322 US 487. *Cf. U.S. v. Interborough Delicatessen Dealers,* 235 F Supp 230.

§ 20. **Immunity.** Both the Federal Constitution (Fifth Amendment) and the New York State Constitution (art. I, § 6) provide "no person shall be compelled in any criminal case to bear witness against himself."

*Murphy v. Waterfront Commission,* 378 US 52, 84 SC 1594, (discussed, § 19.01, *supra*) established the rule authorizing the use of limited immunity. This type of immunity, known as "*use immunity*" bars the prosecutor only from using the witness' own testimony. A federal statute authorizing this type of use immunity was adopted in 1970 (18 USC § 6002) and is in force in a majority of the states. However, a use immunity statute has been held unconstitutional in the Third Circuit, *Catena v. Elias,* 449 F2d 40, and a review of this matter is before the United States Supreme Court for consideration.

The Organized Crime Control Act of 1970 (Pub. L. No. 91–452; 84 Stat. 922; codified in scattered sections of 18, 28 USC) limits the right of a witness to forego his privilege against self-incrimination where the witness is called to testify before a federal court or grand jury, an agency of the United States, or either House of Congress or joint Committee of the two Houses, or a committee or subcommittee of either House.

The limitation of the witness' Fifth Amendment privilege is extended to situations where the testimony sought of the witness "may be necessary to the public interest." 18 USC §§ 6001–6005.

Recalcitrant witnesses may be dealt with summarily. 28 USC § 1826. *See also:* 18 USC § 1623.

Where a statute requires an administrative or judicial grant of immunity, absence such a grant, the witness need not testify. *Security & Exchange Commission v. Olsen,* 354 F2d 166.

Where a grand jury has conferred immunity upon a witness he has an obligation to testify. *U.S. v. Rao,* 296 F Supp 1145.

Additionally, an attorney is under a like duty to answer grand jury questions, where he has been granted immunity and the attorney-client privilege is not applicable. *U.S. v. Pappadio,* 346 F2d 5.

The grant of immunity is discretionary. Failure of the government to confer immunity on a codefendant, where the government was authorized to do so, did not deprive the defendant of a fair trial. *Earl v. U.S.,* 361 F2d 531, cert. den. 388 US 921.

Fear of reprisal against the defendant or members of his family is no valid excuse for refusing to testify before a grand jury, *Piemonte v. U.S.,* 367 US 556.

The federal rule does not prevent the government from calling an individual to testify before the grand jury who is the target of its investigation and who may become a defendant. *U.S. v. De Sapio,* 299 F Supp 436.

*"Transactional immunity"* is immunity from prosecution for

the crime or transaction that the witness testifies about. This is the minority rule and has been adopted in New York. CPL art. 50; *cf. People v. Masiello,* 28 NY2d 287. This type of immunity does not bar a conviction for perjury or contempt. *People v. Tomasello,* 21 NY2d 143, 234 NE2d 190. It is to be noted further that even under the New York (minority) rule, when a person has testified before a grand jury under a subpoena, he does not gain thereby complete immunity from prosecution even though any indictment or information returned against him must be dismissed. *People v. Steuding,* 6 NY2d 214, 160 NE2d 74. He may still be reindicted if sufficient untainted evidence can be adduced to support the new indictment. *Matter of Ryan v. Supreme Court,* 7 NY 2d 989; *People v. Ryan,* 11 AD2d 155; *People v. Laino,* 10 NY2d 161, 176 NE2d 571; *People v. DeFeo,* 308 NY 595 (revd other grounds); *cf. Malloy v. Hogan, supra; Murphy v. Waterfront Comm., supra.*

§ 20.01. **Withdrawal of Waiver of Immunity.** The privilege against self-incrimination is a constitutional right. A potential defendant may waive that right, but he also has a right to withdraw his waiver. The Supreme Court so ruled in a case involving a police officer who, as a potential defendant, executed a waiver of immunity after he was subpoenaed to appear before a New York Grand Jury.

"Even were we to assume, without deciding, that a State may constitutionally exact, on pain of loss of employment and in the absence of counsel, the waiver of a constitutional right, we would be unable to find any justification for denying the right to withdraw it [the waiver of immunity]." *Stevens v. Marks,* 383 US 234, 243–244.

Nor can such a person be held in contempt, in the absence of immunity provisions clearly made applicable to him for invoking the privilege against self-incrimination.

"A witness has a constitutional right to stand on privilege against self-incrimination until it has been fairly demonstrated to him that an immunity, as broad in scope as the privilege against self-incrimination, is available and applicable to him." *Stevens v. Marks,* 383 US 234, 246; *Stevens v. McCloskey,* 383 US 234. *See also: Albertson v. Subver-*

*sive Activities Control Board,* 382 US 70; *cf. Counselman v. Hitchcock,* 142 US 547; *People v. Ryan,* 11 AD2d 155; CPL § 190.45(4).

It is to be noted, however, that when a public officer voluntarily and freely waives immunity, he becomes a proper witness before the grand jury. He cannot thereafter dispute the constitutionality of the provision of the state constitution pertaining to removal and disqualification of officers who refuse to sign a waiver of immunity. *Regan v. New York,* 349 US 58; *People v. Trammel,* 267 NYS2d 434.

Generally there can be no punishment for contempt for refusing to testify before a grand jury unless the court has shown that evidence demanded may be relevant and proper. *See:* N.Y. Judiciary Law, § 750(A)(3). However, relevancy need not be conclusively established, and it is enough if its bearing on the subject of investigation was susceptible of intelligent estimate or there was justifiable suspicion of relationship between the questions and the subject of the investigation. *Koota v. Colombo,* 25 AD2d 497, 267 NYS2d 489, affd 17 NY2d 147; cert. den. 348 US 1001.

In a case of alleged assault committed by a defendant who had an unblemished record, it was held unfair for the district attorney not to have notified the defendant that the matter was being submitted to the grand jury so that the defendant could appear before that body as is his right under state statute and testify in his own behalf, where this action would not have been prejudicial to the People. The court, in setting the subsequent indictment aside, pointed out that the function of a grand jury is not to assist the prosecution, but to protect the individual from oppression. *People v. Lazar,* 51 Misc2d 233, 272 NYS2d 898; *People v. Seward,* 51 Misc2d 415. *Cf.* CPL § 190.50.

There is no constitutional or common law right to testify before a grand jury. The right to do so is purely statutory and arises only after the defendant has complied with the statutory requirements. *See, e.g.,* CPL §§ 190.50(5,6), 210.20 (1)(c), 210.35(4); *People ex rel DeGroat v. Wallack,* 16 AD2d 994; Fed R Crim P 6; *U.S. ex rel McCann v. Thompson,* 144 F2d 604, 605–606, cert. den. 65 SC 1082, 323 US 790.

**§ 20.02. Challenge of Waiver of Immunity.** Where a waiver of immunity has been executed but later challenged by the defendant, the People must establish that the defendant knew its import and its use, as well as its voluntariness. *People v. Guidarelli,* 22 AD2d 336, 255 NYS2d 975.

## § 21. Testimonial Compulsion.

**§ 21.01. Federal (Majority) Rule.** Does testimony given under a subpoena constitute testimonial compulsion? The federal law, followed in a majority of the states, "holds that a subpoena is not per se compulsion. *U.S. v. Kimball,* 117 F. 156, 2nd Circ. 1902." *People v. Werkes,* 46 Misc2d 1020, 1022, 261 NYS2d 726. *See also: U.S. v. Interborough Delicatessen Dealers,* 235 F Supp 230.

"Whatever may be the rule in the State of New York, the Fifth Amendment does not proscribe the practice here inveighed against. Repeately this Court has so ruled, declining to equate the position of a 'potential' defendant called before a grand jury with that of one already on trial.* * * * To suggest that once an individual is named by witnesses before a grand jury under circumstances which may lead to his indictment he thereby automatically gains immunity from subpoena would denude that ancient body of a substantial right of inquiry." *U.S. v. Winter,* 348 F2d 204, 207. *See also: People v. Laino,* 10 NY2d 161, 176 NE2d 571; *U.S. v. Cleary,* 265 F2d 459, cert. den. 360 US 936; *U.S. v. Pappadio,* 346 F2d 5; *cf. Malloy v. Hogan, supra; U.S. v. Tramunti,* 343 F2d 548.

**§ 21.02. New York (Minority) Rule.** The New York Rule, which is the minority rule, holds that the mere service of a subpoena upon the target of an investigation or a prospective defendant followed by the giving of testimony is compulsion per se. *People v. Gillette,* 126 AD 665, 111 NYS 133. *See also: People v. Laino, supra.*

Thus, a prospective defendant or the target of an investigation may not be called and questioned before a grand jury under the New York (minority) rule. If he is, his constitutional privilege against self-incrimination is deemed violated even if he does not assert it. *People v. Steuding,* 6 NY2d 214,

160 NE2d 74; *People v. DeFeo,* 308 NY 595 (reversed on other grounds); *People v. Yonkers Cont. Co.,* 24 AD2d 641, 262 NYS2d 298, mod. 17 NY2d 322.

**§ 22. Perjury.** Immunity does not include immunity from prosecution for prejury committed before the grand jury. In so far as *Gillette, DeFeo, Laino, Steuding* and *Yonkers Contracting Co., supra,* have held otherwise, those cases are now overruled by *People v. Tomasello,* 21 NY2d 143.

The rule now is that a prospective defendant or target of an investigation who is called before a grand jury is *not* immune from indictment and prosecution for perjury if his testimony is found to be willfully false. *Cf.* 18 USC §§ 1621–1623.

In grand jury perjury cases, the old distinctions between "possible defendants," "target" and "mere witness" are eliminated, since it is difficult if not impossible to draw these distinctions.

The immunity granted a prospective defendant who is compelled to testify before a grand jury is for past substantive crimes, based on his testimony. But this does "not endow (him) with a license to commit perjury"—a "present" *new* crime. *Glickstein v. U.S.,* 222 US 139, 142. The "compulsion" involved in compelled testimony "is not to testify falsely but to testify truly." One does not incriminate oneself by giving false testimony. 8 Wigmore, *Evidence,* § 2282, p. 512 (McNaughton ed. 1961).

"Since Tomasello, as a prospective defendant or target, acquired a protection from prosecution for substantive crimes based on his 'compelled' testimony, he may not, and should not, be permitted to escape prosecution for perjury committed in connection with the very testimony that cloaked him with such protection." *People v. Tomasello,* 234 NE2d 190, 21 NY2d 143, 150, revg 27 AD2d 562, affg 48 Misc2d 156, 264 NYS2d 686.

*Tomasello* was decided in 1967. In *People v. Ianniello,* 21 NY2d 418, decided a few months later, the Court of Appeals continued to follow the rationale of *Tomasello* and applied the same rule to contempts committed before a grand jury, holding that a defendant is subject to prosecution for criminal contempt before a grand jury *whether or not* he was a *possible defendant* or the target of the grand jury investigation. *People v. Ianniello,* 21 NY2d 418, 176 NE2d 571. To the same effect see also *Matter of Gold v. Menna,* 25 NY2d 475, 255 NE2d 235.

The failure by a public employee to sign a waiver of immunity (New York City Charter, Sec. 1123) need not necessarily require an immediate summary dismissal of the employee from public service. A reasonable opportunity must be afforded the person to consider the question of signing the waiver or consulting with an attorney. The refusal to sign must be an "informed, intentional refusal to sign."

Thus, where a police officer, in the early morning hours, was directed to appear before a grand jury forthwith and at the appearance refused to sign the waiver "at this time," and was therefore summarily dismissed from the police department, reinstatement was ordered by the New York State Supreme Court. *Gardner v. Murphy,* 46 Misc2d 728, 260 NYS2d 739, *See also: Sauerbrey v. Murphy,* 44 Misc2d 909; *Conlon v. Murphy,* 24 AD2d 737, 263 NYS2d 360. In the *Conlon* case, a police officer was asked to testify before a grand jury concerning bribery and graft in the police department. He refused to do so without first consulting with counsel and was summarily dismissed. It was held that every person interrogated concerning the commission of crime is entitled to counsel upon his request. Summary dismissal without giving Conlon the opportunity to explain his refusal was held to be arbitrary and a denial of due process.

However, where the police officer's discharge without notice and a hearing was in accord with statutory provisions, and the officer had opportunity to test its validity that was equal to a hearing prior to discharge, and where there was a prima facie showing of a good reason for expeditious action by the Police Commissioner, and the officer advanced no tenable grounds for holding that after a fair hearing he would not have been dismissed, his discharge would be upheld. *Koutnik v. Murphy,* 25 AD2d 197.

**§ 23. Limited Waiver and Waiver.** The petitioner, a city employee, executed a limited waiver of immunity, pursuant to section 6 of Article 1 of the New York Constitution, on pain of losing his job and without benefit of counsel. He appeared before a grand jury which was inquiring into acts of bribery. When asked general questions about his participation in acts of bribery, he responded, but when asked about a specific instance, he asserted his privilege.

In *Bohland v. Markewich,* 26 AD2d 545, the First Department held that the execution of a limited waiver of immunity does not in and of itself irreovocably waive the constitutional right against self-incrimination and, when confronted with a question that would be incriminating, the witness may refuse to answer without being subject to punishment for contempt. Citing *Stevens v. Marks,* 383 US 234, the court stated:

> "However, a witness who has without objection submitted himself to examination and who has answered questions pertinent to the inquiry cannot thereafter withdraw his consent (*Rogers v. United States,* 340 U.S. 367). 'Once he waives his privilege against self-incrimination, a witness may not withdraw his waiver to prevent matters which he has already gone into from being explored in greater detail' (*United States ex rel. Carthan v. Sheriff, City of New York,* 330 F.2d 100, 102, cert. den. 379 U.S. 929). That is the situation here."

As mentioned above, the new York (minority) rule does not hold true under federal law. Thus, where a witness was subpoenaed and testified before a New York grand jury, without asserting his privilege, his testimony was held admissible in a federal prosecution under *Murphy v. Waterfront Comm., supra,* as the testimony was deemed "not compelled" testimony under the federal rule. As the court observed in that case, the Fifth Amendment does not preclude voluntary self-incrimination. *U.S. v. Interborough Delicatessen Dealers,* 235 F Supp 230.

A parallel result was obtained in a case involving a waiver of immunity signed by a public contractor under the General Municipal Law. In that case, after conviction, he applied for habeas corpus in the federal court. The writ was denied. The General Municipal Law required that public contractors waive immunity before investigative bodies. Failure to do so may result in possible disqualification from receiving contracts from municipalities. The district court held that this sanction does not violate the constitutional privilege against self-incrimination and the prisoner was not "compelled" in a federal constitutional sense to give testimony against himself when he was subpoenaed to appear before a New York Grand Jury, even though the New York constitutional privilege against self-incrimination was broader. *U.S. ex rel Laino v. Warden,* 246 F Supp 72.

However, in a landmark decision, the United States Supreme Court has held in *Garrity v. State of New Jersey,* 385 US 493, 496, 497, 499, 500, that the constitutional guarantee against self-incrimination bars, during the criminal trial of local police officers, statements obtained from them under a state statute compelling them to make such statements or be discharged from their employment, since such statements were coerced. In reversing the conviction, the Court said:

"The choice imposed on petitioners was one between self-incrimination or job forfeiture. Coercion that vitiates a confession under Chambers v. State of Florida, 309 U.S. 227, 60 S.Ct. 472, 84 L.Ed. 716, and related cases can be 'mental as well as physical'; 'the blood of the accused is not the only hallmark of an unconstitutional inquisition.' Blackburn v. State of Alabama, 361 U.S. 199, 206, 80 S.Ct. 274, 279, 4 L. Ed.2d 242."

Citing *Boyd v. U.S.* 116 US 616 and *Miranda v. Arizona* 384 US 436, as well as *Spevack v. Klein* 385 US 511, the Court continued: "The option to lose their means of livelihood or to pay the penalty of self-incrimination is the antithesis of free choice to speak out or to remain silent."

The question in this case, the Court added, was, "whether a state, contrary to the requirement of the Fourteenth Amendment, can use the threat of discharge to secure incriminatory evidence against an employee."

"We conclude that policemen, like teachers and lawyers, are not relegated to a watered-down version of constitutional rights.

"There are rights of constitutional stature whose exercise a State may not condition by the exaction of a price. . . . We now hold the protection of the individual under the Fourteenth Amendment against coerced statements prohibits use in subsequent criminal proceedings of statements obtained under threat of removal from office, and that it extends to all, whether they are policemen or other members of our body politic."

The Court ruled similarly in a New York disbarment proceeding. *Spevack v. Klein,* 385 US 511. There the Court held that a New York attorney's disbarment, based upon his refusal to testify and produce financial records before a state judicial inquiry into unethical practices on the ground of self-incrimination, violated his constitutional guarantee under the Fifth Amendment. But in *Cohen v. Hurley,* 366 US 117, it was held "that the constitutional privilege against self-incrimination was not available" to an attorney situated as *Spevack.*

In *Spevack,* certiorari was granted to determine whether *Cohen v. Hurley, supra,* had survived *Malloy v. Hogan,* 378 US 1. Construing the privilege against self-incrimination liberally and holding it applicable to the states, the Court held that the phrase "no person," includes lawyers, who also enjoy first class citizenship. *Spevack v. Klein, supra. See also: Slochower v. Bd. of Ed.,* 350 US 551; *Garrity v. N.J., supra.*

*Garrity* and *Spevack* were 1967 decisions. In April, 1968 the New York Court of Appeals decided *State v. Perla,* 21 NY2d 608. In *Perla,* the court held that by virtue of Section 6, Article 1 of the New York State Constitution, any public officer is subject to removal from office when he refuses to sign a waiver of immunity when subpoenaed to testify before a grand jury as to his official acts.

In *Perla,* the court noted:

> "A public official has the undoubted right to claim a constitutional privilege against self-incrimination; but the State has a concommitant [*sic*] right to discharge him from his job if his refusal to testify relates to his public employment." 21 NY2d 608, 615.

Whether a public official might exercise his constitutional privilege on pain of forfeiting his office for invoking his Fifth Amendment rights was a question that the United States Supreme Court did not reach in either *Garrity* or *Spevack. Garrity v. New Jersey, supra,* op. Douglas, J., at 516, n. 3;

and op. Fortas, J., at 519. Spevack was an attorney who refused to disclose his financial records or to testify at an Appellate Division inquiry into his professional conduct, claiming Fifth Amendment privilege. He was subsequently disbarred, but the Supreme Court reversed.

*Garrity,* decided the same day as *Spevack,* held that policemen who made confession of a crime when confronted with a choice either of incriminating themselves or losing their jobs were entitled to reversal of conviction because the confessions were not voluntary and in this respect the Fourteenth Amendment protected them.

Two months after *State v. Perla, supra,* in June 1968, the United States Supreme Court answered the questions left open in *Garrity* and *Spevack.* In two cases, *Gardner v. Broderick,* 392 US 273, and *Uniformed Sanitation Men v. Commissioner,* 392 US 280, the Supreme Court held that public officers (employees), like all persons, are entitled to the benefit of all constitutional privileges, including the privilege against self-incrimination. Such an employee cannot be forced to incriminate himself on pain of forfeiture of his job.

In view of these two decisions, the ruling in *State v. Perla, supra,* is now plainly incorrect.

*Gardner, supra,* involved a New York City policeman and *Sanitation Men, supra,* involved an employee of the New York City Sanitation Department. However, this is not to say that a public employee who violates his trust cannot be dismissed if he refuses to account for his performance as a public employee. This may be done after a proper proceeding which does not involve an attempt to coerce him into relinquishing his constitutional rights.

For a discussion of a public employee's refusal to sign a waiver of immunity solely because of his privilege against self-incrimination, *see: Slochower v. Board of Higher Education,* 350 US 551; *Wieman v. Updegraff,* 344 US 183; *cf. Beilan v. Board of Education,* 357 US 399; *Lerner v. Casey,* 357 US 468, dealing with discharge from public employment, constitutionally based upon incompetency or misconduct (insubordination) flowing from the individual's refusal to answer, *i.e.,* lack of candor.

"By engaging in teaching in the public schools, petitioner

did not give up his right to freedom of belief, speech or association. He did, however, undertake obligations of frankness, candor and cooperation in answering inquiries made of him by his employing Board examining into his fitness to serve it as a public school teacher." *Beilan v. Board of Education,* 357 US 399, 405.

In *Beilan,* the "Pennsylvania Supreme Court has held that 'incompetency' includes petitioner's 'deliberate' and insubordinate refusal to answer the questions of his administrative superior in a vitally important matter pertaining to his fitness. 386 Pa. at 91, 125 A2d at 331. This interpretation is not inconsistent with the Federal Constitution." *Beilan,* 357 US 399, 408. *See also: Lerner v. Casey,* 2 NY2d 355, and *Malloy v. Hogan, supra.*

§ 23.01. **State Narcotics Addiction Hearings.** In narcotic addiction cases, where a defendant has been examined by a physician by order of the court, in order to determine if he is a narcotic addict, admissions made to the physician do not violate the rule against self-incrimination.

"These medical examinations, however, are used solely for diagnostic purposes. Any admission made to the doctor may not be received in evidence at the trial on the criminal charges (Mental Hygiene Law, § 207, subd. 5). As the [narcotics addiction] program is intended solely for the addict's benefit, self incrimination becomes irrelevant. The addiction hearing is not designed as a means of giving an added sentence, but is intended to serve the function of assuring that the physician's conclusion that the defendant is an addict is soundly based. It is the nonincriminating purpose of the examination that makes the privilege against self incrimination and the right to counsel inoperative at the physical examination." *People v. Fuller,* 24 NY2d 292, 301–302, 248 NE2d 17.

§ 24. **Contempt Proceedings: Interplay of Federal and State Immunity Rules.** Where a witness has received full and complete immunity, failure to testify subjects him to contempt proceedings under both federal and state law. It must be emphasized that, although a state grand jury cannot confer immunity from federal prosecution per se, a state witness, upon whom immunity has been conferred by state law, may not refuse to testify on the ground that he will be or may be subjected to federal prosecution. As stated above, the reason for this rule is bottomed on *Murphy v. Waterfront Comm.,* 378 US 52, which holds that while a federal prosecution is not barred by a state grant of imunity, the federal authorities may not use the testimony thereby obtained in the state proceedings, or the fruits thereof. Additionally, the federal authorities have the burden of establishing that their evidence had an independent and legitimate source. *People v. John Doe (Ralph Berger)*, NYLJ, 2/15/65, p. 17, col. 2; *Mtr. of Ushkowitz v. Helfand,* 15 NY2d 713, 204 NE2d 498; *Prensky v. Geller,* 22 AD2d 559, 257 NYS2d 492.

As the Supreme Court pointed out in *Stevens v. Marks,* 383 US 234, and *Stevens v. McCloskey,* 383 US 234, in conferring immunity, there must be strict compliance with the procedural requirements of the statute. Though the *Stevens* cases (citing *People v. Laino,* 10 NY2d 161, 173, 176 NE2d 571) held that immunity is not automatically conferred "merely by testifying," it must be borne in mind they involve contempt proceedings where complete immunity had not been conferred. The New York Court of Appeals rulings, therefore, in *Laino,* as well as in *People v. Steuding,* 6 NY2d 214, are essentially undisturbed. "[A]ccordingly the *Steuding-Laino* immunity—if otherwise applicable—cannot now be invoked to validate this contempt conviction." *Stevens v. Marks, supra,* at 246. *See also: People v. Woodruff,* 50 Misc2d 430, 270 NYS2d 838, affd 26 AD2d 236, 272 NYS2d 786.

While no statute authorizes a grant of immunity for the crime of adultery, endangering life or health of a child, or permitting use of a building for opium smoking, the grand jury investigation dealt with conspiracy to commit these crimes for which immunity as to the conspiracy may be conferred. Such immunity covers crimes disclosed by the testimony but as to which there is no specific immunity statute. *See, e.g.,* CPL §§ 50.10, 50.20, 50.30, 190.40.

Where defendant received the maximum immunity that the state could grant, it was held sufficient to require her to testify even though there was a possibility of prosecution in other jurisdictions. *People v. Woodruff, supra. See also: Mal-*

*loy v. Hogan,* 378 US 1; *Murphy v. Waterfront Comm.,* 378 US 52.

§ 25. **Compelled Self-Incrimination.** The use of defendant's voice to identify him does not violate his privilege against self-incrimination. *People v. Livingston,* 15 NY2d 977, 207 NE2d 530.

A "defendant cannot give testimony and demonstrative evidence in his favor, and then object to legitimate cross-examination, upon the grounds of self-incrimination." *State v. Taylor* (Arizona), 407 P2d 59.

This holding is in accord with the line of cases which refuse to recognize a partial waiver of the privilege. Once a defendant has elected to take the stand in his own defense, he is subject to legitimate cross-examination. *People v. Sorge,* 301 NY 198.

In *Taylor,* the defendant testified on direct examination that he owned a hat like the one found at the scene of the robbery but had lost it prior to the date of the robbery. Requiring him on cross-examination to try on the hat, did not violate his privilege against self-incrimination.

Historically the privilege against self-incrimination has been limited to oral testimonial compulsion and the compulsory production of documents or other articles. Thus it has been held that an order for the extraction of blood samples of a wife and child for a blood grouping examination in a divorce case, for the purpose of proving adultery, does not violate the privilege. *Mestichelli v. Mestichelli,* 44 Misc2d 707, 255 NYS2d 185; *Schmerber v. Calif.,* 384 US 757.

Since the Fifth Amendment does not apply to physical evidence obtained by compulsion, such as fingerprints, photographs, measurements, etc., writing, speaking for identification of voice, or a compelled handwriting specimen is not inadmissible in defendant's prosecution.

In *People v. Goldberg,* 19 NY2d 460, 227 NE2d 575, defendant was required to sign a receipt for monies obtained from him by the police, upon their return to him. His signed receipt was admitted in evidence at his trial. The Court of Appeals rejected defendant's contention that this amounted to compelled self-incrimination.

The right to invoke the privilege in a federal deportation proceeding (a civil action) was also denied in *U.S. ex rel Bilokumsky v. Tod,* 263 US 149.

*Bilokumsky* is not to be interpreted as a phohibition against invoking the privilege in civil cases. *See: U.S. ex rel Vajtauer v. Commissioner,* 273 US 103. However, it must be carefully noted, as the court stated in *Vajtauer* at page 113, "The privilege may not be relied on and must be deemed waived if not in some manner fairly brought to the attention of the tribunal which must pass upon it."

On the other hand, in a case involving arbitration under a collective bargaining agreement with a trade union, the employer would not be compelled to produce his books for examination pursuant to a subpoena duces tecum, where he had been indicted with respect to the same subject matter during the arbitration hearings, and where he asserted the privilege against self-incrimination.

Accordingly, the deletion from the subpoena of the words "for examination," even though the books would not be received in evidence, was proper. "The testimony of a written instrument is given as soon as the eye falls upon it and the mind thereby becomes posessed of its contents. *Matter of Foster,* 139 App Div 769." *Matter of Local Union No. 964* [*Langemyr*], 25 AD2d 534.

In an action in which the defendant had sought to examine the plaintiff before trial, the New York Court of Appeals said in *Laverne v. Village,* 18 NY2d 635, 638, 219 NE2d 294:

> "As to plaintiff's constitutional argument that by compelling disclosure the court is denying him the privilege against self-incrimination, the issue was thoroughly discussed and resolved in *Levine v. Bornstein* (13 Misc2d 161 [Sup. Ct. 1958], affd. 7 AD2d 995 [2d Dept.], affd. without opn. 6 NY2d 892 [1959]. The privilege against self-incrimination was intended to be used solely as a shield, and thus a plaintiff cannot use it as a sword to harass a defendant and to effectively thwart any attempt by defendant at a pretrial discovery proceeding to obtain information relevant to the cause of action alleged and possible defenses thereto (See, also, *Franklin* v.

*Franklin,* [283 SW2d 483,] 365 Mo. 442; *Hazlett* v. *Bullis,* 12 AD2d 784 [2d Dept., 1961].)"

A defendant may not refuse to testify before a grand jury on the ground that it violates her religious freedom. Religious freedom may not be invoked in justification of acts detrimental to the public good and safety. *West Virginia State Board of Education v. Barnette,* 319 US 624, 643–644; *People v. Woodruff,* 50 Misc2d 430; 270 NYS2d 838, affd 26 AD2d 236, 272 NYS2d 786.

The Minnesota Supreme Court has declared that, in the absence of statutes governing the procedure in cases where the accused pleads insanity as a defense and providing the necessary machinery and guidelines for the protection of the accused from self-incrimination, the courts have no legal basis, without the defendant's consent, for ordering an examination either to determine his mental condition at the time of the alleged criminal acts or to qualify an expert psychiatric witness by virtue of such examination to testify at the trial. *State v. Olson,* 143 NW2d 69.

Testimonial compulsion may be present where a defendant has been indicted, based in part on inculpatory statements made by him following the granting of immunity by a district attorney under the provisions of the statute. *People v. Caserino,* 16 NY2d 255, dissent by Desmond, Ch. J.

In *State v. Tyson* (New Jersey), 204 A2d 864, cert. den. 380 US 987, defendant and another were charged with robbery and possession of a dangerous weapon. The second defendant had pleaded guilty to robbery but had not yet been sentenced. Tyson called him as a defense witness, but he refused to answer on the ground of self-incrimination. On the authority of *Malloy v. Hogan,* 378 US 1 and *Hoffman v. U.S.,* 341 US 479, it was held he could assert his constitutional privilege since he might incriminate himself on the weapons charge and he could still apply to withdraw his robbery plea.

**§ 26. Compelled Testimony in a Federal Contempt Proceeding.** A witness before a federal grand jury who had been directed to answer but who refused to do so even though he had been granted complete immunity, could not be summarily adjudged in contempt and punished. He was entitled to notice and a hearing (Fed Rule Crim P 42[b]), as the alleged contempt did not actually take place in the presence of the court. *Harris v. U.S.,* 382 US 162, overruling *Brown v. U.S.,* 359 US 41.

The dissenting opinion of four justices highlighted a problem which has disturbed many judges and lawyers, to wit, the absence of "clear and consistent guidance to the federal judiciary in the application of ground rules of our own making. We are not faithful to our duty, I think, when we overturn a settled construction of those rules for no better reasons than those the Court has offered in this case." 382 US at 168.

Where a witness appeared before a federal grand jury investigating alleged federal narcotics law violations, refused to answer questions even after a grant of immunity, and the court thereupon imposed a conditional sentence giving the witness an unqualified right to be released if and when he obeyed the order to testify, it was held, (1) that the conditional nature of the sentence rendered the action a civil contempt proceeding for which indictment and jury trial were not constitutionally required, (2) since the term of the grand jury before whom the petitioner was contumacious had expired, the judgment would be vacated and the case would be remanded for dismissal, and (3) the sentence could be reimposed if appellant persisted in his refusal to testify before a sucessor grand jury. *Shillitani v. U.S.,* 384 US 364, 86 SC 1531.

But note, that the U.S. District Court has held that a partner was entitled to exercise his privilege against self-incrimination and to refuse to produce, pursuant to a subpoena for grand jury inspection, books of a small general partnership in which he was a partner *U.S. v. Cogan,* 257 F Supp 170.

The prohibition of double jeopardy is not violated by the reiterated adjudications of contempt. In *U.S. ex rel Ushkowitz v. McCloskey,* 359 F2d 788, each of several grand jury witnesses was granted immunity after pleading the Fifth Amendment, but still refused to answer. They were adjudged in contempt and sentenced. After serving their sentences, they were again called and again refused to answer and were again fined and imprisoned. This happened a third time. After exhausting their state remedies they filed a federal court petition for habeas corpus. In dismissal of the petition, the Second Circuit held:

> "We need not here discuss again the extent to which the double jeopardy clause of the Fifth Amendment may limit state power, see United States ex rel. Hetenyi v. Wilkins, 348 F.2d 844 (2d Cir. 1965), cert. denied, Mancusi v. Hetenyi, 383 U.S. 913, 86 S.Ct. 896, 15 L. Ed.2d 667 (1966), for by no accepted standard do the repeated prosecutions of these appellants constitute double jeopardy.
>
> "Appellants were not tried or punished more than once for a single offense. Each episode before the grand jury was a separate and distinct contempt. The conduct for which the sentences were imposed was similar conduct, but it was engaged in on three occasions separated from each other by appreciable periods of time." *Id* at 789. *Cf. Yates v. U.S.,* 355 US 66, 72.

"The public has a right to every man's evidence." *Piemonte v. U.S.,* 367 US 556; *accord: Reina v. U.S.,* 364 US 507.

In a contempt proceeding, the Second Circuit held that where a federal grand jury was conducting an investigation under the Federal Communications Act, which authorized a grant of immunity, and immunity was conferred on the witness, the immunity extended to all compelled testimony that bore a substantial relationship to the subject matter of the investigation even though it related to other statues as well. The witness also enjoyed immunity from the use of that testimony by state prosecuting agencies under *Murphy, supra. U.S. v. Harris,* 334 F2d 460, revd 382 US 160.

Where a defendant had been acquitted of conspiracy to violate the federal narcotics laws and was thereafter subpoenaed to testify before a grand jury, his refusal to answer certain questions relating in part to the conspiracy charge, after immunity had been conferred, constituted contempt. Defendant's claim of double jeopardy, res adjudicata, and collateral estoppel, were defenses without merit. The court pointed out that even had the defendant been convicted, the conviction would not have created a right to refuse to answer questions relating to the underlying cause. The only question before the court in the contempt proceeding was whether the defendant wrongfully refused to obey the court order to answer. *U.S. v. Castaldi,* (2d Cir) 338 F2d 883, cert. granted 384 US 886, jdgt vacated and case remanded.

It must be noted that the Fifth Amendment privilege against self-incrimination is a purely personal one. Accordingly, it may not be asserted by an officer or agent of a corporation on its behalf or on witness' own behalf as regards books and papers of the corporation. *Okla. Press Pub. Co. v. Walling,* 327 US 186; *Wilson v. U.S.,* 221 US 361; *Hale v. Henkel,* 201 US 43.

**§ 27. Comment by Court or Prosecutor on Defendant's Failure to Testify.** Heretofore, certain states, notably Ohio, Connecticut, New Jersey, California, Iowa, and New Mexico, permitted comments by the trial judge or prosecutor, where a defendant failed to testify at his criminal trial. *Griffin v. California,* 380 US 609, n.3.

In an Ohio case, *U.S. v. Tehan,* 337 F2d 990, 991, one Tehan was prosecuted for violation of that state's "blue-sky" laws. He did not testify in his own behalf and the prosecutor commented extensively on this, as permitted then by Ohio law. After his conviction, the case came before the United States Court of Appeals in a habeas corpus proceeding, where the court explained the federal rule:

> "[I]t is sufficient to state that if this case had been tried in the United States District Court for an alleged federal offense, it would have violated appellant's constitutional rights against self-incrimination under the Fifth Amendment to the Constitution of the United States. The right contained in the Fifth Amendment that the accused in a criminal trial in the federal court shall not be compelled to be a witness against himself includes both the right not to testify and the right that such failure to testify shall not be subject of comment by the attorney for the prosecution [cases cited]."

In the past, this federal rule had been held not applicable to state criminal prosecutions. *Twining v. New Jersey,* 211

US 78; *Adamson v. California,* 332 US 46, rehrg den. 332 US 784; *Knapp v. Schweitzer,* 357 US 371, 374; *Cohen v. Hurley,* 366 US 117, 127–129.

The day before the argument of the appeal of *U.S. v. Tehan, supra,* the Supreme Court decided *Malloy v. Hogan,* 378 US 1, in which it held that the Fifth Amendment's exception from self-incrimination is also protected by the Fourteenth Amendment against abridgement by the states.

A year after *Malloy,* in *Griffin v. California,* 380 US 609, 614, 615 the Supreme Court reaffirmed *Malloy* in the following language: "We . . . hold that the Fifth Amendment, in its direct application to the Federal Government, and in its bearing on the States by reason of the Fourteenth Amendment, forbids either comment by the prosecution on the accused's silence or instructions by the court that such silence is evidence of guilt." The Court noted, that to permit comment, "is a penalty imposed by courts for exercising a constitutional privilege. It cuts down on the privilege by making its assertion costly."

*See also:* 28 USC § 2111; Fed R Crim P §§ 52(a), 61; *Fahy v. Connecticut,* 375 US 85; *Chapman v. California,* 386 US 18.

§ 27.01. **Retroactivity.** *Griffin* was decided on April 28, 1965. In January, 1966, *U.S. v. Tehan,* 337 F2d 990, appeared on the Supreme Court docket as *Tehan v. Shott,* 382 US 406, on a writ of certiorari to determine if *Griffin v. California, supra,* "is to be given retrospective application."

Basing its decision on the rationale of *Linkletter v. Walker,* 381 US 618, the court answered the question in the negative. Thus, the cut-off date is April 28, 1965.

Comment on a defendant's failure to testify may be insinuated in the charge to the jury. In a prosecution involving possession, custody or control of an illicit still case (26 USC § 5601(a)(1)), the instructions to the jury included this: "unless the defendant by the evidence in the case and by proven facts and circumstances explains such presence to the satisfaction of the jury." This was held to be a proper charge in that it could not be fairly understood as a comment on the defendant's failure to testify in contravention of the Fifth Amendment. *U.S. v. Gainey,* 380 US 63, 70. *See also: U.S. v. Piccioli,* 352 F2d 856; *cf. Bruno v. U.S.,* 308 US 287.

**§ 28. Defendant's Prior Record.** In the District of Columbia, the law provides that a person's conviction may be given in evidence to affect his credibility as a witness, although it has been held that the statute is not mandatory in its application. While a prior conviction may have some bearing on credibility, the court is not bound to permit impeachment in every case. This is discretionary, since there well may be cases in which the trial judge may think that the cause of truth may be better served by allowing the jury to hear the defendant's story than by the defendant's foregoing that opportunity because of fear of prejudice founded on a former conviction. *Luck v. U.S.,* 348 F2d 763; *Brown v. U.S.,* 375 F2d 310, cert. den. 388 US 915.

New Jersey, which has a similar statute, has held to the contrary. With respect to the *Luck* decision it said, "We consider that construction strained and not justified by the context of the statute." *State v. Hawthorne,* 49 NJ 130, 228 A2d 682.

New York CPL § 60.40 referring to the same matter of evidence of prior convictions has avoided any reference to the rule in *Luck, supra.*

Thus, it would seem that in New York, the applicability of the *Luck* rule is discretionary with the trial judge, pending an appellate court's interpretation of that rule.

Additionally, in New York the people may put into evidence the defendant's prior criminal record even though he does not testify, where the defendant offers evidence of his good character. In other words the people may independently prove any prior convictions of the defendant for an offense which would tend to negate any character trait or quality attributed to the defendant in such witness' testimony. *See:* N.Y. CPL § 60.40(2).

Where defense counsel first commented at length on defendant's failure to testify, and the prosecutor replied briefly thereto, the doctrine of invited error was applicable and the defendant could not profit from the error. *People v. Davenport,* 49 Cal Rptr 575.

§ 28.01. **Entrapment.** Where the defense is entrapment, the People may introduce defendant's earlier fingerprint record as part of the case, to show his predisposition, even if the defendant does not take the witness stand. *People v. Chambers,* 56 Misc2d 683, 289 NYS2d 804.

In *U.S. v. Leon,* 441 F2d 175, 178–179, the court held that where defendant sought to introduce evidence tending to negate intent, the government would be permitted on rebuttal to introduce evidence of prior convictions for the same offense.

The defense of entrapment cannot be asserted in federal habeas corpus proceedings as grounds for a collateral attack on a state conviction. *Burdick v. Allgood,* 270 F Supp 614, affd 402 F2d 480.

§ 29. **Habeas Corpus, Self-Incrimination, Due Process and Constitutional Rights.** Habeas corpus may be invoked to challenge a conviction on the ground that evidence was introduced in violation of due process or of the privilege against self-incrimination or on the ground that the one convicted was deprived of a fundamental or constitutional right, even though the convicting court had jurisdiction of his person and of the crime charged and had power to impose the sentence given.

In *Hoover v. Beto,* 439 F2d 913, the federal courts entertained jurisdiction on a writ of habeas corpus in a case involving consent to a search, following defendant's conviction in a Texas court.

The federal authority and requirements for such habeas corpus relief, are contained in 28 USC § 2254.

Subdivision (a) of this section authorizes federal judges to entertain an application for a writ of habeas corpus in behalf of a person in custody pursuant to the judgment of a State court only on the ground that he is in custody in violation of the Constitution or laws or treaties of the United States.

Factual issues decided by a State court will be presumed to be correct if a hearing on the merits had been had before a court of competent jurisdiction, and in which both the State and the applicant for the writ were parties. 28 USC § 2254(d).

However, there are exceptions to this provision: (1) where the merits of the factual dispute were not resolved in the State court hearing; (2) the State court factfinding procedure was not adequate to afford a full and fair hearing; (3) that the material facts were not adequately developed at the State court hearing; (4) the State court lacked jurisdiction of the person of the applicant or of the subject matter; (5) that applicant was indigent and the State court failed to appoint an attorney to represent him in violation of his constitutional rights; (6) that the applicant did not receive a full, fair and adequate hearing in the State court; (7) that the applicant was otherwise denied due process of law in the State court proceeding; and (8) where the State court record of the proceedings in question fails to fairly support the factual determination made therein. 28 USC § 2254(d).

State remedies, where available, must be exhausted before the federal courts will take jurisdiction. § 2254(b)(c).

Habeas corpus proceedings are not intended as another means to provide additional appeal or collateral review of matters involving alleged errors committed during applicant's trial unless constitutional errors are presented and are in issue. *Norris v. State of South Carolina, Greenville County,* 309 F Supp 1113.

Alleged unfairness in a State proceeding which is not of constitutional stature does not furnish grounds for issuance of a federal writ of habeas corpus. *U.S. ex rel Lopinson v. Bookbinders,* 237 F Supp 180.

On the other hand, § 2254(d)(7) specifically authorizes the issuance of the writ where due process has been violated. *Barnett v. Gladden,* 375 F2d 235; U.S. Const. amend XIV.

The denial of fundamental fairness must be of such a nature that it fatally infected the trial, and the acts complained must be of such a quality as necessarily prevents a fair trial before it can be said that due process has been violated. *U.S. ex rel Irwin v. Pate,* 357 F2d 911; *Schiers v. California,* 33 F2d 173; *U.S. ex rel Cannon v. Maroney,* 255 F Supp 235, affd 373 F2d 908.

As the Supreme Court said in *Rochin v. California,* 342 US at 165, 169–172, the Due Process Clause of the Fourteenth Amendment,

> "[I]mposes upon this Court an exercise of judgment upon the whole course of the proceedings . . . in order to ascertain whether they offend those canons of decency and fairness which express the notions of justice of English-speaking peoples even toward those charged with the most heinous offenses."

As the Court noted in *Rochin* "conduct that shocks the conscience" offends against the Due Process Clause.

Perjury knowingly used by the prosecution in a state trial, violates state prisoners' right to a fair trial and constitutes a deprivation of due process, requiring the issuance of a writ of habeas corpus. *Clark v. Warden,* 293 F2d 479, cert. den. 369 US 877.

## Chapter 4

# ESCOBEDO AND MIRANDA: POISONED OR TAINTED EVIDENCE—RIGHT TO COUNSEL

**§ 38. Confessions and Admissions Defined.** "An admission might very well be called a confession's little brother. A confession includes an acknowledgment of all of the essential elements of the crime charged and is generally defined as an acknowledgment of guilt. Admissions, however, are merely acknowledgments of one or more facts which fall short of supplying all of the essential elements to constitute the offense charged. Accordingly, an admission, if it is to be distinguished from a confession, must be something short of an acknowledgment of guilt." *Journal of Criminal Law and Criminology,* Vol. XXXIX, No. 6, March-April 1949, p. 743.

## § 39. The Escobedo and Miranda Cases.

**§ 39.01 The Pre-Escobedo-Miranda Rules.** The philosophy which engendered holding confessions and admissions inadmissible if they were coerced by physical force or threats (*People v. Crossman,* 184 AD 724, 172 NYS 567; *People v. Mummiani,* 258 NY 394; *Payne v. Arkansas,* 356 US 560); or because they were obtained under circumstances inherently coercive (*Payne v. Arkansas, supra; Haley v. Ohio,* 332 US 596; *Aschcraft v. Tennessee,* 322 US 143); or because they were obtained after protracted interrogation of a defendant and unnecessary delay in arraignment (*McNabb v. U.S.,* 318 US 332; *Mallory v. U.S.,* 354 US 449; *Coleman v. U.S.,* 317 F2d 891; *People v. Vitagliano,* 15 NY2d 360, 206 NE2d 839; *cf. U.S. v. Price,* 345 F2d 256); or because they were obtained during a delay in defendant's arraignment in order to permit him to complete a voluntary statement (*Walton v. U.S.,* 334 F2d 343; Fed R Crim P 5(a); *cf: People v. Everett,* 10 NY2d 500, 180 NE2d 556; *Killough v. U.S.,* 315 F2d 241; *People v. Weinstein,* 11 NY2d 1098, 184 NE2d 312, [dissent]); or because they were obtained from a defendant during a period of detention following an illegal arrest (*People v. Everett, supra; Stein v.* N.Y., 346 US 156; *People v. Alex,* 265 NY 192); or because they were obtained following failure to advise an indigent defendant of his right to the assignment of counsel (*Gideon v. Wainwright,* 372 US 335; *People v. Witenski,* 15 NY2d 392, 207 NE2d 358); or because they were obtained after the defendant was represented by counsel (*Massiah v. U.S.,* 377 US 201; *People v. Gunner,* 15 NY2d 226, 205 NE2d 852; *People v. Pizarro,* 20 AD2d 900, 248 NYS2d 1007, revd 15 NY2d 803, 205 NE2d 694); or because they were obtained after judicial process against the defendant had begun (*Massiah v. U.S., supra; People v. Friedlander,* 16 NY2d 248, 212 NE2d 533; *People v. Pizarro, supra*); or because they were obtained as the "fruit of the poisonous tree" (*Wong Sun v. U.S.,* 371 US 471; *Nueslein v. D. of C.,* 115 F2d 690; *People v. Rodriguez,* 11 NY2d 279, 183 NE2d 651); or because of failure to equate members of a defendant's family with counsel (*People v. Taylor,* 22 AD2d 524, 256 NYS2d 944, mod 16 NY2d 1038, 213 NE2d 321; *People v. Hocking,* 15 NY2d 973, 207 NE2d 529), are questions that have now become largely academic, though historically interesting, by virtue of the decision of the U.S. Supreme Court in *Miranda v. Arizona,* 384 US 436.

To understand how the Supreme Court determined the rules it laid down in *Miranda,* an understanding of *Escobedo v. Illinois,* 378 US 478, is necessary.

**§ 39.02. The Escobedo Decision.** *Miranda v. Arizona, supra,* was a landmark decision in the area of admissions and confessions. Certain basic questions posed in *Miranda* were resolved earlier by the Supreme Court in *Escobedo v. Illinois,* 378 US 478.

Escobedo was arrested on a murder charge, without a warrant and prior to indictment; he was kept in custody at police headquarters and interrogated for many hours as a prime suspect. His request for counsel was denied by the police although his retained attorney was present in police headquarters at the time. The attorney's request to speak with his client was also denied by the police on the ground that they had not completed their interrogation. The obvious purpose of this interrogation was to obtain his confession.

He was not informed of his right to remain silent or of his right to counsel and was told by the police that his lawyer "did not want to see him."

After a protracted interrogation and a confrontation with a co-defendant, Escobedo made some inculpatory statements and thereafter, still in police headquarters, he signed a confession. His timely motion to suppress his incriminating statements was denied.

Writing for the majority of the Court, Justice Goldberg stated:

> "The critical question in this case is whether, under the circumstances, the refusal by the police to honor petitioner's request to consult with his lawyer during the course of an interrogation constitutes a denial of 'the Assistance of Counsel' in violation of the Sixth Amendment to the Constitution as 'made obligatory upon the States by the Fourteenth Amendment,' Gideon v. Wainwright, 372 U.S. 335, 342, . . . , and thereby renders inadmissible in a state criminal trial any incriminating statement elicited by the police during the interrogation." 378 US at 479.

The basic facts in the case were not in dispute. Escobedo was a prime suspect in a murder case. He was interrogated in custody, not in the course of a general police investigation into an unsolved crime, but as a target upon whom the police were concentrating and from whom, during the course of a lengthy interrogation, they sought to elicit incriminating statements. He had been denied an opportunity to consult with his lawyer and additionally he was not "effectively warned of his absolute constitutional right to remain silent." 378 US at 491.

Under these facts, the court held that no statement elicited by the police during the interrogation could be used against him at a criminal trial. His murder conviction was reversed.

The majority opinion concluded:

> "Nothing we have said today affects the powers of the police to investigate 'an unsolved crime' . . . , by gathering information from witnesses and by other 'proper investigative efforts.' . . . We hold only that when the process shifts from investigatory to accusatory—when its focus is on the accused and its purpose is to elicit a confession—our adversary system begins to operate, and, under the circumstances here, the accused must be permitted to consult with his lawyer." *Id.* at 492.

**§ 40. Meaning and Effect of Escobedo.** The *Escobedo* decision apparently merges the privilege against self-incrimination with the right to counsel. However, the seeming ambiguity of the language of the decision led to confusion, uncertainty and various interpretations.

For instance, in his opening statement (p. 479), Mr. Justice Goldberg stated that the "critical question" presented in this case was the effect of the denial of the right to counsel on petitioner's incriminating statements. Yet the opinion contains observations regarding self-incrimination which the court did not mention as part of the "critical question" posed.

Additionally, the court stated that it is proper to question witnesses in a general investigation of an unsolved crime, but once the police develop a prime suspect in the course of their investigation, *i.e.,* when the investigation "shifts from investigative to accusatory" and focuses on a particular suspect, then the police must pull up short and advise the suspect of his constitutional rights. Just how one determines when this "shift" takes place or when the "focus" develops, the court does not say.

As Mr. Justice White pointed out in his dissent (*id.* at 495), the majority decision prevents the police from obtaining admissions from a defendant once the investigation begins to "focus" on him.

The applicability of the rule laid down in *Massiah v. U.S.*, 377 US 201, referred to by Goldberg, J., is also unclear since *Massiah* was a federal, post-indictment case, while *Escobedo* was a state pre-indictment case (*See:* dissent by Stewart, J., *id.* at 493).

The question presented to the court based on the facts as recited by Mr. Justice Goldberg in his opening statement, indicates that the *Escobedo* rule applied to the facts of that case only. Mr. Justice White (p. 494) was of this opinion also.

As a result, the legal profession was swamped with treatises on the import and meaning of *Escobedo,* and various courts throughout the country interpreted it differently. *See: U.S. ex rel Russo v. New Jersey,* 351 F2d 429, judgment vacated, 384 US 889; *U.S. v. Drummond,* 354 F2d 132; *People v. Gunner,* 15 NY2d 220, 205 NE2d 852; *People v. Dorado,* 61 Cal2d 890, 40 Cal Rptr 264, 394 P2d 952; *"Escobedo in New York,"* St. John's Law Review, Vol. XL, No. 1, Dec. 1965, pp. 51, 59.

The Supreme Court noted this confusion over the meaning of *Escobedo,* and in referring to *Escobedo,* commented in *Miranda v. Arizona,* 384 US at 440:

> "This case [Escobedo] has been the subject of judicial interpretation and spirited legal debate since it was decided two years ago. Both state and federal courts, in assessing its implications, have arrived at varying conclusions. A wealth of scholarly material has been written tracing its ramifications and underpinnings."

Although, as noted above, Escobedo's conviction was reversed, the court apparently stopped short of striking down the entire interrogation-confession system.

**§ 41. The Scope and Meaning of Miranda.** *Miranda,* and three other cases decided with it, give an entirely new and more liberal definition of a coerced confession or admission obtained from a person in the custody of the police during an investigation. These cases also broaden the privilege against self-incrimination under the Fifth Amendment. Essentially, they deal with (a) the admissibility of statements obtained from an individual suspected or accused of crime who is subject to custodial interrogation, and (b) the necessity of establishing procedures which will assure him of his privilege under the Fifth Amendment not to be compelled to incriminate himself.

*Miranda,* like *Escobedo,* was a 5 to 4 decision. However, unlike *Escobedo, Miranda* is noteworthy, not so much because of the facts involved, but because of the pronouncements it dictates regarding the constitutional prerequisites governing admissions and confessions. As a matter of fact, the Supreme Court dealt with the facts of these cases in a cursory manner.

Miranda and the co-petitioners were arrested on various charges and subjected to incommunicado interrogation by the police "or a prosecuting attorney in a room cut off from the outside world. In none of these cases was the defendant given a full and effective warning of his rights at the outset of the interrogation process. In all the cases, the questioning elicited oral admissions, and in three of them, signed statements as well which were admitted at their trials. They all thus share salient features—incommunicado interrogation of individuals in a police-dominated atmosphere, resulting in self-incriminating statements without full warnings of constitutional rights." 384 US at 445.

It seems, to this writer, that the court was deeply distressed over many police practices used in obtaining incriminating statements from suspects and defendants, and that the facts in *Miranda* were used merely as a backdrop for its determination to eliminate reprehensible methods, physical as well as psychological, too often employed by police officers in their efforts to obtain admissions. *See, e.g., People v. Portelli,* 15 NY2d 235, 205 NE2d 857, cert. den. 382 US 1009, cited in *Miranda v. Arizona, supra,* p. 446, where the police burned a witness with cigarettes in an attempt to obtain statements from him.

By invoking an exclusionary rule, similar to that laid down in *Weeks v. U.S.,* 232 US 383, and extending it to the states, the court, in formulating new procedural safeguards in the area of admissions and confessions, hoped to put an end to improper interrogation practices. These "procedural safeguards" are discussed *infra.*

**§ 41.01. Basic Constitutional Principles of Miranda.** *Miranda* reiterates two basic constitutional principles set forth in *Escobedo:* (1) that " 'no person * * * should be compelled in any criminal case to be a witness against himself,' " and (2) that " 'the accused shall * * * have the Assistance of Counsel.' " *Miranda* (384 US at 442) holds further that these rights (Fifth and Sixth Amendments) are of constitutional dimensions and attach even before the commencement of any formal judicial proceedings against the accused. *See: Spano v. N.Y.,* 360 US 315; *People v. Waterman,* 9 NY2d 561, 175 NE2d 445; *People v. Pizarro,* 20 AD2d 900, revd and remanded for new trial, 15 NY2d 803, 205 NE2d 694.

**§ 41.02. Juveniles.** The rule that "no person * * * should be compelled in any criminal case to be a witness against himself," applies equally to juveniles. They, too, are entitled to the same protection and due process. *Matter of Gault,* 387 US 1; *Matter of Gregory,* 19 NY2d 55, 62. These requirements include adequate notice of the charges to the child and his parents and of the child's rights. Thus, where the child is taken into custody by the police (NY Family Court Act, §§ 721–729), the proper safeguarding of the child's privilege against self-incrimination suggests that he should not be questioned until he and at least one of his parents are notified of his right to remain silent and of the other *Miranda* rights. Accordingly, statements taken by the police from a 15-year old juvenile after *Miranda* warnings were given him, but in the absence of his mother and counsel, violates due process. *Matter of Aaron D.,* 30 AD2d 183, 290 NYS2d 935.

Extending the rationale of *Aaron D.,* the New York Court of Appeals has held that in a Youthful Offender proceeding (Y.O.) the Court must make a specific, unequivocal finding of the voluntariness of a confession made to a police officer before admitting it when challenged by the defendant. *People v. Sykes,* 22 NY2d 159.

There is an obligation, the Court has warned, on the judiciary to apply these rights. *Weems v. U.S.,* 217 US 349. They must be implemented and the rendition of mere lip service to their existence is insufficient. *Silverthorne Lumber Co. v. U.S.,* 251 US 385, 392; *Miranda v. Arizona, supra* at 444.

Although the U.S. District Court held that a "guidance conference" with school authorities for the purpose of determining a child's future right to attend New York public schools indicates that the child "is in enough trouble" to warrant the presence of counsel. *Madera v. Bd. of Ed.,* 267 F Supp 356, the Circuit Court of Appeals reversed, holding that a pupil at a school disciplinary hearing had no right to counsel. *Madera v. Bd. of Ed.,* 386 F2d 778, cert. den. 390 US 1028.

**§ 42. Limitations on Use of Defendant's Statements.** In consonance with these principles, it follows that "the prosecution may not use statements, whether exculpatory or inculpatory, stemming from custodial interrogation of the defendant unless it demonstrates the use of procedural safeguards effective to secure the privilege against self-incrimination." *Miranda v. Arizona,* 384 US at 444. Thus, the court affirmed the merger of the privilege against self-incrimination with the right to counsel, implied in *Escobedo.*

The *Miranda* rules were held to be applicable in the New York State Court of Claims where a claimant sued for false arrest. After his arrest, claimant had made incriminatory statements to the police in violation of the *Miranda* rules. The statements were held to be of no probative value in his civil suit for damages for false arrest. If those statements could not be used in a criminal prosecution against the claimant, the court ruled that they were likewise barred from use against him when he becomes a plaintiff in a civil suit or proceeding. *Dixson v. State,* 54 Misc2d 100, 281 NYS2d 912.

**§ 43. Definition of Terms Used in Miranda.** The *Miranda* rules refer to "custodial interrogation" of suspects and defendants. This term is defined as the questioning of a suspect or an accused, initiated by the police "while the defendant is in custody or otherwise deprived of his freedom of action in any significant way." pp. 444–445. *Cf. People v. Allen,* 50 Misc2d 897, revd 28 AD2d 724.

However, as to what constitutes "custodial interrogation" the New York Appellate Division in *People v. Allen, supra,* did not accept the rule laid down by the lower court. In effect, the court adopted the rule that coercion would be measured by the defendant's state of mind. Accordingly, the inculpatory statements made to a police officer by a defendant who had not been given the *Miranda* warnings would be admissible when at the time in question, the defendant had not been taken into custody or otherwise deprived of his freedom of action even though the officer had gone to the defendant's home for the purpose of making the arrest and would not have permitted the defendant to leave the room before interrogation.

There was no compulsion present in the defendant Allen's mind at the time he made the statements. He did not know what was in the officer's mind at the time of the interrogation. The defendant was in his own home with members of his family, at the time. Coercion was not present under these circumstances "and we see no reason to go beyond what the Supreme Court has required in applying" the rules announced in *Miranda.*

In *Allen,* the lower court held that the defendant was in custody if the police intended that fact. However, another justice of the New York State Supreme Court has held that this test is incorrect.

"In my view, the test whether there is 'custodial interrogation' under *Miranda v. Arizona,* (384 U.S. 436) is rather the belief of the person under interrogation as to whether he is in custody." *People v. Colleran* (3/13/67), 35 USLW 2540. If the person being questioned is not in custody or is not under the impression that he is in custody, the compulsion to self-incrimination, inherent in custodial surroundings, is absent and the procedural precautions laid down in *Miranda* are not required. *See, e.g., People v. Portelli,* 15 NY2d 235, 205 NE2d 857, cert. den. 382 US 1009.

The *Miranda* warnings must be given to "protect the individual's freedom of choice—to answer or not answer—in situations which are inherently coercive. . . . The custody requirement of *Miranda* does not depend on the subjective intent of the law enforcement officer-interrogators but upon whether the subject is physically deprived of his freedom of action in any significant way or is placed in a situation in which he reasonably believes that his freedom of action is restrained by such interrogation." *People v. Hazel,* 60 Cal Rptr 437.

The *Hazel* test has been adopted in New York, and thus the *Miranda* warnings need not be given where there is no arrest or other detention or where the defendant is not physically deprived of his freedom of action in any significant way and where the person interrogated is not led to believe, as a reasonable person, that he is so deprived. *See also: People v. Arnold,* 58 Cal Rptr 115, 426 P2d 515.

The theory of *People v. Colleran, supra,* and *People v. Arnold,* has been followed by the New York Court of Appeals in *People v. Yukl,* 25 NY2d 585, 256 NE2d 172.

Additionally, the court in *Yukl* stated that its review of the question of the existence of custodial interrogation would be limited as to whether the evidence was sufficient to support the determination of the hearing court. A determination would accordingly not be disturbed absent a finding that the hearing court's conclusion was not erroneous as a matter of law.

Thus, *Miranda* does not require that its warnings be administered in "routine police investigation of crimes or suspicious conduct at a person's home, his place of business or on the street." Moreover, "the fact that he might have been restrained, had he attempted to leave, is not controlling." *People v. Hazel, supra; Guadia v. State,* 1 Md App 455, 230 A2d 700; *Williams v. U.S.,* 381 F2d 20 (9th Cir).

The test to be applied is, was he in fact restrained in any significant way or was he, "as a reasonable person," led to believe that his freedom was restrained in any significant way. *People v. Rodney P.,* (*Anonymous*), 21 NY2d 1, 286 NYS2d 225, 233 NE2d 255.

*See also: People v. Colleran, supra; People v. Allen, supra; cf. People v. Shivers,* 21 NY2d 118.

The strict application of the *Miranda* rules has been followed by the New York Court of Appeals. That court has held that admissions of a defendant made by him on being shown a search warrant, covering him and his apartment, does not constitute custodial interrogation, for the mere existence of a search warrant covering defendant and his apartment, exhibited to him by an officer who was present to execute it, does not constitute custodial interrogation, and statements voluntarily made by the defendant are admissible. *People v. Torres,* 21 NY2d 49, 233 NE2d 282.

> "Defendant's inculpating remark is admissible, then, unless one is to conclude that the mere existence of the search warrant coupled with the officer's presence amounted to a 'compelling influence.' Such an interpretation would extend the *Miranda* rules beyond their avowed purpose, namely, to forbid 'custodial interrogation' by law enforcement officials of suspects who have not been informed of certain constitutional rights. Absent interrogation, post-*Miranda* decisions have consistently held that voluntary or 'spontaneous' statements made by suspects who were plainly in custody are admissible." *People v. Torres, supra* at 54.

On the other hand, interrogation of a suspect by a police officer, at gun point, constitutes custodial interrogation requiring the *Miranda* warnings. *People v. Shivers,* 21 NY2d 118, 233 NE2d 836.

In *Henry v. U.S.,* 361 US 98, the court stated that an arrest is normally deemed to occur automatically at the point when a suspect's freedom of movement is curtailed. In the area of admissions and confessions, *Miranda* has broadened this definition by defining custodial interrogation as interrogation that occurs after a suspect "has been taken into custody or otherwise deprived of his freedom of action in any significant way." 384 US at 444, 445.

Thus, under *Miranda,* a person will be deemed "arrested" not only if he is formally placed in custody or detention in a police station, but also if he is taken into custody in any other place, *i.e.,* if in such other place he is "deprived of his freedom of action in any significant way."

The target of an investigation must be given the *Miranda* warnings prior to interrogation, regardless of the fact that he had not yet been arrested. *People v. Oramus,* 25 NY2d 825, 250 NE2d 723.

The mere fact that the defendant was interrogated in a police station, where he came of his own volition after federal authorities said that they would meet with him at any place he suggested to talk to him about some stolen automobiles, does not constitute custodial interrogation. At the time in question, the authorities had no evidence against the defendant. *Freije v. U.S.,* 386 F2d 408.

On the other hand, where the defendant in a murder case was interrogated in her own home which was dominated by the police, she was held entitled to the *Miranda* warnings. *People v. Paulin,* 25 NY2d 445, 255 NE2d 164.

There is no requirement that the police in giving the four *Miranda* warnings are required to recite them from memory. They may read them from a card. It is sufficient if the officer testifies that he read the warnings to the defendant and then reads into evidence what appears on the card. *People v. Swift,* 32 AD2d 183, 300 NYS2d 639; *Hale v. State,* 247 A2d 409.

A probationer is not entitled to *Miranda* warnings upon questioning by his probation officer with respect to possible violations of probation. Thus, where probationer visited the probation officer, who noticed needle marks on his arm when accompanying another to the probation office, and defendant confessed to violation of probation, he was not in custody and was not entitled to *Miranda* warnings. *People v. Ronald W. (Anon.),* 24 NY2d 732, 233 NE2d 255. However, it was held in *Bey v. Connecticut,* 443 F2d 1079, and *People ex rel Menechino v. Warden,* 27 NY2d 376, 267 NE2d 238, that a defendant is entitled to be represented by counsel at a parole revocation hearing.

In Ohio it has been held that the *Miranda* warnings are not required in misdemeanor cases. Although the case (*State v. Pyle,* 19 Ohio St2d 64, 249 NE2d 826), involved a charge of driving while intoxicated, the Ohio court, in its language, did not limit its rule to that type of case. Certiorari was denied, 396 US 1007.

§ 44. **The Four-Fold Miranda Warnings.** By "procedural safeguards" the court means that before any questioning of the suspect is undertaken by the authorities, he must be warned: (1) of his right to remain silent, (2) that anything he says may be used against him in a court of law, (3) that before any interrogation is undertaken he is entitled to the presence and aid of counsel, (4) if he cannot afford an attorney, one will be furnished to him free of charge. The purpose of this rule is to apprise the suspect of his right to silence and to assure his "continuous opportunity to exercise it."

§ 44.01. **Right to Remain Silent.** He must be warned that he has a right to remain silent. This warning must be given in clear and unambiguous terms. The knowledge that a suspect may possess, based on his age, education, intelligence or prior contact with the authorities, is immaterial, for "whatever the background of the person interrogated, a warning at the time of the interrogation is indispensable. . . ." 384 US at 467. *Cf. Betts v. Brady,* 316 US 455.

§ 44.02. **Use of Statement Against Suspect.** The warning must be accompanied by the explanation that anything said can and will be used against him in court. 384 US at 469.

§ 44.03. **Right to Counsel.** He must be warned that he has the right to the aid and presence of counsel to assist him. The right to counsel is of constitutional dimensions and this warning is an absolute prerequisite to interrogation, and "an individual held for interrogation must be clearly informed that he has the right to consult with a lawyer and to have the lawyer with him during interrogation. . . ." 384 US at 471. The presence of counsel, the court said, would guarantee the absence of compulsion.

The right-to-counsel warning does not carry with it the right to "instant" counsel. After proper *Miranda* warnings have been given, a defendant may choose to speak of his own free will without the aid or assistance of counsel. *Mayzak v. U.S.,* 402 F2d 152. Nor need the warning include a statement that defendant might have counsel assigned at police headquarters. *People v. Swift,* 32 AD2d 183, 300 NYS2d 639. This warning "does not mean, as some have suggested, that each police station must have a 'station house lawyer' present at all times to advise prisoners." *Miranda v. Arizona,* 384 US at 474.

*Miranda* is satisfied if the warnings are given in writing or orally, and substantially in accordance with the rules enunciated. "The rule does not demand the mouthing of 'a ritualistic formula' (cf. *United States* v. *Vanterpool,* 394 F.2d 697, 698–699; *Irving* v. *Breazeale,* 400 F.2d 231, 234)." *People v. Swift,* 300 NYS2d 639, 644, 32 AD2d 183.

**§ 44.04. Appointment of Counsel.** Finally, the suspect must be warned that if he is indigent, the court will appoint a lawyer to represent him. *See: Gideon v. Wainwright,* 372 US 335, *Douglas v. California,* 372 US 353; *McLeod v. Ohio,* cert. granted and remanded, 378 US 582.

Failure of the police to warn defendant that, if indigent, counsel would be assigned does not vitiate the confession where there was no claim of indigency. Accordingly, his confession will not be excluded unless there is some evidence of indigency at the time of his interrogation. And this is the rule, even though a suspect is not required to inform the police of his indigency. *People v. Post,* 23 NY2d 157, 242 NE2d 830.

**§ 44.05. Repeating the Miranda Warnings.** *Miranda* warnings need not be repeated. Thus, after the warnings had been given to the defendant twice, a request to search his motel room was acceded to by "be my guest." This was a valid consent to the search which required no further *Miranda* warnings. *Gorman v. U.S.,* 380 F2d 158 (2d Cir); *Coyote v. U.S.,* 380 F2d 305 (NM); *U.S. v. Mansfield,* 381 F2d 961 (Ill).

**§ 45. Waiver of Rights.** *Miranda* holds that there is no obligation on a suspect, in the first instance to request counsel. He must be advised of his right to counsel, and his failure to request counsel after the warnings, does not constitute a waiver of his constitutional right to the aid of counsel. "No effective waiver of the right to counsel during interrogation can be recognized unless specifically made after the warnings . . . have been given." 384 US at 470.

*See also: Carnley v. Cochran,* 369 US 506, 513; *People v. Dorado,* 394 P2d 952.

"Moreover, any evidence that the accused was threatened,

tricked, or cajoled into a waiver will, of course, show that the defendant did not voluntarily waive his privilege." *Miranda v. Arizona,* 384 US at 476.

The accused may waive his right to silence and to counsel, if the waiver is "made voluntarily, knowingly, and intelligently."

Where a defendant waives counsel, the court should satisfy itself, before accepting a plea of guilty, that the defendant understands the consequences of the waiver (*see, e.g., von Moltke v. Gillies,* 332 US 708, 724), and that the defendant in fact committed an act which constituted the crime and would furnish basis for the plea. *People v. Serrano,* 15 NY2d 304, 308, 206 NE2d 330; *People v. Seaton,* 19 NY2d 404, 280 NYS2d 370, 227 NE2d 294.

**§ 45.01. Waiver: Burden of Proof.** The burden of establishing a waiver by the accused is on the prosecution. This is based on the rule that the waiver of a constitutional right will not be lightly inferred. *Johnson v. Zerbst,* 304 US 458. This rule applies to in-custody interrogations, and "a heavy burden rests on the government to demonstrate that the defendant knowingly and intelligently waived his privilege against self-incrimination and his right to retained or appointed counsel." *Miranda v. Arizona,* 384 US at 475.

Mere silence by the accused after he has been advised of his rights creates no presumption of a valid waiver. Nor will a valid waiver be presumed simply from the fact that a confession was obtained. *Carnley v. Cochran,* 369 US 506. A statement made by the accused closely following an express statement that he wishes to make a statement and does not want an attorney, could constitute a valid waiver of his right to silence and his right to counsel.

An in-custody interrogation, during which the accused made some statements or answered some questions, does not constitute a waiver as to other questions that may be asked of him. He may invoke his privilege at any time during in-custody interrogation. *Cf. Rogers v. U.S.* 340 US 367.

**§ 45.02. Presumptions.** Regardless of testimony by the authorities as to waivers exercised by the accused "the fact of a lengthy interrogation or incommunicado incarceration before a statement is made is strong evidence that the accused did not validly waive his rights. In these circumstances the fact that the individual eventually made a statement is consistent with the conclusion that the compelling influence of the interrogation finally forced him to do so. It is inconsistent with any notion of a voluntary relinquishment of the privilege." 384 US at 476.

**§ 46. Incident Search and Request for Counsel.** "The usual rule is that, when a person is arrested for an offense committed in the presence of an officer, portable, personal effects in the possession of the arrested person may be searched without a warrant (Museums v. State of New York, 20 Misc.2d 960, 195 N.Y.S.2d 798; 79 C.J.S. Searches and Seizures, § 68). The law is the same where the person is arrested under circumstances where there was probable cause for believing that he is or was engaged in the commission of a crime (United States v. Scott, 149 F.Supp. 837; 79 C.J.S. Searches and Seizures, § 68). No different situation ought to obtain because defendant requests counsel before the otherwise permissible search is completed." *People v. Dunleavy,* 26 AD2d 649, 651, 272 NYS2d 795, 798.

**§ 47. Mental Defective—Right to Counsel—Waiver.** A mental defective does not have the mental capacity to waive his right to counsel. *People v. Drake,* 26 AD2d 729, 271 NYS2d 930.

**§ 48. The Right Not to Talk and the Right to Stop Talking.** Once the warnings have been given, if the suspect indicates in any manner at any time prior to or during the questioning that he wishes to remain silent, the interrogation must cease.

> "If, however, he indicates in any manner and at any stage of the process that he wishes to consult with an attorney before speaking there can be no questioning. Likewise, if the individual is alone and indicates in any manner that he does not wish to be interrogated, the police may not question him." *Miranda v. Arizona,* 384 US at 444–445.

If he states that he wants an attorney, the interrogation must cease until an attorney is present. He must be accorded the right to consult with his attorney and the attorney must be present during any subsequent questioning. If he indicates that he wants an attorney before speaking to the police and he cannot obtain one, the police may not question him.

Once the police know or have been apprised of the fact that defendant is represented by counsel, or that an attorney has communicated with the police for the purpose of representing him, the accused's right to counsel attaches and this right is not dependent upon the existence of a formal retainer.

> "Nor is it significant that [the attorney] did not, immediately upon his arrival at Police Headquarters, instruct the police not to take any statements from the defendant. . . . Once an attorney enters the proceeding, the police may not question the defendant in the absence of counsel unless there is an affirmative waiver, in the presence of the attorney, of the defendant's right to counsel." *People v. Arthur,* 22 NY2d 325, 329, 239 NE2d 537.

*See also: People v. Vella,* 21 NY2d 249, 234 NE2d 422; *People v. Gunner,* 15 NY2d 226, 205 NE2d 852; *People v. Donovan,* 13 NY2d 148, 193 NE2d 628; *cf. People v. Friedlander,* 16 NY2d 248, 212 NE2d 533.

§ 49. **Failure to Assign Counsel to Accused Indigent.** If the authorities fail to provide the accused with counsel during a reasonable period of time in which investigation is carried out, it will not constitute a violation of the accused's rights under the Fifth Amendment, so long as he is not questioned during that period.

§ 50. **Confessions and Admissions Equated.** The Court makes no distinction between confessions and admissions. Within the purview of *Miranda,* these terms are equated. The privilege does not distinguish between degrees of incrimination.

§ 51. **Exculpatory Statements.** The exclusion from evidence of confessions and admissions obtained in violation of the procedural safeguards laid down in *Miranda* applies equally to exculpatory statements. There is no such thing as an actual exculpatory statement in a criminal prosecution according to *Miranda*.

**§ 52. Coercion: Psychological and Inherent Coercion.** Custodial surroundings, coupled with incommunicado interrogation, creates a situation that is inherently and psychologically coercive. This atmosphere carries with it its own badge of intimidation, and there is thus an intimate connection between the privilege against self-incrimination and police custodial questioning. The end result is compelled self-incrimination in violation of the Fifth Amendment.

Since the privilege against self-incrimination has consistently been accorded a liberal constructon, (*Albertson v. SACB,* 382 US 70; *Hoffman v. U.S.,* 341 US 479; *Arndstein v. McCarthy,* 254 US 71; *Counselman v. Hitchcock,* 142 US 547), and since the privilege applies to compulsion exerted by law enforcement officers during in-custody questioning, the results of this type of interrogation, absent the warnings that must be given the defendant, constitute testimonial compulsion, requiring exclusion. "[A] confession obtained by compulsion must be excluded whatever may have been the character of the compulsion, and whether the compulsion was applied in a judicial proceedings or otherwise." *Wan v. U.S.,* 266 US 1, 14–15. The "Fifth Amendment is available outside of criminal court proceedings and serves to protect persons in all settings in which their freedom of action is curtailed in any significant way from being compelled to incriminate themselves." *Miranda v. Arizona,* 384 US at 467.

**§ 52.01. Harmless Error.** The introduction of a coerced confession can never be treated as harmless error. *Chapman v. California,* 386 US 18.

For that reason, the California Supreme Court has held that where an extra-judicial confession was made, subsequently followed by a judicial confession, the burden is on the People to show that the causative link between the two has been broken. "We must therefore recognize that it is always possible that an improperly obtained confession will induce the defendant to render a later admission of guilt."

*People v. Spencer*, 424 P2d 715, 722, 57 Cal Rptr 163. *See also: Fahy v. Conn.*, 375 US 85; *U.S. v. Bayer* (1937), 331 US 532, 540.

§ 52.02. **Witnesses: Compelled Testimony.** The interrogation of witnesses and persons not under restraint does not come within the mandate of the procedural safeguards prescribed in *Miranda.*

However, the court, by implication, strongly condemned the practice of coercing testimony from a prosecution witness. *See, e.g., People v. Portelli,* 15 NY2d 235, 205 NE2d 857, cert. den. 382 US 1009; *Miranda,* 384 US at 446.

§ 53. **Applicability of the McNabb-Mallory Rule.** This rule requires prompt arraignment of a person charged with the commission of a crime in order that he be apprised promptly and properly of his constitutional rights.

The requirement of the Fifth Amendment, and its statutory concomitant, Rule 5(a) (Fed R Crim P) as implemented in *McNabb v. U.S.*, 318 US 332, and *Mallory v. U.S.*, 354 US 449, (the *McNabb-Mallory* Rule), requires exclusion of evidence obtained in violation of a defendant's right to prompt arraignment.

Interrogating a suspect in custody without following the procedural safeguards laid down in *Miranda,* constitutes a violation of the *McNabb-Mallory* Rule under both constitutional and statutory law.

However, the Federal Omnibus Crime Control and Safe Streets Act of 1968 (Pub. L. No. 90–351) modifies the *McNabb-Mallory* Rule by permitting a 6 hour delay between arrest, detention and arraignment. 18 USC § 3501(c).

Section 3501 lays down other new rules in testing voluntariness of admissions and confessions in federal criminal prosecutions. The sole test of admissibility is "voluntariness" and the absence of *Miranda* warnings need not be conclusive on the issue of voluntariness of the confession or admission, although it is one of the factors to be considered by the judge before submitting the same question to the jury as provided for in *Jackson v. Denno,* 378 US 368. 18 USC § 3501. *See also:* Sen. Rep. No. 1097, 90th Cong., 2d Sess., pp. 2123–2153 (1968).

**§ 54. Applicability of Miranda to the States.** The procedural safeguards now required by *Miranda* apply equally to state courts since the privilege against self-incrimination is applicable to state court proceedings. *Malloy v. Hogan,* 378 US 1; *Murphy v. Waterfront Commission,* 378 US 52; *Griffin v. California,* 380 US 609; *Rogers v. Richmond,* 365 US 534.

> "The voluntariness doctrine in the state cases, as *Malloy* indicates, encompasses all interrogation practices which are likely to exert such pressure upon an individual as to disable him from making a free and rational choice. The implications of this proposition were elaborated in our decision in Escobedo v. Illinois, 378 U.S. 478, . . . decided one week after *Malloy* applied the privilege to the States." *Miranda v. Arizona,* 384 US at 464–465.

Unless the warnings against self-incrimination and the right to counsel are given in the state courts as well as in the federal courts, "all the careful safeguards erected around the giving of testimony, whether by an accused or any other witness, would become empty formalities in a procedure where the most compelling evidence of guilt, a confession, would already have been obtained at the unsupervised pleasure of the police." *Mapp v. Ohio,* 367 US 643, 685, dissenting opinion.

Therefore, the accused must be adequately and effectively advised of his constitutional rights and the exercise of those rights must be fully honored.

Whether the states will now follow the new guidelines laid down in the Federal Omnibus Crime Control and Safe Streets Act, remains to be seen.

**§ 55. Escobedo-Miranda Application in Cross-Examination.** A statement obtained from a defendant in violation of the rule laid down in *Miranda* and *Escobedo* may nevertheless be used by the People for the purpose of attacking defendant's credibility as a witness. *People v. Kulis,* 18 NY2d 318, 322, 221 NE2d 541.

> "Although the statement would not have been admissible as part of the People's direct case (*Escobedo* v. *Illinois,* 378 U.S. 478; *People* v. *Donovan,* 13 NY2d 148),

> it was admissible on the question of defendant's credibility as a witness (*Walder* v. *United States,* 347 U.S. 62; *Tate* v. *United States,* 283 F.2d 377; *Bailey* v. *United States,* 328 F.2d 542; *United States* v. *Curry,* 358 F.2d 904).
>
> "The prosecution cannot 'use the fruits of such unlawful conduct to secure a conviction' but '[i]t is quite another [thing] to say that the defendant can turn the illegal method by which evidence in the Government's possession was obtained to his own advantage, and provide himself with a shield against contradiction of his untruths. Such an extension of the *Weeks* doctrine [*Weeks* v. *United States,* 232 U.S. 383] would be a perversion of the Fourth Amendment.'" *People v. Kulis, supra at* 322–323.

This opinion seems to be at a variance with the philosophy and intent of *Miranda* and *Escobedo. See:* dissenting opinion, *Kulis,* at 323; *Cf. People v. Shivers,* 21 NY2d 118, 121.

Nevertheless, the *Kulis* doctrine is still followed in New York (*People v. Harris,* 25 NY2d 175, 250 NE2d 349, affd 91 SC 643), and in some federal jurisdictions (*U.S. v. Vanterpool* (2d Cir), 394 F2d 697; *Martin v. U.S.* (9 Cir), 400 F2d 149).

**§ 56. Admissibility of Volunteered Statements.** *Miranda* does not make all confessions and admissions, or exculpatory statements inadmissible. Volunteered statements are not interdicted. "Any statement given freely and voluntarily without any compelling influence is, of course, admissible in evidence. . . . There is no requirement that police stop a person who enters a police station and states that he wishes to confess a crime, or a person who calls the police to offer a confession or any other statement he desires to make. Volunteered statements of any kind are not barred by the Fifth Amendment and their admissibility is not affected by our holding today." 384 US at 478, citing *People v. Dorado,* 398 P2d 361, 371 (1965).

An example of a volunteered statement is found in *People v. Bell,* NYLJ, 11/29/66, p. 18. In that case, spontaneous, unsolicited statements made by a defendant during the interrogation of another, were held to be admissible and not violative of the rule in *Miranda.* The defendant's wife was arrested in her home and taken to the precinct squad room where she was interrogated. Her husband insisted on accompanying her over the objections of the police. He was permitted to do so, and sat about ten feet from his wife while she was being questioned. During this interrogation and without any questions being directed at him, he spontaneously made some statements which he sought to suppress. Suppression under these facts was denied.

§ 57. **On-The-Scene Questioning.** "General on-the-scene questioning as to facts surrounding a crime or other general questioning of citizens in the fact-finding process is not affected by our holding. . . . In such situations the compelling atmosphere inherent in the process of in-custody interrogation is not necessarily present." 384 US at 477–478.

It is not custodial interrogation when a police officer stops a person and asks him for his name, address and explanation of his activities under the Stop and Frisk Law. *See:* CPL § 140.50. *See also: Terry v. Ohio,* 392 US 1; *People v. Rivera,* 14 NY2d 441, 201 NE2d 32, cert. den. 379 US 978.

§ 58. **Extradition Procedings Under Miranda.** The *Miranda* warnings have been held inapplicable in an extradition proceeding or in a hearing on a petition for habeas corpus that is incident thereto. Thus, it was held that failure of an arresting officer to warn a narcotics suspect of his rights under *Miranda* before taking a statement from him does not bar the use of the statement in an extradition proceeding to prove that he was in Florida on the date of the assault charged in the Florida fugitive warrant. Interstate extradition proceedings are summary in nature and the accused is not entitled to all of the procedural safeguards of a criminal trial. There is no sound reason to impart into civil proceedings of this kind principles analogous to those enunciated in *Miranda* for criminal proceedings. *U.S. ex rel Vitiello v. Flood,* 374 F2d 554.

A hearing before a United States Commissioner on extradition to another state was not "a critical stage" in a criminal proceeding requiring the presence of counsel. *U.S. v. Smith,* 379 F2d 628.

§ 59. **Retroactivity.** Since *Miranda* is bottomed on *Escobedo,* the retroactive effect of the former must be determined by an examination of the import of the decision in the latter case.

In two recent cases, the question of retroactivity was examined by the Supreme Court. Those cases established the principle that in criminal litigation involving constitutional claims, the court may in the interest of justice make the rule prospective where the exigencies of the situation requires such an application. *Linkletter v. Walker,* 381 US 618. *See also: Tehan v. Shott,* 382 US 406.

The criteria for these rulings are (1) the purpose of the new standards set in *Escobedo* and *Miranda;* (2) the reliance placed upon prior decisions on the subject; and (3) the effect on the administration of justice if retroactivity is accorded.

Where the constitutional rule of criminal procedure affects the very integrity of the fact-finding process and averts the clear danger of convicting the innocent, such as is present where an indigent defendant is deprived of the aid of counsel (*Gideon v. Wainwright,* 372 US 335), or where an involuntary confession was permitted in evidence at the trial (*Jackson v. Denno,* 378 US 368) then the rule will be given retroactive effect (*Linkletter v. Walker, supra; Tehan v. Shott, supra*).

Although all constitutional guarantees are important, the application of retroactivity as to each guarantee depends on its particular function and its impact on the administration of justice. This requires each case to be judged separately. Another factor to be determined is whether a deviation from strict application of the constitutional guarantee in criminal procedures enhances the reliability of the fact-finding process, and to what degree. In weighing these probabilities, the extent of the availability of other safeguards to protect the integrity of the truth-determining process at trial, must be considered also.

Whatever errors may have occurred by reason of a failure to follow the safeguards set forth in *Escobedo* and *Miranda* as to in-custody interrogations are subject to correction by direct or collateral attack on the question of voluntariness. *Haynes v. Washington,* 373 US 503; *Spano v. New York,* 360 US 315; *Townsend v. Sain,* 372 US 293.

Furthermore, the practice of failing to advise a suspect of his right to silence and right to the aid of counsel, had heretofore not been expressly condemned. *Crooker v. California,* 357 US 433; *Cicenia v. Lagay,* 357 US 504. As a result, law enforcement officers relied on these prior authorities now proscribed by *Escobedo* and *Miranda.* In this connection it is to be noted that in *Mapp,* the States at least knew that they were constitutionally forbidden from engaging in unreasonable searches and seizures under *Wolf v. Colorado,* 338 US 25 (1949). *Johnson v. New Jersey,* 384 US 719, 731.

Additionally, to give retroactive effect to *Escobedo* and *Miranda* "would seriously disrupt the administration of our criminal laws." Amplification of the argument would be superfluous.

"In the light of these various considerations, we conclude that *Escobedo* and *Miranda,* like Mapp v. Ohio, and Griffin v. California, [380 US 609], should not be applied retroactively." *Johnson, supra,* 384 US at 732.

Whereas *Mapp* and *Griffin* were held to apply to cases still on direct appeal at the time they were decided, the court held that *Escobedo* and *Miranda* should have "prospective application only to trials begun *after* the standards were announced . . ." in *Escobedo* and *Miranda.* 384 US at 732 (emphasis supplied).

This ruling does not prevent the states from adopting stricter standards than those announced in *Johnson, supra.*

**§ 59.01. The Escobedo "Date."** Because *Escobedo* is to be applied prospectively, this holding is available only to persons whose trial began after June 22, 1964, the date on which *Escobedo* was decided.

**§ 59.02. The Miranda "Date."** Because of the disagreement among various jurisdictions of the full import of *Escobedo, Miranda* is "therefore available only to persons whose trials had not begun as of June 13, 1966. See Tehan v. Shott, 382 U.S. at 409, n.3, in relation to Malloy v. Hogan, 378 U.S. 1

(1964), and Griffin v. State of California, supra." *Johnson v. N.J.*, 384 US 719, 734.

§ 59.03. **Retrials.** The courts are still not in accord as to whether *Miranda* warnings are applicable in a post-*Miranda* retrial held where the original trial was pre-*Miranda.*

Where defendants, tried prior to *Miranda* (June 13, 1966), made confessions obtained without following the guidelines established for custodial interrogation required by *Miranda,* the confessions were held not admissible at their retrial, conducted subsequent to June 13, 1966. The theory behind this conclusion is that a retrial is a trial *de novo.* It places both parties in the same position as if no trial had been had.

A majority of decisions on this issue in other jurisdictions is to the same effect. *See: People v. Sayers,* 28 AD2d 227, 228; revd 22 NY2d 571, 240 NE2d 571, cert. den. 395 US 970.

California has also held that *Miranda* makes no distinction between trials and retrials. *People v. Doherty,* 429 P2d 177, 59 Cal Rptr 857.

Delaware holds to the contrary, and is the minority view. *Jenkins v. State,* 240 A2d 146.

However, the United States Supreme Court has now held in *Jenkins v. Delaware,* 395 US 213, that the *Miranda* warnings regarding the admissibility of in-custody statements do not apply to a retrial held after June 13, 1966. *See: Johnson v. New Jersey,* 384 US 719, in which the court held that the *Miranda* rule would apply only to cases in which the trial—not retrial—began after June 13, 1966, the date of the *Miranda* decision.

The New York rule is in accord with *Jenkins v. Delaware, supra. People v. Sayers, supra. Cf.* CPL §§ 330.50(4), 470.55.

It seems reasonable to assume that all states will adopt the non-retroactive rule applying to retrials, as enunciated in *Jenkins v. Delaware, supra,* and *People v. Sayers, supra.*

§ 59.04. **Retroactivity Application to Pending Appeals.** Although the states are not compelled to limit the retroactive effect of *Miranda,* the New York Court of Appeals has held in *People v. McQueen,* 18 NY2d 337, that a case, pending appeal, does not avoid the non-retroactivity of the rules laid down in *Miranda.*

In arriving at this decision, the court pointed out that *Johnson v. New Jersey, supra,* "stated categorically that 'these decisions [*Miranda* and *Escobedo*] should apply only to trials begun after the decisions were announced * * * *even though the cases may still be on direct appeal'. . . .*" *People v. McQueen,* 18 NY2d 337, 343, 221 NE2d 550.

§ 60. **Applying the Miranda Rules.** No opinion has ever been written that is so definitive as to constitute an answer to all of the questions posed with respect to a particular problem. *Miranda* is no exception. Within a week after *Miranda,* the Supreme Court was required to decide the type of compelled testimony that constitutes self-incrimination and whether in that case, the right to counsel attached. *Schmerber v. California,* 384 US 757.

Other refinements of the various facets of *Miranda* will undoubtedly be explored in future Supreme Court decisions. Some cases have already been decided which may shed additional light on the various questions not decided in *Miranda.*

*Schmerber v. California, supra,* was decided the week following *Miranda.* Two important questions were raised. (1) Is a person's privilege against self-incrimination violated when, over his objection after he had been arrested for driving while intoxicated—a misdemeanor—a sample of blood is taken by a physician at the direction of a police officer? (2) Is a defendant deprived of his right to counsel where his objection to the taking of blood was based on the advice of his attorney?

The Supreme Court answered both of these questions in the negative. Schmerber had been arrested for driving while intoxicated. While he was in a hospital being treated for injuries received in an accident involving the automobile he had apparently been driving, a sample of his blood was taken by a physician at the direction of a police officer. Blood analysis indicated intoxication and was admitted in evidence at his trial. Schmerber, on advice of counsel, had objected to the extraction of his blood.

Although the Court conceded that puncturing Schmerber's body to draw blood for analysis constituted compulsion to submit to an attempt to discover evidence that might be used to convict him, it did not constitute compulsion "to be a witness against himself." Under the Fifth Amendment, the Court stated, the privilege against self-incrimination reaches an accused's communications, whatever form they might take. The privilege is a bar against compelling "communications" or "testimony." Thus, a subpoena duces tecum of records made by a defendant which might be used to convict him would be a "compelled response" which is equivalent to a communication and is therefore barred by the privilege. *Boyd v. U.S.,* 116 US 616.

On the other hand, "that compulsion which makes a suspect or accused the source of 'real or physical' evidence does not violate it." Examples of "real or physical" evidence are: compelling an accused to put on a blouse that fitted him, over his protest and prior to the trial, *Holt v. U.S.,* 218 US 245; comparing the defendant's features with a photograph in evidence, *Holt, supra.*

"[B]oth federal and state courts have usually held that it [Fifth Amendment] offers no protection against compulsion to submit to fingerprinting, photographing, or measurements, to write or speak for identification, to appear in court, to stand, to assume a stance, to walk or to make a particular gesture." Compelled tests that are seemingly directed to obtain physical evidence which measure changes in body functions during interrogation, such as the lie detector, "may actually be directed to eliciting responses which are essentially testimonial." Thus, compelled testing involving a physiological response of the accused would violate the Fifth Amendment. *Schmerber v. California,* 384 US at 764.

However, the Court held that the taking of a blood sample in no wise implicated the petitioner's testimonial capacities, "indeed, his participation, except as a donor, was irrelevant to the results of the test, which depended on a chemical analysis and on that alone. Since the blood test evidence, although an incriminating product of compulsion, was neither petitioner's testimony nor evidence relating to some communicative act or writing by the petitioner, it was not inadmissible on privilege grounds." 384 US at 765.

Since petitioner was not entitled to assert the privilege, he had no "greater right because counsel erroneously advised him that he could assert it." 384 US at 766.

The Court in *Schmerber* also sustained the blood sample on the ground that it was a search incident to a lawful arrest. *See also: People v. Chiagles,* 237 NY 193; *U.S. v. Rabinowitz,* 339 US 56, (Frankfurter, J., dissenting); *Weeks v. U.S.,* 232 US 383.

The Court did not pass on the question of compelled submission of a defendant to a test using the analysis of his breath obtained by such instruments as the breathalyzer and the Hagar Drunkometer. Do such tests during interrogation involve seeking compelled responses aimed at obtaining physical evidence which measure changes in body functions—physiological changes—"directed to eliciting responses which are essentially testimonial?" The *Schmerber* decision would seem to answer this in the negative, equating a person's breath with his blood. But assuming that the question is moot, it should be resolved, at least at the trial level in favor of the prosecution, since a reasonable doubt on the law should be resolved in favor of the People. *People v. Reed,* 276 NY 5.

Some jurisdictions request a defendant to undergo questioning and testing in a drunk driving case. In New York, the police use a form U.F. 127 for that purpose. The defendant is asked certain questions, such as, was he driving, was he drinking, when did he last eat, how much sleep had he had the night before, is he ill or injured, does he suffer from diabetes, and similar questions.

Obviously, under *Miranda,* these questions and their answers are inadmissible unless the procedural safeguards of *Miranda* have been applied.

On the other hand, observations of the defendant's appearance, such as watery or blood-shot eyes, condition of his clothing, clarity of speech, his attitude, *i.e.,* friendly, cocky, antagonistic, etc., are admissible at a trial.

The last portion of the U.F. 127 is a coordination test directed by the police officer. This consists of tests of muscular and physical control exercised by the defendant, in standing with both feet together and eyes closed; walking a straight line; touching the tips of the index fingers to his nose with each hand alternately and with eyes closed; walking and turning; picking up small coins. Another test employed is shining a bright light into the defendant's eyes at a distance of about six inches, to determine the reaction of the pupils—do they remain dilated or do they contract?

Does the administration of these coordinating tests by the police, at their direction, violate the rule in *Miranda* and *Schmerber* unless the defendant was first apprised of his right to silence and his right to counsel?

As the Court pointed out in *Schmerber,* the privilege against self-incrimination protects an accused only from being compelled to testify against himself or otherwise provide the State with evidence of a testimonial or communicative nature. In a footnote, the court added, "A nod or headshake is as much a 'testimonial' or 'communicative' act in this sense as are spoken words." This can be misleading. The nod or headshake mentioned refers to a question put to the suspect. This act may well be "testimonial."

Observations made of a defendant's ability to coordinate, when requested to perform certain physical acts, such as balancing, walking, turning, finger-to-nose test, etc. (*see:* N.Y.P.D., Form 127) cannot be termed responses of a testimonial or communication nature. It cannot be said that, absent *Miranda* warnings, the results, of those tests conducted at the request of the police, are inadmissible at a defendant's trial for driving while intoxicated. *Contra: People v. McLaren,* 55 Misc2d 676, 285 NYS2d 991. *McLaren* also held that the questions and answers propounded after defendant had been arrested were not admissible. This ruling is fully in accord with *Schmerber.*

**§ 61. Miranda Warnings in Misdemeanor Cases.** In a far-reaching decision, the Supreme Court of Ohio holds that *Miranda* warnings are not required in misdemeanor cases. Although the case involved driving while intoxicated, the opinion is not limited to that charge but encompasses all misdemeanors. *State v. Pyle,* 19 Ohio St2d 64, 249 NE2d 826, cert. den. *Pyle v. Ohio,* 396 US 1007.

Denial of certiorari may cause other jurisdictions to adopt the Ohio rule, although denial of certiorari carries with it no implication whatever regarding the court's views on the merits of the case. *Beck v. Winters,* 407 F2d 125, 127 and cases cited.

**§ 62. Evidence Obtained During Custodial Interrogation in Violation of Miranda.** Where a metal cooking pot allegedly used by defendant to strike decedent was seized as a result of oral statements received by police during improper custodial interrogation, the pot was inadmissible since it was obtained as a direct consequence of incompetent oral admissions. The trial court properly excluded it. *People v. Paulin,* 25 NY2d 445, 255 NE2d 164.

**§ 63. Handwriting Identification.** A defendant compelled to submit a specimen of his handwriting was held not to have been compelled to incriminate himself in violation of his privilege under the Fifth Amendment.

> "Defendant's motion to suppress a specimen of his handwriting which he is alleged to have unwillingly given is also denied at this time. Counsel's citation of *Vignera v. New York* (384 U.S. 436, included in *Miranda*) might be very persuasive had not the same Supreme Court one week later decided *Schmerber v. California,* 384 U.S. 757, . . . . In the *Schmerber* case, which involved compulsory extraction of defendant's blood over defendant's objection, * * * the Supreme Court states: 'both Federal and State courts have usually held that it [privilege against self-incrimination] offers no protection against compulsion * * * to *write* for identification, etc. The distinction which has emerged * * * is that the privilege is a bar against compelling "communication" or "testimony" but *that compulsion which makes a suspect or accused the source of "real or physical evidence" does not violate it.*' " *People v. Kelly,* NYLJ, 8/25/66, p. 8.

The rule announced in *Kelly, supra,* has been approved by the United States Supreme Court in *Gilbert v. California,* 388 US 263, where the court held that neither the Fifth nor Sixth Amendment bars use of handwriting exemplars obtained from the defendant in the absence of counsel and without advice that the exemplar could be used against him. *Cf. Miranda v. Arizona, supra.* Basing its ruling on *Schmerber v. California, supra,* the court said:

"[T]he privilege reaches only compulsion of 'an accused's communications, whatever form they might take, and the compulsion of responses which are also communications, for example, compliance with a subpoena to produce one's papers,' and not 'compulsion which makes a suspect or accused the source of "real or physical evidence" '* * * Schmerber v. State of California, 384 U.S. 763–764." *Gilbert v. California, supra* at 266.

Granted that one's voice and handwriting are means of communication, "It by no means follows, . . . that every compulsion of an accused to use his voice or write compels a communication within the cover of the privilege." *Id.* at 266. These are merely identifying physical characteristics.

Additionally, the court, (at p. 267), held:

"The taking of the exemplars was not a 'critical' stage of the criminal proceedings entitling petitioner to the assistance of counsel. Putting aside the fact that the exemplars were taken *before* the indictment and appointment of counsel, there is minimal risk that the absence of counsel might derogate from his right to a fair trial." (emphasis supplied). *See: Schmerber v. California, supra; Holt v. U.S., supra; cf. U.S. v. Wade* (1967), 388 US 218.

**§ 64. Voice Identification.** The compelled use of one's voice, for identification purposes, likewise does not violate one's constitutional rights under the Fifth or Sixth Amendments. *Gilbert v. California, supra, Schmerber v. California, supra; Holt v. U.S. supra; U.S. v. Wade, supra.*

Voiceprints and voicegraphs are devices used for voice identification by recording on paper resonance bars and voice volume or loudness. It is claimed that this system of voice identification is similar to that used in fingerprint identification. Although some jurisdictions have accepted voiceprints and vociegraphs in evidence, they have not been generally accepted.

The California Court of Appeals has held that the admission in evidence concerning identification opinion based on the "voiceprint" is reversible error, as the technique of spectographic speech analysis has not yet been proven scientifically acceptable. The court noted that scientists are not in agreement on the reliability of this technique as evidence in court, and that no competent authorities in the field accept these tests as scientific. The inventor himself, who testified, admitted that his process is entirely subjective and founded upon his opinion alone. *People v. King,* 266 Cal2d 437, 72 Cal Rptr 478, 493.

In New Jersey, a similar challenge to the use of "voiceprints," impelled the court to remand the matter to the lower court to determine the scientific basis, if any, underlying "voiceprints," since "the interests of justice required that as complete a record as possible be compiled before a decision is made concerning the admissibility of such a new detection of crime." *State v. Cary,* 250 A2d 15, 16, 53 NJ 256.

Requiring a defendant, prior to trial, to don certain clothing, and, for voice identification, to repeat words of the alleged assailant, does not violate the privilege against self-incrimination. *U.S. v. Wade,* 388 US 218, 221–223; *Schmerber v. California,* 384 US 757, 761. "However, a pretrial identification procedure, even though not violative of the defendant's right to counsel or of his privilege against self-incrimination, may be so unfair as to amount to a denial of due process of law." *People v. Ballott,* 20 NY2d 600, 606, 233 NE2d 103. *See also: People v. Brown,* 20 NY2d 238, 243–244, 299 NE2d 192, cert. den. 390 US 928; *Stovall v. Denno,* 388 US 293, 299, 301–302; *Palmer v. Peyton,* 359 F2d 199.

In-court identification is not per se excludable. Should there be a showing that a pretrial identification was held under circumstances "impermissible and improper" (*Gilbert v. California,* 388 US 263), in-court identification is to be excluded unless it can be determined at a pre-trial hearing before a judge and out of the presence of the jury by "clear and convincing evidence" that the in-court identification was not tainted by observing the defendant at the police line-up or show-up identification. *People v. Ballott, supra.*

Following the philosophy in *Schmerber, supra, Holt, supra,* and *Wade, supra,* the New Jersey Essex County Court has held that compelling a defendant to submit to a tape recording of his voice for comparison with a voicegraph prepared from a recording in possession of the prosecutor's office would not violate the Fifth Amendment, or the sense of justice and fairness implicitly guaranteed in the Constitution. Defendant's argument of violation of the privilege against self-incrimination was rejected by the court. *State v. McKenna,* 226 A2d 757. *See also: State v. King,* 209 A2d 110; *State v. Cary, supra.*

**§ 65. Deportation Proceedings.** Under 8 USC § 1251(a)(4), an alien is deportable if he has been convicted of two separate crimes involving moral turpitude not arising out of a single scheme of criminal conduct. An alien who appeared voluntarily at the Immigration and Naturalization office, was questioned about his convictions after being warned that anything he said might be used against him. He was held not to have been entitled to have an attorney present at the interrogation. His statements at the interrogation were not made inadmissible at a subsequent deportation hearing because he was not told that he was entitled to have an attorney present. The right to counsel, under section 1251(a)(4), was held to apply to a hearing and not to interrogation by an investigator prior to a hearing.

> "We think petitioner was not entitled to have a lawyer present at the preliminary interrogation and that it was not error to fail to advise him that he had a right to counsel or to receive in evidence at the hearing his sworn statement made at the preliminary interrogation." *Nason v. Immigration and Naturalization Service,* 370 F2d 865, 867.

**§ 66. Volunteered Statements.** Statements volunteered by a defendant are not inadmissible under *Miranda.* In *Copeland v. US.,* 343 F2d 287, the defendant was identified as having participated in a robbery of a Western Union office. He was placed in a line-up where he was questioned about the robbery of a paint store two months earlier. During this questioning, the victim of the paint store robbery arrived. As he entered, the defendant stood up, put out his hand, and apologized for shooting him. This admission in the form of an apology was held to be admissible as a spontaneous, unsolicited and unexpected comment to the victim of the defendant's crime.

Similarly, *People v. Hill,* 17 NY2d 185, 216 NE2d 588, cert. den. 383 US 960, 385 US 875, a pre-*Miranda* case, would still seem to be good law under *Miranda.* In *Hill,* the defendant made an inculpatory statement while the arresting officer was attempting to subdue him in an effort to effect his arrest. The court held that there "was not even a causal connection between the defendant's admissions and the force properly employed to apprehend him." *Id.* at 190. At such a moment, it would be unrealistic to require the police to advise the defendant of his rights under the Fifth and Sixth Amendments. *See also: People v. Burwell,* 279 P2d 744, 44 Cal2d 17, 30–31, cert. den. 349 US 936.

**§ 66.01. Statements Prompted by Drugs or Polygraph.** In *People v. Horton,* 30 AD2d 709, the court said that although statements made under the influence of drugs are inadmissible, their use as an investigative tool is not unusual.

> "There seems little difference between the use of drugs as a possible prompter and that of the so-called lie detector, which has, of course, triggered confessions found valid, if voluntary. (*See,* e.g., *Tyler* v. *United States,* 193 F. 2d 24, cert. den. 343 U.S. 908; *Commonwealth v. Hipple,* 333 Pa. 33.) Thus, if there was voluntary consent to the tests, the court would have to find untenable any argument that, the tests triggered the . . . confession, and the subsequent written confession, so that they became fruit of the poisonous tree. It is only when submission to such investigative aids as drugs or the polygraph is involuntary that the fruit of the poisonous tree doctrine is applied (62 Yale L.J. 315, 334, 335, . . .)." *People v. Horton,* 30 AD2d 709–710.

In *Horton,* defendant's confessions were admissible since he voluntarily submitted to the drug tests. Although two tests were administered with negative results, he became amnesiac after the second test. Fearful that he may have made some incriminating statements during the latter test, he spoke to another hospital patient, expressing his fears, and then confessed his guilt to this patient. This oral confession and a subsequent written confession under these facts were ruled admissible.

The fact that a defendant was under sedation at the time he made a confession does not of itself render the confession untrustworthy. *People v. Moore,* 23 NY2d 673, 243 NE2d 146; *People v. Schompert,* 19 NY2d 300, 226 NE2d 305, cert. den. 389 US 874.

Most jurisdictions have refused to accept the results of lie-detector (polygraph) tests as probative evidence of truth or deception because the polygraph has not yet gained acceptance in its own scientific field.

Accordingly, the results of such tests are not admissible as evidence in criminal prosecutions. It was noted that the prosecution failed to show to the satisfaction of the Court that there is a general recognition of the efficacy and accuracy of such tests. *People v. Leone,* 25 NY2d 511, 255 NE2d 696; *People v. Forte,* 279 NY 204; *Sowa v. Looney,* 23 NY2d 329, 244 NE2d 243.

**§ 66.02. Grand Jury Appearance.** Nor would *Miranda* seem to apply to the appearance of a potential defendant before a grand jury. *U.S. v. Winter,* 348 F2d 204. Such a person has other and adequate safeguards. *See: Testimonial Compulsion,* § 21, *supra.*

**§ 66.03. Admissions and Confessions Made to Private Persons.** Inculpatory statements made to private persons are admissible under *Miranda.* In *People v. Gunner,* 15 NY2d 226, 205 NE2d 852, the defendant who was being transported by the police from California to New York while under arrest and after counsel had appeared on his behalf, made certain inculpatory statements to the airplane stewardess on his plane. The statements were held admissible.

**§ 66.04. Statements Made to Security Guards.** New York in *People v. Frank,* 52 Misc2d 266, 275 NYS2d 570, has held that department store employees under the N.Y. General Business Law, § 218, are not to be equated with police officers. Accordingly, the court held that the warnings required by

*Miranda,* need not be given by department store security guards when they apprehend a suspected shoplifter.

> "While it is true that under this 'Shoplifting Statute' (applicable to mercantile establishments) either a peace officer, the owner, or the owner's agent may detain and question a suspected shoplifter, if there be reasonable grounds to believe the person has committed larceny, nothing contained therein can be interpreted as placing any duty upon the self-same peace officer, owner, or owner's agent to warn a suspect of her rights. Consequently, we hold that this statute has no application to the issues in this case.
>
> "Accordingly, we find that the 'security guards' herein were under no duty to warn the defendant prior to obtaining any statements from her, and consequently, there is no issue presented warranting a hearing under the guidelines found in *Miranda v. Arizona* (*supra*)." *People v. Frank,* 275 NYS2d 570, 52 Misc2d 266, 267, 268; *see also: People v. Williams,* 53 Misc2d 1086.

As in *Frank,* the California Court of Appeals held that a security guard in a county hospital had no obligation to advise defendant of his constitutional rights to counsel and to remain silent prior to receiving an inculpatory statement. Neither *Miranda* nor *People v. Dorado,* 394 P2d 952, it was noted, catalogued the persons who must give the constitutional warnings. *People v. Wright,* 57 Cal Rptr 781.

Although it has been held that department store detectives are not bound by *Miranda,* in certain situations *Miranda* may apply.

Thus, where a defendant was placed under arrest by a police officer, and was interrogated either by the officer or a store detective while the officer for the most part stood silently by, inculpating statements and real evidence obtained from the defendant, in the absence of a *Miranda* warning, were inadmissible. *People v. Ryff,* 28 AD2d 1112, 284 NYS2d 953.

## § 67. Privileged Communications.

**§ 67.01. Husband and Wife.** Conversations (containing inculpatory statements) between a husband and wife in the presence of a third party are admissible. The objection on the ground of privilege is invalid since privilege does not attach while a third party is present. *People v. Ressler,* 17 NY2d 174, 216 NE2d 582. *See also: People v. Melski,* 10 NY2d 78, 176 NE2d 81; *People v. McCormack,* 278 AD 191, affd 303 NY 782; *People v. Daghita,* 299 NY 194.

As a general rule, statements and acts between spouses are privileged. But this privilege extends only to those disclosures which would not have been made but for the absolute confidence engendered by the marriage relationship. *People v. Dudley,* 24 NY2d 410, 248 NE2d 860. That is to say, not all communications between a husband and wife, when alone, are confidential.

Thus, evidence that at the time of a murder, defendant threatened to kill his wife if she disclosed what she had seen, established very strongly that defendant was not then relying on the confidential relationship of his marriage to preserve the secrecy of his acts. Standing alone, it was enough to remove the protection of the privilege from testimony of the wife at her husband's prosecution. *People v. Dudley, supra.*

**§ 67.02. Clergyman.** The same rule applies to the clergyman-penitent relationship, absent a waiver by the penitent. Thus, where statements are made by a person to a clergyman in his professional capacity, they are privileged.

In *Yates v. Breazeale,* 402 F2d 113, the defendant requested that a minister of his own choosing be sent to him. He conferred with the minister who advised him to confess if he was guilty. The conference with the minister was not suggested by the police nor were they present.

After the conference, the defendant confessed to the police. The confession was held to be admissible.

**§ 68. Constitutional Inadequacy of Counsel.** Of course, the provisions of *Miranda* would not be satisfied if constitutionally inadequate retained or appointed counsel represented the accused. One of the necessary ingredients to substantiate a contention that defense counsel represented a defendant in a constitutionally inadquate manner is proof that counsel's advice "was so fundamentally erroneous as to constitute a deprivation of defendant's basic rights . . . or where counsel's 'representation was such as to make the trial a farce and a mockery of justice' (*People v. Brown, supra* [7 NY2d 359, 361]) that the court is justified in setting aside prior proceedings." *People v. Pirone,* 33 Misc2d 124, 128. *Cf. People v. Ibarra,* 30 Cal Rptr 223, 228.

Indigent defendant whose "lapses" of appointed counsel resulted in apparent prejudice was held to have been denied effective assistance of counsel, especially since it was a close case. *Dyer v. U.S.,* 379 F2d 89.

A federal court (D.C. Pa) has held that an attorney is representing conflicting interests in violation of an accused's constitutional right to counsel, when at the same time he both represents the victims of the crime in an unrelated civil suit and defends the accused without informing him of this dual representation and without obtaining his knowledgeable consent. *U.S. ex rel Miller v. Myers,* 253 F Supp 55.

There is no "basis for a claim that the defendant, an indigent, was deprived of the effective assistance of counsel if the only showing is that he was not represented by the same attorney when he was arraigned, when he pleaded guilty, when he was arraigned on an information charging him with a prior felony, and when he was sentenced." *People v. Comacho,* 16 NY2d 1064, 1065, 213 NE2d 464. *Miranda* should not disturb this holding.

**§ 69. Armed Forces: Courts-Martial.** A member of the armed forces who was represented at a court-martial by an officer without substantial experience or training in the law would likewise not satisfy the requirements of *Miranda. Application of Stapely,* 246 F Supp 316. The right to counsel applies to court-martial proceedings within the ambit of *Miranda* and *Escobedo. U.S. v. Tempia,* USCMA, 4/25/67, 35 USLW 2625.

An accused before a military court was held not entitled as a matter of right under the Sixth Amendment to representation by legally trained counsel except at a general court-martial.

With respect to adequacy of counsel, the Tenth Circuit has held that the qualifications for counsel prescribed in the Uniform Code of Military Justice, whereby defense of special courts-martial may be conducted by non-legally trained officers when the prosecution is conducted by counsel co-equal in training, fully comply with the right to counsel requirements of the Sixth Amendment and satisfy the due process requirements of the Fifth Amendment. *Kennedy v. Commandant* (*Kansas*), 377 F2d 339.

On the other hand, a conviction by a general military court-martial in 1943 was held to be a valid felony conviction upon which to predicate a "second" felony conviction sentence, even though the defendant was ably represented at his court-martial by two commissioned officers, neither of whom was an attorney. *People v. Benjamin,* 22 NY2d 723, 239 NE2d 206.

The law is to the contrary now. *See:* Uniform Code of Military Justice, 10 USC § 827.

Today, *Miranda* is applicable to court-martial proceedings. Thus, it was held that *Miranda* bars use in a court-martial of a confession obtained by miltary police during in-custody interrogation of an airman, who was not advised of his right to have appointed counsel present at his interrogation. The protection of the Bill of Rights applies to all members of the Armed Forces. *U.S. v. Tempia,* USCMA, 35 USLW 2625.

Where, as in *Ashe v. McNamara,* 355 F2d 277, a defendant is represented at a court-martial by counsel with conflicting loyalties, such representation has been held to be inadequate and in contravention of the Sixth Amendment. In that case, the defendant and several codefendants were all represented in an assault charge by the same counsel. One of the co-defendants testified that the defendant-petitioner committed the assault. This presented an obvious conflict of interest, but defendant and counsel were ordered over objection, to proceed with the trial. Defendant was convicted and ordered dishonorably discharged. It was held that a federal court was not precluded under 10 USC § 1552 from reviewing the Correction Board's refusal to alter the defendant's dishonorable discharge under these circumstances. *See also: Glasser v. U.S.,* 315 US 60.

**§ 70. Traffic Infractions.** In New York, one charged with a traffic infraction has no statutory or constitutional right to assignment of counsel, if indigent, nor need he be apprised of his right to the aid of counsel. *People v. Kohler,* 16 NY2d 307, 213 NE2d 670, cert. den. 384 US 911; N.Y. County Law, § 722-a. *Cf. People v. Witenski,* 15 NY2d 392, 207 NE2d 358.

It is doubtful if *Miranda* will be held applicable to traffic infraction cases. *Cf. People v. Kohler, supra,* dissent Desmond, Ch. J.

New Jersey has held to the same effect: "Here we have a prosecution under the Motor Vehicle Act resulting in a fine. We hold that, at least in such a case, *Miranda* does not apply." *State v. Zucconi,* 93 NJ Super 380, 226 A2d 16.

**§ 71. Pro Se Representation.** *Miranda* does not prevent a defendant from representing himself in a criminal case. He has an absolute right to do so under both the Federal and State Constitutions. Nor may counsel be foisted upon him. However, the court may assign counsel to aid and assist a defendant in the exercise of his constitutional right to defend himself, although he may refuse that assistance also. *People v. Pitman,* 25 AD2d 637, 268 NYS2d 83. *Cf. U.S. ex rel Maldonado v. Denno,* 348 F2d 12; *People v. Price,* 262 NY 410. So too, the peremptory substitution at the time of sentencing of assigned counsel in place of defendant's absent retained counsel, without defendant's express consent, was in violation of his constitutional rights requiring vacatur of the sentence. *People v. Fitch,* 25 AD2d 783.

Barring special circumstances, a defendant will not be permitted to act as his own attorney when he is represented by counsel. The rationale behind this rule is based on the fact that an inexperienced layman might make prejudicial statements that redound to his disadvantage. Additionally, to permit pro se representation would be inimical to the proper administration of justice. *People v. Richardson,* 4 NY2d 224, 149 NE2d 875. The rule is the same in many other jurisdictions.

In the 5th Circuit, it has been held where a defendant represented himself during a trial and entered a guilty plea at the end of the People's case, that before entering the plea, he is entitled to be advised of his right to counsel and assignment of counsel, if required. The court reasoned that the defendant's waivers at his arraignment and trial cannot be interpreted to apply prospectively, that the waiver of the right to counsel was a waiver of a constitutional right and that the "courts should indulge every reasonable presumption against waiver of fundamental constitutional rights, Johnson v. Zerbst, 1938, 304 U.S. 458, 58 S.Ct. 1019, 82 L.Ed. 1461." *Davis v. Holman,* 354 F2d 773, 776. Further, it was held, that a defendant must be apprised of the right to the aid of counsel at a critical stage of the proceedings against him, and that the time of the entry of a plea of guilty was such a critical stage. *Davis v. Holman, supra.*

Apparently a defendant has no right to be advised that he has a right to defend himself. This contention was raised by a defendant who was convicted after trial at which he was represented by assigned counsel after he failed to obtain his own attorney though he was given an opportunity to do so. The conviction was affirmed without opinion. *People v. Jackson,* 17 NY2d 817, 218 NE2d 311.

§ 71.01. **Coram Nobis Hearing.** The New York Court of Appeals has held that the right to counsel, including assignment of counsel, attaches in a coram nobis hearing. *People v. Monahan,* 17 NY2d 310, 217 NE2d 664. *Miranda* would not disturb such a holding. The court has also stated that the exclusive remedy for deprivation of counsel is coram nobis. *Hogan v. Culkin,* 18 NY2d 330, n.1 at 332, 221 NE2d 546. *Cf. People v. Gillespie,* 27 AD2d 642, 275 NYS2d 435.

§ 72. **Sanity Hearings: Habeas Corpus.** Nor would *Miranda* disturb a New York decision holding that an indigent mental patient who had been committed to an institution, is entitled to assignment of counsel as a constitutional right in a habeas corpus proceeding to establish his sanity. *People ex rel Rogers v. Stanley,* 17 NY2d 256, 217 NE2d 636.

Although habeas corpus is technically a civil proceeding, such formalistic distinction is no valid basis, in a proper case, for denying an indigent defendant assigned counsel where the relief sought is on the basis of error or defect in a criminal proceeding. *People ex rel Williams v. LaVallee,* 19 NY2d 238, 225 NE2d 735.

In New York, a preliminary hearing is not a critical stage of a criminal proceeding, and the absence of counsel at such hearing does not vitiate a conviction based on a later indictment and proceeding in which the defendant had counsel. *People v. Wolochen,* 15 AD2d 538; *People v. Steinhauer,* 19 AD2d 837. *See also: People ex rel Hirschberg v. Close,* 1 NY2d 258, 134 NE2d 818.

But, in some states, the preliminary hearing may be a critical proceeding in which the rights of the defendant can be asserted or lost. Accordingly, the absence of counsel would be violative of defendant's constitutional rights, *White v. Maryland,* 373 US 59; *People v. Sykes,* 23 AD2d 701; *Application of DeToro,* 222 F Supp 621, 624; *cf. U.S. ex rel Cooper v. Reincke,* 333 F2d 608; *Pointer v. Texas,* 380 US 400, 402–403.

Without directly meeting the contention that a criminal defendant's psychiatric examination is a "critical stage" at which counsel must be present, the Nebraska Supreme Court found no violation of the Sixth Amendment in a refusal to permit counsel to be present at a court ordered examination requested by defendant while represented by counsel. *State v. Snyder,* 180 Neb 787, 146 NW2d 67.

The New York Appellate Division, citing *People ex rel Stanley v. Rogers, supra,* has held that in a habeas corpus proceeding, an indigent prisoner is entitled, upon request, to the assignment of counsel at a hearing held upon the return of a writ of habeas corpus. *People ex rel Rodriguez v. LaVallee,* 26 AD2d 8.

**§ 73. Appeals.** The right to assignment of counsel to an indigent defendant on an appeal at his request is a constitutional right. *Miranda* would not disturb this rule either. *People v. Hughes,* 15 NY2d 172, 204 NE2d 849, cert. den. 384 US 980; *People v. Pascocello,* 15 NY2d 629, 203 NE2d 924; *People v. Maybusher,* 24 AD2d 765, 263 NYS2d 625. But an order revoking probation is not appealable. *People v. Quick,* 26 AD2d 599, 271 NYS2d 547. *Cf. People v. Reynolds,* 25 AD2d 487; *People v. Hamilton,* 26 AD2d 134; *Mempa v. Rhay,* 389 US 128.

**§ 74. Violation of Probation.** Prior to *People v. Hamilton,* 26 AD2d 134, both federal and state courts, limited a defendant's right to counsel at a hearing for violation of probation to the discretion of the court. *Burns v. U.S.,* 287 US 216; *Escoe v. Zerbst,* 295 US 490. In *Hamilton,* the court reasoned that since a defendant had a right to be heard on a charge of violation of probation (CPL § 410.70(4)), he implicitly had the right to counsel. Such a hearing was "a critical stage of the proceedings and in order that sentence be 'constitutionally acceptable' accused was entitled to be represented by counsel" including the assignment of counsel for indigent defendants, on request. 26 AD2d at 136.

The United States Supreme Court has now adopted the same rule based on the same reasoning. Heretofore, the rule has only been in effect in eleven states. It now applies to all of the states. *Mempa v. Rhay,* 389 US 128.

The rule is retroactive. *McConnell v. Rhay* (1968), 393 US 2.

Where a defendant, arraigned for violation of probation, refused aid of counsel after being advised of his right thereto and pleaded guilty to the charge, he cannot thereafter attack his conviction for probation violation on the ground that he had been deprived of counsel. *People v. Quick,* 26 AD2d 599, 271 NYS2d 547, citing *People v. Ryder,* 24 AD2d 808, 263 NYS2d 742, affd 17 NY2d 880, 218 NE2d 340.

Also, it was held in *Bey v. Connecticut,* 443 F2d 1079, and *People ex rel Menechino v. Warden,* 27 NY2d 376, 267 NE2d 238, that a defendant is entitled to be represented by counsel at a parole revocation hearing. *See also: Bearden v. South Carolina,* 443 F2d 1090.

**§ 75. Investigations.** Where there is an investigation in progress to determine whether a crime has been committed, *Escobedo* has been held inapplicable. *Kohatsu v. U.S.,* 351 F2d 898. In such a situation involving a routine civil tax investigation, *Miranda* would not seem to apply.

In *U.S. v. Neves,* 269 F Supp 158, the defendant turned over his corporation books to an I.R.S. agent for a tax examination of the corporation of which he was president and half owner. The court held that there was no need to advise him of his right to counsel, since he appeared voluntarily and was not in custody or deprived of his freedom in any way. *See also: U.S. v. Bachman,* 267 F Supp 593.

In *Mathis v. U.S.,* 391 US 1, the Supreme Court held that *Miranda* warnings must be given by law enforcement officers to persons in custody for whatever reason, who are the subjects of a federal tax investigation where a criminal prosecution might result.

> "It is true that a 'routine tax investigation' may be initiated for the purpose of a civil action rather than criminal prosecution. To this extent tax investigations differ from investigations of murder, robbery, and other crimes. But tax investigations frequently lead to criminal prosecutions, just as the one here did." *Id.* at 4.

When a person is arrested, *i.e.,* taken into custody or otherwise deprived of his freedom of action in any significant way by the authorities, and is interrogated, his privilege against self-incrimination is jeopardized. This jeopardy requires the establishment of certain procedural safeguards to protect that person's constitutional rights and to assure the fact that those rights will be scrupulously honored.

Accordingly, the person must be warned *prior* to questioning, (a) of his right to remain silent, (b) that anything he says can be used against him in a court of law, (c) that he has the right to the aid and presence of counsel, (d) that if he cannot afford an attorney, one will be assigned to him prior to any questioning, if he so desires.

A person may choose to exercise these rights throughout the interrogation. He has the right to stop talking at any time.

However, he may waive these rights and agree to make a statement or answer questions. The waiver must be made knowingly, freely and intelligently. Volunteered statements freely made do not come within the purview of the procedural safeguards laid down in *Miranda.*

*Miranda* also equates confessions with admissions and bars the use by the prosecution of exculpatory as well as inculpatory statements where the procedural safeguards have not been applied.

The burden is on the prosecution to show at the trial that the warnings as to the right to silence and the right to counsel have been properly given, and that the waiver, if any, has been properly made by the accused. Absent such proof, evidence obtained as a result of the interrogation is inadmissible.

The term "coercion" as violative of the Fifth Amendment is defined to include psychological methods of coercion. This means that ploys such as apparent sympathy for the accused, false statements that he has been identified as the culprit, that he should confess for his own good, that he was justified in committing the crime, are all prohibited. Statements obtained by the use of any of these police interrogative methods in the "menacing atmosphere" of a police station where the suspect is alone and has not been advised of his rights, are not statements truly the product of his free choice, and are accordingly inadmissible at the trial.

Such a ploy was condemned in *People v. Paulin,* 25 NY2d 445, 255 NE2d 164, where the defendant was deemed in custody in her own home. *Paulin* involved the murder of defendant's husband. There the ploy used by the interrogating officer was " 'this [is a] terrible tragedy' . . . 'have you any thoughts about an undertaker?' " This ploy elicited incriminating statements from the defendant which, it was held, were inadmissible absent the *Miranda* warnings. In effect, this ploy was psychological coercion.

On the other hand, deception in confronting the defendant with a false confession of another, while not approved, did not render defendant's confession inadmissible. *People v. Robinson,* 31 AD2d 724.

**§ 76. Fruit of the Poisonous Tree and Independent Proof.** *Miranda* seeks to impel the authorities to gather proof of a defendant's guilt from sources other than the defendant himself. The procedural safeguards prescribed are nothing more than an extension of the philosophy of the decision of *Wong Sun v. U.S.,* 371 US 471, which prohibits the authorities from exploiting their own basically illegal action.

However, even if the safeguards prescribed in *Miranda* have not been followed in a given case, but independent of that fact, the police have obtained evidence of the defendant's guilt, *Miranda* does not proscribe the use of the independently obtained evidence. *Copeland v. U.S.*, 343 F2d 287. This conclusion is logical and consonant with the reasoning in *Wong Sun, supra; Malloy v. Hogan,* 378 US 1; *Murphy v. Waterfront Commission,* 378 US 52.

**§ 77. Miranda and Escobedo Summarized.** The thrust of these decisions is to guarantee two specific rights, (a) the privilege against self-incrimination and (b) the right to counsel. Retroactivity was not an issue in these cases. That question was decided a week later in *Johnson v. New Jersey,* 384 US 719.

*Cf. U.S. ex rel Everett v. Murphy,* 329 F2d 68; *People v. Pollock,* 21 NY2d 206, 234 NE2d 223.

**§ 77.01. Right to Counsel Summarized.** The following general rules with respect to the right to the aid of counsel and the right to assignment of counsel to indigents may be noted.

A person subjected to in-custodial interrogation must first be advised of his right to counsel, and, if indigent, his right to assignment of counsel without charge, if he so requests. *Miranda* and *Escobedo, supra.*

A person arrested under a warrant, after indictment, or after a grand jury information has been filed against him, or after judicial proceedings against him (including arraignment) have commenced, must be advised of his right to counsel. *Miranda* and *Escobedo, supra; People v. Donovan,* 13 NY2d 148, 193 NE2d 628; *Massiah v. U.S., supra; People v. Witenski,* 15 NY2d 392, 207 NE2d 358.

In a pre-*Miranda* decision, *People v. Bodie,* 16 NY2d 275, 278–279, 213 NE2d 441, the New York Court of Appeals said that "an inculpatory statement made in the absence of counsel after an information had been filed," would make that statement inadmissible, "because no valid distinction may be made between a postindictment and a postinformation statement."

But, in a subsequent pre-*Miranda* case, *People v. Stockford,* 24 NY2d 146, 148, 247 NE2d 141, that court modified its position in *Bodie* by holding that although the issuance of a warrant is a stage in the commencement of a criminal proceeding, it "has not yet been fully equated to that which would exist where, after arraignment and the appearance of counsel in a court, the police attempted to question a defendant not in the presence of that counsel."

Nevertheless, this rule does not eliminate the requirement of the *Miranda* warnings in a proper case. *Stockford* because of *Miranda,* has no validity today and can be regarded only as of historic interest.

An indigent defendant in a criminal prosecution in a state court has a right under the Fourteenth Amendment to have counsel appointed to represent him. *Gideon v. Wainwright,* 372 US 335; *Douglas v. California,* 372 US 353; *People v. Witenski, supra.*

This right is to be given retroactive effect. *Smith v. Crouse,* 378 US 584; *Doughty v. Maxwell,* 376 US 202; *U.S. ex rel Durocher v. LaVallee,* 330 F2d 303, cert. den. 377 US 998.

A hearing before a United States Commissioner on extradition to another state is not "a critical stage" in a criminal proceeding requiring the presence of counsel. *U.S. v. Smith,* 379 F2d 628; *Vitiello v. Flood,* 374 F2d 554.

Nor is petitioner entitled to the presence of counsel at a preliminary interrogation in a deportation proceeding. *Nason v. I.N.S.,* 370 F2d 865.

The right to counsel attaches at every critical stage of a criminal trial. *White v. Maryland,* 373 US 59, 60; *Hamilton v. Alabama,* 368 US 52, 54; *People v. Sykes,* 23 AD2d 701; 258 NYS2d 275.

The sentencing process is a critical stage of a criminal trial. *Carter v. Illinois,* 329 US 173, 178; *Powell v. Alabama,* 287 US 45, 69; *Hamilton v. Alabama, supra.*

An indigent defendant is entitled to the assistance of appointed counsel without charge at the time of sentencing. *Townsend v. Burke,* 334 US 736; *Gideon v. Wainwright, supra. See also:* 3 *Later Case Service* 288; *cf.* 20 ALR2d 1240.

In certain jurisdictions, the time of arraignment is a critical stage of the proceedings. *Pointer v. Texas,* 380 US 400; *White v. Maryland, supra; Hamilton v. Alabama, supra; U.S. v. Reincke,* 333 F2d 608.

A change of plea to guilty during a trial conducted by the defendant *pro se* has been held to be a critical stage of the proceedings. *Davis v. Holman,* 354 F2d 773; *Matter of De Toro,* 222 F Supp 621; *People v. Thompson,* 26 AD2d 938. Emphasizing that the defendant has a right to counsel at the time he enters a guilty plea, the court stated that the record must establish a deliberate and intentional waiver of this constitutional right. Where the defendant said he was not properly informed of his right to assigned counsel without charge, a hearing was ordered on this contention. The court noted that the record does contain the brief monitions of the trial court informing defendant of his rights. However, ". . . the defendant may well have been unaware of the purport of the recited statement." Although similar applications have been rejected in the past, the court said, ". . . it is sufficient to note that the courts now stress the importance of the rights of the defendant to the assistance of counsel before a plea of guilty is taken." *People v. Mulligan,* 24 NY2d 948, 250 NE2d 70.

Pretrial identification line-up is a "critical stage" of the criminal proceedings, requiring that line-ups be held only with notice to or in the presence of counsel. *U.S. v. Wade* (1967), 388 US 218; *Gilbert v. California* (1967), 388 US 263. This rule is not retroactive and applies only to those cases in which a line-up was held after June 12, 1967. *Stovall v. Denno,* 388 US 293.

The right to counsel does not extend to pretrial voice identification and the taking of handwriting exemplars of a defendant. *Schmerber v. California,* 384 US 757; *Holt v. U.S.,* 218 US 245; *U.S. v. Wade, supra; Gilbert v. California, supra.*

Defendant has no right to be advised that he may defend himself (*pro se*). *People v. Jackson,* 17 NY2d 817, 218 NE2d 311.

Accused is entitled to be represented by counsel where he is charged with a violation of probation. This is a "critical stage" of a criminal proceeding. *Mempa v. Rhay,* 389 US 128; *Bey v. Connecticut,* 443 F2d 1079; *Bearden v. South Carolina,* 443 F2d 1090; *People ex rel Menechino v. Warden,* 27 NY2d 376, 267 NE2d 238; *People v. Reynolds,* 25 AD2d 487; *People v. Hamilton,* 26 AD2d 134.

Where the assistance of counsel is a constitutional requisite, the right to the assignment of counsel does not ordinarily depend on a request for counsel. *Miranda* and *Escobedo, supra; Carnley v. Cochran,* 369 US 506, 513; *Doughty v. Sacks,* 175 Ohio St 46, 191 NE2d 727, revd per curiam sub nom *Doughty v. Maxwell,* 376 US 202. And if indigent, it is the duty of the court to inform him of his right to have counsel appointed. *Miranda* and *Escobedo, supra; Gideon v. Wainwright, supra; People v. Witenski, supra.*

Counsel may not be foisted upon an accused who does not want an attorney. *Moore v. Michigan,* 355 US 155, 161; *People v. Pitman,* 25 AD2d 637, 268 NYS2d 83. In that event, defendant's refusal of the aid of counsel should affirmatively appear on the record. *Carnley v. Cochran, supra.* The burden of proving that defendant refused counsel is on the people. *Miranda-Escobedo, supra; Carney v. Cochran, supra; Moore v. Michigan, supra; People v. Machado,* 17 NY2d 440, 213 NE2d 804, cert. den. 383 US 921; *People v. Jones,* 17 NY2d 404, 218 NE2d 291.

An indigent defendant is entitled to assignment of counsel in a habeas corpus hearing, *People ex rel Stanley v. Rogers,* 17 NY2d 256, 217 NE2d 636; *People ex rel Rodriguez v. LaVallee,* 26 AD2d 8; and in a coram nobis hearing, *People v. Monahan, supra.*

The remedy for deprivation of the right to counsel is coram nobis. *People v. Hannigan,* 7 NY2d 317, 165 NE2d 172; *People v. Shaver,* 26 AD2d 735, 272 NYS2d 175.

Constitutionally inadequate counsel is no counsel at all. *People v. Brown,* 7 NY2d 359, 165 NE2d 557, cert. den. 365 US 821; *cf. People v. Ibarra,* 30 Cal Rptr 223.

An attorney representing conflicting interests is "constitutionally inadequate." *U.S. v. Myers,* 253 F Supp 55; *Ashe v. McNamara,* 355 F2d 277.

A novel "conflict of interest" situation appeared in *People v. Kennedy,* 22 NY2d 280, 281, 239 NE2d 510. In that case defendant sought to withdraw his guilty plea prior to sentence on the ground that he was innocent of the charge, and claiming an alibi. "The court, properly concluding that the defendant was entitled to a hearing on his application (see, *e.g., People* v. *Nixon,* 21 NY2d 338, 355), requested the defendants assigned attorney to investigate the merits of the defendant's asserted alibi and report his findings. . . . When the trial judge asked the defendant's lawyer to check on the facts bearing on the alibi, the defendant was 'deprived of the effective assistance of counsel' at a 'critical stage of the proceeding' (*People* v. *Rozell,* 20 NY2d at p. 713). The defendant's attorney was being asked, in effect, to abandon her role of active advocate for the defendant and to become, in a sense, an investigator for the court." Accordingly, ". . . it was then incumbent upon the court to assign another attorney. . . ." *People v. Kennedy, supra,* 281–282.

In a court-martial, an officer, who is without substantial experience or training in the law, would be "constitutionally inadequate" where he represents the accused at the trial. *Application of Stapely,* 246 F Supp 316.

The right to counsel applies to court-martial proceedings within the ambit of *Miranda* and *Escobedo. U.S. v. Tempia,* USCMA, 4/25/67, 35 USLW 2625.

The right to counsel attaches to trials by a general court-martial but in a trial by a special court-martial, accused may be defended by a non-lawyer if the Army prosecuting officer is also a non-lawyer. *Kennedy v. Commandant,* 377 F2d 339.

A court-martial conviction under former U.S. Code Title 10, § 1482, where defendant was not represented by an attorney, may be used as a predicate conviction for multiple offender sentence. *People v. Benjamin,* 28 AD2d 106; 281 NYS2d 405, revd 22 NY2d 723, 239 NE2d 206. The reason for this holding is that, under the then existing law (circa 1943), there was no requirement that the accused be represented by an attorney. Any commissioned officer was eligible to serve as attorney in a court-martial proceeding, including a general court-martial.

The accused is not entitled to counsel in New York and other jurisdictions in cases involving traffic infractions. *People v. Kohler,* 16 NY2d 307, 213 NE2d 670, cert. den. 384 US 911.

Persons appearing before a grand jury are not entitled to representation by counsel. *U.S. v. Winter,* 348 F2d 204; *People v. Steuding,* 6 NY2d 214, 160 NE2d 74.

It seems to be generally accepted that the right to the assignment of counsel to indigent defendants attaches in misdemeanor as well as in felony cases. *Gideon v. Wainwright, supra; People v. Witenski, supra; Martson v. Oliver,* 324 F

Supp 691; but note *Winters v. Beck,* 407 F2d 125, cert. den. 395 US 963, involving a jail sentence because of inability to pay a fine, imposed after trial for violation of a city obscenity ordinance, at which trial defendant was not represented by counsel.

# Chapter 5

# POLICE LINEUPS AND IDENTIFICATION



---

§ 85. **The Wade, Gilbert and Stovall Cases.** A trilogy of cases decided by the United States Supreme Court at the June, 1967 term (*U.S. v. Wade,* 388 US 218; *Gilbert v. California,* 388 US 263; *Stovall v. Denno,* 388 US 293) radically altered the rules respecting police lineup or showup identification.

In *Wade* and *Gilbert* the suspects were subjected to lineup identifications after indictment and after counsel had been assigned to represent them. The lineups were held on an illuminated stage before an audience of about a hundred persons. Their attorneys were not notified of the impending lineup nor were they present. The stage lights were so arranged that neither suspect could see into the audience.

In *Wade,* the lineup consisted of six additional persons. All, including Wade, were required to wear strips of tape on their faces and to say "Put the money in the bag." The crime was a bank robbery. Two bank employees identified Wade at the lineup. At the trial, on direct examination, they again identified Wade. Their pretrial lineup identification was then elicited from them on cross-examination.

In *Gilbert,* a robber used a handwritten note demanding money. The police took handwritten exemplars from the suspect, unlawfully seized photographs from his apartment, and required him to appear in the lineup, with others, conducted without notice to his attorney. He was identified in court at his trial by witnesses who had also identified him at the lineup.

In *Stovall,* the accused was identified by the victim from her hospital bed, two days after an assault in which her husband had been killed. Her condition was such (she had been stabbed eleven times) that it was doubtful if she would live. In this case, the suspect was not in a lineup, as he was the only person brought before the identifying witness, a "one-to-one" confrontation. The victim survived and identified him at the trial. Stovall had no attorney at his identification in the hospital. At the confrontation with the victim he was required to speak some words for voice identification.

In all three cases the petitioners were convicted. In *Wade* and *Gilbert* the lineups were conducted after indictment and after they had counsel. In *Stovall,* an arraignment was promptly held, but was postponed until he could retain counsel.

The defendants argued that their constitutional rights under the Fifth, Sixth and Fourteenth Amendments had been violated. Their contentions were disposed of as follows.

**§ 85.01. Fifth Amendment (Self-Incrimination).** There is no violation of the Fifth Amendment in compelling an accused to appear in a lineup to exhibit his features to a prosecution witness, nor to repeat words for voice identification, nor to give handwriting exemplars. These acts do not constitute testimonial compulsion. *Wade, supra,* 388 US at 221–223; *Gilbert, supra,* 388 US at 265–267. *See also: Schmerber v. California,* 384 US 757; *Holt v. U.S.,* 218 US 245.

**§ 85.02. Sixth Amendment (Right to Counsel).** This Amendment does not guarantee the right to have counsel present at the time of taking the accused's fingerprints, taking and analyzing a blood sample, clothing, hair and the like. *Wade, supra,* 388 US at 227; *Gilbert, supra,* 388 US at 267. *See also: Schmerber v. California,* 384 US 757. A pretrial identification lineup is a "critical" stage of a criminal proceeding. *Wade, supra,* 388 US at 227; *Gilbert, supra,* 388 US at 235–237; *Stovall, supra,* 388 US at 298. *See also: Pointer v. Texas,* 380 US 400. Accordingly, an accused is entitled to the presence and aid of counsel at a lineup. *Gilbert, supra,*

388 US at 236–238. *See also: Powell v. Alabama,* 287 US 45, 60–65. Presence of counsel may be waived, but it must be an "intelligent waiver." *Gilbert, supra,* 388 US at 237. *See also: Carnley v. Cochran,* 369 US 506.

The Federal Omnibus Crime Control and Safe Streets Act of 1968 (Pub. L. No. 90–351), Title II, eliminates the requirement of the presence of counsel at lineup indentification procedures in federal criminal prosecutions. Assuming that the constitutionality of this provision is upheld, it will be applicable only to federal prosecutions, absent enactment of similar legislation by the states.

A violation of an accused's right to counsel at the lineup does not render courtroom identification of witnesses who also identified him at the lineup, per se, excludable. But, lineup identification based on evidence seized unlawfully from the accused's apartment, *e.g.,* a search in violation of the Fourth Amendment, requires per se exclusion at the trial. *Gilbert, supra,* 388 US at 239. *Cf. People v. Rodriguez,* 11 NY2d 279. In that situation the People must be given an opportunity to "a hearing to determine whether the in-court identifications had an independent source," or were the tainted fruits of the invalidly conducted lineup, or were mere harmless errors. *Wade, supra,* 388 US at 239–242; *Gilbert, supra,* 388 US at 268. *See also: Chapman v. California,* 386 US 18; *Wong Sun v. U.S.,* 371 US 471; *People v. Ballott,* 20 NY2d 600, 233 NE2d 133; *People v. Brown,* 20 NY2d 238, 165 NE2d 557; CPL § 470.05(1).

§ 86. **Burden of Proof.** The People have the burden of establishing their contentions by "clear and convincing" evidence. *Wade, supra,* 388 US at 239.

§ 87. **The Identification Hearing.** Logically, the hearing should take place in the absence of the jury, and, absent legislation or guidelines from an appropriate court, *Huntley* procedures will undoubtedly be followed. *Wade, supra,* 388 US at 239. *See also: Mapp v. Ohio,* 367 US 643; *People v. Huntley,* 15 NY2d 72, 255 NYS2d 838, 204 NE2d 179; *People v. Huntley* 46 Misc2d 209; *People v. Wright,* 27 AD2d 718, 277 NYS2d 695; *People v. Smiley,* 54 Misc2d 826, 284 NYS2d 265.

**§ 88. The Wong Sun Rule.** The *Wong Sun* test to be applied is, " 'whether, granting establishment of the primary illegality, the evidence to which instant objection is made has been come at by exploitation of that illegality or instead by means sufficiently distinguishable to be purged of the primary taint.' " *Wong Sun v. U.S.,* 371 US 471, 488, citing Maguire, *Evidence of Guilt,* p. 221 (1959).

Application of the *Wong Sun* test in the three cases requires an examination of the following factors: prior "opportunity to observe the alleged criminal act, the existence of any discrepancy between any pre-lineup description and the defendant's actual description, any identification prior to lineup of another person, the identification by picture of the defendant prior to the lineup, failure to identify the defendant on a prior occasion, and the lapse of time between the alleged act and the lineup identification." *Wade, supra,* 388 US at 241.

Also to be considered is the way the lineup was actually conducted. Prior relationship between the accused and the witness, if any, should be explored. Were they acquaintances, friends, relatives? How long were they together during the commission of the alleged crime? *See: People v. Brown,* 20 NY2d 238, 242–243, 299 NE2d 192, cert. den. 390 US 928, and concurring op. Fuld, Ch. J., at 244.

**§ 89. Exceptions to the Wong Sun Rule.**

**§ 89.01. Court Room Identification.** Courtroom identification is not barred "where there has been no previous identification in the presence of the police although the defendant is known to be in custody and charged with the commission of a crime." *Wade, supra,* 388 US at 253. The logical interpretation of this rule would apparently include a situation where the courtroom witness sees the defendant handcuffed or otherwise observes that he is the defendant in the very case in which he will be called upon to identify him as the culprit.

**§ 89.02. Due Process.** Even though the accused may not be able to avail himself of the Sixth Amendment right-to-counsel-claim at the lineup identification, at which he had no attorney present, he may nevertheless attack the lineup identification on the ground that it was made under circumstances so unfair as to constitute a denial of "due process of law" guaranteed by the Fourteenth Amendment, that is, that it was conducted in a manner so unnecessarily suggestive, as to be conducive to irreparable mistaken identity. Showing a suspect singly face to face, and not as a part of a lineup, has been widely condemned and may constitute an important element of unfairness. *Stovall, supra,* 388 US at 302.

However, a single, one-to-one confrontation is not, *ipso facto,* unfair. It must be considered in the "totality of the circumstances" present. A "totality of circumstances" as in *Stovall v. Denno,* 388 US 293, requires the conclusion that the "single showing" was "imperative." Identification in the hospital was imperative, because it was doubtful if the victim would live. A situation similar to a dying declaration seems to have been present. Additionally, the victim was the only person who could exonerate the defendant. *See: People v. Brown,* 20 NY2d at 244, 299 NE2d 192, cert. den. 390 US 928; *Palmer v. Peyton,* 359 F2d 199.

Under such a "totality of circumstances" making a "single showing" of the accused imperative, creates no violation of the due process clause of the Fourteenth Amendment. Accordingly, no hearing as to the lineup identification is required in this type of situation. *Cf. People v. Ballott,* 20 NY2d 600, 606, 233 NE2d 133.

**§ 89.03. Retroactivity.** The cut-off date of the *Wade* and *Gilbert* decisions is June 12, 1967. They affect only the *Wade* and *Gilbert* cases "and all future cases which involve confrontations for identification purposes conducted in the absence of counsel." The new rule excludes *Stovall* also, as well as "convictions at various stages of trial and direct review." Thus, cases still in the trial or appeal stage are also excluded from the *Wade* and *Gilbert* decisions. *Wade* and *Gilbert* alone are the "chance beneficiaries" of the new rule, even though there are other litigants who may have raised the same issues. *Stovall, supra,* 388 US at 296, 300–301. *See also: Johnson v. New Jersey,* 384 US 719, 725–727; *Linkletter v. Walker,* 381 US 618; *Tehan v. Shott,* 382 US 406; *cf. Mapp v. Ohio, supra,* and *Miranda v. Arizona,* 384 US 436.

**§ 89.04. Action of Counsel at the Lineup.** May counsel advise his client not to participate in the lineup or to participate only under specified conditions? *See: Wade, supra,* conc. op. Clark, J., 388 US at 246. These questions posed, but not answered by Mr. Justice Clark in his concurring opinion, have been answered in part by the enactment of the Federal Omnibus Crime Control Act of 1968 (Pub. L. 90–351). This Act applies only to federal prosecutions.

Whether or not the Act is held to be constitutional, it is doubtful if *Wade-Gilbert* authorizes an attorney to interfere in the conduct of a lineup or showup procedure. The intent of these decisions is to insure the accused of fairness at the pretrial identification stage. It is indicated in these decisions that the mere presence of the attorney would insure such fairness and his presence and observations thereat would enable him to attack any unfairness by cross-examination during a *Wade-Gilbert* hearing.

In the author's view, however, the attorney's presence at the out-of-court lineup is fraught with grave tactical dangers. For example, if it were asserted that an unfair lineup were employed, an astute prosecutor could be expected to point out that the defense attorney who was present did nothing about it. On the other hand, should counsel attempt to correct what he deemed to be an unfair lineup, his acts would be an invitation to the prosecutor to call him as a witness in an attempt to show that defense counsel tried to prevent the victim from identifying the defendant as the culprit. This would be very damaging to the defendant, if the victim persisted in his identification.

# Chapter 6

## JOINT TRIALS



---

§ 93. **Confessions by an Accomplice.** Where in a joint trial, that part of a lawfully obtained confession by an accomplice which implicates the defendant, is severable, it is error to admit the entire confession under New York Law. *People v. Vitagliano,* 15 NY2d 360, 206 NE2d 839.

Since *Vitagliano,* the New York Court of Appeals has adopted the rule laid down in *People v. Aranda,* 47 Cal Rptr 2d 353, 407 P2d 265, holding: "There [in California] unless 'all parts of the extrajudicial statements implicating any co-defendants can be and are effectively deleted *without prejudice to the declarant'* they are inadmissible in a joint trial. (407 P.2d 265, 272–273; emphasis supplied.)" *People v. LaBelle,* 18 NY2d 405, 411, 222 NE2d 727.

The U.S. Circuit Court of Appeals (2d Cir) seems to have adopted a similar rule as *Aranda,* but its basis is not clear. *U.S. v. Bozza,* 365 F2d 206.

Admission of one defendant's confession from which the names of other defendants were deleted but which corroborated an accomplice's testimony after denial of motion by other defendants for a severance was held to be error requiring reversal of conviction of those defendants who had not confessed as a violation of defendant's rights under the Sixth Amendment.

"Either accept the severance of the trial of the confessor or forego use of the confession." *U.S. v. Bozza,* 365 F2d 206, 217.

California and New Jersey have gone further. They have held that if the confession or an accomplice's incriminating references to other defendants cannot be effectively deleted during a joint trial, a severance on motion of a co-defendant may be granted. If the severance is not granted, the confession must be excluded from the joint trial. *People v.*

*Aranda, supra; State v. Young* 46 NJ 151, 215 A2d 352; *Delli Paoli v. U.S.*, 352 US 232, dissent by Frankfurther, J.; *Jackson v. Denno,* 378 US 368; *People v. Hannon,* 50 Misc2d 297.

In view of the *Miranda* decision, it would seem that the U.S. Supreme Court would adhere to the California-New Jersey rule.

Similarly, admissions or confessions as to the commission of crimes other than the one for which the defendant is currently on trial, should be deleted from a confession offered by the People, *People v. Sorrell,* 24 AD2d, 783, 263 NYS2d 776, although admissible "to show intent or a common scheme." *People v. Molineux,* 168 NY 264; *People v. Marino,* 271 NY 317.

The leading case in this area is *Bruton v. U.S.*, 391 US 123. *Bruton* holds that the admission upon a joint trial of a confession by a co-defendant who does not testify, violates the rights of the implicated defendant under the confrontation clause of the Sixth Amendment.

> "It is a fundamental principle of evidence, embodied in the confrontation clause of the Sixth Amendment, that statements made outside the courtroom, without the opportunity for cross-examination, are admissible only against the person who made them. (See, e.g. *Bruton* v. *United States,* 391 U.S. 123; *Douglas* v. *Alabama,* 380 U.S. 415, 418–420; *Pointer* v. *Texas,* 380 U.S. 400, 403–406.) Consequently, when two or more defendants are tried jointly, a confession given by one defendant which inculpates a codefendant may not be received in evidence unless 'all parts of the extrajudicial statements implicating [the latter] can be and are effectively deleted [cited cases omitted].' Where such effective redaction is not possible, where a defendant's admission of guilt is 'so interrelated in the involvement of an accomplice as to render it impossible for practical purposes to separate them' (*People v. Pollock,* 21 NY2d 206, 214, *supra*), a joint trial must be eschewed and separate trials directed." *People v. Jackson,* 22 NY2d 446, 450, 239 NE2d 869.

The *Bruton* rule is applied retroactively. *Roberts v. Russell,* 392 US 293.

But *Bruton* is not applicable where both defendants have made a full and voluntary confession which is received in evidence and where the evidence is so overwhelming that failure to follow *Bruton* was harmless error "beyond a reasonable doubt." *People v. McNeil,* 24 NY2d 550, 552, 249 NE2d 383. *See also: Chapman v. California,* 386 US 18; *U.S. ex rel Catanzaro v. Mancusi,* 404 F2d 296.

Where a codefendant's confession, implicates the defendant by name and the confession is held inadmissible as to the codefendant requiring a reversal of his conviction and a new trial as to him, it also requires a new trial for the implicated defendant.

> "The defendant was tried with a codefendant and was implicated by name in the latter's confession which was received into evidence. Since this confession was held by the Appellate Division to be inadmissible and a new trial was ordered as to the codefendant, the Appellate Division should also have reversed this defendant's conviction and ordered a new trial in the interests of justice (*See* e.g., *People* v. *Morgan,* 17 NY 2d 696; * * *)." *People v. Cender* 18 NY2d 610, 611, 219 NE2d 200.

The right to counsel encompasses more than the right to have an attorney represent an accused. It includes the right to have compulsory process, *i.e.,* to subpoena witnesses on behalf of a defendant.

Thus a Texas procedural statute, which provided that persons charged as principals, accomplices or accessories in the same crime cannot be introduced as witnesses for each other, was invalidated by the United States Supreme Court, as violative of the Sixth Amendment. *Washington v. Texas* (1967), 388 US 14.

But, the Second Circuit has held that the refusal to grant defendants' request for deletion of references to them from a codefendant's statement was not abuse of discretion, where the statement was admissible against the codefendant and the jury was instructed not to consider the statement with respect to the defendants. *U.S. v. Lovejoy,* 364 F2d 586.

**§ 94. Past Recollection Recorded.** *Miranda* would seemingly authorize the admissibility of a confession, under this rule, if the procedural safeguards have been followed. In a case of first impression, the New York Appellate Division (2nd Dept) held that the rule of past recollection recorded is applicable to a confession in a criminal action. The rule is as follows: "When a witness is unable to testify concerning facts recited by or through him in a memorandum, the memorandum is admissible as evidence of the facts contained therein if he observed the matter recorded, it was made contemporaneously with the occurrence of the facts recited and the witness is able to swear that he believed the memorandum correct at the time made. (See 3 Wigmore, Evidence [3d ed.], §§ 745–754.) When admitted, the memorandum becomes part of the witness' present testimony." *People v. Caprio,* 25 AD2d 145, 150, 268 NYS2d 70, affd 18 NY2d 617, 272 NYS2d 385, 219 NE2d 204.

# Chapter 7

## VOLUNTARY CONFESSIONS AND ADMISSIONS



---

## § 98. Definition of Voluntariness.

> "If an individual's 'will was overborne' or if his confession was not 'the product of a rational intellect and a free will,' his confession is inadmissible because coerced. These standards are applicable whether a confession is the product of physical intimidation or psychological pressure and, of course, are equally applicable to a drug-induced statement." *Townsend v. Sain,* 372 US 293, 307.

To be voluntary, a confession must be the "product of a rational and meaningful act of volition . . . (see *Blackburn* v. *Alabama,* 361 U.S. 199)." *People v. Howard,* 27 AD2d 796, 279 NYS2d 79, 80.

Thus, at a preliminary hearing the uncontroverted facts established that defendant was "insane and a mental defective" at the time he made certain statements to the police which were later used at his trial. This required suppression of these statements. *People v. Howard, supra.*

Nor will a confession be deemed voluntary where it was obtained in violation of the procedural safeguards laid down in *Miranda v. Arizona,* 384 US 436.

An epileptic is responsible for his actions, except when he is suffering from an epileptic disturbance. *People* v. *Barber,* 115 N.Y. 475; *People v. Codarre,* 20 AD2d 98, 102, affd 14 NY2d 370, 200 NE2d 570, cert. den. 379 US 883; *People v. Baksys,* 26 AD2d 648, 649, 272 NYS2d 488.

Following the rationale of *Townsend v. Sain, supra,* the New York courts have indicated that pleas of guilty entered by defendants while allegedly under the influence of a narcotic drug would not be a "product of a rational intellect and a free will." Accordingly, on a motion to withdraw the plea, a hearing is required to determine the issue, where the claim was made prior to sentence. *People v. Swenson and Boyd,* NYLJ, 11/15/66, p. 18, col. 6; *see also: People v. Wilson,* 15 NY2d 634, 203 NE2d 925.

A pre-arraignment confession of a defendant who voluntarily accompanied FBI agents, and which was made during his detainment but prior to his arrest, was held admissible in *U.S. v. Vita,* 294 F2d 524.

The fact that after a voluntariness hearing, following defendant's conviction, his conviction was set aside because the People had failed to establish beyond a reasonable doubt that it was voluntary, the defendant must nevertheless stand retrial since the legal evidence before the grand jury was sufficient upon which to base the indictment. (CPL § 190.65(1)). The question of voluntariness of his confession is a matter of defense at the trial, for the consideration of the jury. *People v. Pariser,* 50 Misc2d 727.

**§ 99. The Voluntariness of Confessions and Admissions: How Determined.** Pending future legislative enactments or clarification by appropriate judicial tribunals, the determination of "voluntariness" under the *Townsend v. Sain* and *Miranda* rules, *supra,* should be decided at least in New York under the present Code provisions (CPL § 60.45), and the cases decided thereunder, with one exception—the date of retroactivity of cases decided under *Miranda.*

The decision in *Escobedo v. Illinois,* 378 US 478, affects only those cases in which the trial began after June 22, 1964, the date of that decision. The decision in *Miranda v. Arizona* 384 US 436, affects only those cases in which the trial began after June 13, 1966, the date of the *Miranda* decision. *Johnson v. N.J.,* 384 US 719.

As was pointed out above, *Miranda* applies only to those trials which had not begun as of June 13, 1966. "The failure to advise defendant of his right to counsel and to remain silent does not require the reversal of the judgment of conviction rendered after trial in 1954 (Johnson v. State of New Jersey, 384 U.S. 719, 86 S.Ct. 1772, 16 L.Ed. 2d 882 . . .)." *People v. Starkins,* 26 AD2d 657, 272 NYS2d 673, 674.

These decisions, therefore, do not preclude an attack on the voluntariness of a confession in cases tried prior to June 22, 1964 under *Escobedo* and prior to June 13, 1966 under *Miranda* if a full and fair hearing under this aspect of voluntariness had not already been afforded a defendant. *See: Townsend v. Sain, supra; Miranda v. Arizona, supra.*

Additionally, it can reasonably be anticipated that in cases tried after the effective date of *Escobedo* and *Miranda,* some defendants will attack their confessions as involuntary in cases in which the police will assert that the procedural safeguards of *Miranda* have been complied with. Hearings on these divergent claims will be required to determine the issue of voluntariness. In New York State the format and procedure to be followed was laid down in *People v. Huntley,* 15 NY2d 72, 255 NYS2d 838, 204 NE2d 179 and 46 Misc2d 209, and is now set forth in CPL art. 710.

**§ 100. Voluntariness Hearings.** The U.S. Supreme Court in *Jackson v. Denno,* 378 US 368, which involved a New York State conviction, held that the voluntariness of a confession will first be passed upon by a judge in the absence of a jury. Heretofore, the New York rule (followed in many states) stated that it was for the jury to decide if a confession was voluntary. *People v. Everett,* 10 NY2d 500, 180 NE2d 556; *People v. Malloy,* 21 AD2d 904, 251 NYS2d 752. The conflict in these rulings between the state and federal appellate courts raised the question as to which appellate court ruling New York courts were to follow. Some New York courts have held that they were bound to follow the rulings of the New York appellate courts. *People v. Malloy,* 21 AD2d 904; *People v. McNerlin,* 44 Misc2d 340, 253 NYS2d 912. *But see: Lego v. Twomey,* 30 L Ed2d 618, 92 SC 619.

This question has now been settled by the New York State Court of Appeals in *People v. Huntley,* 15 NY2d 72, 255 NYS2d 838, 204 NE2d 179. New York will now follow the federal rule as enunciated in *Jackson, supra,* and 18 USC § 3501, in those cases involving the question of voluntariness of confessions. This means that a defendant is entitled to a separate trial by the court alone, of the issue as to the voluntariness of his confession sought to be introduced in evidence. *People v. Mitchell,* 24 AD2d 609, 262 NYS2d 192; *People v. Korda,* 24 AD2d 577, 262 NYS2d 217; *People v. Thomas,* 24 AD2d 466.

The correctness of the New York rules has been underscored by the United States Supreme Court in *Sims v. Georgia,* 385 US 538. In the trial of that case, the issue of the voluntariness of a confession was crucial. The trial judge failed to make a matter of record his conclusion that the defendant, who claimed police brutality, had confessed voluntarily. This omission, the Supreme Court held, violated defendant's Fourteenth Amendment right to a fair trial and vitiated his conviction.

In the Supreme Court of Georgia, it was clearly indicated that both the trial judge and the Georgia Supreme Court were following the Georgia rule on voluntariness of confessions and not the United States Supreme Court rule enunciated in *Jackson v. Denno, supra.* The "Georgia rule presents the question [of voluntariness] to the jury without giving them the judgment of the court." *Sims v. Georgia, supra.*

This Georgia rule was held to be in error. "A constitutional rule was laid down in that case, [*Jackson v. Denno, supra*] that a jury is not to hear a confession unless and until the trial judge has determined that it was freely and voluntarily given." Thus, the judge's conclusions "that the confession is voluntary must appear from the record with unmistakable clarity." *Sims v. Georgia,* 385 US 538, 543, 544. The rule in *Jackson v. Denno, supra,* is binding upon the states.

"The right to a hearing and determination on the issue of voluntariness allowed by the Huntley decision is not limited to confessions but also includes statements containing admissions. (*People* v. *Harden,* 17 NY2d 470; *People* v. *Catanzaro,* 17 NY2d 185; *People* v. *Hocking,* 15 NY2d 973, 975.)" *People v. Nadile,* 26 AD2d 765–766, 271 NYS2d 723, 724.

Where, after trial, the question of voluntariness of a confession is raised on appeal and the case is remanded for a hearing to resolve that question, the prior record may be used on the hearing. However, both sides may submit additional proof. The hearing, when possible, should be held before the judge who presided at the voir dire, if any, or the trial judge. *People v. Alberti,* 23 AD2d 543, 256 NYS2d 177.

When the voluntariness of a confession is challenged, the defendant is entitled to a separate trial on that issue. *Jackson v. Denno,* 378 US 368; *People v. Huntley,* 15 NY2d 72, 255 NYS2d 838, 204 NE2d 179.

A voir dire examination held in the jury's presence, during the trial, and over defendant's objection, does not constitute a "separate trial" of that issue and is a violation of defendant's constitutional rights. *People v. Jones,* 26 AD2d 652, 272 NYS2d 439.

Additionally, it has been held that where the judge, in a

hearing, has found defendant's statements to have been voluntary but failed to charge the jury that they must pass on the question of voluntariness, failure of defendant's counsel to except to the charge and failure to "request that the issue of voluntariness be submitted to the jury" nevertheless constituted reversible error.

"Absent a clear concession of voluntariness or a clear waiver of the right to a jury trial of that issue, such issue must be submitted to the jury, despite the fact that it has preliminarily been passed upon by the trial court in the jury's absence. . . . In our opinion, there has been here no concession of voluntariness and no clear, affirmative waiver of the basic right to have the issue of voluntariness submitted to the jury; and that issue has been preserved for appellate review, depite the failure to except to the charge or request addition of the issue to the charge. . . ." *People v. Mials,* 27 AD2d 944, 945, and cases cited therein.

It is obvious that if the jury is informed as to the judge's findings on the question of voluntariness, that such disclosure would undoubtedly influence it in its independent determination of the same question.

Thus, the New York Appellate Division has held that where a defendant requested a closed hearing but a public hearing is held, the details of which and the court's findings thereon, having been reported in the public press, a change of venue of the trial is required on defendant's application.

Implicit in the court's reasoning in this case is the requirement that "In the future, decisions rendered upon *Huntley* hearings should not be made public prior to the determination of the action." *People v. Pratt,* 27 AD2d 199, 202, 278 NYS2d 89, 93. Where the defendant specifically requests a closed hearing, the request should be granted.

**§ 100.01. Voluntariness: Question of Fact.** Even though the only witnesses who testify at a voluntariness hearing are the People's witnesses, the question of the voluntariness of the proffered admission or confession, is still a question of fact to be determined by the jury. In other words, it does not become a mere question of law simply because a defendant offers no testimony in rebuttal. The jury still has the power and the right to disbelieve the People's witnesses. "The plea of not guilty and the presumption of innocence make the credibility of every witness for the People in a criminal action a question of fact for the jury." *People v. Walker,* 198 NY 329, 334.

To charge, under such circumstances, that it was merely a question of law was held to be error. "Not only was the burden of proof of voluntariness on the People, but the fact of voluntariness had to be established beyond a reasonable doubt. (*People* v. *Huntley,* [15 N.Y.2d], p. 78)." *People v. Veitch,* 25 AD2d 494, 266 NYS2d 688, 689.

In determining the question of voluntariness, the defendant's age and denial of access of his parent are "germane, but in no wise controlling on the question of voluntariness. Nothing in the present case requires, . . . that we abandon our position in *Hocking* and *Taylor* [*People v. Hocking,* 15 N.Y.2d 973; *People v. Taylor,* 16 N.Y.2d 1038]. . . . This case was tried long before June of 1966. The case of *Miranda* v. *Arizona* (384 U.S. 436) is not applicable (*People* v. *McQueen,* 18 NY2d 337 . . . )." *People v. Burd and Hocking,* 18 NY2d 832, 833, 222 NE2d 600.

In *People v. Horton and Alvarez,* 18 NY2d 355, 360–361, 221 NE2d 909, cert. den. 387 US 934, the Court of Appeals stated "that the Judge refused to consider evidence that the authorities failed to advise the defendants of their rights to counsel and to remain silent. That this ruling constituted error [was] unquestionable, since such facts are relevant to the issue of voluntariness. (See *Miranda* v. *Arizona,* 384 U.S. 436 [1966]; *Johnson* v. *New Jersey,* 384 U.S. 719 [1966]; *Davis* v. *North Carolina,* 384 U.S. 737 [1966].)" This was also a pre-*Miranda* trial.

A voluntariness hearing is inapplicable to traffic violations. *People v. Marsh,* 20 NY2d 98, 228 NE2d 783; *People v. Coleman,* 24 NY2d 1005, 250 NE2d 237.

**§ 100.02. Judge's Findings.** The decision of the judge shall set forth specific findings of fact and conclusions of law. The question of voluntariness need not be resubmitted to the jury in those cases which have already been concluded. The voluntariness of a confession as well as its admissibility can only be determined by the trial court.

A magistrate, conducting a preliminary hearing, ruled that a confession was involuntary. The ruling made during the preliminary examination is not the law of the case. Such a hearing is not a prosecution, but merely an inquiry. Regardless of the magistrate's determination, the case could still be presented to the grand jury. *People v. DeIorio,* 45 Misc2d 68, 256 NYS2d 248; *U.S. ex rel Boone v. Fay,* 231 F Supp 387, 390.

The determination by a magistrate made during a preliminary hearing that a confession was involuntary is no more binding than a determination by him that the confession was voluntary.

In such a situation, the defendant is still entitled to a hearing on the issue of voluntariness if he is indicted. *People ex rel Ruppert v. Hoy,* 50 Misc2d 326.

**§ 100.03. Preponderance of Evidence and Burden of Proof.** In deciding *Jackson v. Denno,* 378 US 368, followed in New York, *People v. Huntley,* 15 NY2d 72, and in other jurisdictions, the Supreme Court held that before submitting a purported confession to a jury, the trial court must first determine if the confession is voluntary. The Court, however, did not lay down the gauge by which voluntariness should be measured. Some jurisdictions, like New York, held that voluntariness had to be established beyond a reasonable doubt. Others, like Illinois, held that it should be measured by a preponderance-of-the-evidence rule.

The Supreme Court has now resolved this question in *Lego v. Twomey,* 30 L Ed2d 618, 92 SC 619, by approving the "preponderance" test, although it left the States free to adopt a more stringent test, *i.e.,* the "reasonable doubt" rule.

The Court also held that the admissibility of a challenged confession was an evidentiary question for the trial court alone to determine. Accordingly, once the trial court finds the confession is voluntary and therefore admissible, there is no constitutional requirement that the question of voluntariness be submitted to the jury anew. *Duncan v. Louisiana,* 391 US

145. *Cf.: In re Winship,* 397 US 358; *People v. Huntley,* 15 NY2d, 204 NE2d 179; *People v. Malinsky,* 15 NY2d 86, 204 NE2d 188.

§ 101. **Retroactivity.** *Jackson* is retroactive and requires a separate hearing on the voluntariness of confessions as applicable to all criminal judgments which are no longer in normal appellate process. *People v. Huntley, supra,* also specifically overruled *People v. Hovnanian,* 22 AD2d 686, insofar as it held otherwise. *Cf. People v. Berry,* 14 NY2d 975, 202 NE2d 552; *People v. Bloeth,* 14 NY2d 975, 202 NE2d 552; *People v. Pugach,* 14 NY2d 976, 202 NE2d 553.

§ 101.01. **Coram Nobis Remedy.** *Huntley* also directs that, in the future, defendants seek remedy by coram nobis motion as to those trials which have been concluded, and in which the voluntariness of confessions were contested, and where the normal appellate processes had been exhausted or are no longer available.

The issue of voluntariness of confession cannot be entertained by habeas corpus. (CPLR, § 7002(b)2). The remedy is to be sought by coram nobis in those post-conviction situations which are out of the stream of the normal appellate process. *People ex rel Graham v. Wilkens,* 23 AD2d 523, 255 NYS2d 892; *People ex rel Goodman v. Wallack,* 23 AD2d 514.

Coram nobis is not available to a defendant who had pleaded guilty voluntarily in 1958, with his attorney present, even though, prior to entering the plea, he had confessed to police after he had requested and been denied the right to consult with counsel. Nor is the "new" law (*People v. Howard,* 12 NY2d 65, 187 NE2d 65), as subsequently enunciated in *Huntley,* available to him as a basis for relief by coram nobis in such a situation.

Nor can a defendant contest the voluntariness of his confession by an application for a writ of error coram nobis, after pleading guilty and after sentence. *People v. White,* 26 AD2d 657, 272 NYS2d 410; *see also: People v. Nicholson,* 11 NY2d 1067; *People v. De Renzzio,* 19 NY2d 45, 50, 224 NE2d 97.

In *People v. Muller,* NYLJ, 3/18/66, p. 18, col. 3, the question posed was: Where the defendant, during trial and after the admission into evidence of an inculpatory statement over his objection that the confession was involuntary, withdrew his not guilty plea and pleaded guilty, may he maintain a coram nobis application for a hearing?

In *Muller,* defendant, during trial, entered his plea of guilty prior to the enactment of secs. 813-f, 813-g, 813-h and 813-i of the Code of Criminal Procedure, and appealed solely on the ground that the sentence was excessive. The conviction and sentence were affirmed. He then sought coram nobis relief. This was denied on the authority of *People v. Piracci,* 24 AD2d 892. By his plea of guilty, it was held, defendant had waived his challenge as to the voluntariness of his inculpatory statements.

In a case in which a post-conviction hearing on voluntariness had been granted, defendant sought a commission to take testimony of his former wife, a California resident. The Supreme Court (Erie County, N.Y.) granted the commission. The court held that authority to do so lay in the *Huntley* decision itself as well as in the statutory provisions. *People v. Augello,* 45 Misc2d 402, 257 NYS2d 125, 265 NYS2d 509.

**§ 101.02. When Not Deemed Retroactive.** *Jackson* will not be deemed retroactive where a confession was admitted without objection by the defendant, or without any assertion by him or his witnesses as to voluntariness. *People v. French,* 24 AD2d 657, 261 NYS2d 239; *People v. McQueen,* 24 AD2d 499, affd 18 NY2d 337, 221 NE2d 550.

On the other hand, where the conviction was obtained prior to *Jackson v. Denno, supra,* in a trial without a jury, "there was, of course, no jury to be 'charged * * * on voluntariness' (*People* v. *Huntley,* 15 NY2d 72, 77)," and, therefore it was not a case required to be remanded for a *Huntley* hearing, where the inculpatory admissions were admitted without objections and there was no assertion by the defendant or his witnesses as to involuntariness. *People v. Rogers,* 25 AD2d 794, 269 NYS2d 189, 190.

However, if the trial judge had charged a jury on voluntariness, that issue was in the case and a new hearing was indicated. *People v. French, supra; People v. McQueen, supra.*

In a case where confessions were allegedly made to private persons, which defendant categorically denied, and where no issue of duress was otherwise presented, judge's charge which included a reading of the applicable criminal procedure statute, and his explanation as to when a confession may be considered as part of the evidence of a case, does not constitute injecting the question of voluntariness of the confession into the case. *People v. Rizzi,* 47 Misc2d 948.

In *People v. Green,* 46 Misc2d 812, the court followed the ruling in *Rizzi.* However, a contrary ruling was made in *People v. Wilkes,* 46 Misc2d 511, 259 NYS2d 973, and in *People v. Bartlam,* NYLJ, 9/24/65, p. 17, col. 4. These are all lower court rulings.

New York has held that it was not necessary under the theory of the retroactivity of judicial pronouncements to impose a subsequently developed theory of law upon a trial which had taken place 30 years ago.

In *People v. De Renzzio,* 19 NY2d 45, 224 NE2d 97, the defendant had been convicted of first degree murder in 1938. His appeal was dismissed for failure to prosecute. At his trial, statements made by him after indictment and arraignment and in the absence of counsel were received in evidence without objection. His appeal was reinstated in 1964. In the interim the rule regarding the admission in evidence of his statements had been changed, making them inadmissible. *People v. DiBiasi,* 7 NY2d 544, 166 NE2d 825 and *People v. Waterman,* 9 NY2d 561, 175 NE2d 445.

The conviction was affirmed by a divided court. One judge held that absent an objection at the trial, the objection to the introduction of the statements could not be raised on the appeal. Two judges concurred, stating that the changed rule was not retroactive, citing *Johnson v. New Jersey,* 384 US 719, and *People v. McQueen,* 18 NY2d 337, 221 NE2d 550. Two other judges concurred without opinion. The two dissenting judges held that the changes in the rule should be available to the defendant on the ground that the case was in the appellate process. *See also: Jenkins v. State,* 395 US 213, and *People v. Sayers,* 22 NY2d 571, 240 NE2d 540.

It is to be noted that both *Johnson* and *McQueen, supra,* specifically stated that *Miranda* and *Escobedo* should apply only to trials begun after the decisions in those cases were announced *even though the cases may still be on direct appeal.*

In distinguishing *People v. Gunner,* 15 NY2d 226, the majority of the Appellate Division held in *People v. Baker,* 28 AD2d 24, 281 NYS2d 161, that a statement made by the defendant contrary to the advice of his attorney, known and so understood by him and the police, is admissible. There was no claim by the defendant of the use of coercion, trickery, unduly prolonged insistence or any other pressure.

> "To hold that such a statement is interdicted requires a holding that, once counsel is retained and advises, the defendant loses all volition and control of the conduct of his defense and is powerless to adopt the course that he believes will best either satisfy his conscience or produce the most desirable outcome. Obviously, this is not the law. The defendant himself is the final arbiter of the conduct of his defense (Carter v. People of State of Illinois, 329 U.S. 173, 174 . . .). We find no authority for an exception in this one respect." *People v. Baker,* 281 NYS2d 161, 163. However, *Baker* was reversed on another theory (23 NY2d 307, 244 NE2d 232).

**§ 102. Voluntariness Hearing Where Defendant Denies Having Made Any Confession.** In *People v. Famous,* 47 Misc2d 943, 263 NYS2d 546, the defendant attacked the voluntariness of his confession by coram nobis twelve years later. The court granted a voluntariness hearing only because the trial minutes were missing. The defendant testified in his own behalf and at no time during the trial was the issue of voluntariness "raised by objection, cross-examination, summation or in any form." Defendant's defense on this issue was that he made no confession at all. The issue of voluntariness was not in the case. *Famous* was tried before the decision in *Jackson v. Denno,* 378 US 368.

Subsequently, in *People v. Wright,* 21 NY2d 1011, 238 NE2d 330, the same question appeared before the New York Court of Appeals. In this case, there was some evidence of physical coercion as to a codefendant, Cicatelli, who was alleged to have confessed. As to him, the court said he was entitled to full inquiry into the voluntary nature of his purported confession even though he denied having made any confession.

The cases can be distinguished. It would seem to be the rule that where a defendant does not testify at the trial, he would be entitled to a post-conviction voluntariness hearing on his petition. However, where he does testify at the trial and he denies making any confession and where, in addition, no issue of voluntariness is raised at the trial, no hearing is required. On the other hand, even though he testifies and evidence of coercion is presented at the trial, he is entitled to a hearing even though he denies having made any confession at all.

"The admission in evidence, over objection, of a post-indictment statement is reversible error (*People* v. *DiBiasi,* 7 NY2d 544, [200 N.Y.S.2d 21])." *People v. DeRennzio,* 25 AD2d 652, 653 affd 19 NY2d 45, 224 NE2d 97. *See also: People v. Friola,* 11 NY2d 157, 159, 182 NE2d 100. But where no objection is made to the admission, there is no question of law preserved for review.

Additionally, where the trial judge did not charge on the issue of voluntariness, and there was no exception taken to the charge and no requests to charge were made, there is no necessity for a non-jury hearing on the issue of voluntariness. *People v. DeRennzio, supra.*

Distinguishing *DeRenzzio* from *People v. Friola, supra,* the Appellate Division held that where no objection as to the voluntariness of statements made by the defendant was made by him, that issue is not preserved for appellate review.

Where the issue of voluntariness of an admission is raised during trial, failure to submit that issue to the jury is reversible error, but: "Absent a clear concession of voluntariness or a clear waiver of the right to a jury trial of that issue, such issue must be submitted to the jury, despite the fact that it has preliminarily been passed upon by the trial court in the jury's absence. (*People* v. *Huntley,* 15 NY2d 72; N.Y.S. Const., art. I, § 2)." *People v. Mials,* 27 AD2d 944, 278 NYS2d 1020, 1021. *See also: People v. DeRenzzio, supra; cf. People v. Friola, supra.*

In *People v. Huntley,* 15 NY2d 72, 77, 204 NE2d 179, the court stated:

> "No *Jackson-Denno* hearing will be necessary in cases where a confession was admitted without any objection by the defendant or any assertion by him or his witnesses as to voluntariness. Even in these cases, however, if the trial court charged the jury on voluntariness . . . a new hearing is indicated."

However, it has been held that this rule is not applicable to a pre-*Jackson-Huntley* case even where the defendant vigorously contested the admission of his confession on the ground of involuntariness, but where the defendant's counsel, for strategic reasons, prior to the court's charging the jury, stated that the defendant did *not* contend that his statements were involuntary and where consequently the trial court did not charge this point.

The denial of a hearing by the Appelate Division on the question of voluntariness and judgment of conviction was affirmed accordingly. *People v. Castro,* 19 NY2d 14, 244 NE2d 80.

**§ 102.01. Question and Answer Statements.** A coram nobis petitioner was held entitled to a hearing on the voluntariness of his confession, where objection to the introduction of the confession was made at the trial, even though the objection was not made specifically upon the question of voluntariness, and where in addition the court charged the jury as to voluntariness.

In this case, the court held that the question and answer statements given to the District Attorney were in the nature of a confession.

> "The question and answer statements to the District Attorney were certainly in the nature of a confession and although there was no objection specifically made upon the question of voluntariness the objection was made to introducing them into evidence at the trial. In addition, the trial court charged the jury as to voluntariness and *both these acts would be sufficient* to bring defendant within the rule of *People* v. *Huntley,* (15 NY2d 72). It is our opinion that defendant is entitled to a hearing on

> his petition." *People v. McElroy,* 26 AD2d 598, 599, 271 NYS2d 391, 392 (emphasis supplied).

§ **102.02. Confessions to Private Persons.** Where incriminating statements were alleged to have been made to department store employees by a suspected shoplifter under compulsion, the New York State Supreme Court has held that a voluntariness hearing was required.

> "Therefore, inasmuch as defendant is now objecting to the use of these alleged statements at trial (cf. *People* v. *Terry,* 16 NY2d 731) the trial court is obliged to grant a preliminary hearing (*Jackson* v. *Denno,* 378 U.S. 368) on the issue of voluntariness, no matter to whom these statements were made (*People* v. *Harden,* 17 NY2d 470)." *People v. Frank,* 52 Misc2d 266, 267, 275 NYS2d 570, 572. *See also: People v. Williams,* 53 Misc2d 1086.

However, *Frank* has been overruled in *People v. Mirenda,* 23 NY2d 439, 245 NE2d 194. In *Mirenda,* the court said that although the statute does not distinguish between confessions and admissions made to the police or private individuals,

> "We do not, however, interpret the legislative intent as requiring the District Attorney to notify defendants of admissions made to private parties who were not police agents.
>
> "When an admission is made to a private person the procedure established by section 813-f is inapplicable." *Mirenda, supra,* 23 NY2d at 448.

On the other hand, if the private person is a police informant or a police agent, his admissions in the absence of counsel and absent *Miranda* warnings would be inadmissible. *People v. Mirenda, supra* at 448. *See, e.g., People v. Gunner,* 15 NY2d 226, 231, 205 NE2d 852, and *Corngold v. U.S.,* 367 F2d 1, 5–6.

Upon an allegation by the defendant that the private individual to whom he made admissions was a police informant, a voluntariness hearing is required.

> "When a defendant raises at trial the voluntariness of an admission made to a private person who, it is also

> claimed, was acting as a police agent, the court should conduct a hearing at that time. (See *People* v. *Hooper,* 22 NY2d 655; *People* v. *Ross,* 21 NY2d 258, 262–263, . . .)." *Mirenda, supra* at 449.

*Mirenda, supra* and *People v. Huntley,* 15 NY2d 72, 255 NYS2d 838, 204 NE2d 179, and 46 Misc2d 209 must be deemed modified by virtue of the enactment of CPL § 60.45. This new section interdicts statements, made by a defendant, whether inculpatory or exculpatory, when made to a private person as well as to the police, if obtained as a result of coercion. The basic definition of involuntariness laid down in *Townsend v. Sain,* 372 US 293, 307, *supra,* is left unchanged. But, the acts described in *Townsend,* as inducing involuntariness, now, under New York law apply equally to such acts if performed by private persons.

The ploys, which result in statements made by a defendant, condemned in *Miranda v. Arizona,* 384 US 436 as resulting in "involuntary" statements, are specifically proscribed in New York by virtue of CPL § 60.45(2)(b).

The statements referred to include written as well as oral statements. CPL § 60.45(1).

**§ 102.03. New Jersey Rule: Corpus Delicti.** While, under the law in New York (CPL §§ 60.45, 60.50) and many other jurisdictions, a confession without additional proof of the full existence of the corpus delicti is insufficient to warrant conviction, New Jersey has adopted a less stringent rule:

> "Full proof of the body of the crime, the corpus delicti, independently of the confession, is not required. It may be proved by the confession itself, corroborated by other evidence." *State v. Banusik,* 84 NJL 640.
>
> "When there is a voluntary confession of the offense by the defendant in a criminal case, full proof of the body of the crime is not required in addition to the confession, but sufficient proof thereof may arise out of evidence corroborating some fact or facts in the confession itself." *State v. Geltzeiler,* 101 NJL 415.

This rule was reaffirmed by the Supreme Court of New Jersey in *State v. Portee,* 46 NJ 239, 216 A2d 227, 231 in which the court stated: "The crime here was a simple possessory one declared by the Legislature to be a misdemeanor. The defendant's voluntary statement unequivocally admitted the relevant circumstances and his commission of the crime. There was no danger of confusion or mistake and there has been no suggestion of falsity. The corroborating testimony of *Moses* and *Johnson* [both witnesses], while it was admittedly insufficient of itself to establish the presence of the revolver, nevertheless served to fortify the truth of the admissions in the defendant's statement on the basis of which the trial judge found guilt beyond reasonable doubt. His finding had adequate legal support in the evidence within the flexible standard of proof required by the New Jersey precedents."

Nevertheless, there is a strong inference in this opinion that New Jersey might follow the more stringent rule adopted in New York if the crime charged were a felony.

In any event, whatever rule New Jersey adopts, it will have to be in conformity with procedural safeguards set forth in *Miranda v. Arizona, supra.*

§ **103. Notice by Prosecutor.** When the prosecutor intends to introduce a confession or admission into evidence at a trial, he must give the defendant reasonable notice. *See, e.g.,* CPL § 710.30.

This notice must be given before trial. A second trial, following a declaration of a mistrial over defendant's objection, ordered by the court to afford the prosecutor an opportunity to give reasonable notice to the defendant that a confession would be offered in evidence, was held to constitute double jeopardy. *Roth v. District Attorney,* 46 Misc2d 489, 259 NYS2d 983.

The required notice is applicable to Youthful Offender Proceedings and the use of an admission or confession in evidence against a youthful offender in those proceedings without notice is error. *People v. Lee,* 27 AD2d 700; CPL art. 710.

"[A]t the sentencing stage a defendant is not entitled to prior notice that the District Attorney is planning to introduce a confession and he is not automatically entitled to a *'Huntley* hearing' on its voluntariness prior to its introduction." *People v. Jackson,* 20 NY2d 440, 456, 231 NE2d 722.

**§ 104. Notice by Defendant.** If the defendant intends to attack the voluntariness of a confession or admission, he must notify the prosecutor of his desire for a preliminary hearing on that issue. CPL art. 710.

Where a defendant demands a voluntariness hearing, he must serve notice on his codefendants, if any. There is no explicit duty on the prosecution to serve the notice, since the statute says "the moving party" must do so.

"However, it would be desirable for courts, before the hearing proceeds, to determine whether other codefendants were notified. . . . This is not to say that other codefendants must be present in order to proceed with the hearing, but only that the Judge should inquire whether the proper notice to these defendants has been given." *People v. Mirenda,* 23 NY2d at 447–448, 245 NE2d 194.

The hearing should be held as to *all* inculpatory statements made by the defendant. Thus, where a voluntariness hearing involved two inculpatory statements made to a police officer and which the court (pretrial) found to be voluntary, but where a third inculpatory statement was offered at the trial as part of the People's case, the case was "held" pending a determination as to the voluntariness of the third alleged admission. "At a hearing of the *Huntley* type, all confessions and inculpatory admissions introduced as part of the People's case at the trial should be considered and voluntariness determined. (*People* v. *Harden,* 17 NY2d 470.)" *People v. Colavecchio,* 25 AD2d 812.

It has been held in *People v. Silverman,* 26 AD2d 890, 274 NYS2d 190, that where the District Attorney has advance knowledge of an admission to a police officer, he is obligated to notify the defense attorney of his intention of introducing the admission in evidence.

"In any event, . . . if the admission is to be offered by the People, there must be a *Voir dire,* as outlined in People v. Huntley and, additionally, it will be necessary to consider the mandate outlined in Miranda v. State of Arizona, 384 U.S. 436. . . ." *People v. Silverman, supra,* 274 NYS2d at 192.

This decision indicates that voluntariness under *Huntley,* alone, is not the determining factor of admissibility. The rules prescribed by *Miranda* must also be followed before admissions or confessions may be received in evidence.

However, the motion to suppress made by the defendant will be denied when "he [the defendant] has not been served with a notice by the District Attorney under section 813-f of the Code of Criminal Procedure of an intention to offer a confession or statement at his trial." *People v. Dubard,* 52 Misc2d 244, 275 NYS2d 275, 276.

**§ 104.01. Objection Must Be Specific.** In *U.S. v. Indiviglio,* 352 F2d 276, 277, a generalized objection of an admission or confession based on constitutional grounds has been held insufficient to preserve the question for review on appeal. 1 Wigmore, *Evidence,* § 18(c)(1), (3rd ed. 1940). Fed R Crim P §§ 41(e), 9(c)(1). *Also see: U.S. v. Anderson,* 394 F2d 743.

The court stated that objections must be specific so that the trial court can be reasonably apprised of the grounds therefor. Furthermore, an objection will be reviewed as to the specific point raised, whereas an overruled general objection cannot be reviewed on appeal. "We reject appellant's claim of error because he failed to specify in his objection to the admission of the challenged evidence the Massiah or Escobedo issues on which he now seeks to rely." *U.S. v. Indiviglio,* 352 F2d at 279.

In New York, the courts have ruled that if the constitutional question was somehow raised by the defendant during trial of search and seizure cases, that issue is preserved for review, even in the absence of a specific objection. New York now follows the federal rule in cases pertaining to admissions and confessions. *See: People v. Ross,* 21 NY2d 258, 234 NE2d 427.

**§ 105. Voluntariness Hearing in Non-Jury Case.** Where the judge is the trier of the facts and the law in a case antedating the *Huntley* and *Jackson* cases, no separate hearing on the question of the voluntariness of an admission or confession is required.

> "In the instant case [manslaughter], the defendant waived his right to a jury trial and implicitly made the

presiding judge the trier of the law and the facts of the case. Having elected to have the judge determine the law and the facts, the defendant may not now, under the circumstances of the case, demand that an independent hearing be held to determine the issue of voluntariness." *People v. Brown,* NYLJ, 12/14/65, p. 15.

The application of the decisions in *Jackson v. Denno, supra,* and *People v. Huntley, supra,* "is limited to jury trials and not nonjury cases when raised retroactively." *People v. Brown, supra.*

The same rule also applies to current non-jury cases, whether they are conducted without a jury on defendant's waiver or pursuant to statute. *See, e.g.,* New York City Criminal Court Act, § 40.

The thrust of *Jackson v. Denno, supra,* is concerned with the inability of juries to separate factors relating to voluntariness of confessions from those bearing on guilt or innocence. "There is a critical difference between a jury and nonjury trial and, therefore, [we] hold that the rationale of *Jackson* is inapplicable to the latter situation," (p. 173) in that a judge "is uniquely capable of distinguishing the issues and making an objective determination as to voluntariness, . . ." (p. 172). *People v. Brown,* 24 NY2d 168, 172, 173, 247 NE2d 153.

Nevertheless, the Appellate Division, Fourth Department, in *People v. Williams,* 25 AD2d 612, 267 NYS2d 350, has held that in a non-jury case, the judge must make specific findings as to the voluntariness of admissions made, "and if found to be voluntary, whether the proof established voluntariness beyond a reasonable doubt." *Cf. Lego v. Twomey,* 30 L Ed2d 618, 92 SC 619.

A confession is presumed to be voluntary. The issue of voluntariness must be raised before it is required to be submitted to the jury. If that issue is somehow raised, the jury is required to pass on that question, even though no formal objection to the confession is made at the trial. *People v. Cefaro,* 23 NY2d 283, 285–287, 244 NE2d 42.

A defendant is entitled to have the question of voluntariness of his confession determined uninfluenced by other evidence of guilt under *Jackson v. Denno,* 378 US 368. *People v. Brown,* 24 NY2d 168, 247 NE2d 153.

Even though the defendant denies making any statement, he is nevertheless entitled to a full inquiry into the voluntary nature of any purported confession. *People v. Wright,* 21 NY2d 1011, 238 NE2d 330; *cf. People v. Stigler,* 9 NY2d 717, 719, 174 NE2d 324.

A defendant has the right to testify on the voir dire as to his alleged confession. *People v. Prager,* 30 AD2d 848, 293 NYS2d 22.

**§ 106. Guidelines to Be Followed in Conducting a Post-Conviction Hearing on the Question of Voluntariness in a Case Out of the Normal Appellate Process.** In *People v. Huntley,* 46 Misc2d 209, on remand, the court conducted a post-conviction hearing to determine the voluntariness of the defendant's purported confession, and suggested certain guidelines to be followed. The official reporter (46 Misc2d 209) omitted this portion of the court's opinion, but, the full text of the opinion (Geller, J.) appeared in the New York Law Journal, April 9, 1965, page 16, col. 4, and in the files of the New York State Supreme Court (New York County), Special Term, Part XXXI, entitled *People v. Huntley,* Indictment Number 1083–59.

The suggested guidelines are:

> 1. *Prior Police Action*
>
> "[S]ubterfuge or artifice, [employed by the police], not amounting to a deprivation of due process, does not render invalid a confession otherwise valid (cf. *People v. Leyra,* 302 N.Y. 353, 363, and *People v. Everett,* 10 N.Y.2d 500, 507)."

Note that in *Everett, supra,* at p. 507, the court said:

> "Almost a century ago, Chief Judge Davies stated that 'a confession is admissible, although it is * * * obtained by artifice or deception' (*People* v. *Wentz,* 37 N.Y. 303, 306). This rule has been reaffirmed by our court in *People* v. *Buffom* (214 N.Y. 53, 57); *People* v. *White,* (176 N.Y. 331, 348–349). (See, also, *United States ex rel. Caminito* v.

*Murphy,* 222 F.2d 698, cert. den. 350 U.S. 896; *State* v. *Exum,* 213 N.C. 16; *Commonwealth* v. *Johnson,* 372 Pa. 266, cert. den. 345 U.S. 959; 3 Wigmore, Evidence, § 841.) Deception alone will not render a confession invalid, unless the deceiving acts amount to a deprivation of due process (*People* v. *Leyra,* 302 N.Y. 353, 363)." *See also: Rogers v. Richmond,* 365 US 534, 542.

[Note also, the subterfuges or artifices employed by the authorities may not be any of the ploys proscribed by *Miranda v. Arizona, supra.*]

2. *Prior Action By the Defendant*

The evidence at the hearing disclosed that Huntley attempted to suborn perjury by asking the superintendent of the building where he was employed intermittently to say that he had been working on the day of the robbery. This constituted "a serious impeachment of credibility of [the defendant's] own truthfulness as a witness."

3. *Other Elements to be Considered by the Court.*

Other factors, although not playing a significant part should be noted. These are:

(a) Was defendant's interrogation prolonged or unremitting? *People v. Lane,* 10 NY2d 347, 179 NE2d 339.
(b) Was there any unnecessary delay in his arraignment?
(c) The manner of the arrest, if related in point of fact to a resultant induced confession. Was the arrest lawful?

"[T]he fact that a confession is obtained during a detention following an unlawful arrest does not, as a matter of law, render it inadmissible. *People v. Everett,* 10 N.Y.2d 500, 507." *Cf. Wong Sun v. U.S.,* 371 US 471, 485–486.

§ 107. **Cross-Examination of Defendant.** The general rule under both *Huntley* and *Jackson* is that cross-examination on guilt or truth of the confession should not be permitted, because of irrelevancy and prejudice to a fair and reliable determination of the issue, unless the defendant on his direct examination has affirmatively stated his innocence of the crime.

In *Huntley,* after defendant had testified that he had been coerced into confessing "there was an implication that an innocent man had confessed solely because of coercion. In that circumstance the District Attorney was entitled to prove on cross-examination the question of guilt or innocence and attempt to dispel the implication suggested on direct. A defendant has no right to set forth facts on a subject to his advantage without laying himself open to a cross-examination upon that entire subject (*Brown* v. *United States,* 356 U.S. 148, 154; *People* v. *Cassidy,* 213 N.Y. 388, 394)." *People v. Huntley,* 46 Misc2d at 212.

Where the defendant testifies at a post-conviction, *Huntley* hearing on the issue of voluntariness of his purported incriminating statements, he may be cross-examined as to prior convictions and criminal acts affecting his credibility as a witness, and acts involving moral turpitude, the manner and extent thereof being largely within the discretion of the trial judge. *People v. Tice,* 131 NY 651; *People v. Trybus,* 219 NY 18; *People v. Sorge,* 301 NY 198.

But the determination of voluntariness must not be beclouded or influenced by knowledge that the accused is a bad man with a long criminal record. *Stein v. New York,* 346 US 156, 200, dissenting op. Frankfurther, J.

The determination of voluntariness must be based upon a finding or persuasive relevant factors, whether in addition to or apart from the matter of credibility as affected by defendant's criminal record.

**§ 108. The Use of Defendant's Voluntariness Hearing Testimony at the Trial.** Testimony given at a preliminary proceeding is not a waiver at the trial of defendant's constitutional privilege against self-incrimination. 8 Wigmore, *Evidence,* § 2276, pp. 470–471, (McNaughton rev. 1961).

> "[A]ny admissions of a self-incriminatory nature obtained in a *Jackson-Denno* 'proceeding separate and apart from the body trying guilt or innocence,'. . . , may not be used at a subsequent trial of that charge (see *People* v. *Cassidy,* 213 N.Y. 388, 395; *Matter of Neff,* 206 F.2d 149, 152). . . . The rationale of *Jackson* is that a defen-

> dant should be given the opportunity to contest voluntariness and testify at a separate hearing to secure and certainly not to endanger his rights for the main trial. But, of course, if defendant should take the stand at a subsequent trial and deny his guilt, his privilege would be waived and the door would be opened to using these admissions (*Walder* v. *United States,* 347 U.S. 62, 65)." *People v. Huntley,* 46 Misc2d 209, 212.

This *Huntley* decision indicates that failure to advise a defendant prior to interrogation of his right to silence and his right to counsel are also factors to be considered in weighing the question of the voluntariness of a confession. However, these elements of *Huntley* may now be disregarded as obsolete in view of the decision, one year later, of the case of *Miranda v. Arizona,* 384 US 436.

The Court of Appeals for the District of Columbia, held that a judge is not obliged to order a hearing on the voluntariness of a confession when defendant not only failed to object to a statement attributed to him but also denied making it.

If, at a hearing on a remand, the defendant were to testify that he made an incriminating statement but that it was coerced, he could be impeached by his testimony that he denied making the statement. If, on motion to surpress, defendant testifies that he made a statement that was coerced and his motion is denied, he cannot with impunity testify at his trial that he made no statement. *Woody v. U.S.,* 379 F2d 130.

As pointed out above, the Federal Omnibus Crime Control and Safe Streets Act of 1968 in 18 USC § 3501 seeks to modify the rule of *Miranda v. Arizona, supra,* in federal criminal prosecutions, by prescribing "voluntariness" as the sole test for the admissibility of confessions and admissions, even in the absence of the *Miranda* warnings, by stating that the absence of these warnings "need not be conclusive on the issue of the voluntariness of the confession" or admission.

The constitutionality of this new rule is still to be tested. Whether the states, *e.g.,* New York (*People v. Huntley, supra*) will follow 18 USC § 3501 is also still to be seen.

**§ 109. Admissions After Commencement of Judicial Proceedings.** When the prosecuting authorities (including the police) are notified by the defendant that he desires counsel, or, when they are notified that he has counsel, any inculpatory statements made by the accused thereafter are barred if made in the absence of counsel. *People v. Gunner,* 15 NY2d 226, 205 NE2d 852; *People v. Sanchez,* 15 NY2d 387, 207 NE2d 356; *People v. Livingston,* 15 NY2d 977, 207 NE2d 530. The term "counsel" in this context does not include a parent. *People v. Taylor,* 16 NY2d 1038, 213 NE2d 321; *People v. Hocking,* 15 NY2d 973, 207 NE2d 529; *Miranda v. Arizona, supra.*

Once judicial proceedings against the accused have commenced either by indictment, a grand jury information or arraignment, inculpatory statements made by the accused are also barred when made in the absence of counsel. *People v. Waterman,* 9 NY2d 561, 175 NE2d 445; *People v. Meyer,* 11 NY2d 162, 182 NE2d 103; *People v. Donovan,* 13 NY2d 148, 193 NE2d 628; *Spano v. New York,* 360 US 315. *Cf. People v. Pizarro,* 20 AD2d 900.

Careful note should be made of those cases decided after the *Miranda* decision, but to which *Miranda* warnings did not apply. In *People v. Stockford,* 24 NY2d 146, 247 NE2d 141, the court permitted questioning of a defendant in the absence of counsel after arrest on an arrest warrant but before arraignment. In *People v. Simons,* 22 NY2d 533, 240 NE2d 22, cert. den. 393 US 1107, the court sustained police questioning, in the absence of counsel, of a parolee who had been arrested on a parole violation warrant, but who had been interrogated respecting a robbery. In these two cases, it must be observed, the prosecutions arose pre-*Miranda,* although the decisions of the Court of Appeals were made after *Miranda.* Since *Miranda* was held not to be retroactive (*Johnson v. New Jersey,* 384 US 719), its requirements of giving the warnings were not applicable to those cases.

*Under the present law, after an arrest, whether with or without a warrant, the police are required to inform the accused of all of his constitutional rights including the right to counsel. Miranda v. Arizona,* 384 US 436.

The *Miranda* ruling would clearly render untenable the decision in *People v. Stanley,* 15 NY2d 30, 203 NE2d 475, cert. dism. 382 US 802, which sanctioned, in the absence of counsel, questioning of a defendant about a second crime, although he had been arrested for a different crime, where there had been no "formal commencement of the second action against him."

Thus, although the decisions in *Stockford* and *Simons, supra,* are historically interesting (in overruling *People v. Bodie, infra*), the rule in those cases pertaining to the commencement of a criminal prosecution by the mere issuance of an arrest warrant, is of no validity today in the area of admissions, confessions, and the right to counsel, by virtue of *Miranda.*

In *People v. Vella,* 28 AD2d 563, 21 NY2d 249, 234 NE2d 422, where the defendant was charged for one crime in New York County, at which time he was represented by counsel, and subsequently charged with another crime in Suffolk County after he was turned over to the State Police for investigation, the Appellate Division held there was no "carry over" of representation of counsel to the Suffolk County case. As to the Suffolk County case, the accused was at liberty to waive counsel (*see: People v. Bodie,* 16 NY2d 275, 213 NE2d 441) and defendant could be lawfully interrogated without notice to, or the presence of, the attorney representing him in the former case. However, the Court of Appeals did not concur and reversed the conviction. *People v. Vella,* 21 NY2d 249, 234 NE2d 422.

Conversely, absence of counsel on consent during the administration of a polygraph test, without more, does not operate as a consent to interrogate defendant after the administration of the test.

In *People v. Campbell,* 28 AD2d 735, defendant and counsel consented to a polygraph test, and counsel left after having been advised that it was not good practice to have counsel present during the examination. After having been informed that there were discrepancies in the results of the examination, defendant, in the absence of counsel, was further questioned and made certain incriminating statements. These statements were held inadmissible, since the consent that was given was solely for the administration of the lie-detector tests.

The theory behind this rule is that when the accused has become a defendant, he is entitled to prompt arraignment, which includes his right to be advised promptly of his privileges under the Fifth and Sixth Amendments. Additionally, in a misdemeanor case as well as in a felony case, a defendant is entitled to the aid of assigned counsel if he is indigent and requests it. *Gideon v. Wainwright,* 372 US 335; *People v. Witenski,* 15 NY2d 392, 207 NE2d 358. A defendant is entitled to the aid of counsel, in a criminal prosecution, at all stages of the proceedings against him.

The decision in *People v. Witenski,* 15 NY2d 392, 207 NE2d 358, has now received legislative sanction by both the federal and New York State governments. Both jurisdictions have enacted legislation providing for public defenders or their equivalent. The federal statute (Pub. L. No. 88–455, 78 Stat. 552, 18 USC § 3006(a)) became effective August 20, 1964. The New York State law became effective December 1, 1965 (L. 1965, Ch. 878), and provides for free investigative, expert and other necessary services for an indigent defendant, as well as free legal services. It is to be noted that such services are to be supplied free of charge not only for prosecutions for crimes, but also for prosecutions for the breach of any New York State law, or of any local law or ordinance of a political subdivision of the state, traffic infractions excepted.

However, "the right of counsel at every stage of a criminal proceeding is, of necessity, subject to the rule of reason. A defendant requesting assigned counsel is not entitled to one he names. Neither is he entitled to have his assigned counsel with him 24 hours a day." *People v. San Souci,* 23 AD2d 352, 354, affd 17 NY2d 684, 216 NE2d 616.

Although *San Souci* represents the law today, there are indications that in some situations the rule may be modified to permit a defendant to have assigned to him an attorney he requests, where the attorney consents to the assignment.

The New York rule as to waiver of counsel by the defendant is as follows: The right to the aid of counsel, after the commencement of judicial proceedings, may be waived by defendant. If the waiver is knowingly made, inculpatory statements made by a defendant thereafter are admissible. A defendant's previous experience with the law, such as a prior conviction, may be considered by the court as probative value of what a defendant understood at the time he was asked if he required an attorney.

The police, as a matter of law, are not incapable of advising a defendant of his right to the aid of counsel. *People v. Bodie,* 16 NY2d 275, 213 NE2d 441. With the exception that a defendant's prior contact with the law may be considered in determining if he understood the warnings given him by the police, *Bodie* is still good law. *Cf. Miranda v. Arizona, supra.*

Thus, voluntary statements made by the defendant in the absence of counsel after arraignment are barred. *Massiah v. U.S.,* 377 US 201; *People v. Robinson,* 13 NY2d 296, 196 NE2d 261; *cf. People v. Pizarro,* 20 AD2d 900.

*McLeod v. Ohio,* 1 Ohio St2d 60, 203 NE2d 349, points up this rule. Petitioner, after indictment but before he was represented by counsel, made an oral confession to the police while assisting them in searching for a murder weapon used in a hold-up murder. Based on the authority of *Massiah v. U.S.,* 377 US 201, the Supreme Court vacated McLeod's conviction (378 US 582), reversed and dismissed (381 US 356).

However, inculpatory statements made voluntarily by a defendant to an undercover agent after he, the defendant, had been arrested and indicted unbeknownst to the undercover agent are admissible.

Thus, in *U.S. v. Garcia,* 377 F2d 321, a federal officer who did not know that the defendant had been arrested and indicted for assaulting a federal narcotics agent, asked defendant if he had ever been in trouble with the police, and defendant allegedly replied that in attempting to avoid arrest with narcotics in his possession he had intentionally driven his automobile at a federal narcotics agent. It was held that admission of testimony of the federal officer concerning this conversation did not violate the rule that the Sixth Amendment right to counsel is denied a defendant where, after indictment, law enforcements authorities deliberately elicit incriminating statements from a defendant by surreptitious means.

In distinguishing this case from *Massiah v. U.S., supra,* the court said:

> "*Massiah* was thus not aimed at all post-indictment evidence gathered by the prosecution, but at the narrow

situation where, after indictment, law enforcement authorities have 'deliberately elicited' incriminating statements from a defendant by direct interrogation or by surreptitious means. The rule does not apply to spontaneous or voluntary statements made by the defendant in the presence of government agents [cited cases omitted], or when the person hearing the statement is not a government agent at the time the statement is made. Paroutian v. United States, 370 F. 2d 631 (2d Cir) . . . (1967). Nor should it apply in a case in which the questioner was completely unaware of the existence of the indictment and was not seeking information about the crime the indictment charged had been committed. *Massiah* does not immunize a defendant from normal investigation techniques after indictment, United States v. Edwards, 366 F.2d 853, 873 (2d Cir. 1966); it only protects against deliberate efforts of law enforcement agents which are specifically aimed at eliciting incriminating statements relative to the crime under indictment. Cf. Escobedo v. State of Illinois, 378 U.S. 478, 490–491 . . . , (1964)." *U.S. v. Garcia,* 377 F2d 321, 324.

Proof of the waiver of counsel is required beyond a reasonable doubt. Failure to do so requires a reversal where statements made in the absence of counsel were received in evidence. *See: People v. Bodie,* 16 NY2d 275, 213 NE2d 441; *People v. Malloy,* 282 NYS2d 45.

**§ 110. Admissions and Confessions Obtained as a Result of an Unlawful Search and Seizure or an an Unlawful Arrest.** Such inculpatory statements are inadmissible, undoubtedly on the theory that the police should not be permitted to exploit their primary unlawful acts. *Mapp v. Ohio,* 367 US 643; *Nueslein v. D. of C.,* 115 F2d 690; *Wong Sun v. U.S.,* 371 US 471; *People v. Rodriguez,* 11 NY2d 279, 183 NE2d 651; *People v. Entrialgo,* 19 AD2d 509, affd 14 NY2d 733, 199 NE2d 384.

In *Rodriguez,* the New York Court of Appeals stated, *inter alia,* that if any of Rodriguez' statements were the product or fruit of an illegal search and seizure, it should have been excluded. *Mapp v. Ohio* applied not only to items obtained as a result of an unlawful search and seizure, but also to any evidence, such as a confession, which stems from their use. *See also: People v. Paulin,* 25 NY2d 445, 255 NE2d 164.

With respect to the identification of the defendant, the court, in *People v. Tortorice,* 26 AD2d 902, 274 NYS2d 532, held that requiring defendant to don a jacket taken from his apartment by the police in his absence and without a search warrant was illegal, and, admitting over objection, testimony that shortly thereafter the complainant identified the defendant and later again identified him in the police line-up when he was still wearing the same jacket, was improper and required reversal of his conviction.

This rule as to the excludability of "verbal fruits" has been adopted by the Supreme Court of California, which cited as its authority *Wong Sun v. U.S.,* 371 US 471. *People v. Bilderbach,* 401 P2d 921.

Both states hold that inculpatory statements obtained from a defendant as a result of an unlawful search and seizure must be excluded in state as well as federal prosecutions.

A United States District Court in Texas was faced with a similar question, though the case was decided on other grounds. Tuttle, C.J., in his opinion, agreed with the rulings in both *Rodriguez* and *Bilderbach, supra. Collins v. Beto,* 245 F Supp 639.

Maryland has rejected the reasoning of *Rodriguez* and *Wong Sun, supra.* In *Dailey v. State,* 212 A2d 257, the Maryland Court of Appeals held that the defendant's admissions, even though obtained during detention following an illegal arrest, were admissible, solely on the basis of their voluntariness.

This decision is not in accord with the usual interpretation accorded the holding in *Wong Sun, supra,* or *Silverman v. U.S.,* 365 US 505. Both of these cases equate oral admissions with illegally seized real evidence. However, the Federal Omnibus Crime Control and Safe Streets Act of 1968 (Title II, § 3501) and *Dailey, supra,* are inapposite.

The inadmissibility of the inculpatory statements made in *Nueslein, Wong Sun, Rodriguez, Entrialgo, Bilderbach, Silverman, supra,* would not be disturbed even if there were compliance with the procedural safeguards of *Miranda, supra.*

In reaffirming the rule in *People v. Rodriguez,* 11 NY2d 279, the court said in *People v. Chennault,* 20 NY2d 518, at 521, 232 NE2d 324: "The fruit of the poisonous tree rule was designed to discipline law-enforcement officers rather than because of any bearing which it has on the guilt or innocence of a defendant." *See also: People v. Paulin,* 25 NY2d 445.

**§ 111. Admissions and Confessions: Juveniles.** A child charged with being a juvenile delinquent is not to be deprived of his constitutional rights. An involuntary confession, therefore, will be excluded. It was held, however, that notice to use an inculpatory statement under the New York statute is not required of the prosecution. *Matter of Williams,* 49 Misc2d 154, 267 NYS2d 91.

For a comparable situation involving a District of Columbia statute, the necessity of the right to counsel and assignment of counsel for a juvenile was emphasized. Discovery and inspection of the juvenile's social history record was approved. *Kent v. U.S.,* 383 US 541; *see also: Black v. U.S.,* 355 F2d 104, and *Watkins v. U.S.,* 343 F2d 278.

A parallel, although slightly different situation, is found in a New York case involving a youth under investigation for possible Youthful Offender treatment. In such a case, the youth is interrogated by the Youth Counsel Bureau with the understanding, concurred in by the district attorney, that anything he says to the Y.C.B. is confidential and may not be used against him upon his trial. Absent consent, the district attorney is obligated not to use upon his trial information obtained from the Y.C.B. Cross-examination of the youth, based on such information or leads therefrom, violates the youth's constitutional and statutory rights. N.Y. Family Ct. Act, § 784; Adm. Code, §§ E1-3.0, E1-6.0; CPL § 720.20(6); *People v. Rhem,* 24 AD2d 517, 261 NYS2d 808, 276 NYS2d 751.

Consonant with the ruling in *Rhem, supra,* the Appellate Division, Second Department, has held that although the prosecutor was entitled to cross-examine a defendant for purpose of impeachment, regarding a vicious or immoral act which had been the basis for a prior adjudication as a youthful offender, he may not elicit testimony that defendant was adjudged a youthful offender and may not characterize the act upon which that adjudication was based a "crime." *People v. Geller,* 278 NYS2d 41.

The rule that due process requires that juveniles are entitled to the assistance of counsel in juvenile court proceedings is receiving wider acceptance, particularly since the decision in *Kent v. U.S.,* 383 US 541. *See also: Henry B. v. Williams,* 27 AD2d 529, 275 NYS2d 775.

The U.S.D.C. (New Jersey) has adopted the same rule. In that case, the court also stated that the Due Process Clause of the Fourteenth Amendment requires juvenile court hearings, with presence of counsel, on referral for prosecution of a 17-year old New Jersey felony murder suspect.

> "However, even if the opinion in *Kent,* supra, is not of constitutional dimensions, it strongly suggests, and we now hold, that the constitution requires a hearing on the waiver issue at which the juvenile has the right to have the assistance of counsel." *Brown v. New Jersey* (USDC NJ), 3/9/67, 35 USLW 2553.

In a proceeding in the matter of a person alleged to be a juvenile delinquent (*Henry B. v. Williams, supra*), an order was entered accordingly. The proceeding was based on a finding that the alleged delinquent had committed an act, which, if committed by an adult, would constitute the crime of rape. The appellant was 14 years old. This finding, prior to *In re Winship,* 397 US 358 (1970), required proof by a fair preponderance of the evidence, which the majority found lacking. In his concurring memorandum, Botein, then P.J., indicated that in a close case there should be some evidence of corroboration of the charge, as required by former Penal Law, § 2013, even though none is required in a juvenile delinquency proceeding. *Cf. People v. Oyola,* 6 NY2d 259, 262, 160 NE2d 494; *but see:* N.Y. Family Court Act, sec. 744.

The decision of *Matter of Williams, supra,* has now received the official imprimatur of the New York Court of Appeals in *Matter of Gregory W.,* 19 NY2d 55, 224 NE2d 102. This occurred in a juvenile court proceeding in which two juveniles confessed to the commission of a serious crime after a long police interrogation which lasted 24 and 10 hours respectively.

Part of the interrogation took place after arraignment and after the assignment of counsel, but in the latter's absence. The interrogation also occurred in violation of the statutory requirements of secs. 711, 741, 724 of the Family Court Act and without advising the juveniles of their right to silence and of their right to counsel.

Specifically overruling *People v. Lewis,* 260 NY 171, the court said that juveniles, too, were entitled to due process and to their constitutional rights under the New York State and Federal Constitutions.

Under these circumstances, the court held that confessions so obtained were involuntary as a matter of law. While proceedings held under the Family Court Act "are not criminal in nature, . . . such proceedings, resulting as they do in a loss of personal freedom, are at the very least quasi-criminal in nature." *Matter of Gregory W.,* 19 NY2d at 62, 224 NE2d 102. *See also: Haley v. Ohio,* 332 US 596; *In re Carlo,* 48 NJ 224, 225 A2d 110.

Completing the trend set in *Kent v. U.S., supra,* the United States Supreme Court in *Matter of Gault,* 387 US 1, has cloaked children with the mantle of protection afforded by the Fourteenth Amendment and the Bill of Rights to the same extent as afforded to adults.

Juvenile Court proceedings, it said, are criminal trials and must consequently be conducted under procedures that meet constitutional standards of due process.

Accordingly, in delinquency hearings before Juvenile Court judges children must be accorded the following safeguards of the Bill of Rights:

1. Timely written notice of the charges against them, "so that reasonable opportunity to prepare will be afforded and it must 'set forth the alleged misconduct with particularity'."

2. The right to have a lawyer and the right to be advised that he may have a lawyer represent him, court-appointed if indigent. The fact that the parent knew he might retain counsel, does not constitute a waiver. The parent and child must be specifically advised to that effect. "They had a right expressly to be advised that they might retain counsel. . . ."

3. The right to confront and cross-examine complainants and other witnesses.

4. Adequate warning of the privilege against self-incrimination and the right to remain silent (*Miranda*). "The language of the Fifth Amendment, . . . is unequivocal and without exception. * * * We conclude that the constitutional privilege against self-incrimination is applicable in the case of juveniles as it is with respect to adults." *Matter of Gault* at 33–34, 42–47, 55. *See also: Goldwyn v. Allen,* 54 Misc2d 94, 281 NYS2d 899. "[N]either the 14th Amendment nor the Bill of Rights is for adults only." *Gault* at 13.

The United States Supreme Court has now completed the full cycle in according juveniles full due process. *In re Samuel Winship,* 397 US 358 (1970), now requires that the same criminal standards of guilt necessary to convict an adult must be applied in juvenile courts, *i.e.,* proof of guilt beyond a reasonable doubt.

In *U.S. v. Lovejoy,* 364 F2d 586, the court held that two hour detention by F.B.I. agents of 15-year old boy arrested for possessing goods stolen from interstate commerce did not constitute such a violation of Federal Juvenile Delinquency Act provision that juveniles shall not be detained in jail or similar places of detainment as to make his statement to agents inadmissible, where agents were ignorant of boy's age. *See:* 18 USC § 5035.

Discovery after trial that a codefendant was only 15 years old and vacating of his conviction as juvenile offender did not require vacating the conviction of the adult defendants (18 USC § 3032; Fed R Crim P 8(b)).

Since, under 18 USC § 5032, a juvenile "had no absolute right to be tried as a juvenile, appellants' claim that they had an absolute right not to be tried with him must surely be rejected." *U.S. v. Lovejoy,* 364 F2d 586, 590.

**§ 112. Effect of Plea of Guilty.** By a plea of guilty, the defendant waives his present objection that his confession was unlawfully obtained. Under both state and federal law, one who voluntarily pleads guilty waives forever any constitutional defenses that he might have asserted at his trial, or subsequent appeal. Nor may he raise constitutional questions by coram nobis in our state courts, once he voluntarily pleaded guilty. *People v. Mahoney,* NYLJ, 10/13/64, p. 19, col. 2. *See* *also: People v. Jones,* 11 NY2d 1070, 184 NE2d 192; *People v. Nicholson,* 11 NY2d 1067, 184 NE2d 190; *People v. DeFlumer,* 16 NY2d 20, 209 NE2d 93, cert. den. 384 US 1018, *People v. McDonald,* 20 AD2d 907, 248 NYS2d 955.

There is no statutory requirement that the court question a defendant prior to accepting a plea of guilty, *People v. Hernandez,* 8 NY2d 345. However, before accepting a plea, it is the better practice for the court to conduct a hearing to eliminate any possible ambiguities and to make certain that the defendant committed the acts constituting the crime to which he offers to plead guilty. To quote from *People v. Beasley,* 25 NY2d 483, 255 NE2d 239:

> "No questions were asked about defendant's participation in the crime, nor was there any discussion [between the court and the defendant prior to accepting the plea] of the facts involved."

In New York, juvenile delinquency proceedings are limited to persons under the age of 16 years. Family Court Act § 712. A similar rule prevails in other jurisdictions.

It is not incumbent upon the petitioner to prove respondent's age, for jurisdictional purposes, where respondent is represented by counsel and "failure of respondent to raise any objection was a tacit admission as to the fact that he was under the age of sixteen at the time of the occurrence of the act." *Matter of Don R. B.,* 66 Misc2d 279, 320 NYS2d 813. Accordingly, the respondent was adjudged a juvenile delinquent. This ruling may be questioned as age is a jurisdictional requirement.

A person charged with being a juvenile delinquent is not entitled to a trial by jury in New York. Jury trials, in such cases, are not constitutionally required or desirable. *In re D.,* 27 NY2d 90, 261 NE2d 627.

The United States Supreme Court in *McKeiver et al. v. Pennsylvania,* 403 US 528, has held to the same effect. In these cases, the Supreme Court, in reviewing all of the leading juvenile delinquency cases commencing with *Haley v. Ohio,* 332 US 596 through *In re Winship,* 397 US 358, noted that while "Some of the constitutional requirements attendant upon the state criminal trial have equal application to that part of the state juvenile proceeding that is adjudicative in nature," such as "the rights to appropriate notice, to counsel, to confrontation and to cross-examination, and the privilege against self-incrimination" and the standard of proof beyond a reasonable doubt, "The Court, however, has not yet said that *all* rights constitutionally assured to an adult accused of crime also are to be enforced or made available to the juvenile in his delinquency proceeding. Indeed, the Court specifically has refrained from going that far."

The Court then concluded that a jury trial is not constitutionally required in a juvenile court's adjudicative stage although a jury may be used by a juvenile court judge in an advisory capacity. Juvenile delinquency proceedings are not "criminal prosecutions" and absence of a jury is not violative of the Sixth Amendment made applicable to the states by the Fourteenth Amendment. *See: Malloy v. Hogan,* 378 US 1.

*In re Winship,* 397 US 358, holds that proof of juvenile delinquency must be established beyond a reasonable doubt. New York holds that this rule is not retroactive *Matter of D (Daniel), supra; Matter of Ronald H,* 35 AD2d 845; *Matter of Ivan,* 35 AD2d 806.

In New York, juvenile delinquency proceedings are governed by the Family Court Act. Accordingly, where the petitioner seeks to introduce into evidence admissions made by the respondent, neither notice under statute, nor a voluntariness hearing is required. *In re D.,* 27 NY2d 90, 261 NE2d 627.

An admission to a juvenile delinquency petition should have the same force and effect as a plea of guilty to a criminal charge in a criminal case. *In re D., supra.*

> "Although there is no mandatory catechism required on sentencing, the court should conduct a hearing when at plea-taking or upon sentencing it appears the defendant misapprehends the nature of the charges or the consequences of his plea. (*People v. Nixon,* 21 NY2d 338)." *People v. Beasley,* 25 NY2d at 488, 255 NE2d 239. *See also: People v. Serrano,* 15 NY2d 304, 206 NE2d 330; *People v. Shipman,* 14 NY2d 883, 200 NE2d 733; *Machibroda v. U.S.,* 368 US 487, 493; *Von Moltke v. Gilles,* 332 US 708, 724.

In *Boykin v. Alabama,* 395 US 238, 242, 243, 244 (1969), the United States Supreme Court has held "It was error, plain on the face of the record, for the trial judge to accept petitioner's guilty plea without an affirmative showing that it was intelligent and voluntary." When a plea is entered in a state trial, the court said, the defendant waives several constitutional rights. Accordingly, a trial judge should ascertain that an accused fully understands the plea and its consequences and ought to make "a record adequate for any review that may be later sought." Additionally, the court noted: "[W]e cannot presume a waiver of these . . . important federal rights from a silent record."

### § 112.01. Retroactivity.

> "We hold that nothing in *Jackson* v. *Denno* (378 U.S. 368), or *People* v. *Huntley* (15 NY2d 72) requires this court to overrule our decision in *People* v. *Nicholson* (11 NY2d 1067) whose holding and reasoning we now approve. . . . The defendant, therefore, is not now entitled to a hearing before the trial court on the issue of the voluntariness of his confession. Nor has any argument been advanced to justify or warrant any change or modification of our conclusion, in *People* v. *Howard* (12 NY2d 65, 68–69) that retroactive effect is not to be accorded decisions of this court respecting right to counsel." *People v. Dash,* 16 NY2d 493, 494. *See also: People v. Griffin,* 16 NY2d 508.

Neither may the question of illegally seized evidence be raised by the defendant, once he has voluntarily pleaded guilty. In *People v. Seidenberg,* 221 NYS2d 761, affd 19 AD2d 699, the court held that coram nobis is not available to a defendant asserting an illegal search and seizure who, being represented by counsel, failed to move to suppress and pleaded guilty. *See also: People v. Brown,* 20 AD2d 570, 245 NYS2d 799; *People v. Anderson,* 8 AD2d 731; *People v. Angelet,* 221 NYS2d 834.

**§ 112.02. Withdrawal of Plea of Guilty.** Once a plea is withdrawn, it may not be used as a confession at a subsequent trial. It is out of the case forever and is inadmissible. *People v. Spitaleri,* 9 NY2d 168, 173 NE2d 35.

To the same effect, see *People v. Haycraft,* 221 NE2d 317, where the defendant had originally entered a plea of guilty but was then permitted to withdraw it and enter a not guilty plea. At his trial, a witness disclosed that the defendant had previously pleaded guilty. Even though the trial judge promptly ordered the statement stricken and directed the jury to disregard it, nevertheless, the Appellate Court held that the disclosure deprived the defendant of a fair trial.

**§ 113. Other Unlawful Police Activity Rendering the Fruits Thereof Inadmissible.**

(1) Things a police officer saw in premises unlawfully entered. *Williams v. U.S.,* 263 F2d 487; *People v. D'Amico,* NYLJ, 4/5/63, p 16; *cf. People v. Sperber,* 40 Misc2d 13, 242 NYS2d 652, affd 15 NY2d 566, 203 NE2d 219.

(2) Books, records, copies or photographs of evidence illegally seized. *Flagg v. U.S.,* 233 F 481; *cf. Silfa v. Kennedy,* 5 Misc2d 375, affd 3 NY2d 734, 143 NE2d 518.

(3) Fingerprints of the defendant obtained by virtue of an unlawful detention are subject to suppression even though they are the best kind of evidence.

Where there was no probable cause to arrest the defendant and where no warrant had issued, it is immaterial if the fingerprints were obtained during the investigatory stage, or if the defendant's apprehension was not a "technical arrest," or if taken during a "full-blown" search. *Terry v. Ohio,* 392 US 1, 19. *See also: Davis v. Mississippi,* 394 US 721. *Bynum v. U.S.,* 262 F2d 465, 467.

(4) Knowledge obtained by reason of an unlawful search and seizure. *Silverthorne Lumber v. U.S.,* 251 US 385; *People v. Ferrara,* NYLJ, 11/18/63, p. 16, col. 5, citing *Wong Sun v. U.S., supra; People v. D'Amico, supra; People v. Robinson,* 13 NY2d 296, 196 NE2d 261; *cf. People v. Sperber, supra.* But when knowledge is obtained by a government agency from documents stolen or unlawfully seized by a private citizen, where no connivance by a government agency in the theft or seizure has been established, the documents may be used in a governmental prosecution. *Burdeau v. McDowell,* 256 US 465; *People v. Randazzo,* 34 Cal Rptr 65; *People v. Trimarco,* 41 Misc2d 775, 245 NYS2d 795.

A search made by a private citizen at the behest of the police was held illegal and the evidence so obtained was ordered suppressed. In *People v. Fierro,* 46 Cal Rptr 132, 134, the search was made by a hotel clerk of the defendant's room. The clerk suspected that the defendant was either a user or seller of narcotics. He notified the sheriff, who told him to return to the room and take samples of pills that the clerk had discovered there. His second search revealed heroin.

The appeals court rejected the argument that, in getting the heroin, the clerk had acted as his own agent. "[O]fficial involvement in the lawless quest for evidence was so deep as to evoke the exclusionary rule."

(5) Links or leads to such evidence, held inadmissible. *People v. Laino,* 10 NY2d 161, 176 NE2d 571.

(6) Knowledge obtained as a result of an unreasonable search and seizure may not be used to arrest a defendant at a later time. *U.S. v. DiRe,* 332 US 581.

**§ 114. Psychological Coercion.** If psychological coercion is used in obtaining a confession, it would render the confession involuntary. *Culombe v. Conn.,* 367 US 568; *People v. Carbonaro,* 48 Misc2d 115; *People v. Leyra,* 1 NY2d 199, 34 NE2d 475; *Miranda v. Arizona, supra; People v. Ulisano,* 18 AD2d 432, 239 NYS2d 983.

In this area of psychological coercion, a person's physical condition may be considered as having some relationship to his mental state during an interrogation in determining the question of voluntariness of an admission or confession.

Such a situation was present in a voluntariness hearing ordered in *People v. D'Iorio,* 16 NY2d 551, 208 NE2d 465. That hearing, (*People v. D'Iorio,* 49 Misc2d 30, 266 NYS2d 664), disclosed that the confession was obtained on the day following a four-hour surgical operation. The court found that the defendant's ability to resist his interrogation was impaired and the People had failed to establish the voluntariness of the confession beyond a reasonable doubt. *But see: Lego v. Twomey,* 30 L Ed2d 618, 92 SC 619.

In *People v. Leyra,* 1 NY2d 199, 202, 134 NE2d 475, the court had reversed defendant's first conviction on the ground that the confession made to Dr. Helfand was inadmissible as it had been the product of mental and psychological coercion. In the ensuing trial of *Leyra,* his confession to Dr. Helfand was again excluded but other subsequent confessions alleged to have been made by the defendant were introduced into evidence and he was convicted. The defendant then applied for federal habeas corpus relief.

> "However, the Supreme Court, in a habeas corpus proceeding instituted after its denial of certiorari (345 U.S. 918), reversed, holding that those subsequent confessions, being 'simply parts of one continuous process,' [*i.e.,* the psychological coercion exercised by Dr. Helfand], were tainted by the same poison that invalidated the statement to the psychiatrist [Dr. Helfand] (347 U.S. 561)." *Leyra, supra.*

A statement to a murder suspect during interrogation to determine if he had been upon his wife's premises when she sustained fatal injuries, to the effect that the officer did not want to bring the children into this but would if he had to, did not render the suspect's subsequent inculpatory statement involuntary.

> "This is not the case of a relative threatened by police with arrest, disgrace or physical harm; and the theory that this defendant formed any belief that harm would come to these small children in any of these forms, or in some other fashion, at the hands of these civilized men or, in particular, the officer especially assigned to handle children, seems to us incredible." *People v. Graham,* 27 AD2d 203, 204, 277 NYS2d 943, 945.

Where defendant claimed he was induced to enter a plea of guilty by a threat that his wife would be arrested unless he entered a guilty plea, a hearing was required on a coram nobis application to determine the voluntariness of the plea. *People v. Hicks,* 26 AD2d 906, 274 NYS2d 430, 431.

**§ 115. Intoxication and Drugs: Voluntariness.** Confessions made by a person who is intoxicated are not inadmissible per se. Conversely, a confession by one in a state of self-induced intoxication is not always admissible. Important guidelines as to admissibility of these confessions were laid down by the New York Court of Appeals in *People v. Schompert,* 19 NY2d 300, 226 NE2d 305, cert. den. 389 US 874.

In *Schompert,* the specific issue was, "whether a defendant's severe alcoholism and intoxication at the time he made confession to the police rendered his confession inadmissible as involuntary." (p. 303). The defendant was a chronic alcoholic. While he was drinking in a bar, he sent for the police and when they arrived, he told them that he had committed certain burglaries. When they disbelieved him, he said he had the proceeds in a Greyhound bus station locker and that the key to the locker was in his pocket. The locker was opened and the proceeds of the burglary found.

At the coram nobis hearing, both police officers "testified that the defendant explained in meticulous and rational detail the commission of the burglary."

> "[T]he *coram nobis* court found as a fact, that defendant was sufficiently 'in touch with the realities of his situation' when he made his confession so that one was entitled to accept it as reliable despite defendant's evident advanced intoxication." *Id.* at 304.

The Court of Appeals also explained:

> "In this case, of course, the intoxication and the history of alcoholism, as well as psychosis, make the circumstances limiting volitional competency much stronger than might be expected usually. . . . [T]he exclusion of confessions, otherwise trustworthy, because of coercion or other unfairness was designed to prevent abuse of power by officials and not to protect proven wrongdoers from punishment." *Id.* at 304.

In cases of self-induced intoxication, the standard of admissibility "is whether the confession is reliable." One test of reliability is the specific awareness of the particular facts or general understanding of the circumstances possessed by the defendant. "Another factor is whether the content of the statement was accurate; and accuracy may be tested by subsequent events." *Id.* at 305.

A federal district court has held to the same effect, namely, that statements made by a defendant who was voluntarily intoxicated do not affect their admissibility although the fact of intoxication may affect the weight of such evidence. *Curry v. Wilson,* 269 F Supp 9.

In a parallel situation with respect to a witness under drugs, (*People v. Sorrentini,* 26 AD2d 827), the court said:

> "In our opinion, a witness for the People was not incompetent to testify, even though he may have been under the influence of narcotics during part of the time that he was on the witness stand. That circumstance affected his credibility; and the jury was so instructed. (Cf. *People* v. *Williams,* 6 NY2d 18, Ann. 52 ALR 2d 859–860.)"

§ 116. **Exculpatory Statements.** Exculpatory statements denying guilt are not confessions, *People v. Kingston,* 8 NY2d 384, 388, 171 NE2d 306. Failure of the court to charge on the question of voluntariness of the confession is not error where defendant's statements were protestations of innocence. Therefore, a defendant cannot protest to having been induced by use of force to say what was untrue to his prejudice. *People v. Jones,* 22 AD2d 813. *See also: People v. Fanelli,* 15 NY2d 573, 203 NE2d 299.

However, such exculpatory statements will be admissible if the safeguards of *Miranda, supra,* have been complied with, and if there has been no statutory violations.

§ 117. **Admission as Part of the Res Gestae.** In at least one instance an admission was held to be part of the res gestae. In *State v. Ellis,* 136 NW2d 384, the defendant moments after he had been shot and arrested, told the officer that he had thrown the gun away. This was in reply to a question as to what he had done with the weapon. Under the circumstances, the *Jackson-Denno* rule on the voluntariness of an admission was held not applicable.

Inculpatory statements made as part of the res gestae are not precluded by the decision in *Miranda v. Arizona.* New York has held to the same effect. *People v. Hill,* 17 NY2d 185, 216 NE2d 588. *See also: People v. Burwell,* 44 Cal2d 16, 30–31, cert. den. 349 US 936.

**§ 118. Silence as an Admission.** Prior to *Miranda v. Arizona,* accusatory statements, not denied, were admissible against an accused as admissions if the accusations were fully known and fully understood by him and he was at full liberty to reply. *People v. Koerner,* 154 NY 355; *People v. Allen,* 300 NY 222.

However, even before *Miranda,* it was held that a person in custody had no duty to speak, and evidence of his refusal to make a statement was inadmissible. *People v. Bianculli,* 9 NY2d 46, 174 NE2d 717; *People v. Trovato,* 309 NY 382; *People v. Orgavan,* 14 AD2d 482, 217 NYS2d 740. The same rule was held applicable to statements made by a codefendant inculpating the defendant. *People v. Tisdale,* 18 AD2d 274, 239 NYS2d 226.

As the court noted in *Trovato, supra,* an accused held in custody is under no duty to speak, even to the arresting officer who, at the time of the arrest, questioned the defendant. "And his silence may not be taken as inferential evidence of his guilt."

This rule was followed in *People v. Masters,* 30 AD2d 723, 291 NYS2d 230. In *Masters,* the officer had arrested the defendant on a burglary and grand larceny charge. At the trial the officer was asked repeatedly if the defendant had answered any of the questions put to him by the officer relating to the charges against him. In each instance the officer replied that the defendant remained silent. The Appellate Division held, "Reversal is required because of these repeated violations of the clear rule of *Trovato. . . .*"

New Jersey (*State v. Ripa,* 45 NJ 199, 212 A2d 22) and the Circuit Court of Appeals [2d Cir], (*U.S. v. Piccioli,* 352 F2d 856) have held to the same effect.

The rule of admission by silence (tacit admission) had also been condemned in Pennsylvania. Additionally, that court has held that *Miranda,* which condemned the tacit admission rule, was to be given retroactive effect where the defendant took a direct appeal from the ruling which denied its exclusion.

In *Commonwealth v. Dravecz,* 424 Pa 582, 227 A2d 904, defendant was brought to the police station where an accusatory statement was read to him. In effect, the statement implicated him in a burglary. The defendant remained silent at the completion of the reading. The court held that the statement was inadmissible. There was nothing to show that the accusatory statement read to him required him to reply or that if he did not reply, his silence would be interpreted as an admission of guilt. To hold otherwise, the court held, would compel a violation of the defendant's privilege against self-incrimination.

On the other hand, a Florida court has held that, where constitutional warnings were read to defendant from a card after which he was asked if he wanted an attorney and defendant remained silent but thereafter made a statement, the statement was held admissible. *Brisbon v. State,* 201 So2d 832.

The use in evidence of a conversation between an FBI agent and another in the presence of the defendant, who remained silent, is barred under *Miranda* as violative of the Fifth Amendment. The defendant had a right to remain silent when in custody and when he was accused of a crime. *U.S. v. Pearson,* 344 F2d 430. Admission of evidence by silence would require a warning. "If you say anything it will be used against you, and if you do not say anything, it will be used against you." *McCarthy v. U.S.,* 25 F2d 299. This would result in an anomalous situation. *U.S. v. McKinney,* 379 F2d 259. *See also: U.S. ex rel Smith v. Brierly,* 267 F Supp 274.

*Miranda* has now clearly stated that a defendant need say nothing at all. Nevertheless, the rule in *Miranda* is not applicable where the witness is sworn and under a duty to give testimony that is not privileged. *Vajtauer v. Commissioner,* 273 US 103.

## § 119. Illegally Obtained Evidence No Ground for Dismissal of the Indictment.

> "While the general common-law practice is to admit evidence despite its illegal origins, this Court in a number of areas has recognized or developed exclusionary rules where evidence had been gained in violation of the accused's rights under the Constitution, federal statutes, or federal rules of procedure. *Weeks* v. *United States,* 232 U.S. 383; *Rogers* v. *Richmond,* 365 U.S. 534; *Mapp* v. *Ohio,* 367 U.S. 643; *Nardone* v. *United States,* 308 U.S.

338; *Mallory* v. *United States,* 354 U.S. 449. Our numerous precedents ordering the exclusion of such illegally obtained evidence assume implicitly that the remedy does not extend to barring the prosecution altogether. So drastic a step might advance marginally some of the ends served by exclusionary rules, but it would also increase to an intolerable degree interference with the public interest in having the guilty brought to book." *U.S. v. Blue,* 384 US 251, 255. *See: People v. Gentile,* 20 AD2d 412. *Cf. People v. Colletti,* 42 Misc2d 158, 247 NYS2d 704, which held to the contrary. However, in this case the only evidence to connect the movant to the crime was his unlawfully obtained confession.

*See also: The Motion to Supress, Chapter 25, infra.*

§ 120. **Witnesses: Coerced Statements.** Statements implicating a defendant that are coerced from a witness prior to the trial are not on the same footing as a confession coerced from a defendant. If the witness takes the stand and testifies that the coerced testimony is true and the coercion is disclosed to the jury, the testimony of the witness is admissible.

"Testimony given from the witness stand by a witness who was, some eight months earlier, compelled by police brutality to give a statement implicating a defendant stands on a footing very different from an out-of-court confession coerced from a defendant and sought to be used against him on the trial. While the latter will be excluded as a matter of law, the testimony of a witness who, although previously forced to make a pretrial statement, asserts that his testimony at the trial is truthful is for the consideration and appraisal of the jury. (See 3 Wigmore, Evidence [3d ed., 1940], § 815, pp. 230–231.) The requirements of law are met if the fact of such earlier coercion or other official lawlessness is disclosed to the jurors so that they may pass upon the witness' veracity and credibility and determine whether the testimony given in open court is truthful and worthy of consideration." *People v. Portelli,* 15 NY2d 235, 239, 205 NE2d 857, cert. den. 382 US 1009.

Once the coercion is disclosed, the statement of the witness is admissible when he attests to its truthfulness. The rest—veracity, credibility, weight—is for the jury. *Id.* at 239; *Miranda v. Arizona, supra.*

**§ 120.01. Witnesses: Unlawful, Non-Coercive Interrogation.** Following the theory of *Portelli, supra* (which had been criticized but not disavowed in *Miranda*), the California Supreme Court in *People v. Varnum,* 59 Cal Rptr 108, 427 P2d 772, has held that the unlawful, but non-coercive questioning of an accomplice to be used against one participating in a crime with the person interrogated, was admissible.

*Miranda,* the court said, goes no further than to require that such evidence not be used against the person questioned. Noncoercive questioning is not in itself unlawful, and the rights protected by the *Miranda* exclusionary rule are violated only when the evidence obtained without the required warnings is admitted into evidence. *People v. Varnum,* 59 Cal Rptr 108, 427 P2d 772.

# Chapter 8

## DISCOVERY AND INSPECTION

---

**§ 135. Right to Discovery and Inspection.** The right of a defendant to obtain information about the prosecution's case is based on certain specific statutes under federal law, *i.e.*, Federal Rules of Criminal Procedure. Many states' rules are substantially the same as the federal ones. *See, e.g.*, N.Y. CPL art. 240.

There is a growing tendency to greater liberality in granting pretrial discovery and inspection. *See:* Fed R Crim P; *People v. D'Andrea,* 20 Misc2d 1070; "Pre-Trial Disclosure in Criminal Cases," 60 Yale LJ 625 (1951).

Many jurisdictions provide for a preliminary examination of criminal charges against a defendant. Fed R Crim P; CPL §§ 170.10(3–6), 180.10(2–7), 180.30, 180.40, 180.60.

**§ 135.01. The Pros and Cons of Pretrial Discovery.** The reasons advanced in opposition to pretrial discovery cannot be lightly dismissed. First, there is the duty to safeguard the interests of the People. It is important to note that a defendant cannot be compelled to testify. Pretrial discovery would give a defendant a tactical advantage at his trial. *Coleman v. Alabama,* 399 US 1, 90 SC 1999. Furthermore, in certain types of cases, (more prevalent in federal courts) such as racketeering, shylocking and civil rights, disclosure would enable a defendant to intimidate, bribe and otherwise bring pressure to bear on the People's witnesses if their identities were disclosed.

Those who favor a broad policy which would permit greater pretrial discovery, argue that the diversity of opinion on the subject creates arbitrary and conflicting decisions and that due process demands greater liberality in granting the relief. *State v. Johnson,* 28 NJ 133.

Some states, notably California, Pennsylvania, Texas and Washington, have adopted a liberal policy and permit disclosure of the identities of the People's witnesses. It is interesting to note that, "In England and Canada, . . . all the evidence in possession of the Crown is in the possession of defense counsel before the trial begins. (See *State v. Dorsey,* 207 La. 927.)" *People v. D'Andrea,* 20 Misc2d 1070, 1074.

In *Brady v. Maryland,* 373 US 83, 87, 92, Mr. Justice White, in a separate opinion, observed that the right to pretrial discovery was not of constitutional dimension, although the majority opinion held that failure of the prosecution to disclose to the defendant evidence favorable to him violates due process. In any event, *Coleman v. Alabama, supra,* indicates a departure from the *Brady* pronouncement, subject to the "harmless error" rule enunciated in *Chapman v. California,* 386 US 18. (For a comparable situation, *see: U.S. v. Wade,* 388 US 218, 239–243; *Gilbert v. California,* 388 US 263, 272–274.)

One distinction must be kept in mind, to wit, the right of a defendant to inspect statements of witnesses, including his own, and the right to inspect items produced pursuant to a subpoena duces tecum, *pretrial* must not be confused with his right to such inspections *during trial.*

§ 136. **Federal Preliminary Examination.** The preliminary examination held to determine probable cause for prosecution, as distinguished from a grand jury proceeding, is a valuable means of discovery for a defendant in many cases. The defendant may waive the examination but, if he demands it, he is entitled to a hearing within a reasonable time.

It is unreasonable for the prosecution to delay a hearing until the case has been presented to a grand jury. In *Wheeler v. Flood,* 269 F Supp 194, the court held that failure to grant the preliminary hearing promptly and before presentation to the grand jury, or simultaneous therewith, would entitle the defendant to be released on habeas corpus.

The reason for this is not hard to understand. The right to the preliminary hearing is statutory and carries with it the right to discover important elements of the prosecution's case. At the hearing, it is incumbent upon the prosecution to establish a prima facie case before the defendant may be bound over for trial or for action by a grand jury. This means that the government's witnesses must testify, and, of course, they can be cross-examined by the defendant.

On the other hand, the defendant need not do a thing. He is under no compulsion to testify himself or even to produce witnesses on his behalf. The preliminary hearing is thus a one-way street running in favor of the defendant. Under those circumstances, the defendant is accorded a tactical advantage by obtaining a preliminary hearing. *See: Coleman v. Alabama,* 399 US 1, 90 SC 1999.

In *Coleman,* the United States Supreme Court noted that one of the reasons it held that the defendant was entitled to the aid of counsel at a preliminary hearing was to assist him to discover the People's case and thus prepare a proper defense. The Supreme Court made this ruling even though the applicable Alabama state rule precluded the use at the trial, of anything that occurred at the preliminary hearing where the defendant was not represented by counsel.

**§ 137. The Specific Federal Statutes.** As noted above, federal pretrial discovery in criminal cases is governed by various statutes (Federal Rules of Criminal Procedure, codified in 18 USC). The pertinent rules follow.

**§ 137.01. Rule 6(e).** This rule authorizes disclosure of grand jury procedings, pretrial, to both the government and to the attorneys for the defendant within certain prescribed limits. These limits are broader for the government.

The general rule that grand jury proceedings are shrouded in secrecy is not altered. However, disclosure of grand jury proceedings "other than its deliberations and the vote of any juror may be made to the attorneys for the government for use in the performance of their duties." The ban against disclosure of grand jury proceedings, absent a court order, includes not only the grand jurors and the government attorneys, but also, "interpreter, stenographer, operator of a recording device, or any typist who transcribes recorded testimony."

However, disclosure may also be made to the defendant at his request "upon a showing that grounds may exist for a motion to dismiss the indictment because of matters occurring before the grand jury."

The court also has the power to direct that the indictment

itself be kept secret until the defendant is in custody or gives bail. Under those circumstances, the indictment must be sealed and kept secret.

The reasons for permitting broader rights of disclosure to the government's attorneys are to enable them to use the grand jury transcript to prepare for trial (*U.S. v. Proctor and Gamble Co.,* 19 FRD 122, 47 F Supp 676, revd 356 US 677, 678; *Washington v. American Pipe & Construction Co.,* 41 FRD 59, 62); to enable them to refresh government witnesses' recollection at the trial (*U.S. v. Johns-Manville Corp.,* 259 F Supp 440, 455); and, if necessary, to be able to impeach witnesses at the trial (*U.S. v. Cotter,* 60 F2d 689, 692, cert. den. 287 US 666).

Disclosure of certain grand jury documents to the government attorney for use in the performance of his duties, and which he revealed to F.B.I. agents, did not constitute a violation of Rule 6(e). Accordingly, it was held in *U.S. v. Hoffa,* 349 F2d 20, 43, affd 385 US 293, and *U.S. v. Zirpolo,* 288 F Supp 993, 1015, that the defendants were not entitled to suppression of the documents.

Experience has demonstrated, however, that in spite of the existence of Rule 6(e), pretrial disclosure of matters before a grand jury are virtually unavailable to a defendant. *U.S. v. Potts,* 57 F Supp 204; *U.S. v. Proctor and Gamble,* 47 F Supp 676.

The reasons for this "virtual unavailability" are not difficult to discern, for:

> "Non-disclosure of the [grand jury] minutes before the trial prevents the accused from tampering with the witnesses against him; prevents publication of derogatory information presented to the grand jury against an accused who has not been indicted; encourages complainants and witnesses to come before the grand jury and speak fully without fear that their testimony will be made public (thereby subjecting them to possible repercussions); and encourages the grand jurors to engage in uninhibited investigations and deliberations by barring, before trial, disclosures of their votes and comments." Fontana, *"Discovery in Criminal Cases,"* NYLJ, 12/29/65, p. 1, col. 4.

*See also: People v. McAdoo,* 45 Misc2d 664, affd 51 Misc2d 263, cert. den. 386 US 1031; 8 Wigmore, *Evidence,* § 2360 (3rd ed. 1940). However, there have been exceptions. *U.S. v. Grunewald,* 162 F Supp 621; *U.S. v. Socony-Vacuum,* 310 US 150.

**§ 137.02. Rule 7(f).** This rule governs the right to a Bill of Particulars. "The court may direct the filing of a bill of particulars. A motion for a bill of particulars may be made before arraignment or within ten days after arraignment or at such other time as the court may permit. A bill of particulars may be amended at any time subject to such conditions as justice requires."

Frequently defendants seek to obtain disclosure of government witnesses and of the government's evidence by way of a bill of particulars. As a general rule in such instances a bill of particulars will be denied. *U.S. v. McKay,* 45 F Supp 1007; *U.S. v. Gris,* 146 F Supp 293, affd 247 F2d 860.

Requests via a bill of particulars for names of the government's witnesses will generally be denied. *U.S. v. Elliot,* 266 F Supp 318; *U.S. v. Hasiwar,* 299 F Supp 1053. This is not the function of a bill of particulars. *Yeargain v. U.S.,* 314 F2d 881.

The same rule applies to the names of witnesses who appeared before the grand jury. *Thomas v. U.S.,* 188 F2d 6; *U.S. v. Wolfson,* 294 F Supp 267; *U.S. v. Burgio,* 279 F Supp 843.

This rule against disclosure of names of witnesses in criminal cases is, inter alia, to avoid the danger of tampering with the witnesses. However, there are exceptions, such as where the government witness has knowledge of the transactions charged. *U.S. v. Solomon,* 26 FRD 397. This is particulary true in cases involving informants. *Roviaro v. U.S.,* 353 US 53. *See also: U.S. v. Guterma,* 179 F Supp 417; *U.S. v. Vasquez,* 25 FRD 350; *U.S. v. Pignone,* 189 F Supp 532; *U.S. v. Conforti,* 200 F2d 365, cert. den. 345 US 925.

Motions made under Rule 7(f) for access to books, documents and other tangibles have been generally denied, usually on the ground that the defendant is seeking to inspect evidence and not actually to prevent surprise at the trial. *U.S. v. Elliot, supra; U.S. v. Hasiwar, supra.*

However, there are exceptions. Thus, where justice requires it, a bill of particulars authorizing disclosure of some of the government's evidence or theory of its prosecution will be ordered, even if it results in disclosure. *U.S. v. Smith,* 16 FRD 372; *U.S. v. Bentvena,* 193 F Supp 485.

Where the government intended to rely on certain documents to prove the crime charged, pretrial disclosure under a motion for a bill of particulars was authorized. *U.S. v. Onassis,* 125 F Supp 190.

**§ 137.03. Rule 16.** This rule has been broadened by the amendments effective July 1, 1966. The rule permits pretrial discovery and inspection of books, papers, documents and tangible objects in the hands of the government, obtained from or belonging to the defendant or obtained from others by seizure or by process. Permission to inspect them is discretionary with the court. The inspection may authorize a defendant to copy or photograph the designated article. Prior to July 1966, a defendant was required to show that his request was reasonable and that the items sought might be material to his defense. Rule 16 applied only to defendants. *In re Magnus, Mabee and Reynard,* 311 F2d 12, cert. den. 373 US 902. It limited discovery and inspection to tangibles obtained from the defendant, *U.S. v. Murray,* 297 F2d 812, cert. den. 369 US 828, or which had been obtained from others by seizure or process, *e.g., U.S. v. Black,* 6 FRD 270 (birth certificate); *U.S. v. Haug,* 21 FRD 22, (non-communist affidavits); *U.S. v. Geller,* 163 F Supp 502 (income tax returns); *U.S. v. Patrisso,* 20 FRD 576 (stolen TV tubes); *U.S. v. Schiller,* 187 F2d 572 (diaries); *Ginsberg v. U.S.,* 257 F2d 950 (company books containing alleged unreported sales); *U.S. v. Bentvena,* 193 F Supp 485; *U.S. v. Angelet,* 26 FRD 408; *Bandy v. U.S.,* 296 F2d 882 (inspection of drugs, scientific analyses excluded).

A scientific examination of drugs by defendant's expert was and still is authorized. *U.S. v. Taylor,* 25 FRD 225; Rule 16(a). It is incumbent on the defendant to show that his request is reasonable and that the items sought to be discovered are material as an aid in the preparation of his defense. *U.S. v. Rothman,* 179 F Supp 935.

**§ 137.04. Rule 16(a).** This rule authorizes the court to permit "the defendant to inspect and copy or photograph any relevant (1) written or recorded statements or confessions made by the defendant, or copies thereof, within the possession, custody or control of the government, . . . (2) results or reports of physical or mental examinations, and of scientific tests or experiments made in connection with the particular case, [and in the possession of the government] . . . and (3) recorded testimony of the defendant before a grand jury." Under a 1966 amendment to Rule 16(a), a defendant is no longer required to show that the items sought may be material to the preparation of his defense and that his request is a reasonable one.

The term "statements" mentioned above refers not only to written statements and confessions, but also to statements that may have been recorded in a manner other than in writing. Presumably, this refers to statements recorded by electronic devices. Of course, it specifically includes a defendant's testimony before a grand jury.

In *U.S. v. Murray,* 297 F2d 812, a 1962 case, the court refused pretrial discovery to a defendant of his question-and-answer examination, which had been recorded but not signed by him. This decision was based on the theory that the question-and-answer examination did not constitute "books, papers, documents or tangible objects obtained from or belonging to the defendant" within the purview of the pre-1966 rule. The fact that the defendant had not signed the examination was irrelevant, since the same rule would have been applied if he had signed it.

However, *Murray, supra,* is no longer the law by virtue of the 1966 amendment of Rule 16(a). As the court noted in *U.S. v. Isa,* 413 F2d 244, 246–247, the defendant is now entitled to discovery and inspection of his recorded statements or confessions, as a matter of right by virtue of this amendment. Additionally, "a showing of need" or of applicability to "past occurrences" is not required. *See:* Rule 16(b); *see also: U.S. v. Rosenberg,* 299 F Supp 1241. There is no guaranty that statements discoverable under this rule are complete in all respects. *Castillo v. U.S.,* 409 F2d 762. Whether or not *U.S. v. Isa, supra,* is sustained by the Supreme Court, it has long been held that it is the better practice for the prosecution to exhibit a confession to the defendant, pretrial. *Cicenia v. Lagay,* 357 US 504, 511; *Leland v. Oregon,* 343 US 790, 801. This is a sensible rule, particularly since the defendant will eventually see the confession if it is offered in evidence. *Cf.* CPL art. 710.

**§ 137.05. Rule 16(b).** This new section permits the court to authorize inspection of books, papers, documents and other tangible objects or places, in the government's possession. However, in such instances the defendant is required to show the necessity of the inspection because of the "materiality to the preparation of his defense and that the request is reasonable." Witnesses' statements in the possession of the government are excluded. These statements are of course available to a defendant at the trial under the Jencks Rule, once the witness has testified (18 USC § 3500).

**§ 137.06. Rule 16(c).** This new rule is a radical departure from widely-held constitutional concepts. Its constitutionality had been questioned by two Supreme Court Justices prior to adoption (1966 U.S. Code Cong. Admin. News, 962–965, 966–969).

The rule, if the court grants defendant relief under subdivision (a)(2) or subdivision (b), "permits the government limited, pretrial discovery of certain material within the defendant's possession." However, the "court may condition an order granting defendant pre-trial discovery upon a requirement that the defendant permit the government to discover 'scientific or medical reports, books, papers, documents, tangible objects, which the defendant intends to produce at the trial.' " The government's request must be based on a showing that the items sought for inspection are material to the preparation of its case and that the request is reasonable. Witnesses' statements, except as applicable under *Jencks, supra,* are excluded. *See:* Koplovitz, *"New Amendment,"* Crim Law Bulletin, Vol. 2, No. 4, p. 3.

**§ 137.07. Rule 16(e).** The court on a proper showing by the government may at any time, after an *in camera* inspection, order that the discovery and inspection be denied, restricted or deferred. If the government's application is granted, the statement submitted in support of its application must be sealed and preserved in the record for appellate review purposes. *Taglianetti v. U.S.*, 398 F2d 558; *U.S. v. Schneiderman*, 104 F Supp 405.

**§ 137.08. Rule 16(g).** This rule imposes on both parties a continuing duty to disclose, subject to certain provisions, including the possible penalty of exclusion of certain evidence at the trial.

The concept of Rule 16(g) is neither new nor novel. In 1963, the United States Supreme Court, in *Brady v. Maryland*, 373 US 83, 92, held that, after request, suppression by the prosecutor of evidence favorable to the accused violates due process whenever the evidence would tend to exculpate the defendant or affect the punishment that might be imposed. *See also: Barbee v. Warden*, 331 F2d 842; *cf. People v. Fein*, 18 NY2d 162, 219 NE2d 274.

In *State v. Giles*, 212 A2d 101, 108, the court said:

> "We think that in order for the nondisclosure of evidence to amount to a denial of due process, it must be such as is material and capable of clearing or tending to clear the accused of guilt or of substantially affecting the punishment to be imposed in addition to being such as could reasonably be considered admissible and useful to the defense."

In *U.S. v. Miller*, 411 F2d 825, the court reversed a conspiracy conviction, even though it was convinced that the defendant's guilt was adequately established, on the ground of the Government's failure to disclose to the defense pretrial hypnosis of its principal witness, in part by the attorney who examined him at trial. According to psychiatrists, the fact that the prosecutor who examined the witness at the trial was the same person who interviewed him when he was under hypnosis, induced in part by the prosecutor, would result in putting the witness unduly under the prosecutor's influence making him immune to defense efforts during cross-examination to discredit his identification of the defendant. Evidence of the hypnosis was not discovered until after conviction and defendant then moved for a new trial on the ground of newly discovered evidence. Whether or not this constituted newly discovered evidence, the court would not say since it is unnecessary to pass on this question when there is a duty of the government to disclose the hypnosis. The court held that "a motion for a new trial must be granted if there is a significant possibility that the undisclosed evidence might have led to an acquittal or a hung jury. . . ." *Miller* at 831.

The court added that it could not confidently say what effect this evidence would have had on a jury; however, where the prosecutor had turned over other items for inspection, but failed to offer a memorandum which referred to the hypnosis of his witness, such misconduct creates "a duty of disclosure even if none existed before." There is a significant chance, the court observed ". . . that this added item, developed by skilled counsel as it would have been, could have induced a reasonable doubt in the minds of enough jurors to avoid a conviction." *Miller* at 832.

The United States Supreme Court remanded the *Giles* case, *supra,* for further proceedings following the action of the Maryland Court of Appeal which denied post-conviction relief of defendants convicted of rape. *Giles v. Maryland,* 386 US 66. The basis for the remand was that counsel was denied access to police reports containing statements inconsistent with the prosecutrix' trial testimony and prosecution's information about her subsequent assertion and withdrawal of rape charges against others, and her attempted suicide, and counsel was not permitted, at a post-conviction hearing, to explore evidence of her mental condition and nymphomania.

The denial of due process, condemned in *State v. Giles, supra,* was held to have vitiated a rape-murder conviction in *Miller v. Pate,* 386 US 1.

In *Miller,* the prosecutor represented to the jury that a stained pair of shorts, found one mile from the scene of the crime, belonged to the defendant, and were stained with the blood of the victim, even though he knew that the stains on the garment, which the defendant was not permitted to examine, were actually paint. The "blood-stained" shorts were a vital component of the People's case and the prosecutor made frequent reference to them and the "blood stains" during the trial. The United States Supreme Court found that the prosecution deliberately misrepresented the truth.

> "More than 30 years ago this Court held that the Fourteenth Amendment cannot tolerate a state criminal conviction obtained by the knowing use of false evidence. Mooney v. Holohan, 294 U.S. 103, 55 S. Ct. 340, 79 L.Ed. 791. There has been no deviation from that established principle. Napue v. People of State of Illinois, 360 U.S. 264, 79 S. Ct. 1173, 3 L. Ed.2d 1217; Pyle v. State of Kansas, 317 U.S. 213, 63 S. Ct. 177, 87 L. Ed. 214; cf. Alcorta v. State of Texas, 355 U.S. 28, 78 S. Ct. 103, 2 L. Ed2d 9. There can be no retreat from that principle here." *Miller v. Pate,* 386 US at 7.

In *U.S. v. Tomaiolo,* 378 F2d 26, the court followed the rule laid down in *State v. Giles, supra,* and as indicated in *Griffin v. U.S.,* 183 F2d 990, revd and rem 336 US 704.

It held also that suppression of evidence by a federal prosecutor did not violate due process where such evidence was wholly lacking in probative force because of its speculative quality, since a grand jury witness did not testify that a third party told him who the second robber was nor did the witness in any way explain his surmise that a person other than the defendant was the man.

Similarly, in New York, (*People v. Ahmed,* 20 NY2d 958, 233 NE2d 854), it was error for the district attorney not to have notified the defense either before or during defendant's trial that the robbery victim on the night of the robbery was unable to identify the defendant from a police photograph.

**§ 137.09. Rule 17(c).** Rule 17(c) authorizes the issuance of a subpoena duces tecum. On motion promptly made, the court may quash or modify the subpoena if compliance would be unreasonable or oppressive. The court may direct that books, papers, documents or objects designated in the subpoena be produced before the court at a time prior to the trial or prior to the time when they are to be offered in evidence, and upon their production may permit either of the parties to inspect all or portions of these items. Obviously 17(c) applies only to tangibles.

This subpoena power, available to both parties, is not an additional discovery device. It is merely a method which may be employed for the production of certain items for use as evidence at the trial. *See: Bowman Dairy Co. v. U.S.,* 341 US 214; *U.S. v. Fassler,* 46 FRD 43.

The subpoena must be served in good faith and not for a fishing expedition. *U.S. v. Iozia,* 13 FRD 335; *U.S. v. Scully,* 15 FRD 402; *U.S. v. Hanlin,* 29 FRD 481; *U.S. v. Ward,* 120 F Supp 57; *U.S. v. Solomon, supra.* Good cause must be shown to warrant pretrial production and inspection. *U.S. v. Fassler, supra.*

The party producing the document is not obliged to explain it. *U.S. v. Schluter,* 19 FRD 415.

**§ 138. Lists of Witnesses in Capital Cases (18 USC § 3432).** Although there is no right to the disclosure of witnesses in criminal cases, section 3432 permits disclosure in capital cases. *U.S. v. Haug,* 21 FRD 22. This authority does not include the right to obtain the lists of the witnesses who appeared before the grand jury in capital cases. Federal courts have refused to extend this right to other criminal cases. *U.S. v. Grossman,* 154 F Supp 813; *U.S. v. Brennan,* 134 F Supp 42; *U.S. v. Brandt,* 139 F Supp 367; *U.S. v. Palermo,* 21 FRD 11, affd 360 US 343; *U.S. v. Johnson,* 298 F Supp 58.

There have been exceptions. *U.S. v. Solomon,* 26 FRD 397. For other exceptions where the lists of witnesses have been requested in a bill of particulars, *see:* § 137.01, *supra.*

In interpreting the full meaning of 18 USC § 3432, the D.C. Circuit Court of Appeals reversed a murder conviction in *Gregory v. U.S.,* 369 F2d 185, on the ground, among others, that the prosecutor had advised his witnesses not to talk to defendant's counsel, except in the prosecutor's presence.

> "The purpose of 18 U.S.C., § 3432 requiring that in capital cases the defendant be furnished a list of the names and addresses of the witnesses to be called by the Government is to assist defense counsel in preparing the defense by interviewing the witnesses. . . . It is true

that the prosecutor stated he did not instruct the witnesses not to talk to defense counsel. He did admit that he advised the witnesses not to talk to anyone unless he, the prosecutor, were present.

"We accept the prosecutor's statement as to his advice to the witnesses as true. But we know of nothing in the law which gives the prosecutor the right to interfere with the preparation of the defense by effectively denying defense counsel access to the witnesses except in his presence. . . .

"We cannot indulge the presumption that this tactic on the part of the prosecution is necessary.

* * * *

"A criminal trial, like its civil counterpart, is a quest for truth. That quest will more often be successful if both sides have an equal opportunity to interview the persons who have the information from which the truth may be determined. The current tendency in the criminal law is in the direction of discovery of the facts before trial and elimination of surprise at trial. A related development in the criminal law is the requirement that the prosecution not frustrate the defense in the preparation of its case. . . . It is not suggested here that there was any direct suppression of evidence. But there was unquestionably a suppression of the means by which the defense could obtain evidence. . . . In our judgment the prosecutor's advice to these eye witnessess frustrated that effort and denied appellant a fair trial." *Gregory v. U.S.*, 369 F2d 185, 187–189.

**§ 139. Special Items Discoverable Pretrial.** Items delivered by the defendant to the Securities and Exchange Commission, under a subpoena, are discoverable. *U.S. v. Van Allen,* 28 FRD 329.

In a tax evasion case, all papers which the government had obtained from the defendant are discoverable. *U.S. v. Fancher,* 195 F Supp 448.

Inspection of narcotics in a prosecution for violation of the narcotics law is authorized. Admission by the defendant of possession is not a prerequisite to his motion for discovery. *U.S. v. Lopez,* 26 FRD 174.

In an unusual situation, broad discovery was allowed due to the special circumstances of the case which involved a charge of rape on the high seas. The items allowed were: copy of the plans of the vessel and the section portraying the scene of the alleged crime; a photograph of the complainant taken subsequent to the alleged attack; a photograph of the place where the crime was claimed to have been committed; copies of the medical report made by the physician who examined the complainant immediately after the alleged rape; copies of the defendant's own statements; report of the blood tests taken of the victim and the defendant. *U.S. v. Willis,* 33 FRD 510. *See also: U.S. v. Solomon,* 26 FRD 397, in which a very broad grant of disclosure was allowed.

In a case where a new test was employed by the government in an effort to trace certain narcotics to the defendants, failure to disclose the new test to the defendants required a reversal and a new trial. *U.S. v. Kelly,* 420 F2d 26.

In this case, a new technique, known as the neutron activation test, was employed to prove that certain narcotics, traced to the defendants, came from the same batch as those in the possession of the defendants. Defendants learned of the use of this new test, for the first time, at their trial.

In reversing, the court ruled that the test employed should have been disclosed to the defendants well in advance of the trial, in order to permit them to check the claims of the reliability of the test.

The evidence to be disclosed must be admissible and helpful to the defense, as judged by reasonable standards. When these factors are in doubt, the prosecutor is under a duty to disclose the evidence to the court. ". . . When there is substantial room for doubt, the prosecution is not to decide for the court what is admissible and for the defense what is useful." *Griffin v. U.S.,* 183 F2d 990, 993, revd other grds and rem 336 US 704.

§ 140. **Items Not Discoverable Pretrial.** Rule 16 applies to documents, a defendant's statements and confession and tangibles only. *U.S. v. Wortman,* 26 FRD 183.

The rule is not applicable to items seized from others and returned to them. It applies only to items still in the possession of the government. *U.S. v. Wortman, supra.*

Statements of government witnesses or a summary of their testimony, or their names, are not discoverable. *Peek v. U.S.,* 321 F2d 934, cert. den. 376 US 954; *U.S. v. Telles,* 226 F Supp 670; *U.S. v. Manhattan Brush Co.,* 38 FRD 4.

Statements of co-conspirators and codefendants are not discoverable. *U.S. v. Bentvena,* 193 F Supp 485; *U.S. v. Manhattan Brush Co., supra.*

Evidentiary matter such as the government's evidence and the details of its case are not discoverable. *U.S. v. Smith,* 209 F Supp 907.

Likewise, exploratory excursions (fishing expeditions) to determine the government's evidence are precluded. *U.S. v. Smith, supra; U.S. v. Bentvena, supra.*

Nor is a defendant entitled to a list of the grand jurors. *U.S. v. Wortman, supra.*

The prosecution is under no duty to reveal to a defendant evidence that is equally available to him, *U.S. v. Sorce,* 325 F2d 84, cert. den. 376 US 931, evidence that is lacking in probative value, evidence that is merely circumstantial, or mistaken, false or unreliable. *State v. Giles, supra; Griffin v. U.S., supra; People v. Fein,* 18NY2d 162, 219NE2d 274.

**§ 141. Discovery and Inspection During Trial: Similarity of New York and Federal Rules.** The rule authorizing discovery of prior statements of defendants and witnesses during trial is substantially the same in both the federal and New York courts. At a hearing or trial, the defendant must be permitted to examine a witness' prior statements whether or not they differ from his testimony on the stand. It is for the defendant alone to determine what use, if any, he desires to make of those prior statements on cross-examination. The right is not otherwise circumscribed, providing they relate to the subject matter of the witness' testimony and, if written, contain nothing that must be kept confidential. *Jencks v. U.S.,* 353 US 657, 672; *People v. Malinsky,* 15 NY2d 86; *People v. Rosario,* 9 NY2d 286; *Peek v. U.S.,* 321 F2d 934, cert. den. 376 US 954. *See: § 149, et seq. infra, for further discussion.*

**§ 142. Jencks v. U.S.** Prior statements include testimony given by a witness before a grand jury (*U.S. v. Rose,* 215 F2d 617, 629; *U.S. v. Remington,* 191 F2d 246, 252; *U.S. v. Zborowski,* 271 F2d 661), as well as reports and statements made by the government's witnesses. *Jencks v. U.S.,* 353 US 657; *U.S. v. Manhattan Brush Company,* 38 FRD 4; 18 USC § 3500 (The Jencks Act).

The right to examine prior written or recorded statements or reports of government witnesses at a trial or hearing for the purpose of impeachment, is strictly limited to the provisions of the Jencks Act (18 USC § 3500).

By contrast, the comparable New York rule has evolved through decisional law. *People v. Malinsky,* 15 NY2d 86, 204 NE2d 188; *People v. Pizarro,* 15 NY2d 803, 205 NE2d 694; *People ex rel Lemon v. Supreme Court,* 245 NY 24.

The decision in *Jencks v. U.S., supra,* and the Jencks Act, which was enacted thereafter (18 USC § 3500), were not "cast in constitutional terms. *Palermo v. United States, supra* [360 U.S. 343], at 345, 362. They state rules of evidence governing trials before federal tribunals; and we have never extended their principles to state criminal trials." *U.S. v. Augenblick,* 393 US 348, 356.

"Rough notes" made by a government agent during defendant's interrogation do not constitute "statements" producible under the Jencks Act. *Id.* at 354–355; 18 USC § 3500 (e).

**§ 142.01. The Jencks Act.** As noted above, 18 USC § 3500, was enacted after the decision in *Jencks v. U.S.,* 353 US 657, was handed down. Before *Jencks,* the trial judge inspected certain notes and statements *in camera* and determined their materiality before permitting the defendant to examine them. *Jencks* condemned this practice holding that the defendant is entitled to examine them and decide for himself whether or not to use them, since he alone "is adequately equipped to determine the effective use for purpose of discrediting the government's witnesses and thereby furthering the accused's defense." Accordingly, "the defense must initially be entitled to see them to determine what use may be made of them. Justice requires no less." 353 US at 668–669.

Whether the Jencks Act enlarged or limited the decision

in *Jencks v. U.S., supra,* is moot, but the Act did prescribe certain rules of federal practice with respect to a defendant's access to, and use of, prior statements of witnesses at a trial in a criminal prosecution. Briefly, section 3500 provides:

(a) No statement or report in the possession of the government, made by a government witness or prospective witness (other than the defendant), to an agent of the government, is subject to subpoena, discovery or inspection until that witness has testified on direct examination at the trial. *Cf. U.S. v. Padrone,* 406 F2d 560.

(b) After the witness has testified on direct examination for the government, the court must, on motion of the defendant, order the government to produce any statement of the witness in the government's possession which relates to that witness' testimony, for his examination and use.

(c) If the government claims that the statement covers other matters, the court will examine it *in camera* and excise therefrom the other matter. The rest of the statement may then be used by the defendant.

(d) If the government fails to comply with the court's direction under paragraphs (b) and (c), *supra,* the entire testimony of that witness will be stricken or a mistrial directed if the interest of justice requires it.

(e) If the prior statements cannot be produced (even without any indication of bad faith on the part of the Government, such as their destruction in the ordinary course of government administrative policy), the witness' testimony is required to be stricken, for as the court said in *Lee v. U.S.,* 368 F2d 834, 837, "But the Jencks Act does not embody in terms any 'bad faith' exception."

(f) The term "statement" as used in subsections (b), (c) and (d) in relation to any witness called by the United States means:

(1) a written statement made by the witness and signed or otherwise adopted or approved by him; or

(2) a stenographic, mechanical, electrical, or other recording, or a transcription thereof, which is a substantially verbatim recital of an oral statement made by the witness to an agent of the government and recorded contemporaneously with the making of the oral statement.

In *U.S. v. Padrone,* 406 F2d 560, the prosecution inadvertently failed to comply with an order of the District Court judge directing the government to turn over to the defense a statement taken from the defendant after his arrest. The defendant appealed his conviction for a narcotics violation. The judgment was reversed and new trial ordered solely on the ground that the inadvertent failure to permit counsel to inspect the defendant's statement was a serious detriment to the preparation for trial where it was apparent that the defense strategy may have been undermined by the failure to comply. The court noted that defendant, in his statement, gave police information regarding the source of his narcotics, whereas at the trial he denied any knowledge of drugs. There was a wide discrepancy between what defendant claimed at trial and what he stated after his arrest. Therefore, it was said, had counsel known the contents of the statement, he might well have advised defendant not to testify. The fact that the statement itself was not permitted into evidence does not lessen the prejudice to defendant in not receiving a copy as directed. Defense counsel had a right to inspect the statement.

The right of the defendant to examine prior statements of prosecution witnesses under the Jencks Act may not be so circumscribed or conditioned by the trial court so as to create a situation prejudicial to the defendant, in the eyes of a jury. Thus, where a defendant asked for a Jencks Act statement after a witness had testified, and the trial court required defense counsel to request, receive and read them in the presence of the jury, such direction by the court was held to be improper and the conviction was reversed. *Johnson v. U.S.,* 347 F2d 803.

"Moreover, in order to avoid the undue prejudice which may arise from the jury's knowledge that Jencks Act statements were available to the accused, motions for their production should be made outside the hearing of the jury. The actual handing over of the statements should take place with the jury absent, or at least unaware." *Johnson v. U.S.*, 347 F2d 803, 806.

Section 3500 is intended to restrict the use of those statements to impeachment, *Palermo v. U.S.*, 360 US 343, and to make available at the trial those materials which might lead to impeachment. It was not intended as a license to the defendant to rummage through the prosecution's files before trial, but to protect the government from unwarranted disclosures. *Caldwell v. U.S.*, 338 F2d 385, cert. den. 380 US 984; *U.S. v. West,* 170 F Supp 200, affd 274 F2d 885.

A memorandum report by an F.B.I. agent was held to be a "statement" under this statute. *Mims v. U.S.*, 332 F2d 944, cert. den. 379 US 888.

Requests for statements of a witness' testimony in advance of trial is premature. They may be available to the defendant if the witness testifies at the trial. *U.S. v. Tane,* 29 FRD 131; *U.S. v. Manhattan Brush Co.*, 38 FRD 4.

§ 142.02. **Photographs and Pictures.** A photograph is not a "statement" under the Jencks Act. However, photographs must be produced if they constitute a part of a written statement. *Simmons v. U.S.*, 390 US 377, 387.

In *U.S. v. Zurita,* 369 F2d 474, it was held that the Jencks Act does not require inspection and discovery, at the trial, of a composite picture of bank robbers drawn during an interview with the principal witness to the robbery. This section, it was held, was not applicable to representations of statements since that is, in effect, what the composite picture amounted to. The court held that the composite drawings could not be considered a recordation or reproduction of words.

§ 142.03. **Pre-Sentence Reports.** Pre-sentence reports, sometimes called probation reports, are compiled and presented to the sentencing judge as an aid in sentencing. Disclosure of the contents of the reports, to the defendant or his counsel, is discretionary with the court. *Good v. U.S.,* 410 F2d 1217; *U.S. v. Weiner,* 376 F2d 42. The disclosure may be partial or total. Whatever is disclosed to the defendant or his attorney must also be disclosed to the attorney for the government. Fed R Crim P 32(c).

It is not a denial of due process for a court to impose sentence in reliance on a pre-sentence report without disclosing its contents to the defendant or giving him an opportunity to rebut. *Williams v. New York,* 337 US 241; *Williams v. Oklahoma,* 358 US 576.

It is interesting to note that in England copies of the presentence report are given to the defendant in every case. English Criminal Justice Act of 1948. The same rule prevails in California. Cal. Penal Code, sec. 1203.

**§ 142.04. Grand Jury Proceedings.** Formerly, a transcript of grand jury proceedings was not considered a "statement" within the meaning of the statute. *Ogden v. U.S.,* 303 F2d 724, affd 323 F2d 818, cert. den. 376 US 973. Automatic production of the transcript was not required by the statute. *Pittsburgh Plate Glass v. U.S.,* 360 US 395. However, if the court found an inconsistency between testimony given before the grand jury and testimony given at the trial, the grand jury minutes should be made available to the defendant. *U.S. v. D'Angiolillo,* 340 F2d 453, cert. den. 380 US 955; *U.S. v. Borelli,* 336 F2d 376, cert. den. 379 US 960; *U.S. v. Keegan,* 331 F2d 257, cert. den. 379 US 828.

However, amended Federal Rules of Criminal Procedure, Rule 16(a), specifically includes a defendant's testimony before a grand jury as a "statement." Accordingly, where defendant requests production of grand jury minutes for purposes of cross-examination, they must be produced. Understandably, failure to produce the minutes would frustrate defendant's effort aimed at impeaching a witness. *Palermo v. U.S.,* 360 US 343; *Schlinsky v. U.S.,* 379 F2d 735.

The purpose of section 3500 is to give a defendant the opportunity, through discovery and inspection, of impeaching the witness by showing inconsistencies in his testimony. *Churder v. U.S.,* 294 F Supp 207. The request to examine prior testimony should be made during or after the direct examination of the witness. *Hanger v. U.S.,* 398 F2d 91.

The measure of discovery permitted in federal criminal cases is not intended to be as broad as discovery in civil suits. *U.S. v. Sermon,* 208 F Supp 871. Unlike civil cases, the federal rules (Rules 6(e), 16(c) and 17(c) excepted) apply only to defendants. *In re Magnus, Mabee & Reynard Inc.,* 311 F2d 12, cert. den. 373 US 902. The protection afforded a defendant by the Fourth and Fifth Amendments precludes liberal discovery practices against him. *See: Boyd v. U.S.,* 116 US 616; *U.S. v. Sermon, supra; cf.* Fed R Crim P 16(c).

Thus, during a criminal trial, prior statements or memoranda made by witnesses, whether before a grand jury or at a hearing or trial, are available for inspection by either side, for the purpose of impeaching a witness or refreshing the recollection of a government witness.

In *U.S. v. Youngblood,* 379 F2d 365, the court noted that under *U.S. v. Proctor & Gamble,* 356 US 677, 683, *Pittsburgh Plate Glass v. U.S.,* 360 US 395, 405, and *Dennis v. U.S.,* 384 US 855, 870, the trial court was not obliged to permit the defense to examine grand jury minutes in the absence of a showing of need.

This practice is followed in the Second Circuit. There the practice has been "that the trial court need not allow the defense to examine grand jury minutes in the absence of a showing of a 'particularized need' .... Disclosure may be limited to that portion of the grand jury minutes for which the necessity of examination had been shown, for defendants have no absolute right to any wholesale disclosure of grand jury testimony." *U.S. v. Youngblood, supra* at 367. The judge must examine the grand jury testimony *in camera,* and, if he concludes that they contain no inconsistencies from the trial testimony, he may refuse to allow the defense to examine them. 379 F2d at 367. However, Rule 6(e) gives the court the power to order disclosure, in a proper case, even if no "particularized need" is shown. *Youngblood, supra* at 369.

In any event, *Youngblood* holds that the traditional reasons for grand jury secrecy are largely inapplicable and that disclosure of grand jury testimony should be granted without a showing of "particularized need" by the defendant.

In accordance with this conclusion, the Second Circuit ordered:

> "[W]e direct that at trials commencing after our judgment here is entered, the district courts of this circuit at the request of the defendant should order that the defendant be allowed to examine the grand jury testimony of those witnesses who testify at his trial without requiring him to show any particularized need for this material; we are holding that a defendant should be entitled to see all the grand jury testimony of each witness on the subjects about which that witness testified at the defendant's trial." *Youngblood, supra* at 370.

The court noted two exceptions to this general rule: (1) where disclosure would jeopardize national security, (2) "for other proper reasons." Although the court did not explain "other proper reasons," presumably this refers to situations where disclosure might endanger the life of a witness. *Youngblood, supra* at 370.

> "If the Government seeks such a protective order the court should first examine *in camera* the material sought to be protected before making its ruling; and if material is withheld from the defendant under such an order it shall be sealed by the court and preserved for consideration on appeal. But, *we repeat, absent this unusual situation, a defendant as of right is entitled to examine the grand jury testimony of all witnesses at his trial* on the subjects about which these witnesses testified at the trial." *Youngblood, supra* at 370 (emphasis supplied).

This decision is entirely consonant with the spirit and intent of the Jencks Act. *See also: U.S. v. Manhattan Brush Co.,* 38 FRD 4; *People v. Rosario,* 9 NY2d 286, 173 NE2d 881, citing *Jencks v. U.S.,* 353 US 657, 667, 668.

**§ 142.05. Suppression of Evidence by the Government.** As noted in § 137.07, *supra,* there is a continuing obligation on the government to disclose evidence favorable to the defendant. It is immaterial whether failure on the part of the prosecutor after request, is based on good or bad faith. Rule 16(g); *Brady v. Maryland,* 373 US 83, 88.

On the other hand, in *Earl v. U.S.,* 381 F2d 715, failure of a federal court to compel the U.S. attorney to grant immunity to a government witness who, when called to the stand, claimed his privilege against self-incrimination even if the testimony would have been favorable to the defendant, did not constitute suppression by the prosecution. This is not "suppression" as defined in *Brady v. Maryland, supra,* as violative of due process. In *Earl,* the prosecution had not affirmatively withheld the witness or concealed the evidence. To comply with the defendant's request would have required the court to command the executive branch of the government to exercise the statutory power to grant immunity in order to secure relevant testimony. This power, it was held, is not inherent in the executive, or in the judiciary.

**§ 142.06 Police and Prosecutor Equated.** The general rule is that evidence in the possession of the police, or promises made by the police to a witness for the People (*e.g.,* leniency of treatment) are promises of the prosecutor. *Barbee v. Warden,* 331 F2d 842; *People v. Yamin,* 45 Misc2d 407. *For further discussion, see: § 150, infra.*

**§ 142.07. Due Process.** Failure of the prosecutor to reveal perjured testimony of his witnesses, or exculpatory evidence as mentioned above, constitutes a violation of "due process." *Brady v. Maryland, supra; People v. Savvides,* 1 NY2d 554, 136 NE2d 853; *People v. Yamin, supra.*

**§ 142.08. F.T.C. Hearings.** The Jencks Act is applicable in proceedings before the Federal Trade Commission. *F.T.C.: Inter-State Builders, Inc.,* 34 USLW 2627.

**§ 142.09. Preliminary Hearings Before a Magistrate.** In *Gibson v. Halleck,* 254 F Supp 159, it was held that the provisions of the Jencks Act do not apply to preliminary hearings before a committing magistrate, and statements of government witnesses need not be produced, as the magistrate is not a "court" within the purview of the act. The court observed that many United States commissioners (now magistrates) are laymen, and that it could not have been intended by Congress to vest in a lay magistrate the wide discretion the Jencks Act authorizes.

**§ 143. Grand Jury Proceedings.** While grand jury proceedings are secret (*See, e.g., People v. Dunbar Contracting Co.,* 82 Misc 174; Fed R Crim P 6(e); CPL § 190.25(4)), there are exceptions. Thus, where a grand jury witness is charged with perjury, a member of the grand jury may be required by the court to disclose the grand jury testimony of that witness for the purpose of ascertaining whether it is consistent with that given by the witness before the court; or to disclose the testimony given before the grand jury by any person upon a charge against him for perjury in giving his testimony, or upon his trial. The same rule prevails in prosecutions for contempt of the grand jury. *Knapp v. Schweitzer,* 2 AD2d 579, affd 2 NY2d 913, remittitur amended 2 NY2d 975, affd 357 US 371; *People v. McAdoo,* 45 Misc2d 664, cert. den. 386 US 1031.

A person may, on a proper showing, inspect grand jury minutes to determine if he was lawfully indicted. *People v. Klaw,* 53 Misc 158. This is done to lay a foundation for a motion to dismiss the indictment. Inspection is discretionary with the court and the denial of the motion is not appealable. *People v. Koposesky,* 25 AD2d 777; *People v. Kramer,* 151 Misc 210; *In re Martin,* 170 Misc 919.

The district attorney is authorized to obtain a copy of grand jury minutes to enable him to prepare for trial and to perform his duties. *People v. Supreme Court,* 269 NY 392.

The granting of a motion for pretrial discovery and inspection is discretionary and will be granted when the interests of justice will be served. *People v. Gatti,* 167 Misc 545; *People v. Higgins,* 21 Misc2d 94; *People v. D'Andrea,* 20 Misc2d 1070.

**§ 144. Exploratory Searches.** The leading New York case of pretrial discovery and inspection is *People ex rel Lemon v. Supreme Court,* 245 NY 24, 27, 29, 34, where the Court of Appeals prohibited pretrial inspection where its sole purpose was to pry into the People's case. The defendant was charged with the murder of her husband by administering arsenic. A transcript of a physician's report on the examination of the deceased's stomach, together with the testimony of others as to the cause of death, were given to her. She requested inspection of other evidence submitted to the grand jury. This was granted to the extent of ordering the district attorney to file with the county clerk "each and every written statement, affidavit, letter, memorandum and confession made by William Wegley [an accomplice] . . . the complete written statements and memoranda of the postmortem examination of said Daniel F. Earley referred to in said information and all reports made to said district attorney . . . all reports and information made . . . to said district attorney with reference to any chemical analysis or examinations of the organs or parts of the body. . . ." A penalty of exclusion at the trial was imposed on the district attorney for failure to comply.

In reversing the order, the court held:

> "Documents are not subject to inspection for the mere reason that they will be useful in supplying a clew whereby evidence can be gathered. Documents to be subject to inspection must be evidence themselves. . . . No precedent can be found even in civil causes for compelling disclosure, in advance of the trial, of the office notes or memoranda prepared by an attorney after consultation with his witnesses and summarizing his understanding of the testimony that is likely or expected.
>
> "When we turn to criminal causes, we find a jurisdiction that is even more restricted.
>
> * * * *
>
> "The reason why she asks for a disclosure of the statements of the physicians and the chemists is her belief that their statements to the prosecutor were fuller in all probability than their statements to the grand jury already in her possession. A like reason explains her request for the confessions. In a word, statements and memoranda collected by the prosecutor are to be exhibited to the defendant, though none of them will be admissible

either for her or against her if offered at the trial. She makes no claim that they will be. She takes the ground that she should have them because study of the evidence will be helpful in preparing her defense. This is to enlarge the remedy beyond anything permitted by analogy or precedent.

* * * *

"What concerns us at the moment is the scope of the remedy available in advance. At such a stage of the contest, a remedy so drastic is within the condemnation of the rule that inspection may not be had for the sole purpose of prying into the case of one's opponent. The documents to be exhibited must be evidence in support of the cause of action or defense of the party seeking the discovery (1 Pomeroy's Eq. Juris. § 201; Wigram on Discovery, § 342; Hare on Discovery, pp. 183, 189). . . . The documents to be exhibited to this defendant are not evidence for any one. They are merely mnemonic instruments whereby the prosecutor may be better able to elicit evidence hereafter. A mandate giving them publicity is something more than error in the exercise of power. It is an assumption of power where none has been confided. . . ." 245 NY at 29, 34.

In *People v. Gatti,* 167 Misc 545, 547, 553, 554, the court reemphasized the basic tenets of the *Lemon* decision. It repeated the distinction between pretrial discovery and discovery at trial and the right of the defendant to a bill of particulars.

Where the exhibit itself is the basis of the charge against the defendant, pretrial discovery is authorized. If there are fingerprints on a weapon, discovery is authorized. *See also: U.S. v. Rich,* 6 Alas 670, involving fingerprints on glass.

In sum, *Gatti* holds that where justice and fair play require it, pretrial discovery should be granted. Subsequent New York cases have adhered to this rule.

*People v. Walsh,* 262 NY 140, 150, cited in *People v. Gatti, supra,* sums up the general rule as follows: "[T]he defense has no right to go 'upon a tour of investigation, in the hope that they would find something which would aid them' (*Arnstein* v. *United States* [296 Fed. 946]. . . .) When, however, it does appear that there is evidence in the possession or control of the prosecution favorable to the defendant, a right sense of justice demands that it should be available, unless there are strong reasons otherwise."

Contrary to these general rules, the court, in *People v. Powell,* 49 Misc2d 624, 268 NYS2d 380, granted broad and extremely liberal discovery and inspection. Powell was indicted for murder in the first degree. The gravity of the charge did not require authorization for discovery which was tantamount to a fishing expedition into the People's case. But, the court permitted discovery of purely evidentiary items, such as fingerprints, blood tests and fabric tests, as well as statements made by prospective witnesses and notes made by the police and district attorney with relation to those statements. The court also authorized inspection of "any and all records and photographs made by or for the police and District Attorney during and in connection with defendant's arrest, interrogation, detention and custody prior to arraignment, including but not limited to those police forms UF61, UF6 and DD5. . . ." *People v. Powell,* 49 Misc2d 624, 626. *Cf. U.S. v. Manhattan Brush Co.,* 38 FRD 4; *People v. Gunner,* 21 AD2d 900, 251 NYS2d 1001, affd 15 NY2d 226, 257 NYS2d 924, 205 NE2d 852.

**§ 145. Tangibles.** Only tangibles which are admissible in evidence may, in the court's discretion, be inspected pretrial by the defendant.

A weapon is a tangible. Thus, as noted above, a pistol with defendant's fingerprints on it may be inspected, but mere surmise that defendant's fingerprints are on the weapon is not sufficient to authorize the examination. *People v. Gatti,* 167 Misc 545. *Cf. U.S. v. Rich,* 6 Alas 670, where an examination of a glass with fingerprints was denied because of the absence of express statutory authority or precedent authorizing the inspection.

In *People v. Miller,* 42 Misc2d 794, 796, 797, defendants, charged with the crime of abortion, were permitted to examine visually instruments in the possession of the district attorney which were allegedly used. Although there is no statutory authority for this pretrial discovery, the court noted there is ample case law for supporting the defendant's request. Additionally, the court said:

> "Where there is evidence in the possession or control of the prosecution which is of such a nature that may require lengthy inspection and examination by experts to determine whether it is favorable to the accused, the court will afford to the accused an adequate opportunity, pretrial, to examine the evidence in the interest of justice and to avoid delay at the trial."

Nor need defendant show in advance that the records sought will in fact prove to be favorable to him. *People v. Powell,* 49 Misc2d 624.

*Miller, supra,* observed that no general rule can be enunciated as to pretrial inspection of tangibles but each case must be decided on its own facts. However, certain guidelines are applicable in making this decision: (1) will the pretrial discovery further the ends of justice, *i.e.,* is there evidence that "fundamental requirements of fairness" demand the relief; (2) will the pretrial discovery assist the trier of "the facts in making a more accurate determination of the facts in issue."

Narcotics allegedly seized from the defendant come within this category. Thus, a chemical analysis by defendant's chemist, of narcotics, sought pretrial, was authorized, but with certain safeguards to protect the People's interests, in a case involving a narcotic's sale. *People v. Perrell,* 47 Misc2d 1024, 263 NYS2d 640.

**§ 146. Books, Records and Documents.** One of the great areas of contention in pretrial discovery involves the inspection by defendant of books, records and documents.

As Chief Judge Cardoza said in *Lemon v. Supreme Court,* 245 NY at 24, 32, there is no statutory authority for permitting discovery and inspection by a defendant in a criminal case, but the courts might have inherent power "to compel the discovery of documents in furtherance of justice." This view has been followed. *See: People v. Christiano,* 53 Misc2d 433; *People v. Roldan,* 42 Misc2d 501; *People v. Powell,* 49 Misc2d 624.

It must be borne in mind that the right to examine books, records and documents pretrial must not be confused with the right to examine these items during trial.

**§ 147. Autopsy Reports—Medical Reports—Special Tests.** An autopsy report in a homicide case, comes within this category. *People v. Higgins,* 21 Misc2d 94, 95.

In a case where defendant was charged with driving while intoxicated and vehicular homicide, and where a comparatively long period of time elapsed between the accident and the death of the decedent, the medical issue raised as to causal relationship was vital to the defense. Pretrial discovery and inspection of the hospital records of the decedent was authorized, as the medical examiner stated that the cause of death was massive pulmonary embolus that might well have been formed from causes unrelated to the injury. *People v. Christiano,* 53 Misc2d 433, 278 NYS2d 696.

The People are not entitled to invoke physician-patient privilege to preclude a defendant from discovering hospital records. *People v. Christiano, supra; Matter of Silver v. Sobel,* 7 AD2d 728, 180 NYS2d 699; *cf.* CPLR § 4504.

But, a defendant is not entitled to pretrial discovery of hospital records and physician's reports in a criminal prosecution for grand larceny, robbery and assault. *People v. Johnson,* 55 Misc2d 185.

A defendant has no right to pretrial discovery of the People's evidence. *Lemon v. Supreme Court, supra.*

Thus, the results of a chemical analysis made by the People's chemist in a narcotics case are not subject to pretrial discovery even though the defendant is permitted to make an independent chemical analysis of the substance. *People v. Perrell,* 47 Misc2d 1024, 263 NYS2d 640.

However, as noted above, in *Kelly v. U.S.,* 420 F2d 26, where a new testing method was employed by the government in analyzing narcotics, the defendant was entitled to pretrial discovery of that test to enable him to check its reliability.

## § 148. Matters as to Which Discovery Is Not Authorized.

**§ 148.01. Hearsay.** Statements by others which are hearsay and inadmissible at the trial are not subject to inspection.

*People v. Higgins,* 21 Misc2d 94, case No. 1. Nor are documents in the possession of the district attorney which are themselves inadmissible in evidence. *Lemon, supra.*

Disclosure of transcribed statements taken from a codefendant was not allowed on the defendant's application, on the ground that the codefendant's statements were not competent evidence in support of the defense of the moving party, the defendant. *People v. Torres,* 46 Misc2d 264.

In *People v. Friedberg,* NYLJ, 5/3/65, p. 19, col. 7, defendant moved for an order directing the People to submit to his attorneys for examination miniphone recordings made by the victim when he spoke with the defendant. This was held to be nothing more than a request to compel the People to disclose its evidence in advance of trial. "This the court will not do—not even in the form of a bill of particulars (*People v. Spina,* 14 A.D.2d 505)." The court continued: "Such an examination cannot be equated with the examination which a court may grant of a defendant's statement made to a police officer or assistant district attorney after his arrest in the absence of counsel, or under other circumstances where the issue of the voluntariness of the statement is claimed."

Articles in possession of the prosecution which are items of incriminatory evidence are likewise precluded. *People v. Gatti,* 167 Misc 545; *Wendling v. Commonwealth,* 134 Ky 587.

§ 148.02. **Fishing Expeditions.** Where it appears that the motion for discovery is to indulge in a fishing expedition into the People's evidence, the application will be denied. *People v. Higgins,* 21 Misc2d 94, case No. 2; *People v. Gatti, supra; Lemon v. Supreme Court, supra; People v. Friedberg, supra.*

§ 148.03. **Premises and Witnesses.** Defendant was held to have no right to pretrial inspection of premises where the offense is alleged to have taken place, or of pretrial examination of the People's witnesses. An order to inspect the premises would violate the Fourth Amendment rights of its occupants. The witnesses, whose examination was requested, were not in custody and therefore had a right to speak or to remain silent, as they chose. *People v. Bradford,* 54 Misc2d 54, 281 NYS2d 480.

**§ 148.04 Confessions.** Some New York courts authorize pretrial inspection of a defendant's confession. They base this decision on the admonition of the Supreme Court in *Cicenia v. Lagay,* 357 US 504, that it is the "better practice" to permit defendant to see it. These courts also indicate that if there is a voluntariness hearing, the defendant will see the confession pretrial in any event. *See: People v. Quarles,* 44 Misc2d 955, 963–964; *People v. Harvin,* 46 Misc2d 417, 420; *People v. Abbatiello,* 46 Misc2d 148.

However, in *People v. Nero,* 59 Misc2d 645, 300 NYS2d 223, the court held that the defendant was not entitled to inspect his confession prior to the time the district attorney serves notice that he intends to use that statement at the defendant's trial. *See also: People v. Dubard,* 52 Misc2d 244; CPL art. 710.

**§ 148.05. Entrapment Cases.** Although the general rule precludes disclosure of the identity of the People's witnesses, the rule has been held modified in an entrapment case. *People v. Chambers,* 56 Misc2d 683, 289 NYS2d 804. In *Chambers,* the court held that where the defense is entrapment the defendant is entitled to the disclosure of the names of police officers who worked with the informant as well as to information about the course of dealings with the informant, in order to permit the defendant to prepare his defense (citing *Lemon v. Supreme Court,* 245 NY 24).

**§ 148.06. Probation Reports.** A defendant in a criminal case is not entitled to receive a copy of the probation report upon request, although the judge will use it as an aid in sentencing. CPL §§ 390.30, 390.50, 390.60. Access of defendant to the probation report is a matter of discretion with the sentencing judge.

There is no denial of due process when the court used the probation report as an aid to sentence, which was based upon information supplied by witnesses with whom the accused had not been confronted and as to whom he had no opportunity for cross-examination or rebuttal. *People v. Peace,* 18 NY2d 230, 232–233, 219 NE2d 419, citing *Williams v. New York,* 337 US 241, 243. *See also: People v. Leipzig,* 23 AD2d 854.

**§ 149. Discovery and Inspection During Trial.** During trial, the defendant has a right to examine prior statements of the People's witnesses, whether oral, written or otherwise recorded, to impeach, contradict or to show recent fabrication. *People v. Rosario,* 9 NY2d 286, 173 NE2d 881; *People v. Malinsky,* 15 NY2d 86, 90, 204 NE2d 188. The rule in *Malinsky* states:

> "[D]efense counsel must be permitted to examine a witness' prior statement, whether or not it differs from his testimony on the stand, and to decide for themselves the use to be made of it on cross-examination, *provided only* that the statement 'relates to the subject matter of the witness' testimony and contains nothing that must be kept confidential'. . . ."

"Prior statements" include grand jury testimony and notes, memoranda and reports made by the People's witness which have been adopted by them. *Malinsky, supra.*

Although the People are required to have grand jury minutes available for the defendant's inspection at the trial, in New York the question has arisen as to who must pay for them. In a sharply divided decision, the New York Court of Appeals has ruled that, absent a showing of indigency, the defendant is required to pay for the transcription of grand jury testimony. Absent payment, the defendant cannot be heard to complain that the minutes were not available for his use in cross-examining the witness. *People v. Jaglom,* 17 NY2d 162, 216 NE2d 576.

**§ 149.01. Statements of Defense Witnesses.** The court indicated in *People v. Regina,* 19 NY2d 65, 224 NE2d 108, that the right to discovery by the defendant during trial applied only to the People's witnesses. Thus, a statement given to the prosecution by one of the defendant's alibi witnesses was properly withheld from the defendant who requested inspection after the witness had testified. In this case, the People did not impeach the witness. The court said: "In the present case, we perceive no ground whatever upon which defense counsel could have employed the statement. . . . It could not have been used to impeach appellant's *own* witnesses." 19 NY2d at 76.

On the other hand, the People have the right to inspect statements made by defendant's witnesses. Such examination does not involve any element of self-incrimination as far as the defendant is concerned. That rule of self-incrimination applies only to evidence of a testimonial or communicative nature obtained from the defendant himself. *Schmerber v. California,* 384 US 757, 761.

While the defendant has the right to inspect statements made by the People's witnesses for the purpose of cross-examination in an attempt to impeach them (*People v. Rosario,* 9 NY2d 286, 173 NE2d 881), the same rule is applicable to the People as to witnesses who testified on behalf of the defendant.

> "These statements were not those of the defendant but of witnesses offered by the defendant. In no sense can it be said that he is being compelled to produce incriminating statments of his own. The privilege against self incrimination applies only to evidence of a testimonial or communicative nature obtained from the defendant himself (*Schmerber* v. *California,* 384 U.S. 757, 761; . . .)." *People v. Damon,* 24 NY2d 256, 261, 247 NE2d 651.

**§ 149.02. Statements Made During a Preliminary Examination.** Statements made by a witness during a preliminary examination would constitute a "prior statement" under the *Rosario* rule, even though the examination held before a committing magistrate is not technically a trial. The "hearing" referred to in *People v. Malinsky,* 15 NY2d at 90, 204 NE2d 188, refers to a hearing on a motion to suppress.

In *People v. Anderson,* 16 NY2d 282, 288, 213 NE2d 445, the court defined "trial" saying:

> " 'It may be given a meaning broad enough to include the examination of criminal cases by a court in all their stages.' (*People ex rel. Steckler* v. *Warden,* 259 N.Y. 430, 432–433.) Such is the rule where questions of fact are to be determined."

The purpose of this rule is to enable the defendant to impeach the People's witness if he can. Once the People have rested their case, it is too late to request the testimony of the People's witnesses before the grand jury. It was held, accordingly, that the trial court did not commit error when it denied defendant's request for access to its witnesses' testimony before the grand jury under the circumstances. *People v. Bolster,* 24 AD2d 774.

§ 149.03. **Mandatory Disclosure.** As noted above (§ 137.08, Federal Rule 16(g)), there is a continuing duty on the People to disclose to the defendant evidence which would tend to exculpate him or mitigate his sentence. *Brady v. Maryland,* 373 US 83.

§ 149.04. **The General Rule.** The suppression by the prosecution of evidence favorable to an accused upon request violates due process if the evidence is material to guilt or punishment, irrespective of the good faith of the prosecutor. *Brady v. Maryland,* 373 US 83. "We have noted that this requirement has been stated not to be a *sine qua non* (*United States* v. *Wilkins,* 326 F.2d 135). On the other hand, we cannot believe that it is the law that every statement by a person interviewed by the District Attorney must be disclosed to the defendant regardless of its materiality or probable veracity merely because the defense, after the event, claims that it might have made use of it. . . . Nor do we believe that any such all-embracing rule has been enunciated. . . . Rather, we think the true test of what must be disclosed is that of simple fairness." *People v. Fein,* 24 AD2d 32, 40, affd 18 NY2d 162, 173–176.

§ 150. **Police and Prosecutor Equated.** It is not infrequent in criminal prosecutions to promise a codefendant leniency if he testifies for the People against another defendant, and when he testifies, to deny that he had been promised leniency in exchange for his testimony.

When such a situation develops at a trial, it is a violation of due process when the prosecutor remains silent in the face of false testimony and fails to correct the record. And it matters not whether the promise was made by a police officer or the prosecutor. Disclosure is required in either case.

> "A promise by the police or a different prosecutor is a promise which even if not known to the trial prosecutor violates due process if not revealed." *People v. Yamin,* 45 Misc2d 407, 415; *see: People v. Fein,* 18 NY2d 162, 219 NE2d 274.

The *Fein* decision is in line with the decision in *U.S. v. Tomaiolo,* 378 F2d 26, which also follows the rule in *State v. Giles,* 212 A2d 101, 108, and *Griffin v. U.S.,* 183 F2d 990, revd and rem 336 US 704.

As in *Fein, Tomaiolo* also held that suppression of evidence by a federal prosecutor did not violate due process where the evidence was wholly lacking in probative force because of its speculative quality, since a grand jury witness had not testified that a third party told him who the second robber was, nor did the witness in any way explain his surmise that a person other than the defendant was the man.

**§ 151. Error in Identification.** Similarly, in *People v. Ahmed,* 20 NY2d 958, 233 NE2d 854, it was error for the district attorney not to have notified the defense either before or during defendant's trial that the robbery victim on the night of the robbery was unable to identify the defendant from a police photograph.

**§ 152. Perjury.** The prosecution must reveal to a defendant testimony of a People's witness that is perjured, even if the perjury is elicited by the defense. *People v. Savvides,* 1 NY2d 554, 136 NE2d 853; *Napue v. Illinois,* 360 US 264; *People v. Yamin, infra.* This type of perjury is most frequently found in those cases where a material witness for the prosecution denies that he has been promised leniency in exchange for his testimony, when, in fact, such a promise had been made. *People v. Yamin,* 45 Misc2d 407.

In all disclosure cases, it must be noted that state courts are bound by United States Supreme Court decisions where due process (*e.g.,* mandatory disclosures and basic constitutional rights) are involved. *See: Malloy v. Hogan,* 378 US 1.

**§ 153. Juveniles: Waiver of Jurisdiction of Juvenile Court.** Under a District of Columbia statute, where a juvenile contests waiving jurisdiction of the Juvenile Court to the District Court, he is entitled to a hearing on the validity of the waiver order. This right to a hearing includes access by his counsel to the social records and probation and similar reports which presumably are considered by the court. *Kent v. U.S.,* 383 US 541, 557. Where the juvenile moves for a hearing, it is error not to grant it. 383 US at 561, 562.

Due process requires that on demand, the respondent in a juvenile delinquency proceeding is entitled to pretrial discovery in the form of a bill of particulars. *In re Edgar,* 66 Misc2d 142, 320 NYS2d 570.

# Chapter 9

# DISTINCTION BETWEEN SEARCH AND SEIZURE



---

## § 161. In General.

> "But the authority to search cannot be confused with the authority to seize. It cannot be confused with the power to use seized articles in evidence. . . . The distinction has never been more carefully drawn than in the language used by Mr. Justice Miller in the concurring opinion in the case of *Boyd v. United States,* 116 U.S. 616, 641. . . . It is there he said:
>
> " 'The searches meant by the constitution were such as led to seizure when the search was successful.'
>
> "And again: 'The things here forbidden are two: search and seizure.' " *Takahashi v. U.S.,* 143 F2d 118, 123.

There is a difference between "searches and seizures" and "seizures." "Seizures" are not prohibited by the Constitution. A gun or other contraband, found on the street or other public place, may be picked up. This is a "seizure." There is no invasion of privacy involved, such as is proscribed by the Fourth Amendment. The exclusionary rule under the Amendment is not involved in such a situation nor is the issue of "probable" cause applicable.

Protective custody of property held for the rightful owner may also constitute a "seizure." *People v. Manzi,* 21 AD2d 57, 248 NYS2d 306.

In *U.S. v. Lipscomb,* 435 F2d 795, it was held that an inventory of the personal property of the defendant which was taken while being booked in the police station, did not constitute a search.

Thus, an automobile key found on his person was used to open his car. In doing so to check the car's identification number, it was disclosed that the vehicle had been stolen. Obtaining the automobile's identification under these circumstances did not constitute an unlawful search and seizure.

§ 161.01. **Seizure by Trespass.** If for example, a policeman observes a pistol on private premises, and in order to seize it, he must enter the premises without a warrant, he becomes a trespasser. The seizure is unlawful and the contraband may not be used in evidence against the possessor. *People v. DeLeo,* 12 NY2d 913, 188 NE2d 402 (bookmaking); *People v. Adorno,* 37 Misc2d 36 (drugs); *People v. Caliente,* 12 NY2d 89 (bookmaking); *People v. Jordan,* 37 Misc2d 33 (pistol); *People v. Anthony,* 21 AD2d 666, 249 NYS2d 997; *People v. Mangino,* 236 NYS2d 439; *People v. Kramer,* 239 NYS2d 303; *People v. Ryan,* 14 AD2d 926, 222 NYS2d 92; *People v. Wieczorek,* 16 AD2d 1025, 229 NYS2d 1021; *cf: Abel v. U.S.,* 362 US 217; *Hester v. U.S.,* 265 US 57; *People v. Sperber,* 40 Misc2d 13.

Contraband in plain view, while the police are lawfully upon the premises, may be seized. *Hester v. U.S.,* 265 US 57; *U.S. v. Barone,* 330 F2d 543; *California v. Hurst,* 325 F2d 891; *People v. Jordan, supra.*

Trespassing in the hope of obtaining evidence of probable cause to conduct a search, will render a subsequent arrest and search unlawful. *McDonald v. U.S.,* 335 US 451; *Mattingly v. Comm.,* 247 SW 938; *People v. Woodward,* 183 NW 901.

In *U.S. v. Conti,* 361 F2d 153, the defendant argued that IRS agents who obtained evidence of probable cause to obtain a search warrant did so by trespassing. The alleged trespass took place by making observations of defendant's apartment from a public hallway which was intended to be kept locked and which could be opened only by a tenant's key or by buzzer from tenants. It was contended that this corridor space was protected and semi-private, and when entered without a tenant's consent, a trespass resulted. In rejecting this contention, the court explained:

> "However, the Supreme Court in *McDonald* [335 US 451] did not hold that officials could not peaceably enter common corridors and hallways in a multiple dwelling in the course of a surveillance. In that case, the police gained

entrance to the building by climbing through the landlady's window, and intruded upon the defendant's right of privacy before arresting him by peering through his transom. More recent cases have indicated that peaceable entry which works a technical trespass is permissible in order to gather evidence indicating probable cause, so long as the trespass does not impinge upon some area protected by the Fourth Amendment. United States v. Buchner, 164 F. Supp. 836 (D.D.C.), aff'd per curiam, 268 F.2d 891 (D.C. Cir. 1958), cert. denied, 359 U.S. 908, [citations omitted] (1959); see United States v. St. Clair, 240 F. Supp. 338 (S.D.N.Y. 1965). . . . It follows from *Buchner* and *Miguel* [*U.S. v. Miguel,* 340 F2d 812, cert. denied 382 US 859 (1965)] that the peaceable entry here involved, although perhaps a technical trespass, did not vitiate the surveillance evidence tending to establish probable cause." *United States v. Conti,* 361 F2d at 157.

**§ 162. Mere Seizure and Open View Doctrines.** In *People v. White,* NYLJ, 3/22/65, p. 17, col. 7, Judge Sobel stated with respect to mere seizures:

> "If police observe contraband through an open window within private premises, unless they have a search warrant or can make a lawful arrest of a possessor, they may not enter and seize. This would be a general search.
>
> "The 'mere seizure' doctrine is not to be confused with the 'open view' doctrine. The latter is strictly a probable cause issue in the incidental search area. . . . But under the 'open view' doctrine, it is held that what is observed in 'open view' by the police without a search may furnish the probable cause for an arrest, an[d] incidental search and seizure of the property previously observed." Citing *Hester v. U.S.,* 265 US 57; *U.S. v. Barone,* 330 F2d 543; *David v. U.S.,* 327 F2d 301; *People v. McCracken,* 35 Ill 2d 425, 197 NE2d 35; *People v. Cove,* 39 Cal Rptr 535.
>
> "[A] 'mere seizure' is the 'finding' of property upon a public street or public place rather than upon the person or within private premises. No issue of arrest or probable cause is ever involved in a 'mere seizure'. . . . Obvi-

ously, the 'mere seizure' cases which do reach the courts are those which can be evidentially connected. Almost invariably, these cases are the 'discarding' or 'dropping' cases in the presence of the police." *People v. White, supra.*

*People v. Swanberg,* 22 AD2d 902, affd as modified 16 NY2d 649, 209 NE2d 122, is an example of a "seizure" as distinguished from a "search and seizure." In that case, the police had information that stolen clothing would be found in a detached garage which the defendant had leased. The owner permitted the police to look into the garage through its loose-fitting doors. The police observed 310 suits of clothing, "merchandise that was obviously stolen." The owner broke the lock on the doors and permitted the officers to enter and seize the suits. The court held that looking through the apertures of the loosely hung garage doors and seeing clothing which had obviously been stolen did not constitute an unlawful search. It also held that the police entry into the garage was not for the purpose of searching for the stolen suits (*cf. Chapman v. U.S.,* 365 US 610) but to seize them—a lawful act. *See also: People v. Manzi,* 38 Misc2d 114, affd 21 AD2d 57; *U.S. v. Jankowski,* 28 F2d 800; *Busby v. U.S.,* 296 F2d 328, cert. den. 369 US 876.

Where the police enter private premises without a warrant, for the purpose of acquiring the fruits of a crime (contraband) after following the defendants into the premises, the acquisition constitutes a seizure and not a search. In this type of case (*People v. Ray, et al,* 26 AD2d 560, 271 NYS2d 453), the court followed the reasoning in *Swanberg, supra.*

In the *Ray* case, acting on information suplied by a reliable informant, the police observed the defendants carrying more than 10 television sets into the home of one of them at 1:30 A.M. Two were known to the police to have been involved previously with stolen TV sets. (*See: People v. Teams,* 20 AD2d 803, 248 NYS2d 477.) When approached by the police all attempted to flee. Entering the home was held to have been for the purpose of obtaining the TV sets. As in *Swanberg,* the police knew that the stolen articles were in the premises.

They entered to seize and not to search. *See also: People v. Manzi, supra; Ker v. California* 374 US 23.

In *People v. Jewett,* NYLJ, 3/30/65, p. 17, col. 5, the police, without committing a trespass, observed narcotics and a hypodermic needle through apertures in a door. Under these facts, it was held a crime had been committed in the presence of the officers.

§ 163. **Police Entry by Ruse.** *Jewett, supra,* raised other interesting and concomitant questions. After their observations, the officers obtained entry into the premises by misrepresentations. This was held to be a legally permissible subterfuge. *See: People v. Lawery,* 43 Misc2d 1084, 252 NYS2d 823; *Benson v. California,* 336 F2d 79, cert. den. 380 US 951. As the court said in *Leahy v. United States,* 272 F2d 487, 490, "There is no constitutional mandate forbidding the use of deception in executing a valid arrest warrant."

Observing things in public places, either by use of natural or artificial light does not constitute a search. *People v. Jordan,* 37 Misc2d 33. "A search implies a prying into hidden places." *People v. West,* 300 P2d 729, 733.

# Chapter 10

## REASONABLE SEARCH AND SEIZURE



---

**§ 167. In General.** The Fourth Amendment reads:

> "The right of the people to be secure in their persons, houses, papers and effects, against unreasonable searches and seizures, shall not be violated, and no Warrants shall issue but upon probable cause, supported by Oath or affirmation, and particularly describing the place to be searched, and the person or things to be seized."

The Amendment covers all constitutionally protected areas and these are spelled out in its language. Thus, a package comes within the terms "papers and effects" and is deemed immune from unreasonable searches and seizures within the ambit of the Fourth Amendment. *See: Corngold v. U.S.,* 367 F2d 1, 7.

> "Since the delivery of a package to a common carrier does not forfeit one's right of privacy thereto (see *Ex Parte Jackson,* 96 U.S. 727, 733; *Santana* v. *United States,* 329 F.2d 854, 856; *Oliver* v. *United States,* 239 F.2d 818, 820–821), the fact that the package of marijuana claimed by defendant was in the custody of the Railway Express at an airport does not deprive him [the defendant] of standing to assert an invasion of his privacy in the package opened by Detective Tobin." *People v. Sanders,* 277 NYS2d 487, 489, 52 Misc2d 989, 991.

The Amendment does not concern itself with seizures per se, but with searches and the concomitant seizure. The Amendment contains two clauses. The first clause interdicts the "unreasonable search and seizure." This is aimed at guaranteeing one's privacy against unlawful intrusion by government agents. The second clause states that a search is reasonable, if executed pursuant to a lawful search warrant.

Unfortunately, the term "unreasonable search and seizure" is not defined in the Amendment, nor is the relationship between these two clauses explained. These ambiguities have resulted in much protracted litigation over the intent, meaning and implementation of the Amendment, especially since *Mapp v. Ohio,* 367 US 643, was decided in 1961.

**§ 167.01. Places of Business and Exceptions to Search Warrant Requirement.** One's place of business is also protected.

> "A person's office or place of business is quite as immune from search without a warrant as his kitchen or bedroom." *U.S. v. DiCorvo,* 37 F2d 124, 132. *See also: Silverthorne Lumber Co. v. U.S.,* 251 US 385; *Go-Bart Importing Co. v. U.S.,* 282 US 344; *U.S. v. Lefkowitz,* 285 US 452.

There is an exception, however, as to places of business open to the public:

> "[A] private business whose doors are open to the public is also to be considered open to entry by the police for any proper purpose not violative of the owner's constitutional rights—e.g., patronizing the place or surveying to promote law and order or to suppress a breach of the peace." *State v. LaDuca,* 89 NJ Super 159, 214 A2d 423, 426.

If, on such an entry, they observe a crime being committed in their presence, they may arrest the offender and conduct a search incidental thereto. This incidental search may encompass "as much of the place as is under the control of the arrestee to find and seize things used to carry on the unlawful enterprise." *State v. LaDuca, supra; also see: Smith v. U.S.,* 353 F2d 877; *People v. Reshes,* 39 Misc2d 723; *Smith v. U.S.,* 105 F2d 778; *cf. Chimel v. California,* 395 US 752.

In the early cases, the Supreme Court itself had interpreted the Amendment to mean that any search without a warrant was unlawful. *See: Boyd v. U.S.,* 116 US 616, 641; *Gouled v. U.S.,* 255 US 298, 308.

Nevertheless, the rule today is that all searches and seizures are unreasonable, if conducted without a search warrant, unless the search and seizure comes within the ambit of certain recognized exceptions.

As the Supreme Court stated in *Katz v. U.S.,* 389 US 347, 357: "[S]earches conducted outside the judicial process, without prior approval by judge or magistrate, are *per se* unreasonable under the Fourth Amendment—subject only to a few specifically established and well-delineated exceptions." In footnote 19 at page 357 the court noted some of these exceptions: *Carroll v. U.S.,* 267 US 132, 153, 156; *McDonald v. U.S.,* 335 US 451, 454–456; *Brinegar v. U.S.,* 338 US 160; *Cooper v. California,* 386 US 58; *Warden v. Hayden,* 387 US 294, 298–300.

Other exceptions are:

(1) A search on consent. *Bumper v. North Carolina,* 391 US 543; *Amos v. U.S.,* 255 US 313. *See: Chapter 15, infra.*

(2) A search incident to a lawful arrest. *Chimel v. California,* 395 US 752; *People v. Loria,* 10 NY2d 368, 179 NE2d 478. *See: Chapter 14, infra.*

(3) A search of a vehicle, where probable cause exists for the belief that the vehicle contains contraband. *Brinegar v. U.S.,* 338 US 160, 175–176; *Carroll v. U.S.,* 267 US 132, 161. *See: Chaper 21, infra.*

(4) A search under the "stop and frisk" rule. *Terry v. Ohio,* 392 US 1; *People v. Rivera,* 14 NY2d 441, 201 NE2d 32, cert. den. 379 US 978. *See: Chapter 19, infra.*

(5) A search of impounded vehicles and property subject to forfeiture. *Cooper v. California,* 386 US 58, *Abrams v. State,* 223 Ga 216, 154 SE2d 443. *See: Chapter 21, infra.*

(6) A search conducted in the course of a "hot pursuit." *Warden v. Hayden,* 387 US 294. *See: Chapter 18, infra.*

(7) A search conducted in an emergency situation or

under exceptional circumstances. *Terry v. Ohio, supra; Schmerber v. California,* 384 US 757; *McDonald v. U.S.,* 335 US 451; *Johnson v. U.S.,* 333 US 10; *People v. Taggart,* 20 NY2d 335, 229 NE2d 581; *State v. Gosser,* 50 NJ 438, 236 A2d 377; *People v. Johnson* 48 Misc2d 907. *See: Chapter 18, infra.*

(8) A search of an open field even if private property. *Hester v. U.S.,* 265 US 57; *People v. LaRosa,* 25 AD2d 587. *See: Chapter 17, infra.*

(9) A search of abandoned property. *Abel v. U.S.,* 362 US 217; *People v. Anderson,* 24 NY2d 12. *See: Chapter 17, infra.*

(10) Searches conducted by United States Customs officers. *Thomas v. U.S.,* 372 F2d 252; *Murgia v. U.S.,* 285 F2d 14; *People v. Furey,* 42 Misc2d 579, 248 NYS2d 460. *See: Chapter 16, infra.*

(11) Searches of United States mails. *Webster v. U.S.,* 92 F2d 462; 39 USC §§ 903, 904; *U.S. v. Costello,* 255 F2d 876. *See: § 249, infra.*

(12) Searches by Officers of the Immigration and Naturalization Service. 39 USC § 1357. *See: Chapter 16, infra.*

(13) Searches and seizures by private persons. *Burdeau v. McDowell,* 256 US 465; *Sackler v. Sackler,* 15 NY2d 40, 203 NE2d 481. *See: § 14, supra.*

**§ 167.02. The Right to Search: Summary of General Rules.** A search and seizure under a lawful warrant is sanctioned under both the Federal and New York State Constitutions. U.S. Const. amend. IV; N.Y. Const. art. 1, § 12.

On the other hand, a warrant is not a *sine qua non* to a lawful search (*U.S. v. Rabinowitz,* 339 US 56; *cf. Chimel v. California,* 395 US 752), and in an absolute sense all searches and seizures in a constitutionally protected area, without a warrant, are not inviolable.

In the following instances, warrantless searches have been judicially sanctioned.

(1) Search with consent. *U.S. v. Mitchell,* 322 US 65; *People v. D'Iorio,* 16 NY2d 551, 208 NE2d 465; *Amos v. U.S.,* 255 US 313; *People v. Russell,* 33 Misc2d 851, 227 NYS2d 826; *cf. Johnson v. U.S.,* 333 US 10. *See: Chapter 15, infra.*

(2) Search incident to a lawful arrest. *Cooper v. California,* 386 US 58; *U.S. v. Rabinowitz,* 339 US 56; *Harris v. U.S.,* 331 US 145; *Agnello v. U.S.,* 269 US 20; *cf.: Preston v. California,* 376 US 364; *Chimel v. California,* 395 US 752. *See: Chapter 14, infra.*

(a) "Probable cause" and informers. *Draper v. U.S.,* 358 US 307; *People v. Solomine,* 18 NY2d 477; *McCray v. Illinois,* 386 US 300; *Brinegar v. U.S.,* 338 US 160. *See: Chapter 24, infra.*

(3) A search of a vehicle where probable cause exists to believe that it contains contraband. *Carroll v. U.S.,* 267 US 132; *Brinegar v. U.S., supra. See: Chapter 21, infra.*

(4) A search conducted as an administrative inspection authorized by law, under the police powers of government for the promotion of safety, health or morals, such as inspections of dwellings, factories, food establishments, etc., requires a search warrant. *Frank v. Maryland,* 359 US 360, overruled by *See v. Seattle,* 387 US 541; *Camara v. Municipal Court,* 387 US 523. *See: Chapter 16, infra.*

(5) A search incident to a lawful administrative arrest, as distinguished from an arrest for a crime, such as an arrest for deportation under an administrative warrant. *Abel v. U.S.,* 362 US 217. *See: Chapter 16, infra.*

(6) A search of an open field even though it is private property. *Hester v. U.S.,* 265 US 57; *People v. LaRosa,* 25 AD2d 587. *See: Chapter 17, infra.*

(7) Search of abandoned property. *Abel v. U.S., supra; Hester v. U.S., supra. See: Chapter 17, infra.*

(8) "Border" searches, *i.e.,* those executed by U.S. Customs officers at ports of entry into the United States. *Alexander v. U.S.,* 362 F2d 379; *Blefare v. U.S.,* 362 F2d 870; *People v. Searbie,* 273 NYS2d 965; *Landau v. U.S.,* 82 F2d 285. *See: Chapter 16, infra.*

(9) Searches under the "Stop and Frisk" law. CPL § 140.50; *People v. Pugach,* 15 NY2d 65; *U.S. v. Lewis,* 362 US 759; *People v. Horman,* 29 AD2d 569, 286 NYS2d 642, affd 22 NY2d 378, 292 NYS2d 874, 239 NE2d 625, cert. den. 393 US 1057, 89 SC 698; *cf. Wainwright v. New Orleans,* 248 La 1097, 184 So2d 23, cert. granted, 385 US 1001, cert. vacated 392 US 598; as to right to "stop and frisk" under the common law, *see: People v. Rivera,* 14 NY2d 441, 201 NE2d 32; *Terry v. Ohio, supra. See: Chapter 19, infra.*

(10) Search under exigent circumstances, *i.e.,* where prompt police action is required including breaking and entering into constitutionally protected area, without a warrant, for the purpose of rescuing a victim in peril or to prevent the destruction of vital evidence. *U.S. v. Barone,* 330 F2d 543; *Wong Sun v. U.S.,* 371 US 471; *Wayne v. U.S.,* 318 F2d 205, cert. den. 375 US 860; *People v. Johnson,* 48 Misc2d 907; *State v. Puryear,* 227 A2d 139; *People v. Gallmon,* 19 NY2d 389, 227 NE2d 284, cert. den. 390 US 911. *See: Chapter 18, infra.*

(11) An unreasonable or unlawful search by a private person does not come within the ambit of the Fourth Amendment. *Burdeau v. McDowell,* 256 US 465; *Sackler v. Sackler,* 15 NY2d 40, 203 NE2d 481; *People v. Horman, supra. See: § 14, supra.*

## Chapter 11

# PROBABLE CAUSE



**§ 170. In General.** The general rule is that proof of the existence of probable cause is an essential predicate for the issuance of a valid search or arrest warrant, or for a lawful arrest without a warrant. This rule is of ancient origin. Although different fact situations have caused disagreement among the justices of the Supreme Court, as to the existence of probable cause they are, nevertheless, all in agreement that suspicion alone does not constitute probable cause. *Agnello v. U.S.,* 269 US 20, 33; *Jones v. U.S.,* 357 US 493, 497; *People v. Brown,* 24 NY2d 421, 423, 248 NE2d 867. In *Stacey v. Emery,* 97 US 642, 645, the first classic definition of probable cause was enunciated by that court,—to wit, probable cause is "facts & circumstances . . . such as to warrant a man of prudence and caution in believing that the offense has been [or is being] committed." Subsequently, in *Brinegar v. U.S.,* 338 US 160, 175, the court said, "In dealing with probable cause . . . as the very name implies, we deal with probabilities. These are not technical; they are the factual and practical considerations of every-day life on which reasonable and prudent men, not legal technicians, act." *See also: Carroll v. U.S.,* 267 US 132; *People v. Teams,* 20 AD2d 803, 804. Evidence to sustain a finding of probable cause need not be of such a nature as to be admissible at a defendant's trial. The two are distinct. *Brinegar, supra.* For example, on a hearing to determine probable cause hearsay evidence is admissible. *U.S. v. Ventresca,* 380 US 102, 111.

The issuance of a search warrant, absent probable cause, involves a violation of a constitutional right. The court may, therefore, vacate such a warrant before trial on a motion to controvert. *People v. Gatti,* 16 NY2d 251, 212 NE2d 51; *People v. Politano,* 17 AD2d 503, affd 13 NY2d 852, 192 NE2d 271.

The Court of Appeals as arbiter of constitutional questions must make an independent appraisal in determining if probable cause existed to issue the warrant. *People v. Fino,* 14 NY2d 160, 199 NE2d 151; *People v. Marshall,* 13 NY2d 28, 191 NE2d 798; *People v. Coscia,* 42 Misc2d 978, 250 NYS2d 308; *cf.: Woo Lai Chun v. U.S.,* 274 F2d 708; *U.S. v. Freeman,* 358 F2d 459.

"The People, in order to prevail, are under the necessity of going forward in the first instance with evidence to show that probable cause existed both in obtaining a search warrant and in sustaining the legality of the search made, without a warrant, as incident to an arrest." *People v. Malinsky,* 15 NY2d 86, n.2 at 91 and cases cited.

A valid warrant which was not executed within the statutory time may not be reissued on the basis of the original supporting affidavit because of the danger that the original probable cause factors may have become stale. *Sgro v. U.S.,* 287 US 206; *see also: People v. Kramer,* 38 Misc2d 889, 239 NYS2d 303.

The terms "reasonable grounds," "reason to believe," "reasonable cause" and "probable cause" are equated.

The substance of all definitions of probable cause is a reasonable ground for belief of guilt and lies between bare suspicion and evidence which would justify conviction. *McCarthy v. DeArmit,* 99 Pa 63; *People v. Gold,* 46 Misc2d 495, 499.

It must be emphasized that the underlying circumstances upon which the belief of probable cause rests must be spelled out. *U.S. v. Ventresca,* 380 US 102; *Aguilar v. Texas,* 378 US 108. Unless this is done, the issuing magistrate would, in effect become a rubber stamp for the police. The fact that the applicant for the warrant had sufficient facts and witnesses available who could have established "probable cause," does not validate the issuance of a warrant, where the supporting affidavit is not based on the affiant's personal knowledge, and does not disclose the source of his information or any indication of the reliability of his information. *People v. Gold, supra.* The "probable cause" must exist at the time of the application and the issuance of the warrant.

## § 171. Obtaining the Warrant.

**§ 171.01. Probable Cause.** As indicated above, to obtain a warrant, it must first be demonstrated that probable cause, as distinguished from mere suspicion, exists, that specified property, *i.e.,* fruits, instrumentalities, contraband or evidence of the commission of a crime, will be found in certain specified premises. *People v. Montanaro,* 34 Misc2d 624, 229 NYS2d 677; *U.S. v. Plemmons,* 336 F2d 731; *Aguilar v. Texas,* 378 US 108; *People v. Reinhardt,* 42 Misc2d 45, 247 NYS2d 708; *People v. Fino,* 14 NY2d 160, 199 NE2d 151; *Conti v. Morgenthau,* 232 F Supp 1004, affd 361 F2d 153, conviction vacated on other grounds, 390 US 204.

The term "probable cause" is equated with "reasonable grounds for belief." *Brinegar v. U.S.,* 338 US 160, 175; *Jones v. U.S.,* 362 US 257, 269; *U.S. v. Heitner,* 149 F2d 105, 106.

In *People v. Marshall,* 13 NY2d 28, 34, 191 NE2d 798, the court said: " 'It is enough if the apparent facts which have come to his [the officer's] attention are sufficient, in the cirsumstances, to lead a reasonably discreet and prudent man to believe that liquor is illegally possessed in the automobile to be searched' (*Husty* v. *United States,* 282 U.S. 694, 701)." Or, in general terms, "that the law is being violated on the premises to be searched (*Carroll* v. *United States,* 267 U.S. 132; *Dumbra* v. *United States,* 268 U.S. 435; *Aderhold* v. *United States,* 132 F.2d 858). It is not a matter for technical rules or tight and exact definition. The question always is: what in the common judgment of reasonable men would be regarded as good, sound cause, remembering that we seek only probable, not absolute cause?" *See also: Henry v. U.S.,* 361 US 98, 102.

The supporting affidavit may not rest upon mere suspicion, nor need it set forth sufficient facts to sustain a conviction.

The facts must rest somewhere between bare suspicion and convincing evidence of guilt. *McCarthy v. DeArmit,* 99 Pa 63; *Aguilar v. Texas, supra; People v. Rooks,* 35 Misc2d 598, 229 NYS2d 923; *People v. Perez,* 35 Misc2d 461, 229 NYS2d 882; *Brinegar v. U.S.,* 338 US 160; *Jones v. U.S.,* 362 US 257.

**§ 171.02. Perjury in Supporting Affidavit.** A warrant may be attacked if the supporting affidavit is perjurious, even though the warrant on its face establishes probable cause. A defendant has a right to try to establish perjury by the affiant police officer.

Thus, in a case where the police officer swore in his supporting affidavit that he had received information from an informer, and where, at the hearing on the motion, defendant elicited information from the officer that there had been wiretapping before the issuance of the warrant, defendant had the right to cross-examine further in his effort to establish that the wiretap was illegal.

> "The trial court cut off all questioning on this point without explanation when the prosecution objected that it was irrelevant on the issue of perjury. This clearly was error, as the perjury could be established indirectly by showing that the information which the police officer alleged he had obtained from an informant was in fact gained through a different source—an illegal wiretap." *People v. Munger,* 24 NY2d 445, 452, 248 NE2d 882.

Each case must rest on its own set of facts. *U.S. v. Ramirez,* 279 F2d 712, cert. den. 364 US 850.

Information obtained from an informant, together with the officer's independent observations, or together with other known facts, may establish "probable cause." *People v. Santiago,* 13 NY2d 326, 196 NE2d 881; *People v. Coffey,* 12 NY2d 443, 191 NE2d 263; *U.S. v. Plemmons, supra.*

**§ 171.03. Hearsay and the Supporting Affidavit.** A warrant may be issued where the affidavit is on "information and belief," providing the source of the information and the grounds of the belief are given. *Rugendorf v. U.S.,* 376 US 528; *U.S. v. Plemmons,* 336 F2d 731.

Probable cause cannot be established on "information and belief." Evidential facts must be set forth. *Marcus v. Search Warrants,* 367 US 717; *People v. Roth,* 207 Misc 875; *People v. Malinsky,* 15 NY2d 86, 204 NE2d 188. A mere allegation that an informant of known reliability had placed illegal wagers with a defendant is insufficient unless the dates the wagers were placed are set forth. *People v. Kramer,* 38 Misc2d 889, 239 NYS2d 303.

Where at least part of an affidavit submitted in support of an application for a search warrant is based on hearsay, a reviewing court should accord a preference toward sustaining the warrant (*Jones v. U.S.,* 362 US at 270), even though, on the same set of facts, the reviewing court would not find the existence of probable cause in a search conducted without a warrant. *U.S. v. Ventresca,* 380 US 102; *People v. Rogers,* 15 NY2d 422, 208 NE2d 168. This is undoubtedly based on the rule that, although a reasonable doubt on the facts should be resolved in favor of the defendant, *People v. Carpenito,* 292 NY 498, a reasonable doubt on the law should be resolved in favor of the People. *People v. Reed,* 276 NY 5.

In a subsequent ruling, the New York Court of Appeals in *People v. Williams,* 20 NY2d 388, 391, 229 NE2d 839, said that the issuance of a search warrant by a magistrate would be a factor of some weight in determining the question of probable cause, quoting *U.S. ex rel Rogers v. Warden,* 381 F2d 209, 216:

> "Once there has been a judicial determination of probable cause . . . it will not be handily overturned by an appellate court." *See also: Johnson v. U.S.,* 333 US 10, 13–14.

An information sworn to by a police officer stating that he had talked with the victim of an assault sufficiently states the sources of his knowledge as well as the ground for his belief that the defendant had committed a crime. Failure of the information to recite the substance of what the officer was told by the victim was not fatal. But, an information based on hearsay should recite the substance of what affiant was told. *People v. Tennyson,* 19 NY2d 573, 575, 227 NE2d 876; *cf. People v. Jeffries,* 19 NY2d 564, 567, 227 NE2d 870.

**§ 171.04. Establishing Probable Cause by Hearsay.** Hearsay statements in an affidavit do not render it insufficient, so long as there is a substantial basis for crediting the hearsay. *Rugendorf v. U.S.*, 376 US 528. An affidavit may not contain hearsay based on hearsay to supply probable cause. However, "Observations of fellow officers of the Government engaged in a common investigation are plainly a reliable basis for a warrant applied for by one of their number." *U.S. v. Ventresca,* 380 US 102, 111. *See also: Rugendorf v. U.S.*, 376 US 528; *Chin Kay v. U.S.*, 311 F2d 317; *U.S. v. McCormick,* 309 F2d 367; *Weise v. U.S.*, 251 F2d 867.

An unusual hearsay situation was presented in a case in Oregon. In *State v. Tacker,* 407 P2d 851, an affidavit supporting an application for a search warrant contained hearsay declarations of facts within the personal knowledge of an informant. The Supreme Court of Oregon held that the affidavit was sufficient to establish probable cause for the issuance of a valid search warrant.

The New York Court of Appeals, in *People v. Montague,* 19 NY2d 121, 122, 123, 125, 224 NE2d 873, has held that probable cause for the issuance of a search warrant, based upon information supplied by an undisclosed informant may be established absent personal observations of the officer, where:

(a) The magistrate is informed of circumstances leading the informant to conclude that the narcotics are where he claims they are, and from which the officer concludes that the informant's information is reliable.

(b) The credibility of the informant and the reliability of his information is established by the affiant's statement that the informant is known to him and has in the past furnished information leading to the arrest and conviction of others. *See, e.g., People v. Rogers,* 15 NY2d 422, 424, 208 NE2d 168.

(c) There are other methods by which the credibility or reliability of the informant may be established, such as observations of fellow officers of the government engaged in a common investigation. *People v. Montague, supra,* at 122–123, citing *U.S. v. Ventresca,* 380 US 102, 111.

(d) In a case in which the supporting affidavit spells out in detail circumstances from which a magistrate may independently determine that probable cause exists for the warrant to issue (*see: Aguilar v. Texas, supra,* pp. 114–115), *i.e.,* where the informant evidenced his truthfulness by telling a story which could with ease have been tested, coupled, apparently, with an admission against his, the informant's, penal interest. *People v. Montague, supra,* at 125. *See:* 5 Wigmore, *Evidence,* § 1457, pp. 262–263 (3rd ed. 1940).

As the dissenting opinion in *Montague* points out (Fuld, Ch. J.), test (d) is a dangerous one. "The majority find it significant that the informant had told 'a story which could with ease have been tested' (opinion of court, p. 125, supra). However, the simple fact is that not the slightest effort was made to test or verify the informant's account. In my view, it is both impermissible and dangerous to substitute the 'ease' or facility with which information could be checked for the actual investigation and corroboration itself. Since there is no guarantee that an informant who tells a guileless tale is being truthful and perceptive rather than spiteful and simple-minded, there is as much need to check his story as any other." 19 NY2d at 126. *See, e.g., Wong Sun v. U.S.,* 371 US 471, 480–482, 491; *Riggan v. Virginia,* 384 US 152.

**§ 171.05. The Informant of Known Reliability.** In *People v. McCall,* 17 NY2d 152, 216 NE2d 570, the New York Court of Appeals held that a warrant is as good as its supporting affidavit. *McCall* involved an ex parte wiretap order issued under statutory authority. That order was attacked for want of probable cause. It was held deficient in that its supporting affidavit contained conclusions, not facts. Where the source of the hearsay is a "person of known reliability," his identity need necessarily not be disclosed, yet some factual statement of the affiant's experience with his reliability and some factual showing of what he had revealed in the past are basic requirements. The rule requiring probable cause to be established for a search warrant is applicable to ex parte eavesdropping orders issued. *People v. Gold,* 46 Misc2d 495; *People v. Beshany,* 43 Misc2d 521 and cases cited.

The existence of probable cause depends upon the facts and the emphasis placed thereon. This often leads to divergent rules in the various jurisdictions. The U.S. Circuit Court of

Appeals for the Second Circuit differed from the New York Court of Appeals holding in the *McCall* case ruling that the uncorroborated hearsay of a previously reliable informant is a sufficient basis for the issuance of a search warrant. *U.S. v. Freeman,* 358 F2d 459. The Second Circuit relied on a literal interpretation of the language in *Jones v. U.S.,* 362 US 257, where the Supreme Court said that an affidavit based on hearsay is sufficient "so long as a substantial basis for crediting the hearsay is presented."

As the Second Circuit analyzed the problem in *Freeman, supra,* the issue for decision was whether or not the statement that the source of the hearsay was an informant of previous known reliability offered such a "substantial basis."

In *Jones, supra,* there was corroboration of the informant's story from other sources, and in *U.S. v. Ramirez,* 279 F2d 712, cert. den. 364 US 850, it was suggested that *Jones* may require that the supporting affidavit include some factual information to corroborate the hearsay report. *Cf. People v. McCall, supra.*

However, the Supreme Court has held that corroboration is not required where the affiant attests to the previous reliability of the informant. *U.S. v. Ventresca,* 380 US 102; *Aguilar v. Texas,* 378 US 108; *Rugendorf v. U.S.,* 376 US 528.

In *Aguilar,* the affidavit was held to be inadequate in that it described the informant as a "credible person" without supplying any details as to his background to warrant the conclusion that he was a "credible person."

In *Freeman,* however, the informant had worked for the narcotics bureau for eight years and for the affiant-agent for about one year, during which time he had supplied information which had led to prosecutions in eight cases. Thus, unlike *Aguilar,* there was sufficient background information at hand to warrant the conclusion that the informant in *Freeman* was indeed a "credible person."

The Second Circuit further bolstered its position by citing *Rugendorf* and *Ventresca.* In *Rugendorf* as in *Freeman,* the affidavit rested on statements by informants who had previously furnished reliable information. In *Ventresca,* it was the reason for crediting the source of the informant. Under those circumstances, it was held that the court should not invalidate a warrant by interpreting the affidavit in a hypertechnical manner. *Accord: People v. Rogers,* 15 NY2d 422, 217 NE2d 636.

In *People v. Lawrence,* 31 AD2d 712, 714, the search warrant was held void and the items seized suppressed because the application for the warrant was based in part on hearsay information supplied by a "confidential informant" whose reliability had not been shown. ". . . [T]here is absent any statement as to the informer's reliability, or facts relative to the informant, which would support reliance upon the information supplied by him. The record reveals no basis at all for sustaining a belief by the affiant [the police officer] or the court that the informer was reliable."

The *Lawrence* supporting affidavit stated: (1) that certain information was received from a "confidential informant" (no further reference to, or description of the informant was given); (2) informant stated that "defendant was dealing in narcotics illegally, that he possessed large quantities of marijuana and grew marijuana plants at his home;" (3) that he also operated the Dairy Isle, located at a given address; (4) "that other men went to his home to smoke marijuana cigarettes;" (5) that "on August 27, 1967 a party would take place at defendant's residence."

From these statements there was nothing from which a court could conclude that the informer was reliable nor were facts spelled out to show probable cause for the issuance of the warrant. The court was careful to point out, however, that had there been "a separate objective checking of the informer's story," then probable cause could be established without verifying the informer's reliability.

"An affidavit in support of a search warrant may be based on hearsay information and need not reflect the personal observations of the affiant police officer, and may show probable cause by communications received from an informer, as long as the information related is substantiated by either the character and reputation of the informer, or by a separate objective checking of the story he tells. (*People* v. *Coffey,* 12 NY2d 443, cert. den. 376 U.S. 916; *People* v. *Schnitzler,* 18 NY2d 457; *People* v. *Malinsky,* 15 NY2d 86; *Aguilar* v. *Texas,* 378 U.S. 108; *Riggan* v. *Virginia,* 384 U.S. 152.)" *People v.*

*Lawrence,* 31 AD2d 712, 713. *Accord: Metze v. New York,* 303 F Supp 1359.

In another situation, a search warrant was issued directing a search of two different apartments in a certain building. The supporting affidavit, however, established probable cause to search only one of those apartments. Since the supporting affidavit was insufficient to establish probable cause to search the second apartment, the court held that the affidavit was insufficient as to both—*i.e.,* that probable cause must be shown to exist to search as to each. *People v. Rainey,* 14 NY2d 35, 197 NE2d 527. *See also: People v. Lawrence,* 31 AD2d at 714.

In *People v. Wheatman,* 33 AD2d 67, the defendants appealed from convictions for conspiracy, bid-rigging and bribery which brought up for review the propriety of the lower court's ruling on a motion to suppress evidence which had been seized pursuant to a search warrant. The appellants contended that the affidavit in support of the search warrant was insufficient since it was based solely upon the affidavit of an Assistant District Attorney who had attended grand jury sessions at which testimony was adduced to the effect that certain "man-day estimates" prepared solely for the internal use of the Housing Authority had wrongfully found their way into the defendant's possession. The court held that the affidavit was insufficient since it failed to set forth the identification of the witnesses who appeared and testified before the grand jury or to demonstrate the reliability of their testimony. However, on appeal (27 NY2d 337), the New York Court of Appeals reversed and held that the affidavit was sufficient to establish probable cause and that, consequently, the warrants were valid, the search lawful and the evidence seized admissible. The court stated:

> "[W]here the affidavit is based upon hearsay and not solely on the personal knowledge of the affiant, it must, in order to satisfy the law's requirements, set forth facts which will enable a magistrate to judge for himself (1) the reliability (or credibility) of the informant, and (2) the reliability of his information. Only then can a reviewing court be satisfied that the magistrate has discharged his

'constitutional duty' of reaching a neutral and independent determination that probable cause exists (Spinelli v. United States, 393 U.S. 410, 415, supra), instead of serving merely as 'a rubber stamp' for police or prosecution (Aguilar v. Texas, 378 U.S. 108, 111, supra)."

A basic rule should be borne in mind. The supporting affidavits "must be tested and interpreted by magistrates and courts in a common sense and realistic fashion. They are normally drafted by nonlawyers in the midst and haste of a criminal investigation. Technical requirements of elaborate specificity have no proper place in this area." *U.S. v. Ventresca,* 380 US 102, 108. *See also: People v. Hendricks,* 25 NY2d 129, 250 NE2d 323; *Alderman v. U.S.,* 394 US 165.

Hearsay, in the form of the observations of an informer of known reliability, may constitute probable cause for the issuance of the warrant where in addition there is corroboration from other sources. Hearsay alone will not vitiate the warrant. *Jones v. U.S.,* 362 US 257, 267–273; *Draper v. U.S.,* 358 US 307.

False statement of facts will vitiate a warrant. *King v. U.S.,* 282 F2d 398, 400.

**§ 171.06. Probable Cause at Time of Application for Warrant.** Probable cause must exist at the time of the application for the warrant. "We are concerned only with the question whether the affiant had reasonable grounds at the time of his affidavit and the issuance of the warrant for the belief that the law was being violated on the premises to be searched. . . ." *People v. Marshall,* 13 NY2d 28, 35, 191 NE2d 798, citing *Dumbra v. U.S.,* 268 US 435, 441; *Henry v. U.S.,* 361 US 98, 102.

This point was highlighted by the decision in *Riggan v. Virginia,* 384 US 152. In *Riggan,* the Supreme Court of Appeals of Virginia had sustained a seizure under a search warrant based on a supporting affidavit which stated the material facts constituting probable cause for issuance of the warrant, as "Personal observation of the premises and information from sources believed by the police department to be reliable."

The testimony at Riggan's trial disclosed the existence of

probable cause for the issuance of the search warrant. However, as noted above, there was no showing of probable cause in the supporting affidavit at the time of the execution of the affidavit and the issuance of the warrant. Thus, under the authority of *Aguilar v. Texas, supra,* the Supreme Court granted certiorari and reversed.

The dissenting opinion in *Riggan v. Virginia, supra,* was undoubtedly based on a confusion between establishing probable cause at the trial and establishing probable cause to issue the warrant.

So, too, in *People v. Gold,* 46 Misc2d 495, and *People v. Beshany,* 43 Misc2d 521, an application for search warrants (wiretap order) made 16 months after information had been received was denied on the ground that it was based upon "stale" information. *See also: Sgro v. U.S.,* 287 US 206, 210, which condemned the re-issuance of an unexecuted search warrant unsupported by a current supporting affidavit.

On the other hand, a unique theory was advanced in *People v. Schnitzler,* 18 NY2d 457, 223 NE2d 28. In *Schnitzler,* a search warrant was obtained based on a supporting affidavit which averred, in substance, that the officer (the affiant) received information from a confidential informant, that the defendant, who was described in detail and whose address was given, had a large amount of marihuana in his apartment which the informant had seen there. There were no personal observations made by the officer.

It was not until the hearing to suppress was held that testimony was adduced to the effect that the officer told the issuing judge that the informant was reliable. However, the supporting affidavit as well as the testimony taken at the suppressal hearing is barren of any facts upon which one could substantiate the conclusion that the informant was in fact reliable. In addition, although the officer stated in his affidavit that "upon my personal knowledge there is probable cause to believe," etc., the basis of that "personal knowledge" is also undisclosed by the record.

In a 4 to 3 decision, the court nevertheless sustained the warrant.

It is difficult to agree with this decision in view of all of the previous pronouncements on this issue by our highest courts. *U.S. v. Ventresca,* 380 US 102; *Aguilar v. Texas,* 378 US 108; *Brinegar v. U.S.,* 338 US 160; *People v. Rogers,* 15 NY2d 422, 208 NE2d 168.

As Judge Keating said in his dissent in *Schnitzler, supra,* "there must be more than a mere assertion of an informer's reliability, or of independent corroboration, or of the ultimate conclusion of probable cause. There must be a statement of facts and circumstances from which those conclusions can reasonably be drawn and, when the facts and circumstances are based, not on independent knowledge by the affiant, but on an informer's information, there must also be some basis for crediting the informer's tale other than the affiant's bare assertion of reliability. . . . [T]his record reveals nothing of the informer's 'character and reputation' or of any independent checking of his tale in any particular at all." 18 NY2d at 463 and 464. *See also: Riggan v. Virginia,* 384 US 186, 187.

As in *Riggan,* the court in *Schnitzler* may have been influenced in its decision by the testimony taken at the suppressal hearing, just as the dissenters in *Riggan* may have been influenced by the facts adduced at Riggan's trial.

Judge Keating's strong dissent in *Schnitzler,* found support in *U.S. ex rel Schnitzler v. Follette,* 267 F Supp 337. Schnitzler had applied for a writ of habeas corpus. In granting the writ, the District Court held:

> ". . . In other words, there must be some basis, apart from the mere conclusory statements of the complaining officer, for a determination that probable cause exists. *Giordenello v. United States,* 357 U.S. 480 . . . (1958); *Nathanson v. United States,* 290 U.S. 41 . . . (1933)." 267 F Supp at 341.
>
> "Of course, 'the reviewing court may consider *only* information brought to the magistrates' attention' in deciding whether an adequate basis was presented. *Aguilar, supra,* 378 U.S. 109, fn 1. . . ." *Ibid.,* fn 2.
>
> "Therefore, as Judge Keating concluded, the standards set forth in *Aguilar* for establishing the reliability of the informant were not met." *Ibid.,* at 342.

Nevertheless, the Circuit Court reversed on the unique ground that the defect was cured by affiant's statement to the issuing judge that an arrest had already been made, in effect proving that the information supplied by the informant was reliable and thus was probable cause for the issuance of the search warrant. *Cf. People v. Gold,* 46 Misc2d 495.

**§ 171.07. Attacking the Supporting Affidavit.** Although the United States Supreme Court and the New York Court of Appeals have both held that in a doubtful or marginal case a search under a warrant should be sustained (*U.S. v. Ventresca,* 380 US 102; *People v. Rogers,* 15 NY2d 422, 208 NE2d 168), there had been do definitive ruling in New York which can be read as authorizing a later contest of the facts which were before the magistrate when he signed the warrant. In other jurisdictions, there are decisions both ways. The U.S. Supreme Court "seems to assume although not to hold that such an attack on the underlying affidavit may be made." *Rugendorf v. U.S.,* 376 US 528, 532.

This question was resolved in New York in *People v. Alfinito,* 16 NY2d 181, 211 NE2d 644. In that case, the question raised was, "[I]s it permissible, and has the person against whom the search warrant was executed a right to try out the issue of truthfulness of the sworn assertions on which the warrant was issued?"

"Modern thought which produced the decision in *Mapp v. Ohio* (367 U.S. 643) would make incongruous any holding that a search warrant is beyond attack even on proof that the allegations on which it was based were perjured." 16 NY2d at 185. While it is necessary to protect the rights of the individual in this regard, it is equally necessary that proper and reasonable rules be established so as to protect the rights of the People. Adoption of "overstrict rules" in this area would defeat that purpose.

> "We hold as follows: first, that section 813-c of the Code of Criminal Procedure is to be construed so as to permit an inquiry as to whether the affidavit's statements were perjurious; second, that the burden of proof is on the person attacking the warrant (see *United States* v. *Goodwin,* 1 F.2d 36; *United States* v. *Napela,* 28 F.2d 898), and third, that any fair doubt arising from the

> testimony at the suppressal hearing as to whether the affidavit's allegations were perjurious should be resolved in favor of the warrant since those allegations have already been examined by a judicial officer in issuing a warrant." *People v. Alfinito,* 16 NY2d 181, 186, 211 NE2d 644.

On a motion to controvert a search warrant, it was held to be reversible error not to permit defendant to inspect the wire tap order and its supporting affidavit, where it was clear that the fruits of the wire tap order led to the issuance of the search warrant sought to be controverted. *People v. Mendez,* 28 AD2d 727; *cf. People v. McCall,* 17 NY2d 152, 216 NE2d 570.

However, it has been held in *People v. Solomine,* 18 NY2d 477, 233 NE2d 341, that the rule in *Alfinito* does not apply where the defendant simply contests the truthfulness of the informer's statement on which the affiant police officer based his application for a search warrant, but where he does not "put in issue the truthfulness of the affiant's statements."

In that case the detective-affiant stated that a named informer, who was in prison, had told him that the defendant, together with the informer, had burglarized certain business premises and the proceeds of the burglary were in the possession of the defendant either at his home or in his automobile. He described all the items explicitly. The defendant denied the detective's allegations, averring that they were based entirely on the hearsay statement of a confessed thief.

A hearing on a motion to suppress the items seized under the warrant was denied, and defendant was convicted. The Appellate Division reversed and ruled that the defendant was entitled to a pretrial hearing on his motion to suppress, based on the authority of *Alfinito.*

In reversing the Appellate Division, the Court of Appeals said:

> "A challenge directed at the veracity of the informer does not put in issue the truthfulness of the affiant's statements. When reasons are given for crediting the sources of the information, and the items and their location are particularly detailed, a hearing will not be

granted unless facts are set forth in the moving papers which would imply perjury." 18 NY2d at 480.

Thus, since the supporting affidavit is sufficient and the defendant has produced nothing which tends to impugn the truthfulness of the detective's statements, the Appellate Division was held to be in error in ordering a hearing. The order was reversed and the judgment of the Supreme Court was reinstated.

**§ 171.08. Probable Cause Decided by Issuing Court.** Whether "probable cause" exists to issue the warrant is for the issuing judge to decide, not the officer seeking the warrant. *Jones v. U.S.,* 357 US 493; *People v. Politano,* 17 AD2d 503, affd 13 NY2d 852, 192 NE2d 271; *Carroll v. U.S.,* 267 US 132; *Brinegar v. U.S.,* 338 US 160; *Stacey v. Emery,* 97 US 642; *People v. Roth,* 207 Misc 875. The officer need only show sufficient facts that would lead a cautious, prudent person to act. It can be, and usually is, based on hearsay. Legally admissible evidence, sufficient to convict, is not required for establishing the reasonable grounds or probable cause. *Irby v. U.S.,* 314 F2d 251, 253; *People v. Rooks,* 35 Misc2d 598, 229 NYS2d 923; *Rugendorf v. U.S.,* 376 US 528; *People v. Coscia,* 42 Misc2d 978, 250 NYS2d 308; *Spinelli v. U.S.,* 393 US 410.

Probable cause cannot be established by unsworn oral representations made to the issuing judge. *People v. Carminati,* 236 NYS2d 921.

The rule that the issuing judge determines the existence of probable cause has been criticized in *Milonas v. Schwalb,* 65 Misc2d 1042, 319 NYS2d 327. Milonas applied for a writ prohibiting a judge of the Criminal Court of the City of New York from conducting a prior adversary proceeding to determine whether a search warrant should issue for the search and seizure of an alleged obscene motion picture film.

In granting the writ, the Court attacked the standards set forth in the statute, by which a judge determines probable cause as applied to cases involving First Amendment rights, since the language used in that section imposes a "tenuous burden" on the judge required to make such a determination.

The standards required in such a case, the Court noted, should be more circumscribed and more definitive. The Court indicated that proof of the existence of probable cause beyond a reasonable doubt or by a fair preponderance of the evidence, would be constitutionally acceptable. This concept is novel but is not in accord with the authorities.

**§ 172. Probable Cause to Arrest Without a Warrant.** The authority to arrest is statutory. *See, e.g.,* CPL §§ 140.10, 140.25(1, 2); *People v. Roach,* 44 Misc2d 40, 42. But even these arrest statutes in some instances contain authority to arrest on probable cause.

The relaxation of the rule of strict compliance in interpreting the statutes pertaining to search warrants in New York (CPL, art. 690) as noted in *People v. DeLago,* 16 NY2d 289, 213 NE2d 659 and *People v. Misuraco,* 16 NY2d 542, 208 NE2d 461, has permeated the "probable cause" area with respect to arrests made without a warrant. Recent New York decisions have interpreted "probable cause" situations with new liberality.

In applications for search warrants the courts have consistently held that probable cause for the issuance of the warrant must be based on the issuing court's conclusion based on the facts averred, and not on what the officer requesting the warrant has concluded as to the existence of probable cause. To hold otherwise, it has been said, would make the issuing court a mere rubber stamp for the officer. *Nathanson v. U.S.,* 290 US 41; *Aguilar v. Texas,* 378 US 108. The cases and references cited, *supra,* hold that the facts presented in the affidavit in support of the warrant must be such as "in the circumstances, to lead a reasonably discreet and prudent man to believe" that certain items, subject to lawful seizure, are to be found in specified premises. *Husty v. U.S.,* 282 US 694.

Under the provisions of CPL §§ 140.10, 140.25(1, 2), a police officer is authorized to make an arrest without a warrant if he has reasonable grounds for believing that a crime or offense is being committed in his presence.

In the case of *People v. Valentine,* 17 NY2d 128, 216 NE2d 321, Valentine was arrested without a warrant for gambling (policy). The officer concededly was an expert in matters pertaining to policy. He testified that he had observed six unknown persons approach the defendant at various intervals and hand him money; that on three of these occasions the defendant made notations on a slip of paper; that he had not overheard any conversations between the defendant and any of the unknown persons nor had he seen what the defendant had written on the slip of paper; that following the arrest he had seized a slip of paper from the defendant's hand.

Nevertheless, the court in *Valentine, supra,* held that this was a lawful arrest based on a situation which presented probable cause to an experienced police officer, expert in gambling matters, to believe that the crime of policy was being committed in his presence.

> "The standard of probable cause to be applied in a situation where a police officer makes an arrest without a warrant is the standard of what would be probable cause to 'a reasonable, cautious and prudent police officer' ([*People v. Brady,*] 16 NY2d, p. 189). (See, also, *People* v. *Hook,* 15 NY2d 776, [1965] and *Bell* v. *United States,* 254 F.2d 82, 86, cert. den. 358 U.S. 885.)
>
> ". . . Here each transaction observed by the officer might have been seemingly innocent, but the repeated pattern amounted to probable cause in the eyes of an arresting officer who was well versed in the behavior of a professional policy operator." *People v. Valentine,* 17 NY2d 128, 132, 216 NE2d 321. *See also: Manger v. State,* 214 Md 71, 79.

The same logic was applied by the court in sustaining the arrest without a warrant in *People v. Cassone,* 20 AD2d 118, affd 14 NY2d 798, 200 NE2d 214, which arrest was made under subdivision 4 of sec. 177 of the Code of Criminal Procedure, now embodied in CPL §§ 140.10, 140.25(1, 2).

In *Cassone, supra,* the court held that the statute must be interpreted literally.

> "If he [the police officer] has reasonable grounds for believing both that a felony has been committed and that the person arrested committed it, his belief, resting on

> such grounds, validates the arrest just as if the person arrested had in fact committed the felony (§ 177, subd. 4). So in this situation the reasonableness of the officer's belief becomes very material. . . . If no felony had in fact been committed, it is necessary to show that a reasonable ground for believing the contrary was presented to the officer." *Cassone,* 20 AD2d at 120.

In *People v. Valentine, supra,* the Court of Appeals equates this rule in subdivision 4 with the rule in subdivision 1 of section 177. (*See:* CPL §§ 140.10, 140.25(1, 2)).

> "This amendment [subd. 1, sec. 177] has the effect of allowing a police officer to arrest a person when there is *probable cause* for believing that the person is committing a misdemeanor in his presence. The change allows the same standard of probable cause justifying an arrest without a warrant to prevail for misdemeanors committed in the presence of a police officer as for felonies." 17 NY2d at 131.

The rule enunciated in *People v. Malinsky,* 15 NY2d 86, 204 NE2d 188, requires the People to establish probable cause for an arrest without a warrant before they can assert that the incident search was lawful. *Malinsky* further held that the informer must be disclosed, "where there is insufficient evidence, apart from the arresting officer's testimony as to the informer's communications to establish probable cause." 15 NY2d at 94. The rule is sound, but may become meaningless if facts are strained in order to bring a particular case within the ambit of *Malinsky.*

A close question as to the applicability of the *Malinsky* rule was presented in *People v. White,* 16 NY2d 270, 213 NE2d 438. At a suppression hearing in that case, the facts disclosed that a paid informer (although not paid in this case), of known reliability, told the detective that the defendant whom he described and pointed out, had narcotics in his possession, which he was selling. Ten minutes later, a person whom the detective described as a drug addict, (although the record is bare of any facts to justify such characterization), approached the defendant with money in his hand and conversed with him.

No conversation was overheard nor was any transaction observed. The detective then approached, whereupon the alleged addict hastily departed, putting his money away. The defendant was then arrested and searched. Thirteen glassine envelopes containing a white powder, and a hypodermic needle, were found in his possession. It was later disclosed that the glassine envelopes contained no narcotics.

The motion to suppress was denied in the lower court and in sustaining such denial the Court of Appeals conceded that this was a close question. Hearsay, *i.e.,* the informer's communication to a police officer, may form a basis for an arrest without a warrant, so long as it is disclosed that an informant was involved "whose identity need not be revealed," and who was himself credible or his information reliable. *U.S. v. Ventresca,* 380 US 102; *People v. Rogers,* 15 NY2d 422, 208 NE2d 168.

With this as a premise, the Court reasoned that sufficient facts, observed by the detective, were present to establish the reliability of the informer's information. These facts were: (1) the approach of the known addict, (2) with money in his hand, (3) the conversation between the two, and (4) the addict's rapid departure on the approach of the detective.

**§ 172.01. Examples of Probable Cause to Arrest Without a Warrant.** A classical case of probable cause to arrest without a warrant is found in *U.S. v. Llanes,* 398 F2d 880.

In that case the police followed two suspected narcotics sellers to an apartment on the ground floor of a building. Loud conversations were heard from within concerning the sale and delivery of narcotics. One person was observed filling glassine envelopes, with what the police believed to be narcotics, in the bathroom of the apartment.

Another classical case of "probable cause" is found in *People v. Merola,* 30 AD2d 963. Police in a squad car received a radio alarm at 4:10 A.M., "burglary in progress" at a certain address. They arrived in the area immediately thereafter. It was a store. A window was broken. A "burglar" alarm was sounding from within the store. They observed a man running toward an automobile which had its lights on and motor running. The auto started to leave, but the police stopped it.

They looked into the automobile and saw a large number of coats on the back seat. The occupants refused to respond to police questions. The arrest and the search of the automobile, in which additional coats were found, were upheld. *See also: People v. Hoffman,* 24 AD2d 497.

The court noted that due weight must be given "to the specific reasonable inference which he [the police officer] is entitled to draw from the facts in the light of his experience." In a nutshell, this is a good guide in determining the existence of "probable cause." In this connection see *Terry v. Ohio,* 392 US 1, 27, and *People v. Cassone,* 14 NY2d 798, 200 NE2d 214, and as to "Radio Runs," *see: People v. Wilson,* 16 AD2d 207, and *Daniels v. U.S.,* 393 F2d 359.

In a converse situation, *People v. Brown,* 24 NY2d 421, 248 NE2d 867, a pattern of conduct observed by the police was held insufficient to establish probable cause for an arrest without a warrant.

Thus, in *Brown, supra,* the actions of the defendant were equivocal. The defendant was arrested and convicted for the unlawful possession of narcotics. After the arrest he was searched and the narcotics were found on his person and seized.

The facts leading to the arrest, search and seizure disclosed that the arresting officer testified that he observed the defendant in a high crime area in the company of a suspected narcotics addict who entered a nearby building and then rejoined the defendant. Both then came "close together," and the officer saw a movement of hands. Believing that a narcotics transaction had occurred, the officer walked over to the defendant just as the suspected addict walked away, and arrested him.

This behavior and activity were held to be at most "equivocal and suspicious" and were not supplemented by any additional behavior raising "the level of inference from suspicion to probable cause." There was no overheard conversation (*cf. People v. Cohen,* 23 NY2d 674, 243 NE2d 145), no flight (*cf. People v. White,* 16 NY2d 270, 213 NE2d 438) and no misstatements when questioned (*cf. People v. Brady,* 16 NY2d 186, 211 NE2d 815). *See also: People v. Butterly,* 25 NY2d

159, 250 NE2d 340; *cf. People v. Valentine,* 17 NY 128, 216 NE2d 321.

In a case similar to *Brown, supra,* the court, in *People v. Corrado,* 22 NY2d 308, 239 NE2d 526, found an absence of probable cause when police, acting on an informer's tip that marihuana would be passed on a certain corner, observed defendants hand each other opaque manila envelopes. The uncontradicted testimony of the officer, a Narcotics Bureau detective, that he had never seen loose marihuana in small quantities passed or sold in envelopes other than those described herein, does not raise the level of inference from suspicion to probable cause, since the envelopes could have contained any number of non-contraband items.

It is to be noted that heroin is usually packaged in small glassine envelopes. When these envelopes are seen to contain a white powder, "probable cause" to arrest is present. Some judges have taken judicial notice of the fact that heroin is sold at retail in small glassine envelopes.

The term "reasonable cause," as used in statutes and as used in the Fourth Amendment of the Federal Constitution, is equated with "probable cause." *People v. Malinsky,* 15 NY2d 86, 204 NE2d 188; *People v. Lombardi,* 13 NY2d 1014, 195 NE2d 306.

In *Wong Sun v. U.S.,* 371 US 471, the Supreme Court held, inter alia, that the basis for an arrest without a warrant cannot be any less stringent than the basis for an arrest with a warrant. Otherwise, it would be more expedient for an officer to make a warrantless arrest.

By giving former subdivision 1, section 177 of the CCP, the same literal interpretation that it gave former subdivision 4 (now embodied in CPL §§ 140.10, 140.25(1, 2)), the Court of Appeals in *Valentine,* 17 NY2d 128, avoided conflict with this dictum in *Wong Sun.*

Of course, the inference is clear in *Valentine, supra,* that an arrest in that case by an inexperienced officer, on the facts there presented, would have been unlawful.

The conclusions, therefore, to be drawn from *Valentine* are (1) that the arrest statute is to be given a literal interpretation, and (2) that facts which may not constitute probable cause to an ordinary individual may nevertheless constitute probable cause to a police officer of experience.

In *People v. Santiago,* 13 NY2d 326, 196 NE2d 881, probable cause to arrest without a warrant was found to exist where the following combination of facts was present: information from a reliable informant; confirmation by the police of the information given to them by the informer that the defendant feloniously possessed narcotics; and police knowledge of defendant's reputation as a narcotics seller. *Cf. People v. Martin,* 13 NY2d 332.

In *People v. Maize,* 32 AD2d 1031, 305 NYS2d 37, the court found that the totality of the following circumstances gave rise to probable cause to arrest without a warrant: a police radio alarm of a burglary in a suburb; defendant, answering a general description of the culprit, operating a motor vehicle at 5:15 A.M., 2½ blocks from the scene of the burglary; defendant, when stopped, produced an improper vehicle registration certificate and a duplicate license; defendant gave evasive replies; he was in wet stockinged feet and knees of his trousers were wet, and a pair of wet gloves were on the front seat of the car; and a portable TV set was on the floor of the car.

Another probable cause situation involving TV sets was sustained in *People v. Ray,* 26 AD2d 560, 271 NYS2d 453, on the following facts: information from a reliable informant; police observation of defendants transporting more than 10 TV sets into the home of one of them at 1:30 A.M.; when confronted, two of the defendants fled but were apprehended at the scene; and two of the defendants were previously known to the police to have been involved with stolen TV sets.

In *People v. Teams,* 20 AD2d 803, probable cause to arrest without a warrant was based on the following: two anonymous phone calls to the police station informed a sergeant on duty that a man called "Big Jim" was discharging a gun in front of a certain designated building; "Big Jim" was described; a patrolman who reported to the scene knew the defendant as "Big Jim" and as one who had been arrested many times before; that "Big Jim" had a reputation as the "enforcer" and "strong-arm man" of the area; and that "Big Jim" answered the description given by the anonymous informers.

*See also: People v. Taggart,* 20 NY2d 335, 283 NYS2d 1, 229 NE2d 581.

There seems to be doubt in some quarters as to whether the observations by a police officer of possession of marihuana, constitutes probable cause for an arrest without a warrant. It is often argued that a marihuana cigarette, being hand-rolled and home-made, is no different in appearance from other home-made cigarettes of ordinary tobacco.

However, an expert in dealing with marihuana cigarettes would have probable cause to make a summary arrest. Such an arrest based on probable cause has been upheld in *People v. Glover,* 17 NY2d 429, 213 NE2d 800, in a case where the officer testified "that he had seen marihuana cigarettes on 40 or 50 previous occasions and they differed from ordinary cigarettes in various specified respects; that, when defendant looked in his direction, he immediately took the cigarette from his mouth. . . ."

Obvious falsehoods following questioning by police based on their personal observations of the defendant after he had emerged from a hotel where he had been previously stopped on one of its upper floors with keys to five different rooms in his possession, was held to constitute probable cause for his arrest in *People v. Brady,* 16 NY2d 186, 211 NE2d 815.

As to attempted flight when defendant is approached by police, *see: People v. Yazum,* 13 NY2d 302, 196 NE2d 263.

In *People v. Jackson,* 23 AD2d 635, 257 NYS2d 72, it was held that the personal observation by the police officer of bulges in the defendant's outer pockets plus flight supplied that additional information authorizing an arrest without a warrant for a narcotics law violation, since it supplemented information supplied by an informant who had described the defendant to the officer in detail. *See also: People v. Melchor,* 47 Cal Rptr 235; *U.S. v. Moon,* 351 F2d 464.

Generally, a police officer may, without a warrant, arrest a person for any offense when he has *reasonable cause to believe* that such person has committed such offense *in his presence. See, e.g.,* CPL 140.10.

In defining the term "presence," the New York Court of Appeals in *People v. Goldberg,* 19 NY2d 460, 227 NE2d 575, said that evidence observed by means of any of the senses is "in one's presence." Citing *Beck v. Ohio,* 379 US 89, 94, the court said, "To limit the meaning of 'presence' to observations perceived through one sense, sight, seems unsupportable." 19 NY2d at 465. In footnote 6, the court added,

> "In *Beck v. Ohio,* (379 U.S. 89, 94 [1964]) the court reversed the defendant's conviction, noting that 'the record does not show that the officers * * * saw, heard, smelled, or otherwise perceived anything else to give them ground for the belief that the petitioner had acted or was then acting unlawfully.'" 19 NY2d at 465, n. 6.

Thus, in *Goldberg, supra,* it was held that where the arresting officer heard a voice accepting bets through a closed door, this constituted a crime committed in his presence.

fruits of crime or contraband. . . . Privacy is disturbed no more by a search directed to a purely evidentiary object than it is by a search directed to an instrumentality, fruit, or contraband. A magistrate can intervene in both situations, and the requirements of probable cause and specificity can be preserved intact." *Warden v. Hayden,* 387 US at 301–302.

In *Hayden,* certain clothing was seized which the defendant was alleged to have worn at the time of the commission of an armed robbery. It was the admissibility of this clothing that was in dispute. Since the clothing was related to the crime that prompted the police to make the search, it was ruled admissible. The new rule does not authorize the seizure of articles that are not related to the crime. *See: Cooper v. California,* 386 US 58; *cf.: Preston v. U.S.,* 376 US 364; *U.S. v. Joseph,* 174 F Supp 539, 545, affd 278 F2d 504, cert. den. 364 US 823.

The court in *Hayden* was careful to point out that this new rule is not to be interpreted as authorizing the seizure of written documents which could constitute compulsory self-incrimination. *See: Boyd v. U.S.,* 116 US 616. In *Gouled* and *Boyd, supra,* the seizure of the defendants' papers was for the purpose of using them as evidence against them, in effect, compelling defendants to become witnesses against themselves. *Hayden* does not grant carte blanche authority to seize items of evidentiary value. There may be items "whose very nature precludes them from being the object of a reasonable search and seizure," such as in *Gouled* and *Boyd, supra,* but this is far different from the seizure of clothing in *Hayden.* Those items of wearing apparel are not "testimonial" or "communicative" in nature, and the defendant's privilege under the Fifth Amendment was not violated by their seizure. *See also: Schmerber v. California,* 384 US 757.

Insofar as they have held otherwise, *Mapp v. Ohio,* 367 US 643, and *Malloy v. Hogan,* 378 US 1, must be deemed overruled by *Hayden.*

*Warden v. Hayden, supra,* was a "hot pursuit" case. 18 USC § 3103a authorizes the seizure of mere evidence under a search warrant. This, by implication, seems to enlarge the right of seizure of mere evidence in cases other than "hot pursuit" cases.

In *People v. Grossman,* 27 AD2d 572, it was held:

> "In our opinion, the ultimate fact that the evidence sought to be suppressed herein was evidentiary in character did not preclude its seizure as unreasonable or violative of due process under the Fourth, Fifth and Fourteenth Amendments (*People* v. *Givens,* 26 AD2d 684; *People* v. *Berger,* 18 NY2d 638; *People* v. *McCall,* 17 NY2d 152; *Black* v. *United States,* 385 US 26; *People* v. *Carroll,* 38 Misc2d 630; *State v. Bisaccia,* 45 N.J. 504)."

In a concurring memorandum, Hopkins, J. equated judicially supervised wiretapping with search warrants. Both are intrusions into privacy. He also noted that probable cause to search an automobile, established by the exigencies, has also been sustained, even though such a search is also an invasion into privacy, and that Fourth Amendment rights are not absolute. Citing *Carroll v. U.S.,* 267 US 132; *Ker v. California,* 374 US 23; and *People v. Berger,* 18 NY2d 638, 219 NE2d 426, revd 388 US 41.

Justice Hopkins observed:

> "To put it differently, the reasonableness for the search and detection of conversations must be tested by the need shown by the affidavit in support of the order under section 813-a and, once that need is established under the traditional standards, the search must envelope the use of conversations as evidence of any crime thereby uncovered, just as in the use of evidence and contraband found in the execution of a search warrant (*cf. People* v. *Daily,* 157 Cal. App. 2d 649; *Eisenstein* v. *State,* 200 Md. 593), or found as a result of a legal arrest (*Marron* v. *United States,* 275 US 192; *Harris* v. *United States,* 331 US 145; *United States* v. *Rabinowitz,* 339 US 56; *Abel v. United States,* 362 US 217). Otherwise, we introduce refinements in the test of reasonableness in the use of eavesdropping which are difficult to enforce or to justify." *People v. Grossman,* 27 AD2d at 573.

Thus, in *People v. Grossman,* the New York Appellate Division upheld the constitutionality of the statute; validated a search for "mere evidence"; equated a wiretap and "bugging" order with search warrants; and reaffirmed the rule that it is for the trial court to determine whether a search is reasonable. *See also: Weeks v. U.S.,* 232 US 383.

In *Berger v. New York,* 388 US 41, and *Katz v. U.S.,* 389 US 347, conversations were held to be "things" that may be "seized" under the Fourth Amendment.

A seizure of "mere evidence" under a search warrant has also been sustained by the New Jersey Supreme Court. In that case, the police seized a pair of the defendant's shoes pursuant to the search warrant, for the purpose of comparing them with casts of footprints found at the scene of the robbery. The defendant argued that the seizure was unconstitutional since a search for mere evidence was unlawful under the Fourth Amendment. The court rejected this contention and held that a search for a pair of shoes to match a culprit's footprints was not unreasonable. *State v. Bisaccio* [N.J.], 213 A2d 185. *See also: People v. McDonald,* 47 Misc2d 1040.

California has adopted the same rule. In *People v. Thayer,* 47 Cal Rptr 780, 408 P2d 108, the California Supreme Court held that where a police officer, under a warrant, was searching a doctor's office for records indicating false billings of welfare cases, there was no violation of the Fourth Amendment even though the records were sought for their inculpatory value alone.

The rule has been broadened concerning the requirement that search warrants must specifically state the things to be seized. Now, evidence of a crime may be seized. This allows for wide latitude in the use of language in the search warrant, language that earlier had been repeatedly condemned by the United States Supreme Court. *See, e.g., Stanford v. Texas,* 379 US 476; *Marron v. U.S.,* 275 US 192; *Aguilar v. Texas,* 378 US 108.

A general warrant is a defective warrant and is invalid. *Stanford v. Texas,* 379 US 476; *People v. Matherson,* 16 NY2d 509, 208 NE2d 180; *cf. Marcus v. Search Warrant,* 367 US 717.

However, once the police are lawfully on the premises, they may arrest for any crime committed in their presence. *U.S. v. DiRe,* 332 US 581; *U.S. v. Festa,* 192 F Supp 160, 163.

**§ 183.02. Description of Things to Be Seized.** Description of the things to be searched for and seized must be specific. Thus, where a search warrant specifically described a certain product, and another product is also seized, the search as to the latter is unreasonable. One cannot use a particular warrant as an excuse to make a general search. *Marron v. U.S.,* 275 US 192; *People v. Rainey,* 14 NY2d 35, 197 NE2d 527; *Woo Lai Chun v. U.S.,* 274 F2d 708; Fed R Crim P 41; CPL § 690.45.

The reason for this rule is to prevent general searches, which have long been condemned. *Entick v. Carrington,* [1765] 19 Howells St. Tr. 1029; *Marron v. U.S.,* 275 US 192.

For example, a warrant issued to search for a knife does not authorize an exploratory search. In *People v. Baker,* 23 NY2d 307, 321, 244 NE2d 232, the police did not find a knife, but saw a sweater fitting the description given by the victim. They seized this sweater without a warrant. "The right to search for one item . . . does not permit the inference that there is probable cause for other items."

In *U.S. ex rel Nickens v. LaVallee,* 391 F2d 123, a search warrant was obtained to search defendant's apartment for "key-making machines, blank keys, lock picks." The police searched the apartment and seized newspaper clippings of several burglaries. The court there held that these seizures could not be used as they were not described in the warrant. *See also: People v. Cefaro,* 21 NY2d 252, 244 NE2d 42; *but cf. U.S. v. Alloway,* 397 F2d 105, where clothing was seized as an "instrumentality of crime" although not listed in the search warrant.

However, the rule as to specificity must be reasonably construed. "It is true that warrants must accurately describe the property to be seized (*People v. Coletti,* 39 Misc.2d 580; *Marron v. U.S.,* 275 U.S. 192). But this requirement is at the very least to be construed within the varying latitudes of the nature of the property stolen, contraband, and etc., and manner in which it was seized (*Marron v. U.S., supra*)." *People v. Cody,* NYLJ, 3/3/66, p. 20, col. 5.

The rule in *Cody, supra,* has been reaffirmed in *People v. Solomine,* 18 NY2d 477, 480, 233 NE2d 341. In *Solomine,* the New York Court of Appeals said that minor discrepancies in the supporting affidavit as to the description of the items to be seized under the search warrant "can hardly be deemed to give the affidavit an air of falsity." Such discrepancies are "inconsequential minutiae at best."

Federal courts have held to the same effect:

"It is permissible to seize things other than those described in the search warrant if they have reasonable relation to the purpose of the search." *U.S. v. Joseph,* 174 F Supp 539, 545, affd 278 F2d 504, cert. den. 364 US 823. *See also: Bryant v. U.S.,* 252 F2d 746, 748, 749; *Woo Lai Chun v. U.S.,* 274 F2d 708; *Marron v. U.S.,* 275 US 192; *People v. Rainey,* 14 NY2d 35; U.S. Const. amend. IV.

Some conversations are not "mere evidence" but may be the *corpus delicti* itself. In *U.S. v. Borgese,* 235 F Supp 286, 294, conviction vacated on other grounds, 372 F2d 950, under a prosecution for violation of 18 USC § 1084, in which eavesdropped conversations as to wagering were received in evidence, the Court stated:

> "[I]t should be noted that telephone conversations about wagers by a person in the gambling business would not be simply evidence of a violation of law; they would be themselves criminal acts." *Cf. Katz v. U.S.,* 389 US 347.

*See also: § 189, infra.*

**§ 184. Improper Use of the Search Warrant.** A search warrant may not be used as a substitute for the subpoena duces tecum, nor merely to obtain documentary evidence of a crime. *People v. Richter,* 265 AD 767; *People v. Carver,* 172 Misc 820; *Mancusi v. DeForte,* 392 US 364.

Nor may it be used to conduct a general search. *People v. Bosco,* 56 Misc2d 1080, 290 NYS2d 481, and cases cited.

On the other hand, seizure of evidence as incident to a lawful arrest after police enter premises open to public access, but under a search warrant subsequently determined to be invalid, does not constitute an improper use of the warrant.

As the court held in *People v. Matherson,* 16 NY2d 509, 511, 208 NE2d 180:

> "The seizure of evidence upon which the conviction is based was an incident to a lawful arrest on sufficient

cause in a place open to public access. Therefore, the fact a search warrant was defective, as the People concede, because it was a general warrant (cf. *Marcus* v. *Search Warrant,* 367 US 717; *Stanford* v. *State of Texas,* 379 US 476) did not preclude the reception in evidence of exhibits seized as an incident to the arrest."

**§ 185. Search Warrant: Prima Facie Valid, Subsequently Voided.** A warrant, valid on its face and issued by a court having jurisdiction, is a lawful mandate. Thus, it has been held that a person who forcefully resists such a warrant can be convicted of assault, even though it later develops that the information underlying the warrant (in this case, motor vehicle violations) was insufficient.

"But this kind of deficiency which must ultimately be decided by a court does not render a warrant, valid on its face, and issued by a Judge having jurisdiction, a nullity. It is a 'lawful mandate or process.' Its potential underlying legal insufficiencies do not justify forceful resistance to the execution of a resulting warrant." *People v. Briggs,* 19 NY2d 37, 42, 224 NE2d 93.

Another situation involving a search warrant valid on its face but subsequently declared invalid, arose in *People v. Dentine,* 27 AD2d 139, 276 NYS2d 963, affd 21 NY2d 700, 234 NE2d 462.

Dentine's apartment was searched pursuant to a search warrant. The search lasted from 8:15 P.M. to 9:45 P.M. After the search was completed, some police officers remained in the apartment. About 11 P.M., one Bramante entered. Bramante told the police he had come to make arrangements for an abortion to be performed on a certain female. The name of the female was unknown to the police, but Bramante furnished it to them. Both he and the female testified before the grand jury, and the defendant was thereupon indicted.

However, on a motion to controvert the original warrant, the warrant was vacated and all evidence seized thereunder was ordered suppressed.

The defendant then moved to suppress all the evidence, which resulted in this indictment, *e.g.,* the testimony of Bramante and the female who was to have been aborted, on the ground that it stemmed from "an unlawful trespass under a void search warrant" in violation of the defendant's rights under both the United States and New York State Constitutions.

Defendant argued that the prohibitions recited in *Mapp v. Ohio,* 367 US 643, were applicable to the several states (*Malloy v. Hogan,* 378 US 1; *Murphy v. Waterfront Commission,* 378 US 52), and that, accordingly, the evidence in question must be suppressed because it was the result of an exploitation of a primary illegal act. *People v. Robinson,* 13 NY2d 296, 301, 196 NE2d 261; *see also: Wong Sun v. U.S.,* 371 US 471, 488; *Mapp v. Ohio, supra; Nardone v. U.S.,* 308 US 338, 340–341.

The lower court granted the motion. In reversing, the Appellate Division said:

> "A Constitutionally unreasonable search may be consequent either on a search without a warrant or probable cause, or one resulting from trespass or other illegality. Here involved is a search based on a warrant thereafter vacated after a hearing.
>
> ". . . The initial entry of the officers was with judicial approval. (*Bornstein* v. *Levine,* 7 AD2d 843.) In the circumstances the police officers in defendant's apartment at the time Bramante appeared were not trespassers. (*Fischer* v. *Langbein,* 103 N.Y. 84; *Marks* v. *Townsend,* 97 N.Y. 590; *Bornstein v. Levine, supra; Solomon v. Baar,* 168 Misc. 439, affd. 255 App. Div. 849.)
>
> . . . .
>
> "Here is not involved testimony induced or shaped by the product of illegality. (See *United States* v. *Tane,* 329 F.2d 848, 853 [C.A., 2d Cir]; cf. *Smith* v. *United States,* 344 F.2d 545; *People v. Albea,* 2 Ill. 2d 317 [118 N.E.2d 277]; contra, *Smith* v. *United States,* 324 F.2d 879, 881, 882 [C.A., D.C.]; *Payne v. United States,* 294 F.2d 723, 726, 727 [C.A., D.C.].)" *Dentine, supra,* 27 AD2d at 140, 141; *cf. People v. Perez,* 35 Misc2d 461, 229 NYS2d 882.

A search warrant may not be attacked collaterally. *Meegan v. Tracy,* 220 AD 600, 223 NYS 355.

## § 186. Probative Value of Search Warrant.

> "The introduction into evidence of a search warrant is for the sole purpose of demonstrating that the search was lawful, as distinguished from unlawful. It has no probative value in establishing the guilt of the accused." *People v. Silverman,* 26 AD2d 890, 274 NYS2d 190, 191.

Thus, the court's instructions to the effect that the search warrant which had been introduced in evidence was one of a series of circumstances from which the jury might draw a conclusion, constituted reversible error.

Logically, it would seem, that the same rule is applicable to arrest warrants.

A court of limited jurisdiction has no authority to issue a search warrant for execution outside of the limits of its jurisdiction. Thus, in *People v. Niven,* 35 AD2d 174, 316 NYS2d 393, the court said that a Buffalo City Court Judge, who issued such a warrant, exceeded his jurisdictional powers, unless there was evidence that a crime had been committed within the City of Buffalo *and* the property to be seized is connected with that crime.

Absent proof of these exceptions, defendant's motion for suppression of the things seized must be granted.

**§ 187. Third Party Searches.** A valid search warrant authorizing a search of certain premises and of its John Doe occupant does not carry with it authority to search other persons found in the premises, unless the search of the others is incidental to their lawful arrest. To be lawful, their arrest must have been made pursuant to the statutory authority to arrest. Otherwise, a search of a third party disclosing contraband in his possession will be suppressed on motion. *People v. Rawluck,* 14 NY2d 609, 198 NE2d 266.

A similar ruling was made by the Second Circuit in *U.S. v. Viale,* 312 F2d 595, cert. den. 373 US 903. There the court held that an Internal Revenue agent operating under a warrant, had no reasonable cause to arrest a person who had entered premises two hours after a raid.

**§ 188. Other Discovered Contraband.** If, in the execution of a valid search warrant, contraband not specified in the search warrant is discovered, it may be seized, and the defendant, if he is the possessor thereof, may be charged for this new crime. *Bennett v. U.S.*, 145 F2d 270; *U.S. v. Howell,* 240 F2d 149; *Zap v. U.S.*, 328 US 624; *U.S. v. Old Dominion,* 10 F2d 736; *U.S. v. Howard,* 138 F Supp 376; Sobel, *"The Pleader,"* pp. 56–59, 71–76 (Kings Co. Crim. Bar Assn.). As to the special rule applicable to obscene material, *see: Search and Seizure of Obscene Material, Chapter 22, infra.*

Internal Revenue agents have the power to seize non-tax-paid distilled spirits without a search warrant, apart from incidence of search to a lawful arrest. *U.S. v. Boston,* 330 F2d 937, cert. den. 377 US 1004; 26 USC § 7608.

**§ 189. The Place or Person to Be Searched—Specificity.** The search warrant must specifically describe the place or the person to be searched. A warrant may authorize the search of a person, but not unknown (John Doe) persons. *People v. Brown,* 40 Misc2d 35, 242 NYS2d 555; *People v. Coletti,* 39 Misc2d 580, 241 NYS2d 454; *Keiningham v. U.S.*, 287 F2d 126.

Where a search warrant, authorized a search of "entire premises," which were known to the officer to consist of two separate residential apartments occupied by separate people, but which fact was not disclosed by the officer, and where the police searched the entire building, the warrant was held to be Constitutionally deficient as "not particularly describing the place to be searched." A warrant cannot be partially valid and partially invalid. If it is invalid in part, it is invalid in its entirety. *People v. Rainey,* 14 NY2d 35, 197 NE2d 527; *People v. Feliciano,* 23 AD2d 806, 258 NYS2d 319.

The caption of a warrant is part of the warrant and must be considered with the body of the supporting affidavit in determining if the warrant particularly describes the place to be searched. *People v. DeLago,* 16 NY2d 289, 290, 213 NE2d 659.

In what appears to be an extension of the rule in *People v. DeLago, supra,* the Federal Court of Appeals (2d Circuit) has held in a wagering tax statute case, that the United States Commissioner, when issuing a warrant to search an apartment, could consider facts learned from affidavits presented to him on the same day by the same federal agent in support of applications for search of other apartments, which contained references to bookmaking operations of persons named in the supporting affidavit for the warrant under attack. *U.S. v. Serao,* 367 F2d 347.

A District Court, however, has held that a search warrant describing the premises to be searched as a basement apartment at a stated address was sufficient, although there was more than one basement apartment in the premises, where the officers who had obtained the warrant had familiarized themselves with the apartment through surveillance and could identify the particular apartment to be searched. *U.S. v. Gomez,* 42 FRD 347; *cf. People v. Rainey,* 14 NY2d 35, 197 NE2d 527.

*See also: § 183.02, supra.*

**§ 190. Delay in Obtaining Search Warrant.** In *U.S. v. Van Leeuwen,* 397 US 249, 25 L Ed2d 282, a delay of 29 hours in obtaining a search warrant to open first class registered and insured air mail was held not "unreasonable" within the meaning of the Fourth Amendment in view of the fact that the material mailed consisted of two packages of a suspicious character and the unavoidable delay in contacting a distant point of destination of one of the packages. Each package weighed 12 pounds, and was mailed from a post office in Mount Vernon, Washington (near the Canadian border). One was destined for Van Nuys, California, and the other for Nashville, Tennessee.

In accepting the packages (each was insured for $10,000), the postal clerk became suspicious. A nearby police officer noticed the return address on the packages as the address of a vacant housing area and the sender's car plates as belonging to a man under investigation for dealing in illegal coins. These facts constituted probable cause to justify a delay of 26½ hours in mailing the packages as well as probable cause for the issuance of a search warrant, notwithstanding that:

> "Letters and sealed packages of this kind are as fully guarded from examination and inspection, except as to their outward form and weight, as if they were retained

by the parties forwarding them in their own domiciles. . . . No law of Congress can place in the hands of officials connected with the postal service any authority to invade the secrecy of letters and such sealed packages in the mail; and all regulations adopted as to mail matter of this kind must be in subordination to the great principle embodied in the Fourth Amendment of the Constitution." *Ex parte Jackson,* 96 US 727, 733, quoted in *Van Leeuwen, supra,* 25 L Ed2d at 284–285.

§ 191. **Executing the Search Warrant.** Only a peace officer may execute a search warrant. Some states require that he be named in the warrant. New York limits the execution of search warrants to police officers, although the warrant may be executed by any police officer of a designated classification. CPL §§ 690.05(2), 690.25.

The federal statute authorizes the service of a search warrant "by any officer mentioned in its direction or by an officer authorized to serve such warrant, but by no other person, except in aid of the officer on his requiring it, he being present and acting in its execution." 18 USC § 3105.

Agents of the F.B.I. may make seizures under a warrant for violations of federal laws. 18 USC § 3107. Internal Revenue agents have the same power. *U.S. v. $1,058.00 in U.S. Currency,* 210 F Supp 45; 26 USC §§ 7608 *et seq.*

§ 192. **Execution of the Warrant: "Daytime"—"Nighttime"—Sundays.** Ordinarily a warrant may only be executed in the daytime. Fed R Crim P 41(c); *People v. Malinsky,* 15 NY2d 86, 204 NE2d 188; *People v. Prisco,* 36 Misc2d 357, 232 NYS2d 837; *U.S. v. Merritt,* 293 F2d 742.

A warrant may only be executed in the daytime, unless the issuing judge, upon proof, believes that the warrant cannot be excuted in the daytime, or that the property sought to be seized will be removed or destroyed, if not seized forthwith, in which instance, the judge, in his discretion, may order execution of the warrant at any time of the day or night. Fed R Crim P 41(c); CPL § 690.30(2).

A supplemental affidavit, submitted by the police officer, at the time of the hearing to controvert the warrant, cannot be considered. *People v. Misuraco,* 23 AD2d 722, revd 16 NY2d 542, 208 NE2d 461; *Sgro v. U.S.,* 287 US 206; *People v. Kempner,* 208 NY 16; cf. *Riggan v. Virginia,* 384 US 152.

"Daytime" is between 6 A.M. and 9 P.M., and "nighttime" is between 9 P.M. and 6 A.M. CPL §§ 690.30(2), 690.45.

In *Misuraco, supra,* the lower court vacated a "nighttime" warrant because the supporting affidavit failed to set forth specific facts and detailed statements to show the necessity for authority to execute the warrant during the nighttime. This decision was based to a large extent on the requirement that the statute must be strictly construed. The Appellate Division affirmed, 23 AD2d 722.

An examination of the affidavit submitted in support of the application for the warrant discloses that all of the suspect's activities were observed to have taken place during the nighttime. In reversing both lower court determinations, without opinion, the New York Court of Appeals in effect held that these facts constituted a sufficient showing of probable cause for a "nighttime" execution of the warrant, and that such a conclusion was implicit in the facts set forth in the supporting affidavit. *People v. Misuraco,* 16 NY2d 542, 208 NE2d 461.

In a subsequent decision, *People v. DeLago,* 16 NY2d 289, 213 NE2d 659, the court not only held that the caption of the warrant might be considered in clarifying, for the purpose of specificity, the place to be searched, but also held that it was reasonable to authorize the officers executing the search warrant to dispense with notice of their office and purpose before entry into the premises even though the necessity for this precipitous action was not set forth in the supporting affidavit, as is required by statute. In the *DeLago* case, the officers under the search warrant were seeking gambling paraphernalia. As authority for its position in this latter regard, it was held that a "court could take judicial notice that contraband of that nature [gambling materials] is easily secreted or destroyed if persons unlawfully in the possession thereof are notified in advance that the premises are about to be searched," and that the judge signing the warrant might draw such an inference of fact.

It is to be noted that some federal court decisions hold that with reference to a search warrant, "daytime" continues after sunset for a limited period of time. *Distefano v. U.S.*, 58 F2d 963; *U.S. v. Liebrich*, 55 F2d 341.

Other federal decisions hold that it is "daytime" when there is sufficient natural light to recognize a person's features at a reasonable distance. *Sasser v. U.S.*, 227 F2d 358; *Moore v. U.S.*, 57 F2d 840.

Where no probable cause has been established as to why a warrant cannot be executed in the daytime, a "nighttime" warrant will be controverted. Fed R Crim P 41(e); CPL §§ 690.30 (2), 690.35(3-a), 690.40(2), 690.45(5); *People v. Carminati*, 236 NYS2d 921; *People v. Misuraco*, 16 NY2d 542, 208 NE2d 461; *U.S. v. West*, 328 F2d 16.

A search and seizure executed on a Sunday pursuant to a lawful search warrant which was directed to be executed forthwith, is a lawful search and seizure.

At common law, the execution of a "Sunday" search warrant is also valid. *People v. Childers*, 54 Misc2d 752, 283 NYS2d 336.

Unintentional incorrect dating does not vitiate the warrant. CPL § 690.30(1); *People v. Horton*, 32 AD2d 707, 300 NYS2d 15.

The validity of a warrant directing its execution outside of the hours between 6 A.M. and 9 P.M., because it cannot be executed during the daytime does not require proof by affidavit as to that fact. Additionally, failure to raise the issue at the hearing on the motion to controvert constitutes a waiver. *People v. Horton, supra. See also: People v. DeLago,* 16 NY2d 289, 213 NE2d 659.

**§ 193. Search Warrant: Time Limitation.** A search warrant must be executed within ten days or it becomes void. Fed R Crim P 41; CPL § 690.30(1).

It is implied in *In re McDonald*, 263 AD 967, that once the warrant has become void for failure to execute it within the ten-day period, proceedings had thereunder are also void and they cannot be revitalized merely by the issuance and execution of a second search warrant. To obtain such a lawful "second" search warrant, the proceedings therefore must be instituted *ab initio* and in accordance with the applicable statutory requirements. *People v. Mason,* NYLJ, 3/18/66, p. 18, col. 8. *Also see: Sgro v. U.S.,* 287 US 206.

**§ 194. Notice by Officer in Executing Warrant.** The general rule requires that police, in breaking and entering premises for the purpose of making an otherwise lawful arrest, with or without a warrant, or for the purpose of arresting an escaped prisoner, must give notice to the occupants of their office and purpose. In New York this rule is based both on the common law and statute. *People v. Floyd,* 26 NY2d 558, 260 NE2d 815; CPL §§ 120.80(4, 5), 140.15(4), 140.25(3). The federal rule is the same. *Sabbath v. U.S.,* 391 US 585, 590; *Miller v. U.S.,* 357 US 301.

The rationale of *Sabbath, supra,* which cites *Miller, supra,* is based on the provisions of 18 USC § 3109, which proscribes "unannounced intrusions into a dwelling." The intrusion "is no less an unannounced intrusion whether the officers break down a door, force open a chain lock on a partially open door, open a locked door by use of a passkey, or, as here, open a closed but unlocked door." *Sabbath* at 590.

Exigent circumstances, however, may excuse such notice. *Ker v. California,* 374 US 23; *Sabbath, supra; Miller, supra.*

**§ 194.01 "No-Knock" Law.** The "no-knock" law authorizes the police in executing a search warrant, to break and enter without notice, if authorized to do so in the warrant. The judge issuing the warrant may authorize this action only on proof under oath that the property sought may be easily and quickly destroyed or disposed of, or that danger to life or limb of the officer, or another may result if notice is given. *People v. DeLago,* 16 NY2d 289, 213 NE2d 659.

If notice is to be given, officers need wait a reasonable time after giving the notice before they may break in. Thirty seconds has been held to be a "reasonable time." *U.S. v. West,* 328 F2d 16. Where officers knocked twice and received no response after announcing their presence, and then entered premises through a window, these acts constituted substantial compliance with the statute. *People v. Dacken,* 14 NY2d 653, 198 NE2d 899.

The notice is not required where the premises are unoccupied. *People v. Johnson,* 231 NYS2d 689, affd 19 AD2d 946.

The Federal Statute, the Drug Abuse Prevention Control Act of 1970 (Pub. L. No. 91–513), §§ 509 (a)-(b), also contains a no-knock provision similar to the New York statute. *See:* 1 U.S. Code Cong. and Admin. News 1437 (1970).

**§ 195. The Police as Trespassers.** Although police may be lawfully on premises pursuant to a lawful search warrant, their subsequent actions in executing the warrant may be of such a nature as to constitute them trespassers.

The general rule is that any evidence obtained as a result of a trespass by the police is inadmissible. *McDonald v. U.S.,* 335 US 451; *Johnson v. U.S.,* 333 US 10, 16; *Silverthorne Lumber Co. v. U.S.,* 251 US 385.

"A constitutionally unreasonable search may be consequent either on a search without a warrant or probable cause, or one resulting from trespass or other illegality." *People v. Dentine,* 27 AD2d 139, 140, affd 21 NY2d 700, 234 NE2d 462.

The product of such a search "as well as evidence which stems therefrom—the product of such search—the so-called 'fruit of the poisonous tree'—may not be used against the defendant upon his trial." 21 NY2d at 702 (dissent); *see also: Wong Sun v. U.S.,* 371 US 471, 484.

**§ 195.01. Dissipating the Taint.** However, not all evidence obtained by police trespass is inadmissible.

If the causal relationship between the evidence disclosed as a result of the trespass and the trespass itself had "become so attenuated as to dissipate the taint," the evidence, be it oral or tangibles, may be admissible. *Nardone v. U.S.,* 308 US 338, 341; *Wong Sun v. U.S.,* 371 US 471, 491.

In *People v. Dentine, supra,* for example, Dentine's apartment was entered at 8:15 P.M., pursuant to a search warrant. The search of the apartment was completed at 9:45 P.M., and Dentine was placed under arrest and removed from the apartment. Some of the officers however remained in the apartment. At about 11 P.M., one Bramante entered and disclosed to the officers the name of a woman who was to be aborted by the defendant and whom he was to meet there. Both the woman and Bramante testified before the grand jury and Dentine was indicted.

In the meantime, the original search warrant was declared invalid at a hearing and the items seized thereunder were ordered suppressed.

Thereafter defendant moved to suppress the grand jury testimony of Bramante and the woman. The motion was denied because, as the court noted [in 27 AD2d at 140]; (1) the police were not trespassers in that they had entered the premises initially under what appeared to be a valid search warrant; (2) "Bramante's presence in the apartment was neither related to nor induced by the search." The court then concluded: "Absent a substantial link between the search and the testimony, [before the grand jury] it would seem that the causal relation had 'become so attenuated as to dissipate the taint' [citing *Nardone* and *Wong Sun,* supra]."

**§ 195.02. Latecomers.** Frequently situations arise in which officers are lawfully on private premises upon which they have entered pursuant to a lawful search warrant and after having completed their search, wait in the premises and arrest other persons who had thereafter entered. These persons are often called "latecomers."

As to these latecomers, several questions are presented: (1) may such persons be arrested, and if so under what circumstances; (2) if they are lawfully arrested, may they be searched; (3) how long may the police remain on premises which they have lawfully entered pursuant to a valid search warrant before they can be denominated as trespassers.

In *People v. Perez,* 35 Misc2d 461, 462, 463, 464, the court passed upon these troublesome questions. First, it was noted "that a search warrant contains no authority whatsoever to arrest." Secondly, "After the search has been productive, under ordinary circumstances, the police may no longer remain upon the premises." Third, if they do so, beyond a reasonable but short period of time the police become trespassers. As trespassers they may make an arrest for a crime committed in their presence by any latecomers, but since they are trespassers they may not make a lawful search of these latecomer arrestees "even for a crime committed in their presence." On the other hand latecomers who enter the premises during the search, that is, before the police have become trespassers, may be arrested and searched for a crime committed in the officer's presence.

In conclusion the court said:

> "But of course under any kind of search, if the police remain upon the premises not to search, but with the purpose to arrest any latecomers, they are trespassers, and all such searches are unreasonable."

The prohibition against the right to make an incidental search of latecomers, lawfully arrested, as laid down in this case, is difficult to reconcile with the long-accepted rule authorizing such incident search for weapons, implements which may be used to effect an escape, for contraband and to prevent the destruction of evidence of the crime.

> "The right to search the person of the prisoner as incidental to an arrest had its origin in the English common law and was justified by necessity. A search of the person and, to some extent, of his property was permitted even in the absence of a search warrant in order to protect the lives of the arresting officers, to ensure that the fugitive would not escape and to prevent him from destroying the evidence of his crime." Landynski, *"Search and Seizure and The Supreme Court,"* p. 98. *Cf.: Chimel v. California,* 395 US 752; *Abel v. U.S.,* 362 US 217, 236.

**§ 196. The Inventory.** An inventory of the property taken must be given to the judge, who must give a copy thereof, if requested, to the person from whom it was taken. The officer, seizing the property under a warrant, is also required to give a receipt therefor to the person from whom it was taken. *People v. Kempner,* 208 NY 16; *People v. Montanaro,* 34 Misc2d 624, 229 NYS2d 677; Fed R Crim P 41(d); CPL § 690.50.

**§ 197. The Receipt.** A receipt is defined as a "writing which acknowledges payment or delivery." Shapiro, *Dictionary of Legal Terms.*

The officer must give a detailed receipt for the property taken. The effect of a failure to give such a receipt, and prompt delivery thereof, are questions not wholly resolved. Failure to give such a detailed receipt or failure to deliver it within a reasonable time after the search and seizure may, in certain instances, result in granting the motion to controvert. Fed R Crim P 41(d); CPL § 690.50(4).

It has been held that failure to give such receipt does not invalidate the search warrant, despite the mandatory language of the statute. The weight of authority holds that such failure is a ministerial defect and does not void either the warrant or the search. *People v. Rose,* 52 Misc2d 648. *Cf. Evans v. U.S.,* 242 F2d 534.

Courts should carefully scrutinize the facts surrounding a failure to give such a receipt. *People v. Fusaro,* 53 Misc2d 510, 279 NYS2d 126.

The statute is mandatory. It is not a constitutional requirement—merely statutory. "A search may nevertheless be reasonable if 'defects' in the return are later corrected. (*Evans* v. *U.S.,* 242 F.2d 534.)" *People v. Montanaro,* 34 Misc2d 624, 628, 229 NYS2d 677, 683.

A detailed receipt for items seized, delivered within an hour after the seizure, together with a copy of the search warrant was held not to render the seized property inadmissible. *Martin v. U.S.,* 99 F2d 236.

The items seized under the search warrant and listed in the receipt given to the defendant should be the same as those listed in the inventory delivered to the magistrate concerned.

In *People v. Fusaro, supra,* the court ordered suppression of those articles listed in the inventory which did not appear in the receipt.

If *Fusaro* became a generally accepted rule, the incidence of failure to give a receipt for items seized under a warrant (*People v. Rose, supra*) should decrease sharply. If omission of items in a receipt requires their suppression, why should not the same rule apply where no receipt at all is given? Logic requires an affirmative answer. Good police practice requires no less.

**§ 198. The Return.** Defects in the return of the search warrant will ordinarily not make the search unlawful, and these defects may be corrected, *Evans v. U.S.,* 242 F2d 534.

A search warrant, directed to be executed "immediately," was executed eight days later and the return was made after ten days. The execution was held to be good. It was noted that the statute authorizes execution of a warrant within 10 days after date. *People v. Robles,* NYLJ, 1/17/64, p. 14, col. 2, citing *People v. DiGiacomo,* NYLJ, 11/22/63, p. 13, col. 5.

If either the receipt or return are inaccurate, the defect will adversely affect the other, and a motion to suppress the articles under a lawful search warrant may be granted. *People v. Rose,* 52 Misc2d 648; *People v. Fusaro,* 53 Misc2d 510, 279 NYS2d 126.

It has been held that failure to file the original warrant and return as a public record within ten days of the issuance of the warrant does not mandate suppression of the articles seized thereunder. Thus, where the warrant was issued on December 1, 1965 and executed on December 2, 1965, and the return made to the issuing judge on December 6, 1965, but not filed in the office of the county clerk until the hearing to suppress was held (more than ten days after the issuance of the warrant), the action was held not in violation of statute.

> "It is to be noted from the statutory language that it is the failure to execute the warrant within ten days which renders the warrant void, and not the failure to file the return thereon. While it generally remains unquestioned that the warrant and return should properly and promptly be filed as a public record, the statutes do not command any specific time for filing, failure of which would require the court to vacate that which had theretofore transpired." *People v. Bell,* NYLJ, 11/29/66, p. 18, col. 7.

The return is a ministerial act and any failure therein does not void the warrant. *Evans v. U.S.,* 242 F2d 534; *People v. Massey,* 38 Misc2d 403, 238 NYS2d 531; *Rose v. U.S.,* 274 F 245.

The return may be made to any magistrate, other than the one who issued the warrant. *People v. Massey, supra.*

Failure of the officer to give a copy of the warrant to the defendant at the time of the search and the failure to file the inventory does not invalidate the search and make the evidence seized inadmissible. *U.S. v. Gaitan,* 4 F2d 848.

**§ 199. Substantial Irregularities and Variations in Obtaining Warrant and Making the Return.** Where neither of state troopers seeking search warrants appeared before the judge when the warrants were issued, neither of the peace officers to whom warrants were given for execution made returns of warrants to the judge who issued warrants, and warrants and returns thereon were not delivered to the county court until some eight months after the search and seizure, there were substantial irregularities and variations in procedures which rendered the search warrants void and precluded use of evidence obtained thereunder. Such irregularities were substantial and not merely "ministerial." There is no presumption of regularity as to police activities. *People v. Ricken,* 49 Misc2d 677, 268 NYS2d 677.

**§ 200. The Arrest Warrant: In General.** An arrest warrant is an order of the court directing the arrest of the defendant in the name of the People. It must contain the name of the defendant or other adequate description, together with the nature of the offense charged. The warrant must be signed by the issuing magistrate, dated, and contain a direction as to when the defendant is to be brought before the court.

The issuance of a warrant of arrest must be supported by the same basic criteria as is required for the issuance of a lawful search warrant. In substance, it must be based on probable cause, established by oath or affirmation before a magistrate, particularly describing the person to be arrested and the offense with which he is charged. Fed R Crim P 4; CPL § 120.20. *Bellows v. State,* 30 AD2d 1019, 294 NYS2d 282.

Hearsay testimony is admissible to establish probable cause providing the source of the hearsay is supplied together with facts supporting affiant's belief that the source of the hearsay is reliable and the information supplied is credible. *Barnes v. Texas,* 380 US 253; *Giordenello v. U.S.,* 357 US 480; *People v. Tennyson,* 19 NY2d 573, 227 NE2d 876.

Under the Federal rules, probable cause must be established by oath or affirmation and the same basic criteria for the issuance of a valid search warrant applies to warrants of arrest. Fed R Crim P 3–4; *Jaben v. U.S.*, 381 US 214, rehrg den 382 US 873; *U.S. v. Greenberg,* 320 F2d 467; *cf. Giordenello v. U.S.*, 357 US 480.

In addition to the establishment of probable cause, the warrant must specifically identify the person to be arrested. Under the Federal practice, the warrant may be issued by a commissioner, federal magistrate or other officer authorized by law to commit persons charged with offenses against the United States. Fed R Crim P 3.

The federal practice also authorizes the service of a summons in lieu of the arrest warrant. Fed R Crim P 4. Warrants of arrests are not limited to crimes. Administrative arrest warrants such as are used in deportation proceedings, are also authorized. *Abel v. U.S.*, 367 US 217.

An officer need not have a copy of the arrest warrant with him at the time of the arrest. Knowledge that there is a warrant outstanding is sufficient. *State v. Fultz,* 13 Ohio St2d 79, 234 NE2d 593; *State v. Pedersen,* 424 P2d 810; *U.S. v. One Olivetti Elec. 10-Key Adding Mach.*, 406 F2d 1167; *cf. People v. Valdez,* 65 Cal Rptr 356.

Unlike a search warrant, an arrest warrant does not become stale. The latter remains in effect until executed. *U.S. v. Weaver,* 384 F2d 879, cert. den. 390 US 983; *Wilson v. U.S.*, 325 F2d 224, cert. den. 377 US 1005; *cf. Sgro v. U.S.*, 287 US 206. Nor is there any legal requirement that an arrest warrant be executed immediately or at the first opportunity. *U.S. v. Joines,* 258 F2d 471, cert. den. 358 US 880.

Situations may arise, however, where the warrant is so old and the offense so trivial, that an arrest thereunder, granting good faith, would be improper. This was the case in *Quinnette v. Garland,* 277 F Supp 999, which involved a twelve-year-old warrant for a misdemeanor.

# Chapter 13

## ARREST WITHOUT A WARRANT



---

§ 205. **The Lawful Arrest.** The admissibility of evidence seized in a search incident to an arrest depends on the lawfulness of the arrest. *People v. Floyd,* 26 NY2d 558, 260 NE2d 815. Thus, the legality of the arrest is a basic issue to be resolved by the court in considering the suppression of evidence.

An arrest occurs at the point where a suspect's freedom of movement is curtailed. *Henry v. U.S.,* 361 US 98; *People v. Shivers,* 21 NY2d 118, 233 NE2d 836.

The police have a right to investigate prior to arrest. This includes the right to stop and question persons answering a description received on a police radio. They have the right to approach persons for the purpose of routine investigations and these acts do not constitute arrests. *Rios v. U.S.,* 364 US 253; *People v. Wilson,* 16 AD2d 207; *People v. Carafas,* 14 AD2d 886, affd 11 NY2d 891, 182 NE2d 413; *People v. Entriaglo,* 19 AD2d 509, affd 14 NY2d 733, 199 NE2d 384; *U.S. v. Vita,* 294 F2d 524, cert. den. 369 US 823; *Busby v. U.S.,* 296 F2d 328, cert. den. 369 US 876; *People v. Surplice,* 21 Cal Rptr 826; *People v. Cassese,* 47 Misc2d 1031, 263 NYS2d 734.

In *People v. Morales,* 22 NY2d 55, 57, 58, 238 NE2d 307, the issue was "the authority of law enforcement officials to temporarily detain and question suspects upon less than probable cause for charges of crime after advising them of their Fifth and Sixth Amendment rights." The defendant was taken to a police station for questioning in regard to a murder case in which the victim had been stabbed 21 times. During their investigation, the police "learned that defendant, a known narcotics addict, who constantly frequented the apartment house, [where the victim resided], had not been seen since the killing." Ten days later they located the defendant at his mother's beauty parlor. The police told him they wished to question him. He was not placed under arrest nor did the police have probable cause to do so. They intended to question him for no more than an hour, and they so advised the defendant. They drove to the police station. No physical force was used. "In fact, defendant testified that he was so loosely guarded when taken from the car to the station that he could have safely escaped but did not because he had no reason to do so. However, he was not free to leave at the time he was apprehended and would have been restrained had he attempted to flee."

After being advised of his Fifth and Sixth Amendment rights, he was questioned, and confessed to the killing after some 15 minutes of interrogation. Citing *Culombe v. Connecticut,* 367 US 568, 590–592, the Court of Appeals held that the detention in this case did not constitute an arrest:

> "We hold merely that a suspect may be detained upon reasonable suspicion for a reasonable and brief period of time for questioning under carefully controlled conditions protecting his Fifth and Sixth Amendment rights. Mass detentions for questioning are never permissible. The scope of the authority to question is limited to those persons reasonably suspected of possessing knowledge of the crime under investigation in circumstances involving crimes presenting a high degree of public concern affecting the public safety." *Morales, supra,* 22 NY2d at 64–65. *Cf. Sibron v. New York,* 392 US 40.

However, the United States Supreme Court remanded *Morales* for a hearing to determine the question of probable cause for the original detention. *Morales v. New York,* 396 US 102.

The right of the police to make inquiries of persons concerning unusual or suspicious circumstances which the officer observed does not constitute an arrest, although an arrest may ensue. "This right, pre-existing the statute, continues, and is not impaired by the specifics of [the statute]." *People v. Rosemond,* 26 NY2d 101, 104.

Thus, when a police officer on routine patrol saw a man enter a building late at night, empty-handed, and leave later with some bundles, the officer had the right to inquire and ask questions. This is a common law right. *People v. Rosemond, supra; People v. Rivera,* 14 NY2d 441, 201 NE2d 32, cert. den. 379 US 978.

The "question of precisely when an arrest occurred is one of fact." *Sibron v. New York,* 392 US 40, 67; *see also: People v. Butterly,* 25 NY2d 159, 250 NE2d 340.

The police, it was held, have the right to stop and question motorists found in a parked car at 3 A.M. on a winter's morning. When, upon their inquiry, no vehicle registration or operator's license was disclosed, detention of the defendants for a short time while the police checked the vehicle to determine if it was stolen did not constitute an arrest. *People v. Donnelly,* NYLJ, 8/31/65, p. 18, col. 3.

The continued questioning and holding of the defendant constitutes an arrest. *People v. Jones,* 38 Misc2d 125, 128. However, the time factor alone, is not conclusive. Thus, detention of the defendant for eleven hours by the F.B.I. was held not "unreasonable." *U.S. v. Vita,* 294 F2d 524, cert. den. 369 US 823; *cf. People v. Morales, supra.*

The federal law authorizing "border" searches permits detentions which do not constitute arrests. Detention of defendant incidental to a search by customs inspectors while he was entering the country from Mexico did not amount to an arrest. *People v. Mitchell,* 26 Cal Rptr 89, cert. den. 374 US 845; *U.S. v. Yee Ngee How,* 105 F Supp 517. *See also: Searches by Government Officers and Agents, Chapter 16, infra.*

The legality of an arrest is determined by local law subject to the same constitutional standards as applies to Federal officers. *U.S. ex rel Lupo v. Fay,* 332 F2d 1020; *Miller v. U.S.,* 357 US 301; *People v. Manasek,* 33 Misc2d 832, 837, 225 NYS2d 673; *People v. Lombardi,* 18 AD2d 177, affd 13 NY2d 1014; *Ker v. California,* 374 US 23.

In cases involving arrests by federal officers, made without a warrant in the absence of an applicable federal statute, the arrest is controlled by the law of the place where the arrest took place. *U.S. v. Viale,* 312 F2d 595, cert. den. 373 US 903; *U.S. v. Burgos,* 269 F2d 763.

Nor is the power of a federal officer to make an arrest as a private person (permissible by state law), curtailed by a federal statute authorizing him to make an arrest for another offense cognizable under federal law. *U.S. v. Burgos, supra;* 26 USC § 7607; 8 USC § 1326; CPL § 140.30(1).

The rule in *Burgos* was followed in *U.S. v. Heliczer,* 373 F2d 241. There the court held that since evidence authorized a jury to find that one of the defendants had committed a felony by threatening a government informant, his arrest by federal narcotics agents without a warrant was lawful under New York statute permitting an arrest of another by a private person when the person arrested has committed a felony.

An off-duty policeman is not relieved of his obligations or powers as a police officer. *People v. Peters,* 18 NY2d 238, 219 NE2d 595, affd 392 US 40.

Under the federal rule, where the arresting officer knows that there is an outstanding warrant for the defendant, he may lawfully make the arrest, even though he does not have the warrant in his possession at the time. *U.S. v. Petti,* 168 F2d 221, 223; Fed R Crim P 9(C)(1). The same rule applies to New York police officers. *U.S. v. Burgos,* 269 F2d 763, 766; *People v. Floyd,* 56 Misc2d 373.

**§ 205.01. Arrest by Federal Officers and Agents.** Although there is a popular misconception that the F.B.I. is our federal police force, there is in fact no such thing as a federal police department or force. Nor do we have any general federal arrest statute such as exists in the various states. The power to arrest, to search, to seize and to execute warrants is allocated by statute only to certain federal agencies and bureaus. Federal Bureau of Investigation (F.B.I.), 18 USC §§ 3052, 3105, 3107; Fed R Crim P 41(c); U.S. Marshals, 18 USC § 3053; The Secret Service (Treasury Dept.), 18 USC § 3056; Alcohol Tax Unit (Treasury Dept.), 26 USC § 7608; Bureau of Customs (Treasury Dept.), 19 USC § 1581; Bureau of Narcotics and Bureau of Customs, 26 USC § 7607; Immigration and Naturalization Service (Justice Dept.), 8 USC § 1357; Internal Revenue Service (Treasury Dept.), 26 USC § 7608; Post Office Department, 39 USC § 3523(a)(2)(k).

These statutes must be strictly construed. The officers and agents have no greater power or authority than those contained in the statute governing their agency. For example, in a case where an F.B.I. agent made an arrest without a warrant, the government must establish that the arrest was necessary because there was a likelihood that the suspect might escape before a warrant could be obtained. *U.S. v. Coplon,* 185 F2d 629, cert. den. 342 US 920; *U.S. v. Bianco,* 189 F2d 716; *James v. U.S.,* 280 F2d 443; *Matter of Fried,* 68 F Supp 961; *U.S. v. Haberkorn,* 149 F2d 720.

Another example is *Williams v. U.S.,* 382 F2d 48, which holds that even though the local police may have had the right to search an automobile on probable cause, after it had been abandoned following a chase by postal inspectors and after it had been removed to a garage by the police, the postal inspectors themselves had no authority to search the vehicle at a later time without a search warrant.

Where invalid arrest warrants had been obtained and no new arrest warrants were sought, the arrests were lawful where the defendants were arrested in a public place by F.B.I. agents who had probable cause to believe that they had committed a felony. *U.S. v. Hall,* 348 F2d 837; *Ford v. U.S.,* 352 F2d 927. Both courts indicated, however, that a different result might have been obtained had these arrests taken place in the defendants' home rather than in a public place.

In *Ford,* the court sought to discourage the practice of warrantless arrests by citing *U.S. v. Ventresca,* 380 US 102, 106, which held in part that "in a doubtful or marginal case of probable cause a search may be sustainable on a warrant, where without one it would fall."

However, where an arrest warrant has been issued, in the case of a suspect fleeing or likely to take flight, it is unnecessary to obtain a search warrant to enter and make the arrest. *Johnson v. U.S.,* 333 US 10; *U.S. v. McKinney,* 379 F2d 259.

On a motion to suppress, therefore, the burden is on the government not only of showing probable cause to believe that a crime had been committed or was being committed both in obtaining a warrant prior to arrest and in sustaining the legality of an arrest without a warrant (*Rogers v. U.S.,* 330 F2d 535; *U.S. v. Rivera,* 321 F2d 704), but implicit in these requirements is the necessity on the part of the government to establish the fact that the federal officer or agent was duly authorized to arrest, search, seize or execute a warrant, as the case may be, by the appropriate statute applicable to his bureau or agencies, by the terms, provisions and limitations, if any, of that statute. *U.S. v. Rivera, supra; Rogers v. U.S., supra; U.S. v. Elgisser,* 334 F2d 103; *Wrightson v. U.S.,* 222 F2d 556; *U.S. v. Costner,* 217 F Supp 644; *Matter of Fried, supra; see also: People v. Malinsky,* 15 NY2d 86, 204 NE2d 188.

Of course, this does not preclude a federal officer or agent in a proper case from making an arrest, without a warrant, as a private citizen. *U.S. v. Burgos,* 269 F2d 763, cert. den. 362 US 942.

Also, in the absence of any federal statute setting a standard to apply in testing the legality of an arrest by federal officers, resort must be made to the law of the place of the arrest. *U.S. v. Costner, supra; cf.: U.S. v. Burgos, supra; U.S. v. Viale,* 312 F2d 595, cert. den. 373 U.S. 903. The applicability of the law of the *locus in quo* must be applied in all arrests made by postal inspectors, since there is no statute prescribing the standard when the arrests referred to in the statute may be made (39 USC § 3523), and thus these arrests can only be executed by them as private citizens.

**§ 206. Arrest Without a Warrant.** In general, peace officers and police officers as such, and private persons, are authorized to make an arrest without a warrant under certain circumstances usually prescribed by statute. *See, e.g.,* N.Y. CPL art. 140; *also see:* Fed R Crim P 5.

**§ 206.01. Police Officers.** Generally an officer may make a lawful arrest for any crime committed or attempted in his presence, or where he has reasonable grounds for believing that a crime was committed. *Cf.: Draper v. U.S.,* 358 US 307; *People v. Lane,* 10 NY2d 347, 179 NE2d 339; *People v. Malinsky,* 15 NY2d 86, 204 NE2d 188.

In *U.S. ex rel McCullen v. McMann,* 370 F2d 757, the police received a report at 4 A.M. of a burglary in progress at a candy store. On arriving at the scene, they saw evidence of the burglary and observed the defendant alone on the street not far from the store and questioned him. This was about 4:30 A.M. Defendant was frisked. Without discussing the frisk, the court held that probable cause existed to arrest the defendant without a warrant and to search him incidental to that arrest.

The facts establishing the probable cause were: the police knew that a burglary had been committed; defendant was found at 4:30 A.M. alone on a street not far from the burglarized premises; when questioned, defendant gave evasive and false answers. *Accord: Arnold v. U.S.,* 382 F2d 4.

Such arrest without a warrant is lawful when the officer has reasonable cause to believe that a felony has been committed and that the person arrested committed it, though it should afterward appear that no felony has in fact been committed, or if committed, that the person arrested did not commit it. *People v. Ward,* 32 Misc2d 843, 223 NYS2d 355.

Such arrest without a warrant is lawful when the officer has reasonable cause for believing that a person has been arrested by a citizen as statutorily provided. *U.S. ex rel Lupo v. Fay,* 332 F2d 1020.

Thus, unless there is probable cause to make the arrest, it is unlawful, and any search incident thereto is unreasonable. Mere suspicion cannot be deemed probable cause. *Beck v. Ohio,* 379 US 89; *Stoner v. Calif.,* 376 US 483; *People v. O'Neill,* 11 NY2d 148; *U.S. v. Smith,* 308 F2d 657; *Carroll v. U.S.,* 267 US 132; *Brinegar v. U.S.,* 338 US 160; *People v. Politano,* 17 AD2d 503; *People v. Cassone, infra; People v. Garcia,* 20 AD2d 855, 248 NYS2d 154; *People v. Scalegnio,* 14 NY2d 744, 199 NE2d 509.

*See also: Probable Cause to Arrest Without a Warrant, § 172, supra.*

**§ 206.02. Private Persons.** Under the common law a private individual may arrest a person for an offense committed or attempted in his presence. However, this is regulated by statute in most states today. *See, e.g.,* N.Y. CPL § 140.30(1).

The validity of a citizen's arrest for a felony depends on the guilt of the defendant. No other considerations, such as the reasonableness of the arresting person's belief, is of any significance. *People v. Cassone,* 20 AD2d 118, 120, affd 14 NY2d 798, 200 NE2d 214; *People v. Horman,* 22 NY2d 378, 380, 239 NE2d 625; CPL § 140.30(1).

In *Matter of Fried,* 68 F Supp 961, 964, it was held that "a private person could in no event make a search incidental to an arrest." This rule was modified in *People v. Alberta,* 37 Misc2d 847, which held that such a search was authorized on consent of the arrestee.

However, *U.S. v. Viale,* 312 F2d 595, cert. den. 373 US 903, has overruled both *Fried* and *Alberta* by holding that a private person may make a search incidental to a lawful arrest. See also *People v. Horman,* 22 NY2d 378, 380, where the court did "not reach, . . . the question whether a private person may conduct a search without a warrant incidental to a lawful arrest," although it cited *Viale.*

The rationale of the holding in *Viale* is based on the rule that Fourth Amendment "protections have not been applied to searches and seizures by persons other than government officers and agents. (*Sackler* v. *Sackler,* 15 NY2d 40.)" *Horman, supra,* 22 NY2d at 381. *See also: Burdeau v. McDowell,* 256 US 465; *People v. Defore,* 242 NY 13, 22, 23.

Additional support for the decision in *Viale* may be found in *People v. King,* NYLJ, 9/1/66, p. 15, col. 4, where the court said: "It is well settled that the 'mere evidence' rule does not apply to searches of the person, and that papers so obtained are admissible even though 'mere evidence' (*Abel v. United States,* 362 U.S. 271 [1959]; *Weeks v. United States,* 232 U.S. 383 [1914]; *Grillo v. United States,* 336 F.2d 211; *United States v. Kirchenblatt,* 16 F.2d 202; *United States v. Kraus,* 270 F.2d 578."

Search of defendant by a parole officer (*People v. Randazzo,* 37 Misc2d 80, affd 15 NY2d 526, 202 NE2d 459) for a parole violation, which was sustained as lawful, lends further support to *Viale.*

In *People v. Trimarco,* 41 Misc2d 775, 777, the New York State Supreme Court said, "The defendant's point that a private person may not make a search incidental to a lawful arrest is without legal validity (*United States* v. *Viale,* 312 F.2d 595 . . .)."

Since a private person may lawfully arrest another for an offense committed or attempted in his presence or for a felony, it would logically follow that a search incident thereto is also lawful. In this regard, the lawful incident search made by an officer and by a private person are equated. *People v. Santiago,* 53 Misc2d 264, 278 NYS2d 260. *See also: U.S. v. Viale, supra; U.S. v. Park Ave. Pharmacy,* 56 F2d 753, 756; *Coplon v. U.S.,* 191 F2d 749, 754, cert. den. 342 US 926; *U.S. v. Rabinowitz,* 339 US 56, 60–61.

Where an arrest was made by a civilian who persuaded the defendant to open the trunk of his automobile in which he saw stolen goods, and where the civilian (defendant's employer) thereupon called the police, the police had probable cause to arrest the defendant and open the trunk of his automobile without a warrant and seize the contraband as incident to a lawful arrest. *People v. Zalduondo,* 58 Misc2d 326.

There was no police connivance in this search. As stated in *U.S. v. McGuire,* 381 F2d 306, 313, n. 5, "'The thrust of the Fourth Amendment is to assure protection from official, not private intrusion.'" *See: Hoffa v. U.S.,* 385 US 293, 301.

It has long been the law that evidence wrongfully obtained by a private person, absent governmental connivance, is admissible in both federal and state criminal prosecutions. *Burdeau v. McDowell,* 256 US 465; *People v. Kowalczyk,* 20 NY2d 835, 213 NE2d 772; *People v. Horman,* 22 NY2d 378, 381, 239 NE2d 625; *Sackler v. Sackler,* 15 NY2d 40, 203 NE2d 481; *People v. Defore,* 242 NY 13, 22–23. However, such evidence must be viewed with caution if turned over to the police in the light of "fruit of the poisoned tree" doctrine. *See: Wong Sun v. United States,* 371 US 471.

As noted above, where there is involvement by the police in an unlawful search by a private person, the search and seizure violate the defendant's Fourth Amendment rights.

In a California case, private investigators searched defendant's automobile while assisted by the police. The court found that there was "official participation and implementation" of the overall scheme to arrest and search the defendant which constituted a violation of his rights. *Stapleton v. Superior Court,* 477 P2d 967.

In some cases the status of the person making an arrest or

a search is important. Thus, the question arose in *People v. Custis,* 32 AD2d 966, whether the status of a special policeman at a racetrack was that of a police officer or private person. If his apointment as a special policeman had been approved by the State Harness Commission, he would have the status of a police officer.

In civil cases, "evidence is not excluded because the private litigant who offers it has gathered it by lawless force." *Sackler v. Sackler,* 15 NY2d 40, 203 NE2d 481. *Sackler* was a divorce case instituted by the husband. Proof of the wife's guilt was obtained by a forcible entry into the wife's home by her husband and some private "detectives." The question of law presented for review was, "should the proof as to the wife's guilt have been excluded from evidence because it was obtained by means of an illegal forcible entry into the wife's home by the husband and several private investigators employed by him? Agreeing with the Trial Justice and the Appellate Division, we hold that the evidence was admissible." *Id.* at 42.

Rejecting the contention that *Mapp v. Ohio,* 367 US 643, was controlling, the court noted that "applying the Fourth Amendment is of course not controlling here or even applicable since its impact is on governmental seizures only and not on evidence illegally gathered by private persons." *Ibid.* As additional authority the court cited *Burdeau v. McDowell,* 256 US 465. "In *Burdeau,* the court (p. 475) said flatly and finally that the Fourth Amendment's 'origin and history clearly show that it was intended to be a restraint upon the activities of sovereign authority, and was not intended to be a limitation upon other than government agencies.' " 15 NY2d at 43. *Burdeau* has never been overruled.

In *People v. Horman,* 22 NY2d 378, 308, 239 NE2d 625, the court reaffirmed the rule in *Sackler, supra.* Horman was arrested on a shoplifting charge by store detectives outside a department store for allegedly stealing a small water faucet. He was taken to the security manager's office where he emptied his pockets. He was frisked, and a loaded pistol was forcibly taken from him. His conviction was affirmed in the Appellate Division on the ground that "evidence wrongfully obtained by a private person is admissible in a state criminal prosecution." The Court of Appeals also affirmed, noting: "Therefore, since the evidence in this case was seized without the participation or knowledge of any governmental official, it is admissible in a criminal prosecution." 22 NY2d at 382 and cases cited therein. *See also: Agency v. Dept. of State of N.Y.*, 262 NYS2d 694.

Store detectives are generally equated with private persons. *People v. Frank,* 52 Misc2d 266, 275 NYS2d 570; *People v. Horman, supra,* at 380.

§ 207. **Delay in Arrest and Arraignment.** An arrest, without a warrant, for a misdemeanor committed in the officer's presence may be made within a reasonable time after the commission of the offense. *People v. Sessa,* 43 Misc2d 24, 250 NYS2d 193, and cases cited. However, the delay in the arrest of a defendant after the commission of a crime may be for such a long period of time so as to create a presumption of prejudice to his rights to a fair trial, but not in all circumstances.

In *Powell v. U.S.,* 352 F2d 705, the court held that it was not unreasonable for an undercover agent to delay the arrest of a defendant for five months so that the agent's usefulness would be maintained during that time and that the five months' lapse in time in no way impaired the defendant's rights to a fair trial. *See also: Jackson v. U.S.,* 351 F2d 821; Fed R Crim P 5.

The same rule was held applicable to delays in arraignment in a New York case. "In the instant case, to have attempted to arraign the defendants at an earlier date may well have jeopardized their lives. In matters of this nature, the court must be guided by practical considerations." *People v. Moskus,* NYLJ, 12/14/65, p. 15, col. 6.

The U.S. Court of Appeals (2d Cir.) held in *U.S. v. Hammond,* 360 F2d 688, that in the absence of any other circumstances, a 15-month delay between the commission of the offense and the arrest did not violate due process and did not violate any right of the accused on the ground that the delay prejudiced the accused's ability to recollect the events in question, where although the accused raised such a question at the trial, the government was prevented from offering any explanation of the delay by defense counsel's successful objection to such explanatory testimony.

*See also: § 222, infra.*

§ 208. **Invalid Arrest: Effect of Search.** If no valid arrest is made, a subsequent search is illegal. *People v. Ryan,* 14 AD2d 926, 222 NYS2d 92. The validity of an arrest is primarily of interest to the court on the question of suppression of evidence. Thus, an arrest by a police officer effected by unlawful means requires suppression of the evidence seized incident to such arrest. *People v. Floyd,* 26 NY2d 558, 260 NE2d 815.

Where, at the time of arrest, the police did not know that a felony had been committed by anyone, a search disclosing stolen articles was unlawful, and it was not made lawful by what was subsequently learned. *People v. Malinsky,* 15 NY2d 86, 204 NE2d 188. *People v. Jones,* 38 Misc2d 125; *U.S. v. DiRe,* 332 US 581; *U.S v. Smith,* 308 F2d 657; *Cochran v. U.S.,* 291 F2d 633.

# Chapter 14

## SEARCH INCIDENT TO LAWFUL ARREST



---

**§ 215. In General.** A search absent a warrant may be reasonable where it is executed incident to a lawful arrest. This means that, under these circumstances, the person of the individual arrested may be searched as well as the area under his immediate control. *Weeks v. U.S.,* 232 US 383, 392; *Chimel v. California,* 395 US 752; *Marron v. U.S.,* 275 US 192; *Agnello v. U.S.,* 269 US 20; *People v. Defore,* 242 NY 13. This right, born of necessity, stems from the common law and was permitted to protect the life of the arresting officer, to uncover instruments that might aid the prisoner in escaping, and to prevent the destruction of evidence of the crime for which he is arrested. *Abel v. U.S.,* 362 US 217, 236.

However, the search must be truly incidental to the primary purpose to arrest. *U.S. v. Robinson,* 325 F2d 391; *Palmer v. U.S.,* 192 A2d 801 [D.C.]; *People v. Roach,* 44 Misc2d 40, 43, affd 26 AD2d 561. It may not be used as a pretext to search, *People v. Scalegno,* 14 NY2d 744, 199 NE2d 509; or as a pretext to search for evidence to justify the arrest, *People v. Loria,* 10 NY2d 368, 373, 179 NE2d 478; *U.S. v. DiRe,* 332 US 581, 595; or to search for evidence of another crime, *Jones v. U.S.,* 357 US 493; *State v. Taylor,* 81 NJ Super 296, 308–309; *U.S. v. Harris,* 32 F2d 739.

The Fourth Amendment commands that probable cause to search is a necessary condition precedent to a lawful search even though the arrest was lawful. *People v. Brown,* 45 Cal2d

640; *People v. Roach,* 44 Misc2d 40, 46. On the issue of probable cause, hearsay evidence is admissible. *People v. Loria, supra; Draper v. U.S.,* 358 US 307.

In sum, a lawful incident search requires (1) statutory authority to arrest, and (2) probable cause to search. *See: Sibron v. New York,* 392 US 40; *cf. Peters v. New York,* 392 US 40. If both of these elements are present, the search is reasonable. Nor does an acquittal of an underlying charge stamp the subsequent incident search as unreasonable. There is no operable collateral estoppel. *People v. LoCicero,* 14 NY2d 374, 380, 200 NE2d 622; *cf. People v. Dreares,* 15 AD2d 204, 206, affd 11 NY2d 906, 182 NE2d 812; *People v. Cassone,* 20 AD2d 118, 120, affd 14 NY2d 798, 200 NE2d 214. Neither suspicion nor equivocal behavior alone justifies a search. *People v. Brown,* 24 NY2d 421, 423, 248 NE2d 867; *People v. Corrado,* 22 NY2d 308, 311, 313, 239 NE2d 526; *see also: Agnello v. U.S.,* 269 US 20, 33; *Jones v. U.S.,* 357 US 493, 497. A search is good or bad when it starts. A bad search, *i.e.,* a search in violation of the Fourth Amendment, is not made good by what it discloses. *Byars v. U.S.,* 273 US 28, 29; *Henry v. U.S.,* 361 US 98, 104; *U.S. v. DiRe,* 332 US 581, 595. The critical question revolves around the officer's primary purpose. If his primary purpose was to search, a search warrant is mandatory. *People v. Roach,* 44 Misc2d 40, 43, citing *People v. Shelton,* 60 Cal2d 740 and *People v. Haven,* 59 Cal2d 713.

The search for "mere evidence" in a case of hot pursuit of the defendant is also authorized. *Warden v. Hayden,* 387 US 294; *cf.: U.S. v. Lefkowitz,* 285 US 452; *Abel v. U.S.,* 362 US 217, 238; *Chimel v. California,* 395 US 752. *See also: Exigent Circumstances and Hot Pursuit, Chapter 18, infra.*

§ 216. **What May Be Seized Under an Incident Search.** Items that may be seized as incident to a lawful arrest are (1) instrumentalities and means by which the crime is committed, (2) instruments which may be used to injure the arresting officer, (3) instruments which may aid the suspect to escape, (4) fruits of a crime, (5) contraband, *i.e.,* items the possession of which constitutes a crime, and (6) evidence of the crime. *U.S. v. Nirenberg,* 19 FRD 421, 422; *People v. Carroll,* 38 Misc2d 630, 238 NYS2d 640; CPL § 690.10; *Warden v. Hay-*

*den,* 387 US 294; *Schmerber v. California,* 384 US 757; *Abel v. U.S.,* 362 US 217, 236–239.

Search warrants in federal prosecutions may be issued for the seizure of evidence. 18 USC § 3103a.

The former rule that search for "mere evidence" is *always* unreasonable (*U.S. v. Stern,* 225 F Supp 187; *cf. People v. Grossman,* 45 Misc2d 557, revd 27 AD2d 572; *Entick v. Carrington,* 19 Howells St Tr 1029), has been relaxed in cases involving "hot pursuit" (*Warden v. Hayden,* 384 US 294) and in "driving while intoxicated" cases involving taking of a blood sample (*Schmerber v. California,* 384 US 757; *People v. Young,* 42 Misc2d 540, 248 NYS2d 287).

In *Brent v. White,* 398 F2d 503, cert. den. 393 US 1123, the court has gone so far in an incident search case following an arrest on a charge of rape, as to hold as lawful, the taking of penis scrapings for menstrual blood taken from the defendant. As in *Schmerber, supra,* the court noted that this incident search was necessary to prevent destruction of this evidence.

In *Schmerber, supra,* as in *Brent v. White, supra,* the court held that the incident search, *i.e.,* the forcible extraction of the defendant's blood after his arrest for drunken driving, was lawful, following a valid arrest, since a delay in the extraction of the blood sample threatened destruction of evidence. Although the court recognized the importance of obtaining a search warrant for an intrusion into a person's body unless an emergency exists, the officer in this case "might reasonably have believed that he was confronted with an emergency, . . . [which] under the circumstances, threatened 'the destruction of evidence,' *Preston* v. *U.S.,* 376 U.S. 364, 367. We are told that the percentage of alcohol in the blood begins to diminish shortly after drinking stops, as the body functions to eliminate it from the system. . . . Given these special facts, we conclude that the attempt to secure evidence of blood-alcohol content in this case was an appropriate incident to petitioner's arrest." 384 US at 770.

In *People v. Britton,* 26 AD2d 586, the seizure of defendant's bloodstained trousers, lying in open view, were lawfully seized as incident to a lawful arrest, albeit they were "evidence." The court said:

"We are . . . of the opinion that defendant's bloodstained trousers, lying in open view at the time of his arrest, were properly subject to seizure (cf. *Abel* v. *United States,* 362 U.S. 217; *Morton* v. *United States,* 147 F.2d 28, cert. den. 324 U.S. 875; *United States* v. *Guido,* 251 F.2d 1, cert. den. 356 U.S. 950; *Robinson* v. *United States,* 283 F.2d 508, cert. den. 364 U.S. 919; *People* v. *Chiagles,* 237 N.Y. 193, 196–197)."

Introduction of photographs of blood stains on the exterior and interior of an automobile, and of a handkerchief found in the car, without a search warrant, was sustained in Georgia, although these items were also "mere evidence." *Abrams v. State,* 223 Ga 216, 154 SE2d 443. The vehicle belonged to the petitioner who was charged with rape, alleged to have taken place in his car.

The car was seized at the time of his arrest and impounded. The photographs were made two days later. The court sustained the search and seizure on several grounds: (1) A car can constitute an implement of crime since it was used to commit the rape. Even though the vehicle was not subject to a forfeiture, yet as an implement of crime it is equated with weapons and as such it may be seized, impounded and searched under the circumstances of this case. (2) The photographs of the blood stains were merely evidence of what the officers had observed and this did not constitute a search and seizure. *See also: Cooper v. California,* 386 US 58; *State v. McCoy,* 437 P2d 734 (Oregon); *cf. Preston v. U.S.,* 376 US 364.

A "contemporaneous" search without a warrant extends to things and places under the accused's immediate control. In *Chimel v. California,* 395 US 752, 762, 763, the court defined that term to mean an area which was readily accessible to the accused at the time of his arrest. *See also: Vale v. Louisiana,* 399 US 30, 26 L Ed2d 408, *Cooper v. California,* 386 US 58; *cf.: Preston v. U.S.,* 376 US 364; *U.S. v. Rabinowitz,* 339 US 56; *People v. Daily,* 321 P2d 469. The search must be truly incidental to the primary purpose of the arrest. *U.S. v. Robinson,* 325 F2d 391; *Preston v. U.S., supra; Cooper v. California,* 386 US 58; *People v. Bennett,* 28 AD2d 526, 280 NYS2d 258.

Thus, where a defendant, while in his automobile, was arrested for vagrancy and his car was then removed from the street for public convenience, a subsequent search of the vehicle without a warrant was unlawful. The search of the vehicle was in no wise related to the charge of vagrancy. *Preston v. U.S.,* 376 US 364.

On the other hand, a defendant charged with trafficking in narcotics and who used his car in those acts could not complain that a search of his car without a warrant was unlawful where, under California law, the police were required to impound the car and hold it for forfeiture or other disposition. In this case, the search of the car was truly related to the purpose of the arrest—a search for contraband narcotics in an area under his immediate control. Since the vehicle was also in the custody of the police, the search was held proper for the protection of the police. *Cooper v. California,* 386 US 58, *see, e.g., Preston v. U.S., supra,* opinion by Black, J. *See also: People v. Randazzo,* 37 Misc2d 80, affd 15 NY2d 526, 202 NE2d 459, dissent by Fuld, J.; *People v. Beaman,* 44 Misc2d 336, 253 NYS2d 674.

In a case similar to *Cooper* and *Preston, People v. Webb,* 56 Cal Rptr 902, and in which the vehicle was searched at the police garage, following the defendant's arrest, the Supreme Court of California stretched the "time and place" contemporaneous elements of the incident search, due to the special facts of that case, where there was gun fire and a crash, and a mob had collected at the time of the commencement of the search. The necessity of delaying this incident search is apparent. *See also: People v. Moschitta,* 25 AD2d 686, 269 NYS2d 70.

Of particular interest in *Webb,* however, is the concurring opinion of Peters, J., who stated that *Cooper v. California, supra,* overrules *Preston v. U.S., supra.* "No longer need a warrant be secured if a search is not incidental to a lawful arrest but is separated from the arrest both in time and space. A search is now permissible without a warrant if the vehicle is in valid police custody." *Webb, supra,* 56 Cal Rptr at 916. *See also: People v. Burke,* 394 P2d 67, 39 Cal Rptr 531. *Cf. Chimel v. California,* 395 US 752.

In the incident search area cases, one of the critical questions presented is how far the officer may go in searching the area under the control of the accused at the time of his arrest.

How far does this area extend? In *People v. Daily,* 321 P2d 469 (Calif.), it was held to extend to a car parked on the street when the defendant was arrested in an apartment house. *See also: U.S. v. Cefaratti,* 202 F2d 13. In *Harris v. U.S.,* 331 US 145, it was held to extend to all four rooms of an apartment occupied by the petitioner, although he was seen in only one of the rooms at the time of his arrest.

In all of the cases in this area, the search was held lawful because the place searched was under the control of the defendant at the time and place of his arrest. This rule, however, has been struck down by the decision in *Chimel v. California, supra.*

*Chimel* has limited the search area strictly to what may be called the "arms length" rule. *Chimel* limits the area and places that may be lawfully searched without a warrant, as incident to a lawful arrest, to the area or places readily within the accused's reach. *Vale v. Louisiana,* 399 US 30, reemphasizes the *Chimel* rule, in holding that when a person is arrested outside of his house, the search of his house as incident to that arrest is also unlawful, absent a search warrant.

*Chimel* has specifically overruled *Harris v. U.S.,* 331 US 145, and *U.S. v. Rabinowitz,* 339 US 56. In effect, *Chimel* reinstated the pre-*Harris,* pre-*Rabinowitz* rule enunciated in *Trupiano v. U.S.,* 334 US 699.

In substance *Trupiano* held that even where a lawful arrest has been made, an incident search is not lawful if the circumstances present made it feasible for the officers to obtain a search warrant before the search was executed.

Thus, *Trupiano* restates the basic rule that all searches without a search warrant are unlawful (see the "warrant" clause of the Fourth Amendment) unless the particular facts of the case render the search without a warrant not unreasonable (see the "unreasonable search and seizure" clause of the Fourth Amendment).

Accordingly, it has been held repeatedly that, following a lawful arrest, a search to prevent the destruction of evidence is not an unreasonable search.

In *Hill v. California,* 401 US 797, the Supreme Court validated an incident search of an individual who was arrested in error because the police thought him to be another person, whom they were seeking in connection with a robbery. " 'When the police have probable cause to arrest one party, and when they reasonably mistake a second party for the first party, then the arrest of the second party is a valid arrest.' " *Hill* at 802, quoting from 69 Cal2d at 553. ". . . [T]he police were entitled to do what the law would have allowed them to do if Miller [the person sought] had in fact been Hill, [the one mistakenly arrested as Miller], that is, to search incident to arrest and to seize evidence of the crime the police had probable cause to believe Hill had committed." 401 US at 804. *See also: U.S. v. Holland,* 438 F2d 887.

In *People v. Block,* 93 Cal Rptr 779, the court sustained a search and seizure as incident to a lawful arrest, contraband found in open view while searching a house, on probable cause to believe that a "pot party" (marihuana smoking) was in progress. The marihuana was found while the police were searching the upstairs portion of the house to determine if others were involved in the "pot party" who might be hiding. This search for other "bodies" under these circumstances and the discovery and seizure of marihuana during such search was lawful. *Chimel v. California,* 395 US 752, is not applicable. *See also: People v. Marshall,* 69 Cal2d 51.

The same "search" rules are applicable where an arrest is made pursuant to a warrant of arrest. *Harris v. U.S.,* 331 US 145; *People v. Chiagles,* 237 NY 193; *cf. People v. Montgomery,* 21 AD2d 904, affd 15 NY2d 732, 205 NE2d 206.

Although in *People v. Beaman,* 44 Misc2d 336, 253 NYS2d 674, the search was held unlawful as not contemporaneous with and incident to the purpose of the arrest, in *People v. Moschitta,* 25 AD2d 686, 269 NYS2d 70, a slightly different fact situation, the search was held lawful. Moschitta was arrested when it was ascertained that the car he was driving had stolen license plates. The interior of the car was searched at the scene, and then the defendant drove his car to the police station, followed by the police in their own car. At the station house, and while he was being interrogated, a police officer went to the defendant's car, broke open its trunk and found a gun.

The court found the search lawful because the search at the police station was merely a continuation of the original search made at the scene of the arrest; that the search was incident to the purpose of the arrest, *i.e.,* to ascertain the identity of the owner of the car, believed to have been stolen, citing *People v. Montgomery,* 21 AD2d 904, affd 15 NY2d 732, 205 NE2d 206; that the defendant retained control over the car up until the time he drove it up to the police station where the search was continued; that there were some actions by the defendant in his car which led to the suspicion that the defendant was secreting something in the vehicle. *Cf. Preston v. U.S.,* 376 US 364. Citing the dissent in *Trupiano v. U.S.,* 334 US 699, 714, the court in *Moschitta, supra,* noted that the mere fact that the police had an opportunity to obtain a search warrant is not controlling. "The legality of a search without a warrant turns upon the reasonableness of the search under all the circumstances and not upon the practicability of procuring a warrant (United States v. Rabinowitz, 339 U.S. 56, 64–66 . . .)." *Moschitta, supra,* 269 NYS2d at 72. Since the identical search made at the police station could have been properly made at the scene and time of the arrest, defendant's rights under the Fourth Amendment were not violated. Nor is a search warrant required where its issuance would contribute nothing to the preservation of a defendant's constitutional rights. *Cf.: Preston v. U.S.,* 376 US 364; *People v. Beaman, supra.*

A similar search was held to be contemporaneous and incidental with a lawful arrest in *People v. Hatch,* 25 AD2d 606–607, 267 NYS2d 651. There the defendant was arrested in his car at night. "The arrest having been made in the nighttime on a public highway, it was inadvisable to complete the search in that location, and it was thereafter completed at the police station. The search made there, after a brief and reasonable suspension, was merely a continuation of the search which was initiated at the time and place of the arrest. Hence we hold that the search was incidental to and contemporaneous with a lawful arrest; that the search was valid; and that the exhibits discovered by the search were properly admitted into evidence. . . ." *See also: People v. Montgomery, supra.* As the Court held in *Preston v. U.S.,* 376 US 364, 367, a search cannot be regarded as an incident to a lawful arrest where it is remote from it in time and place. Such a search, to be lawful, requires a warrant. Of course, as indicated above, a search which is truly an incident to a lawful arrest, is a proper search. *Draper v. U.S.,* 358 US 307; *People v. Defore,* 242 NY 13.

In *People v. Lewis,* 26 NY2d 547, 260 NE2d 538, the court underscored the reason for the rule which permits a search without a warrant as incident to a lawful arrest. In effect, it is a recapitulation of the rule.

In this case, a police officer observed Lewis driving a car containing two other occupants. He knew there was an arrest warrant outstanding for Lewis. He stopped him and took him to the nearest precinct where he confirmed the existence of the warrant—a 1965 warrant for criminally receiving stolen property. Some ten minutes later, he took the defendant back to his car where his companions were still seated. On searching the car, he found a loaded revolver. The defendant was arrested on the gun charge. Motion to suppress was denied and defendant was convicted. However, the Court of Appeals reversed and dismissed the indictment on the ground that there was no justification for the search even though it took place only some ten-minutes after the original arrest. The ten-minute time interval is immaterial.

> "[A]t the time of the defendant's arrest on the second floor of the station house, there was absolutely no danger that he would use a weapon concealed in the car to injure one of the officers or to effect escape. Therefore, the warrantless search cannot be sustained on the theory of self-protection.
>
> "Of course, the justification for searches incident to a valid arrest are not only borne out of protection for public officers, but are also conducted for the purpose of discovering (1) the fruits of the crime; (2) instrumentalities used to commit the crime; (3) contraband, the possession of which constitutes a crime; or (4) material which constitutes evidence of the crime or evidence that the person arrested has committed it (*Amador-Gonzales* v. *United States,* 391 F.2d 308). . . . There must exist a reasonable belief that the search will produce the fruits, instrumentalities, contraband or evidence (*Carroll* v.

*United States,* [267 U.S. 132] *supra* at p. 154). Here, the only basis for the arrest was an outstanding warrant dated almost three years before the arrest. All the arresting officer knew was that the defendant was still wanted in connection with a charge of criminally receiving stolen property prior to February 1, 1965. Without more, the search cannot be sustained as an incident to the arrest, since the officer could not formulate the requisite reasonable belief that the search would be productive.

"It must be emphasized, however, that it is not the mere 10-minute lapse of time between the arrest and search which gives rise to our disposition, for we have on several occasions sustained searches of automobiles sometime after the arrest (e.g., *People* v. *Cassone,* 14 NY2d 798 and *People* v. *Montgomery,* 15 NY2d 732, where the car itself was seized as an instrumentality or as evidence of the crime). Rather it is the lack of any justification to make the search after the 10 minutes had elapsed which brings about the result herein." *People v. Lewis,* 26 NY2d 547, 551–553, 260 NE2d 538.

Note, too, that where an officer is executing a lawful arrest, he "is free to take hold of articles which he sees the accused deliberately trying to hide. This power derives from the dangers that a weapon will be concealed, or that relevant evidence will be destroyed." *Abel v. U.S.,* 362 US 217, 238. *See also: In re Marshall K,* 92 Cal Rptr 39.

However, this is not to say that "probable cause for belief that certain articles subject to seizure are in a dwelling cannot of itself justify a search without a warrant. *Agnello v. United States,* 269 US 20, 33. . . ." *Jones, supra,* 357 US at 497–498. The purpose behind this rule is to guard against unwarranted searches. This can be accomplished "by requiring that an impartial magistrate determine from an affidavit showing probable cause whether information possessed by law-enforcement officers justifies the issuance of a search warrant." 357 US at 498.

**§ 216.01. Objects Within Sight.** Looking into a car, even with a flashlight, and seeing things in open view does not constitute a search. *Smith v. U.S.*, 2 F2d 715; *Boyd v. U.S.*, 286 F2d 930; *People v. Jordan,* 37 Misc2d 33. A search implies a prying into hidden places. *People v. West,* 144 Cal App2d 214, 219. It is not a search to observe what is open and patent either in daylight or in artificial light. *People v. Hoffman,* 24 AD2d 497, 261 NYS2d 651.

> "It is incontestible that no search of the automobile occurred when the officers observed the coats in open view unless they had no right to be in a position of attentiveness. . . . 'It has long been settled that objects falling in the plain view of an officer who has a right to be in the position to have that view are subject to seizure and may be introduced in evidence' (*Harris* v. *United States,* 390 U.S. 234, 236; *Davis* v. *United States,* [9 Cir.,] 327 F.2d 301, 305)." *People v. Merola,* 30 AD2d 963, 294 NYS2d 301.

A similar ruling was made in a case prosecuted under the N.Y. Conservation Law. There the defendant was convicted of a statutory violation for possession of undersized clams. The seizure of these clams was held to be lawful in that they were contraband. "The defendant concedes that the Conservation Department inspector was properly looking at the bags to determine if they were tagged. It was while doing this that the inspector saw that the clams were undersized. Since they were, therefore, illegally possessed in his presence he was entitled to seize them as contraband. The judgment of conviction is affirmed." *People v. King,* NYLJ, 3/14/66, p. 20, col. 4.

For other cases involving the "plain view" doctrine, *see Davis v. Eide,* 439 F2d 1077; *Harris v. U.S.*, 390 US 234; *U.S. v. Crow,* 439 F2d 1193; *U.S. v. Morales,* 440 F2d 1332.

A critical test to be applied in "plain view" doctrine cases is whether the officer made the observations complained of from a place that he had a right to be. *Harris, supra,* at 236.

**§ 217. Breaking, Entering and Notice by Police.** The police, in breaking and entering premises for the purpose of making an otherwise lawful arrest, must give notice to the occupants of their office and purpose, unless they encounter physical resistance, flight or other factors rendering such procedure impractical. If entry is made pursuant to statutory authority, neither the search nor seizure is illegal. However, there are cases which hold that exigent circumstances, *i.e.*, danger of bodily harm to the officer or another, likelihood of destruction of evidence, may authorize the police to break and enter without giving prior notice.

In *People v. Wojciechowski,* 31 AD2d 658, 659, the court said:

> "The failure of the officer to give 'notice' of his 'purpose' as required by [statute], prior to his breaking, does not require suppression of the evidence found in the apartment. Where the authorities have reason to believe that the life of an innocent man, who is stationed with the suspect in his apartment, is endangered, the failure to fully comply with [the statute] is not fatal. The circumstances here amounted to a showing of exigent circumstances which would excuse the giving of the notice (see *People v. McIlwain,* 28 AD2d 711)."

Although there is a hint in some cases that notice of office and purpose must precede an officer's entry even where exigent circumstances are present, *Miller v. U.S.,* 357 US 301; *People v. Kaidy,* 14 NY2d 812, 200 NE2d 452, the great weight of authority sanctions dispensing with such notice in emergency situations, *People v. Floyd,* 26 NY2d 558, 260 NE2d 815, and cases cited.

In *People v. Gallmon,* 19 NY2d 389, 227 NE2d 284, entry without prior notice was sanctioned where the purpose of the entry was investigatory and not "to make an arrest or to execute other process (*Miller v. United States,* 357 U.S. 301, 305–310)."

**§ 218. The Search Area.** Where a lawful arrest is made in fixed premises, such as an apartment or office, what area surrounding the point of arrest may the police search?

In *U.S. v. Rabinowitz,* 339 US 56, 60, after lawfully arresting the defendant, the police searched his one-room office looking for forged postal stamps for an hour and a half. They found some stamps which were admitted in evidence and it was held that the police have a right "to search the place where the arrest is made in order to find and seize things connected with the crime."

In a prior case, *Harris v. U.S.,* 331 US 145, 183, the Court sustained a search of an entire four-room apartment as incident to petitioner's arrest under an arrest warrant, even though Harris was arrested in his living room and the contraband was found in his bedroom. The crime for which the warrant had been issued was using the mails to transport forged checks. During the five-hour search Harris was handcuffed and his apartment ransacked. No checks were found, but certain Selective Service documents were uncovered—a totally unrelated crime.

In his dissent, Mr. Justice Murphy stated that under this decision:

> "A warrant of arrest, without more, is now sufficient to justify an unlimited search of a man's home from cellar to garret for evidence of any crime, provided only that he is arrested in his home. . . . In short, all the restrictions put upon the issuance and execution of search warrants by the Fourth Amendment are now dead lettters as to those who are arrested in their homes."

This new rule, he asserted, resurrects the odious general warrant or writ of assistance which presumably had been outlawed in this country forever.

Both *Harris* and *Rabinowitz* were contrary to the early American decisions by which the searches were generally strictly limited in scope to the body of the accused and to goods which were subject to seizure and visible to the arresting officer.

The United States Supreme Court has now reverted to the pre-*Harris-Rabinowitz* rule in the case of *Chimel v. California,* 395 US 752. *See also: Vale v. Louisiana,* 399 US 30, 26 L Ed2 408.

In *Chimel,* the California police, armed with an arrest warrant, but no search warrant, arrested Chimel at his home, on a charge of burglary of a coin shop. Over Chimel's objection, they proceeded to search his entire house, including the attic, garage and workshop. Coins and other items were seized, which were received in evidence, and he was convicted.

In reversing, the Supreme Court specifically overruled *Rabinowitz,* and *Harris, supra,* asserting that those cases cannot withstand historical or rational analysis.

The area of permissible search after the arrest is "justified by the circumstances which rendered its initiation permissible." For example, it is entirely reasonable that an officer in a stop-and-frisk case be permitted a protective search for weapons (*Terry v. Ohio,* 392 US 1), but he may not place his hand in a suspect's pocket to find narcotics (*Sibron v. New York,* 392 US 40). Additionally, it is entirely reasonable to search the arrestee's person to prevent the destruction or concealment of evidence as well as ". . . the area 'within his immediate control'—construing that phrase to mean the area from within which he might gain possession of a weapon or destructible evidence"—what might be called the arms-length rule. *Chimel, supra.*

There is no comparable justification, however, "for routinely searching any room other than that in which an arrest occurs—or, for that matter, for searching through all the desk drawers or other closed or concealed areas in the room itself. Such searches . . . may be made only under the authority of a search warrant." 395 US at 763.

In this case, the Court noted, the search went far beyond Chimel's person and the area from which he might have obtained a weapon or sought to destroy evidence. "There was no constitutional justification, in the absence of a search warrant, for extending the search beyond that area." 395 US at 768.

In *Shipley v. California,* 395 US 818, the Court declined to pass on the question of retroactivity of *Chimel* but the Second Circuit, in *U.S. v. Bennett,* 415 F2d 1113, refused to give *Chimel* retroactive effect. Subsequently, both the United States Supreme Court, in *Williams v. U.S.,* 401 U.S. 646, and the New York Court of Appeals, *People v. LoCicero,* 28 NY2d 525, 527, 200 NE2d 622, held to the same effect. *See also: Von Cleef v. New Jersey,* 395 US 814; *cf. U.S. v. Baca,* 417 F2d 103.

§ 219. **Search Contemporaneous With Arrest.** Generally the search must be contemporaneous with the arrest and limited to items under the immediate control of the defendant. It may not be conducted merely to find evidence to justify the arrest, or evidence of another crime. It may include the interior of fixed premises, including an automobile.

There is no right to search at a time and place remote from the scene of the arrest, but the time of the search may be delayed from the time of the arrest, depending on the circumstances of the case. *People v. Moschitta,* 25 AD2d 686, 269 NYS2d 70; *People v. Webb,* 424 P2d 342, 56 Cal Rptr 902.

> "The Fourth Amendment is not concerned with acquittals or convictions. It is only concerned with searches. It commands that probable cause and statutory authority to arrest, precede every search." *People v. Roach,* 44 Misc2d 40, 43.

An acquittal may follow a perfectly lawful arrest based on probable cause. In such a situation, the People are not estopped from prosecuting on an "unrelated" crime arising out of a reasonable search in an "original" case in which the defendant was acquitted. *People v. LoCicero,* 14 NY2d 374, 380. *Cf.: People v. Dreares,* 15 AD2d 204, affd 11 NY2d 906, 182 NE2d 812; *People v. Cassone,* 20 AD2d 118, 120, affd 14 NY2d 798, 200 NE2d 214; *Preston v. U.S.,* 376 US 364.

In *People v. Molloy,* 22 AD2d 814, affd 17 NY2d 431, 213 NE2d 801, the defendant was arrested and charged with burglary. The arrest was based on probable cause that a felony had been or was about to be committed by him. When arrested he was searched, and a registration for a stolen motor vehicle was found in his possession. The burglary charge was dismissed, but two months later he was charged with grand larceny of the motor vehicle. A motion to suppress was denied with the following observation:

> "The fact that the burglary charge was thereafter dismissed did not render the arrest unlawful. . . . Since there was a reasonable cause for the arrest, the subsequent search incident to the arrest was lawful (*Draper* v. *United States,* 358 US 307, 310–311; *People* v. *Loria,* 10 NY2d 368, 373). The evidence seized at the time of the arrest for burglary, which charge was dismissed, was

admissible on a subsequent charge of larceny (*Paper* v. *United States,* 53 F.2d 184; *Carroll* v. *United States,* 267 US 132, 158; *Harris* v. *United States,* 331 U.S. 145, 155; *People* v. *Lombardi,* 18 AD2d 177, 180, and cases there cited)." *Molloy, supra,* at 814.

Not all items seized at some distance from the point of defendant's arrest are barred under *Chimel v. California,* 395 US 752. In *U.S. v. Hallman,* 438 F2d 94, contraband observed five feet away from the defendant was held to have been seized lawfully.

In *U.S. v. Tozzi,* 322 F Supp 1, a hijacking case, a search of the vehicle a half-hour after the arrest and at a point two and one-half blocks away, was sustained, as a "tightly coupled event [which] makes a unity of the arrest and the search of the motor vehicle." *Id.* at 3. *Cf. Root v. Gauper,* 438 F2d 361.

**§ 220. Search Incident to Arrest for Violation of Parole.** In *People v. Langella,* 41 Misc2d 65, 70, the court held that a parolee remains in the legal custody of the warden of the prison, until the expiration of the maximum term specified in his sentence.

A parolee's rights are qualified. "Crediting and accepting the defendant's contention—that his release on parole did not divest him of all of his rights—does not however require a conclusion that his rights were equal to those of a person enjoying unrestricted and unconditioned liberty." *Langella, supra,* 41 Misc2d at 70.

Because of his particular status, a parolee's rights to claim the protection against unlawful searches and seizures afforded by the Fourth Amendment "are more circumscribed and limited than the rights of citizens not in such status." *People v. Randazzo,* 37 Misc2d 80, 82, affd 15 NY2d 526, 202 NE2d 459; *People v. Santos,* 31 AD2d 508, 298 NYS2d 526.

A search and seizure following a parolee's arrest on a warrant charging him with violation of parole deprives him of no constitutional right. *People v. Randazzo, supra.*

The contraband in *Randazzo* (heroin) was found after a 2½ hour search in a dresser drawer in his bedroom.

In *Langella, supra,* the contraband (a gun) was found in

the trunk of a car the defendant had been driving. He was not in the car at the time of his arrest. The car trunk was not opened until the car had been taken to the station house, where it was opened by the parole officer.

None of these searches can be considered truly "incident" to the arrest for the violation of parole charged in the warrants. *Preston v. U.S.,* 376 US 364; *Abel v. U.S.,* 362 US 217; *People v. Beaman,* 44 Misc2d 336, 253 NYS2d 674; *also see:* dissent by Fuld, J., in *Randazzo, supra,* 15 NY2d at 527, and *Chimel v. California,* 395 US 752.

Nevertheless, the majority of the court in *Randazzo* apparently reasoned that since the parolee was always in constructive custody, though not actually confined (*People ex rel Natoli v. Lewis,* 287 NY 478), a wider latitude must be allowed in defining contemporaneous and incident searches in those cases.

This is not to say that *Randazzo* may be applied as a rule of thumb. A parolee's rights under the Fourth Amendment are suspended "to allow a parole officer to freely search him and his abode when he suspects that the parolee may have lapsed into criminal ways. Similarly, because of his parole status, there is also a suspension of his constitutional rights against self-incrimination under the Fifth Amendment to facilitate interrogation by a parole officer. *People v. W.* (*Anonymous*), 24 NY2d 732, 302 N.Y.S.2d 260, 249 N.E.2d 882." *People v. Way,* 319 NYS2d 16, 21.

Such invasion of a parolee's rights is permitted for his rehabilitation and for the protection of the public. However, such invasion is not authorized for the convenience of law enforcement officers. Thus, where a parole officer without a search warrant, at the instigation of the police searched a parolee's home and seized certain contraband, the search and seizure having been inspired, initiated, arranged and actively participated in by the police, required suppression of the articles seized. *People v. Way,* 319 NYS2d 16 and cases cited. *Way* emphasizes the rationale of *Lustig v. U.S.,* 338 US 74, which condemns the silver platter doctrine—a situation comparable in *Way.*

*Way* enunciates the New York rule. *See: People v. Randazzo,* 15 NY2d 526, 202 NE2d 459, cert. den. 381 US 953;

*U.S. ex rel Randazzo v. Follette,* 418 F2d 1319; *People v. Adams,* 63 Misc2d 52; *People v. Sickler,* 61 Misc2d 571.

Although there are some federal cases to the contrary (*Brown v. Kearney,* 355 F2d 199; *Martin v. U.S.,* 183 F2d 436; *U.S. v. Lewis,* 274 F Supp 184), the weight of authority follows *Way.*

In *U.S. ex rel Sperling v. Fitzpatrick,* 426 F2d 1161, the Second Circuit followed the New York rule. Sperling, who was a parolee, was searched unlawfully by police officers who found a gun on his person. He contended that the fruits of this unlawful search and seizure could not be used as evidence to prove his violation of parole.

The court rejected this argument:

> "We cannot accede to this contention and affirm the denial of appellant's petition for a writ of habeas corpus on the ground that the exclusionary rule is not applicable in a parole revocation proceeding." 426 F2d at 1163.

**§ 221. Search Incident to Traffic Infractions and Non-Criminal Violations.** The fact that traffic infractions are generally not considered crimes has led to some modification of the incident search rule where one is arrested for this offense.

In *People v. Marsh,* 20 NY2d 98, 101, 228 NE2d 783, the court said:

> "Although, as a general rule, when an individual is lawfully arrested, the police officer may conduct a contemporaneous search of his person 'for weapons or for the fruits of or implements used to commit the crime' (*Preston v. United States,* 376 US 364, 367), we do not believe that the Legislature intended to cover arrests for traffic violations. It is obvious that, except in the most rare of instances, there can be no 'fruits' or 'implements' of such infractions and the search, to be upheld, would have to be justified as one for weapons. But there is something incongruous about treating traffic offenders as noncriminals, on the one hand, and subjecting them, on the other, to the indignity of a search for weapons."

Thus, the court concluded that in the ordinary case of an arrest for a traffic infraction, the incident search is "unreasonable" unless, "when the vehicle is stopped, there are reasonable grounds for suspecting that the officer is in danger or there is probable cause for believing that the offender is guilty of a crime rather than merely a simple traffic infraction." *See: People v. Coleman,* 24 NY2d 1005, 250 NE2d 237.

Such a situation appeared in *U.S. v. Frye,* 271 A2d 788. In that case that officer received inaccurate radio information that defendant's car had improper tags. He had also received a tip from an unidentified citizen that a car with these plates was being loaded with shotguns and rifles. Upon seeing the vehicle, the officer stopped it, arrested the defendant and upon frisking him found an illegal weapon under his coat. Although the court acknowledged that a mere traffic arrest may not warrant searching the occupants of a car, nevertheless the informer's tip supplied considerably more of a basis for the frisk than a mere traffic arrest. It was the aggregate of the information supplied that could not be disregarded by the arresting officer, despite the fact that the radio communication as to the improper license plates proved to be false. Here the court noted, there was a moving street scene where quick, reasonable police action was necessary. *Cf. People v. Taggart,* 20 NY2d 335, 283 NYS2d 1, 229 NE2d 581.

It is logical to assume that this rule would be equally applicable to arrests for other "non-criminal" violations. That is to say, that an incident search of a person arrested for a "non-criminal" violation would be "unreasonable" absent probable cause for believing that the arresting officer is in danger.

In *People v. Ford,* 313 NYS2d 454, 455, the court held that *Marsh* and *Coleman, supra,* "are *sui generis* and should not be extended to non-traffic cases," citing *People v. Barnes,* NYLJ, 6/3/64, p. 16, and *People v. Lopez,* NYLJ, 5/18/65, p. 17.

The existence of probable cause to search will be great in "non-criminal" violation cases, because of the very nature of the violations, *e.g.,* trespass, loitering, disorderly conduct, harassment. *Cf.: People v. Rivera,* 14 NY2d 441, 201 NE2d 32; *Terry v. Ohio,* 392 US 1.

**§ 222. Delay in Arresting Defendant.** There is no constitutional right to be arrested. *Hoffa v. U.S.,* 385 US 293. The same rule is applicable to arrests under a warrant. Thus, in *U.S. v. Joines,* 258 F2d 471, cert. den. 358 US 880, it was held that there is no legal requirement that an arrest warrant be executed immediately or at the first opportunity. An arrest under a warrant was also upheld in *Wilson v. U.S.,* 325 F2d 224, cert. den. 377 US 1005, where the warrant was issued in April 1962, charging a narcotics offense in January 1961 and which warrant was executed in September 1962. *See also: U.S. v. Weaver,* 384 F2d 879, cert. den. 390 US 983.

However, it was held in *U.S. v. Cally,* 259 F Supp 539, 541–544, that where the delay was a mere pretense for making an improper search, *i.e.,* an incidental search of an area which would not ordinarily be subject to a search without a warrant, then the items seized in such incident search would be subject to suppression. *See also: Carlo v. U.S.,* 286 F2d 841, cert. den. 366 US 944; *cf. McKnight v. U.S.,* 183 F2d 977. The mere fact that a search immediately follows a valid arrest in point of time does not conclusively establish the reasonableness of the search. *Abel v. U.S.,* 362 US 217, 235; *U.S. v. Rabinowitz,* 339 US 56, 65–66.

*U.S. v. Cally, supra,* involved a tax evasion suit arising, *inter alia,* from alleged failure to report taxable income and earnings received from a Canadian mining corporation stock sale in a joint venture of five defendants. This joint venture netted some two million dollars and the indictment covered the period from 1936 to 1965, at which latter date the defendants were indicted. A warrant of arrest was issued for one of these defendants, Silensky, whose apartment was searched for some 45 minutes by five I.R.S. agents armed with an axe and crowbar. Some 200 items were seized and separated into relevant and extraneous material.

The court granted suppression, holding that this was a rummaging search for evidence in a nonviolent, weaponless crime, committed 5 or 6 years before the arrest, and was not an incident search. *Cf.: Harris v. U.S.,* 331 US 145; *U.S. v. Rabinowitz, supra; Preston v. U.S.,* 376 US 364; *Chimel v. California, supra.*

In *Kremen v. U.S.*, 353 US 346, federal officers arrived with an arrest warrant, entered a cabin to arrest one of three men hiding there. They seized, as incident to the arrest, the cabin's entire contents, which they removed to San Francisco, a distance of some 200 miles. What might have been a perfectly lawful incident search (see dissent, 353 US at 347–348) degenerated into a rummaging about, long condemned since *Entick v. Carrington* (1765), 19 Howell's St Tr 1029. As in *Cally, supra,* the seizure was illegal. *See also: Abel v. U.S.*, 362 US at 239; *U.S. v. Lefkowitz,* 285 US 452.

*See also: § 207, supra.*

**§ 223. Cumulative Harmless Error.** Where the cumulative effect of the erroneous admission into evidence of illegally seized evidence is prejudicial, it may not be called harmless error.

Such a situation was present in the cases of *State v. Miller,* 206 A2d 835 and *Fahy v. Conn.,* 375 US 85, 92. In both of these cases, certain evidence against the accused was obtained as a result of an unlawful search and seizure. Fahy's conviction was affirmed in the state appellate court (149 Conn 577, 183 A2d 256) because the appellate court found the admission of the unconstitutionally obtained evidence to have been harmless error. However, the Supreme Court reversed, stating in effect that such error cannot be called harmless if it is prejudicial.

In *Miller, supra,* the defendant's car was searched without a warrant two days after his arrest and in a town different from the town in which he was confined. The court held that such a search could not be regarded as incidental to the arrest as it was too remote as to time and place. The court had to determine whether the fruits of this search, which were introduced at the trial, was harmless error. Although the Connecticut court stated that prior to *Fahy,* it would have so held, it was constrained to follow the rule laid down by the Supreme Court in *Fahy,* which it quoted: "'We find that the erroneous admission of this unconstitutionally obtained evidence at the petitioner's trial was prejudicial; therefore, the error was not harmless, and the conviction must be reversed. We are not concerned here with whether there was sufficient evidence on which the petitioner could have been convicted without the evidence complained of. The question is whether there is a reasonably possibility that the evidence complained of might have contributed to the conviction.'" *Miller* at p. 837.

The fruits of the unlawful search in *Miller* supported the credibility of the only eye witness to the crime. Under this circumstance and based on *Fahy,* Miller's conviction was reversed.

# Chapter 15

## SEARCH ON CONSENT



---

§ 230. **In General.** The right of the people to be secure in their persons, houses, papers and effects, is guaranteed by the Fourth Amendment. A consent to an illegal search is a waiver of that constitutional right. *Amos v. U.S.,* 255 US 313; *U.S. v. Dornblut,* 261 F2d 949; *U.S. v. Sclafani,* 265 F2d 408; *U.S. v. Martin,* 176 F Supp 262; *People v. Lane,* 10 NY2d 347, 179 NE2d 339.

But, the courts will accordingly indulge every reasonable presumption against such a waiver. *U.S. v. Martin,* 176 F Supp 262; *Johnson v. Zerbst,* 304 US 458; *Green v. U.S.* 355 US 184.

On the question of consent, some basic rules must be borne in mind:

Despite a state court's determination on the findings of fact, in a case involving consent to a search, federal law is controlling on that issue. Additionally, the state court's determination thereof is not res judicata in a federal proceeding. *Hoover v. Beto,* 439 F2d 913, 919.

Where the police assert they have a search warrant, subsequently held to be invalid, and where defendant thereupon says to the police with reference to the search, "go ahead," it cannot be said that this constitutes a free and voluntary consent to a search. Under such circumstances, as indicated in *Bumper v. North Carolina,* 391 US 543, the state must show that the consent was given sufficiently independent of the warrant to remove the taint of its coercive nature. *Hoover v.*

*Beto, supra* at 920. As to "taint" *see Wong Sun v. U.S.*, 371 US 471.

The burden of proving consent which is on the prosecution is not met by a showing of no more than mere acquiescence to lawful authority. *Hoover v. Beto, supra* at 919.

A consent to a search will not be lightly inferred. *Johnson v. Zerbst*, 304 US 458.

§ 231. **Implied Consent.** In certain situations there may be found an implied consent to search.

Consent is implied where an unconscious patient in a hospital is disrobed in preparation for emergency treatment, and a gun found on his person. *People v. Hargrave*, 40 Misc2d 556, 243 NYS2d 773.

In *People v. Capra*, 17 NY2d 670, 216 NE2d 610, the defendant was taken to a hospital following an accident. During an examination his shoes and socks were removed. A packet of heroin fell out of a sock, which was turned over to the police. The Court of Appeals held that the accidental finding of the heroin did not constitute an illegal search, and turning it over to the police was not disclosure of information acquired in a professional capacity by a physician from a patient.

*People v. Young*, 42 Misc2d 540, 248 NYS2d 287, found no implied consent to take a blood sample from an unconscious defendant not under arrest, who was subsequently charged with vehicular homicide and driving while intoxicated.

Failure to comply with provisions of the state's "Implied Consent Law" requiring sterilization of needle in taking blood sample in "driving while intoxicated case," rendered results of a test inadmissible in a Virginia case. *Kyhl v. Commonwealth*, 135 SE2d 768. But, in *Schmerber v. California*, 384 US 757, the U.S. Supreme Court held that a blood sample taken by a physician in a hospital in a "driving while intoxicated case" at the direction of a police officer, and over the defendant's objection, was admissible.

A bullet removed from defendant's head by a doctor at a hospital where the defendant had come for treatment, which the doctor then delivered to the police, was not a product of an unreasonable search and seizure. *State v. Turner*, 416 P2d 409.

In *People v. Butler,* 41 Misc2d 249, 251, 252, 253, the court held that defendant's statement to the police investigating a murder in a restaurant that the rifle was usually kept in the kitchen constituted an implied consent to search that room.

§ 232. **Third Party Consents.** Persons other than the defendant, such as another occupant in defendant's apartment may also give a valid consent to enter and search. *People v. Rodriguez,* 38 Misc2d 949; *People v. Kortwright,* 236 NYS2d 385; *People v. Matthews,* 21 AD2d 883.

In *People v. D'Iorio,* 16 NY2d 551, 208 NE2d 465, the parents of a twenty-five year old defendant, who resided in their apartment, consented to a search of the son's room. Heroin was found. Although the defendant contended that his rights against illegal search and seizure were personal and could not be waived by third parties, the New York Court of Appeals sustained the lawfulness of the search.

The U.S. Court of Appeals has held to the same effect. In *Roberts v. U.S.,* 332 F2d 892, the court held that a wife could effectively consent to a search of premises owned jointly by herself and her husband, and that the product of the search was admissible in evidence in a criminal prosecution against the husband.

Relying on the *Roberts* decision, the Supreme Court of Minnesota has held that consent given by a father to search without a warrant, the room of his son, an adult who had occupied the room for some fifteen years, was a valid consent which effectively waived the rights of the son. *State v. Kinderman,* 136 NW2d 577.

There has been some disagreement among the several federal Courts of Appeal as to whether a wife may lawfully consent to a search of an apartment which she occupied with her husband and whether the consent would be binding on her husband. The Fifth Circuit has now abandoned its thirty-year rule that a wife could not lawfully consent to such a search in *U.S. v. Thompson* 421 F2d 373, and is now in agreement with the Second, Seventh, Eighth and Ninth Circuits.

In *Thompson,* the court found that the wife's consent was voluntary and not coerced in any way. She was informed by the police, prior to the search, that her husband was suspected of complicity in a robbery. She gave oral and written consent to the search. As a result of the search, evidence was uncovered and the husband was convicted. His conviction was affirmed despite his contention that a wife could not give consent to a search of his apartment for the reasons noted above.

> "It is the rule in this [Fifth] Circuit that ' "where two persons have equal rights to the use or occupation of premises, either may give consent to a search, and the evidence thus disclosed can be used against either." ' Gurleski v. United States, 5th Cir. 1968, 405 F.2d 253, 262, quoting United States v. Sferas, 7th Cir. 1954, 210 F.2d 69, 74." *U.S. v. Thompson,* 421 F2d at 375.

A contrary rule was announced in *People v. Gonzales,* 50 Misc2d 508, 509:

> "While the original entry was with the permission of defendant's wife, she could not validly consent to a search of his personal effects which were not exposed to open view (*State* v. *Evans,* 45 Hawaii 622; cf. *Roberts* v. *United States,* 332 F.2d 892, cert. den. 380 U.S. 390). Since consent is the weakest possible basis for a search and must be shown to have been freely and voluntarily given (*Pekar* v. *United States,* 315 F.2d 319; *Hall* v. *Warden,* 313 F.2d 483; *United States* v. *Viale,* 312 F.2d 595; *United States* v. *Smith,* 308 F.2d 657), it is even less persuasive when given by one's wife to effect a waiver of his constitutional right against unreasonable search. Consequently, the motion to suppress should have been granted."

This decision appears to be contrary to the authorities. *See: U.S. v. Thompson, supra.*

Consent to search an apartment, given by the mother of the defendant, was held valid, in the absence of a search warrant in *Combs v. LaVallee,* 417 F2d 523.

It has been held that a woman's consent for the police to enter her motel room could not extend to the search of a person found therein. *Davis v. California,* 341 F2d 982. *Davis* follows the rationale of *People v. Rawluck,* 14 NY2d 609.

In *U.S. v. Botsch,* 364 F2d 542, the court held that in a landlord and tenant relationship, the consent of the landlord to a search of his tenant's apartment without a search warrant did *not* render the search unreasonable, when the tenant had given his landlord a key to his apartment with authorization to accept deliveries. This act, the court held, extended the relationship between the two, beyond that of a mere landlord and tenant. The landlord, fearful that his property was being utilized for illegal purposes and that he might be involved, had a right to promptly and voluntarily exculpate himself by inviting an inspection of the premises. It was held further that failure of the invited officers to obtain a search warrant did not render the search unreasonable, even if no prejudice would have resulted from delay necessary to obtaining a search warrant.

Where the defendant's sleeping quarters were specifically set aside to him by the lessee who permitted defendant to sleep there, consent to search those quarters, given by the lessee, was held to be a valid consent. *U.S. v. White,* 268 F Supp 998; *see also: People v. Kowalczyk,* 20 NY2d 835, 231 NE2d 772.

Where part of a garage was rented to the defendant to be shared by its owner, consent to search the garage given by its owner was valid and the defendant's consent was not required. *People v. Schwartz,* 281 NYS2d 246.

But a search and seizure without a warrant were held to be illegal if defendant's door was not open when the officer arrived, but had been opened by defendant's landlady for the officer. *People v. Mullgrav,* 23 AD2d 855, 269 NYS2d 540. *See also: Stoner v. California,* 376 US 483.

The rule to be deduced from these cases is that a defendant has no constitutionally protected right of privacy where he does not have exclusive possession and control over the place searched. Accordingly, the person who does have present, exclusive possession and control over the place in question, or who shares the premises co-equally with the person claiming to be aggrieved, may give consent to the search.

**§ 233. Consent Given in Advance.** Consent may be given in advance, by the very nature of a person's agreement or obligation of employment, such as policemen, soldiers, etc. *People v. Russell,* 33 Misc2d 851. The use of certain governmental facilities, such as U.S. mails, will constitute consent in advance. *Santana v. U.S.,* 329 F2d 854.

So too, members of the armed forces, under certain conditions, are deemed to have given consent in advance to searches without a warrant. In *U.S. v. Grisby,* 335 F2d 652, a search of a soldier's living quarters on an army post conducted without a warrant on orders of his commanding officer was held to constitute a lawful search.

> "[A] search of property located on a military installation and occupied by persons subject to military law is valid [without a warrant] when authorized by a commanding officer having jurisdiction over the place where the property is." 335 F2d at 654.

Consent in advance has been held applicable to licensed pharmacists in New York. *McKaba v. Bd. of Regents,* 30 AD2d 495. Where the state statute requires pharmacies to keep records of all narcotic drugs received and disposed of, a pharmacist accepts this statutory obligation by accepting his professional license.

Thus, inspection of petitioner's narcotics records without a warrant by department inspectors was deemed consent in advance and was lawful. His contention that this consent did not include counting his inventory of narcotics stock, without a search warrant, was held to be without merit. Aside from the question of actual consent having been given to the inspectors to count the inventory, consent is implied, since the purpose of the inspection is to balance out the purchase and sales of the narcotics. *McKaba,* 30 AD2d at 498–499. *See also: People* v. *Laverne,* 14 NY2d 304.

By the same rule government officers may board and inspect vessels carrying cargo or passengers from foreign ports to the United States within twelve miles of the coast. Pleasure boats are excepted unless probable cause exists that they are engaged in violations of law. *U.S. v. Wischerth,* 68 F2d 161; *Fish v. Brophy,* 52 F2d 198; 19 USC § 1581.

19 USC § 1581 (Boarding vessels) need not be strictly construed in favor of the defendant, since it is a statute designed

to prevent frauds on the revenue. *U.S. v. Yee Ngee How,* 105 F Supp 517; *cf. One 1958 Plymouth Sedan v. Penn.,* 380 US 693.

Compilation or maintenance of public records or reports, or public documents, or corporate books, may also constitute consent in advance. *Davis v. U.S.,* 328 US 582; *Zap v. U.S.,* 328 US 624; *Wilson v. U.S.,* 221 US 361.

§ 234. **Examples of Consent.** Where after vigorous, repeated requests by two federal narcotics agents, who had no warrant, for permission to enter defendant's apartment, defendant admitted them but only after he had opened a window and made a throwing motion and narcotics were recovered by a third agent who also saw the throwing motion and felt something hit him and who then recovered narcotics, it was held that the entry by the first two agents was by consent and the seizure of the narcotics was not illegal. *U.S. v. Cachoian,* 364 F2d 291. *Cf. People v. Williams,* 24 AD2d 274.

In *U.S. v. Callahan,* 439 F2d 852, defendant in a pre-*Miranda* case, went to the F.B.I. office in connection with an armored car robbery investigation, after he was given what is now known as the *Miranda* warnings. He consented to a "pat down" by the F.B.I. agent which disclosed an elastic band used to bundle the stolen money. The consent was held to have been freely and voluntarily given. Callahan permitted the F.B.I. to retain the elastic band apparently under the impression that it was not significant—a thought indulged in by the F.B.I. agent at the time of its discovery.

One general partner in a limited partnership may consent to an examination of the partnership's books and records by the Attorney General, where no personal papers of the other general partner, the defendant, were taken. *People v. Herrmann,* 40 Misc2d 1089. *See also: U.S. v. Sferas,* 210 F2d 69, 74; *U.S. v. Silverstein,* 314 F2d 789.

A United States District Court has held that the alleged seizure of corporate records by a trustee in bankruptcy was not within the exclusionary mandate of the Fourth Amendment. *U.S. v. Masterson,* 251 F Supp 937.

The owner of an automobile, premises or other property, may consent to a search and a third party may not object even where the search discloses property for possession of which the third party is subsequently prosecuted. *People v. Lane,* 10 NY2d 347, 179 NE2d 339; *People v. Kortwright,* 236 NYS2d 385; *People v. Angevine,* 262 NYS2d 784, 47 Misc2d 374. Consent to a search freely given by one in authority destroys any claim of illegal search and seizure. *Amos v. U.S.,* 255 US 313.

*People v. Overton,* 20 NY2d 360, 229 NE2d 596, involved the search of a high school student's locker in which marihuana was discovered. The pertinent facts disclosed that detectives had obtained a warrant directing the search of two high school students and their lockers. They presented the warrant to Dr. Adolph Panitz, the vice-principal of the high school, who summoned the students to his office. The detectives searched the boys and found nothing. After a brief interrogation, two of the detectives took one youth to his locker, leaving Overton with the vice-principal and the second detective. He was asked if he had marihuana in his locker, and nodded in an uncertain manner. The detective persisted and Overton replied either "I guess so" or "maybe." The detective, Dr. Panitz, the school custodian and Overton then went to Overton's locker, where Dr. Panitz opened it with his master key. The detective found marihuana cigarettes in the defendant's jacket hanging in the locker. "Subsequently, it was held that the warrant was ineffective insofar as the search of the locker was concerned." 24 NY2d at 523.

The locker with a combination lock was assigned to Overton who was required to disclose the combination to his official teacher. Both Dr. Panitz and the school custodian possessed master keys to all lockers. Each student had exclusive possession of his locker.

Motion to suppress the marihuana made in the trial court was denied, the court stating: "The Board of Education through Dr. Panitz, retained dominion over the use of the lockers and the court finds that the search was legal." The Appellate Term reversed, stating, "The search was illegal and cannot be justified upon the theory of consent on the part of the vice-principal of said school." (51 Misc2d 140). However, the Court of Appeals reversed the Appellate Term and sustained the trial court. (20 NY2d 360). Certiorari was granted in light of *Bumper v. North Carolina,* 391 US 543 and the case remanded for reconsideration by the Court of Appeals.

The Court of Appeals adhered to its original decision (24 NY2d 522, 249 NE2d 366), declining to extend *Bumper, supra,* to cover the facts in *Overton* even though in both cases the search warrants were invalid, since to do so "would be extending *Bumper* far beyond its logical applicability." The Court noted that there was no "lawful coercion"; that title to the school building and properties was in the Mount Vernon Board of Education represented by Dr. Panitz; that lockers were assigned to students under certain conditions one of which prohibited the storage of unlawful material; that Dr. Panitz had a duty to enforce the rules and regulations of the school and " 'this right becomes a duty when suspicion arises' "; that the locker was opened by a representative of the people of Mount Vernon; that the locker was not the private property of the student. Thus, it was held: "Coercion is absent in this setting, having been displaced by the performance of a delegated duty." 24 NY2d at 526.

Although the question was not raised directly in *Overton,* it would seem that a school official is in *loco parentis.* As such, it would seem, that the teacher could consent to the search. *See: People v. Mummert,* 183 Misc 243, 50 NYS2d 699; *Hogan v. Newton,* 185 Misc 405, 56 NYS2d 779. This theory was in fact adopted in *People v. Jackson,* 65 Misc2d 909, 319 NYS2d 731.

In *Calway v. Williamson,* 130 Conn 575, 36 A2d 377, 378, the court held that a teacher, "in a limited sense," is in *loco parentis* over the pupil and incident to this relationship "may require obedience to reasonable rules and proper submission to his authority."

In *Moore v. Student Affairs Committee,* 284 F Supp 725, the court held that a state university regulation that "the college reserves the right to enter rooms for inspection purposes" was prima facie reasonable as necessary to the college's performance of its duty to operate the school as an educational institution. Thus, the search by college authorities of student dormitories under this regulation was held to be a reasonable rule.

**§ 235. Examples of No Consent.** A consent, to be valid, must be clear, definite and without equivocation. *U.S. v. Vitale,* 312 F2d 595, cert. den. 373 US 903. While there are many cases of varying fact situations in which no consent to a search was found, the following ones are typical.

Consent obtained by obscuring the warning inherent in the request to inspect records. *U.S. v. Sclafani,* 265 F2d 408.

Obtaining the item to be searched by ruse or trick. *Gouled v. U.S.,* 255 US 298.

Obtaining consent by duress or coercion. *Channel v. U.S.,* 285 F2d 217; *People v. Loria,* 10 NY2d 368, 179 NE2d 478.

Defendant arrested at entrance of his parent's apartment, surrounded by five armed government agents, one of whom told him that if he had any guns he should give them up, followed by an alleged consent to search his bedroom where weapons were found, held to be a submission to authority and not a free and voluntary consent to a search. *U.S. v. Marotta,* 326 F Supp 377.

Defendant confronted in his home at 3 A.M. by nine police officers and a justice of the peace, constituted a sufficiently coercive situation as to render a consent to search involuntary even though defendant told officers to "go ahead." *Hoover v. Beto,* 439 F2d 913.

Obeying the orders of a police officer which results in a search or delivery of contraband, fruits, instrumentalities or leads. *People v. Rodriguez,* 11 NY2d 279, 287, 183 NE2d 651.

Opening a door, after threat by the police, to break it down or submit to police authority. *People v. Loria,* 10 NY2d 368; *Johnson v. U.S.,* 333 US 10; *Amos v. U.S.,* 255 US 313; *Catalanotte v. U.S.,* 208 F2d 264.

Where a key was taken by the police and used in opening defendant's apartment, surrender of the key, if it occurred, did not constitute consent. *People v. Porter,* 37 Misc2d 73.

"Defendant's response to a direction to empty his pockets during questioning by three special patrolmen who had apprehended him in a part of Bellevue Hospital to which the public had access and had then taken him to their one-door, one-room headquarters, cannot be deemed a search by consent under these circumstances." *People v. Matera,* 45 Misc2d 864, 258 NYS2d 2.

Mere acquiescence on the part of a defendant to talk to officers, inside of his apartment, did not constitute consent to search it. *People v. Loria, supra.*

An apartment shared with others is nonetheless constitutionally protected against intrusion under the Fourth Amendment. The fact that the door to the apartment was partly open does not make the intrusion by persons not guests of any of the tenants any more lawful. Entry by the police into such an apartment without a warrant, exigencies or probable cause, which entry resulted in finding of contraband, requires suppression of the seized contraband.

> "The connection between the unlawful entry and the discovery of the challenged evidence is too direct to be disregarded (*People* v. *Loria,* 10 NY2d 368; *Badillo* v. *Superior Court,* 46 Cal. 2d 269; *State* v. *DeGrazio,* 39 N.J. 268; *McDonald* v. *United States, supra*)." *People v. Williams,* 24 AD2d 274, 276.

§ 236. **Consent and Primary Taint.** Consent to a search given by a defendant to a police officer, following an unlawful detention and interrogation by the officer, voids the consent to search.

Thus, where police had no reasonable suspicion that defendant was committing a crime or that he had committed a felony, and all that they knew was that the defendant was a character who should be followed, it was held that the officers had no initial right to stop the defendant and interrogate him. Accordingly, the ensuing search, although made with his consent, was fatally infected and the fruits of the search were suppressed. *People v. Albright,* 32 AD2d 878, 302 NYS2d 213. *Cf.: People v. Rivera,* 14 NY2d 441, 201 NE2d 32; *Sibron v. New York,* 392 US 40; *Wong Sun v. U.S.,* 371 US 471.

On the other hand, where a defendant was lawfully arrested and taken to the police station, it was proper for the police to require him, when he was booked, to empty his pockets. In complying with this request, a defendant, in a broad sense, is doing so under police coercion. Nevertheless, this coercion does not invalidate the search, nor taint the consent. In reaching this conclusion, the court noted that the procedure followed is standard and necessary police practice and is in accordance with regulations adopted by the State Commission of Correction and further, that this procedure is necessary for the protection of the police, correction officers, and the defendant himself. In these circumstances, contraband found after defendant had emptied his pockets is admissible. In this case marihuana was found in an unsealed envelope. *People v. Vasquez,* 57 Misc2d 138.

§ 237. **Burden of Proof.** The burden rests heavily on the People to show by clear, positive and convincing evidence that the consent was unequivocal, specific and freely given. *Judd v. U.S.,* 190 F2d 649; *Karwicki v. U.S.,* 55 F2d 225; *Channel v. U.S.,* 285 F2d 217; *People v. Russell,* 33 Misc2d 851; *Bumper v. North Carolina,* 391 US 543.

In *Bumper,* a 66 year old woman consented to a search by four policemen when they showed her a warrant later declared to be invalid. The prosecution contended that the search was valid on the ground of consent and because of what was found. The United States Supreme Court rejected both arguments. On question of consent, the Court said:

> "When a law enforcement officer claims authority to search a home under a warrant, he announces that the occupant has no right to resist the search. The situation is instinct with coercion—albeit colorably lawful coercion. Where there is coercion there cannot be consent." 391 US at 550.

In *People v. Whitehurst,* 25 NY2d 389, 391, 392, the court emphasized the rule that the burden of proving consent is on the People. In that case, defendant recognized a detective from a previous narcotics arrest and exclaimed, "Oh no. Not you again." To this the detective said, "Yes, it's me. What have you got this time?" The defendant understood this as a reference to narcotics and produced two glassine envelopes from his pocket and said, "That's all I've got." On appeal from his conviction, defendant contended that producing the narcotics was not a search based on consent and the burden is on the People to establish consent, since they urged consent in this case, citing *Bumper v. North Carolina,* 391 US 543;

*People v. Malinsky,* 15 NY2d 86, 91, n. 2, 204 NE2d 188; *Nardone v. U.S.,* 308 US 338, 342. The Court of Appeals agreed that the trial court did not apply the burden of proof rule properly. The detective's question was "couched in terms of a request and an affirmative response by word or by deed would constitute a constitutional waiver." Thus the burden in this "consent" case was on the People.

§ 237.01. **Hearings on Question of Consent.** The court is required to conduct an evidentiary hearing on the question of consent to a search, where that issue is raised, and must make a specific finding as to whether consent was given. Consent to search by a defendant who is in custody at the time, should be viewed with caution. *Hubbard v. Tinsley,* 336 F2d 854.

## Chapter 16

# SEARCH BY GOVERNMENT OFFICERS AND AGENTS



---

**§ 245. Administrative Searches.** Without disturbing the rule authorizing the entry into private premises without a warrant under exigent circumstances, exemplified by *Johnson v. U.S.*, 333 US 10, and *State v. Rees,* 139 NW2d 406, the United States Supreme Court has struck down the right of administrative officers to inspect private premises, residential as well as commerical, under local health, fire and safety codes, without a warrant, thus reversing *Frank v. Maryland,* 359 US 360, and *Ohio ex rel Eaton v. Price,* 364 US 263.

It is a well known fact that as cities have grown, the hazards of urban living have multiplied. Congestion in the urban areas has called for increased inspections to check on the sources of fire, disease, pests and pollution. With the lives, health, safety and welfare of millions of people at stake, local governments across the nation have enacted codes authorizing related inspections, and providing penal sanctions against persons who refuse to permit them.

Mindful of the provisions of the Fourth Amendment, the Supreme Court has now held that, absent consent and exigent circumstances, a warrant must be obtained prior to those inspections. More specifically, the Court said that the Amendment bars prosecution of a person who has refused to permit a warrantless code enforcement inspection of his personal residence, absent an emergency.

The issue arose in *Camara v. Municipal Court,* 387 US 523, out of a refusal by Camara to permit an annual routine inspection of his residence under the city (San Francisco) Housing Code, without a warrant. *Cf. People v. Laverne,* 14 NY2d 304, 307–308, 200 NE2d 441.

Basing its decision on the right to privacy and security of individuals against arbitrary invasion by government officials under the Fourth Amendment, enforceable against the states under the Fourteenth Amendment (*see: Ker v. California,* 374 US 23, 30), the Court said:

> "[E]xcept in certain carefully defined classes of cases, a search of private property without proper consent is 'unreasonable' unless it has been authorized by a valid search warrant. See, *e.g., Stoner* v. *California,* 376 U.S. 483; *United States* v. *Jeffers,* 342 U.S. 48; *McDonald* v. *United States,* 335 U.S. 451." *Camara* at 528–529.

Analyzing *Frank v. Maryland, supra,* which it overruled, the court concluded:

> "It is surely anomalous to say that the individual and his private property are fully protected by the Fourth Amendment only when the individual is suspected of criminal behavior." *Id.* at 530.

Having made this pronouncement, the court nevertheless conceded that inspectors must ultimately have access to private property and proceeded to weaken the "probable cause" warrant provision by providing for a new type of warrant in inspection cases. It did this by distinguishing between the "probable cause" which must be established in a criminal case and the "probable cause" required to obtain a warrant to inspect private premises.

> "Unlike the search pursuant to a criminal investigation, the inspection programs at issue here are aimed at securing city-wide compliance with minimum physical standards for private property. . . . In determining

whether a particular inspection is reasonable—and thus in determining whether there is probable cause . . . —the need for the inspection must be weighed in terms of these reasonable goals of code enforcement." *Camara,* 387 US at 535.

As Mr. Justice Douglas said in his dissent in *Frank v. Maryland, supra,* quoted in *Camara,*

> " 'Where considerations of health and safety are involved, the facts that would justify an inference of "probable cause" to make an inspection are clearly different from those that would justify such an inference where a criminal investigation has been undertaken. . . . The test of "probable cause" required by the Fourth Amendment can take into account the nature of the search that is being sought.' " 387 US at 538.

The effectiveness of periodic inspections to seek compliances with various municipal codes is virtually axiomatic. These inspections are unavoidably based on area inspections resulting from an appraisal of conditions in a particular area and *not* on the conditions of a particular structure. Accordingly, the Court said that such area inspections are reasonable within the purview of the Fourth Amendment because: (1) the programs have a long history of judicial and public acceptance; (2) the public interest demands that all dangerous conditions be prevented or abated; (3) the inspections are not personal in nature nor aimed at discovering evidence of crime; (4) they involve a limited invasion of the urban citizen's privacy. *Frank v. Maryland, supra.*

In view of the foregoing, the court held that a lawful warrant to inspect private premises would be valid for conducting an area inspection if certain procedures are adopted. The details for these procedures would have to be worked out in the ordinances of each city. These procedures are as follows:

(1) The inspector will first go to the areas to be checked, without a warrant, to obtain permission to inspect. Experience has shown that at least 85 percent of the people will voluntarily admit them. "[W]arrants should normally be sought only after entry is refused

unless there has been a citizen complaint or there is other satisfactory reason for securing immediate entry," such as exigency. 387 US at 539–540.

(2) Absent consent, or exigent circumstances, a warrant to inspect may be issued by a judge based on general allegations that:
   (a) The premises have not been inspected in a certain length of time;
   (b) The nature of the building, *e.g.*, a multi-family apartment house;
   (c) The condition of the entire area.

(3) Specific knowledge of the conditions of the particular building to be inspected is *not* necessarily required.

Thus, it would seem that if the inspector states that the building in question had not been inspected for some time or that the buildings in the area are old or that the conditions in the neighborhood are bad, a valid warrant could issue.

"If a valid public interest justifies the intrusion contemplated, then there is probable cause to issue a suitably restricted search warrant." *Camara,* 387 US at 539.

In *See v. Seattle,* 387 US 541, the question posed was whether *Camara, supra,* applied to similar inspections of *commercial* structures which are not used as private residences. The question was answered in the affirmative.

> "We find strong support . . . for our conclusion that warrants are a necessary and a tolerable limitation on the right to enter upon and inspect commercial premises." *See,* 387 US at 544.

However, the court was careful to point out that this decision did not strike down such accepted regulatory techniques "which require inspections prior to operating a business or marketing a product." *See* at 546.

The court also indicated that wider latitude would be afforded the right to inspect and obtain warrants in cases involving business premises than residential premises.

As the dissenting opinions point out, the court in these cases is following the form but ignoring the substance of the Fourth Amendment.

> "It prostitutes the command of the Fourth Amendment that 'no Warrants shall issue, but upon probable cause' and sets up in the health and safety codes area inspection a newfangled 'warrant' system that is entirely foreign to Fourth Amendment standards." *See* at 547.

In substance, these two cases bar warrantless, nonemergency inspection of residential and commercial premises by city health and fire inspectors without the occupant's consent; warrants for such inspections need *not* be based on reasonable cause to believe that the violation exists in premises to be inspected, but can be based on reasonableness of need to conduct periodic, area-wide inspections.

In *Parrish v. Civil Service Commission,* 425 P2d 223, decided three months prior to *Camara* and *See, supra,* the California Supreme Court had before it the question of the constitutionality of an administrative search, conducted at dawn, by county welfare officials, of the homes of welfare recipients, to determine their eligibility for continued welfare benefits.

These "raids" were held to be unconstitutional even under the criteria established in *Frank v. Maryland,* 359 US 360, since they were conducted without a search warrant, at night, as a search for evidence of a crime and without effective consent, given freely and voluntarily. *Parrish* at 228.

"We fully recognize the importance of ferreting out fraud in the inexcusable garnering of welfare benefits not truly deserved. Such efforts, however, must be, and clearly can be, conducted with due regard for the constitutional rights of welfare recipients." *Parrish,* 425 P2d at 234.

The question of administrative searches—"raids"—has now become largely academic by virtue of new California and Federal regulations barring such searches (*see* 425 P2d at 225, n.1) and, in addition, by virtue of the decisions in *Camara* and *See.*

Nevertheless, in spite of these new regulations, the lawfulness of such welfare case "raids" is not wholly resolved. In *Wyman v. James* 400 US 309, a 1971 decision, the United States Supreme Court, in referring to the *Parrish* case (Pt. VII of the majority opinion), stated that the facts in *Parrish* "present another case for another day."

*Wyman v. James, supra,* must be read carefully, lest it be misconstrued. *Wyman* does not overrule *Camara, supra,* or *See, supra.*

The *Wyman* case involved the authority of a New York welfare caseworker to visit the home of a welfare recipient periodically and on notice, during reasonable hours, as a condition of continued receipt of Aid to Families with Dependent Children (AFDC), under New York's statute and regulations.

Respondent James had a pre-school age child who suffered a skull fracture, a dent in the head and a possible rat bite. The respondent refused to permit such visits in her home, asserting, inter alia, a violation of her Fourth Amendment rights, although she expressed willingness to be interviewed away from her home.

In rejecting her contentions, the Court noted that Fourth Amendment rights were not involved "for the seemingly obvious and simple reason that we are not concerned here with any search by the New York social service agency in the Fourth Amendment meaning of that term." (Pt. IV of majority opinion.) Nor does the home visit "fall within the Fourth Amendment's proscription. This is because it does not descend to the level of unreasonableness. It is unreasonableness which is the Fourth Amendment's standard. *Terry* v. *Ohio,* 392 U.S. 1, 9 (1968); *Elkins* v. *United States,* 364 U.S. 206, 222 (1960)." *Wyman v. James, supra,* Pt. V, at 318.

The Court further noted (Pt. IV) that, "It is also true that the caseworker's posture in the home visit is perhaps, in a sense, both rehabilitative and investigative," but added "this latter aspect, we think, is given too broad a character and far more emphasis than it deserves if it is equated with a search in the traditional criminal law context. We note, too, that the visitation in itself is not forced or compelled, and that the beneficiary's denial of permission is not a criminal act." *Wyman v. James, supra,* at 317.

As the Court observed in his case, "The focus is on the *child* and, further it is on the child who is *dependent*" and it is the child's needs that are paramount. (Pt. V of majority opinion; emphasis is the Court's.)

Accordingly, the Court concluded that the home visits requested herein were not unreasonable. In addition, the Court observed, that since the state provides the money specifically for the care of dependent children, it has an obligation to see, by "gentle means" that such care is properly provided. *Wyman v. James, supra,* Pt. V.

The Court concluded (Pt. VII):

> "Our holding today does not mean, of course, that a determination of benefits upon refusal of a home visit is to be upheld against constitutional challenge under all conceivable circumstances. The early morning mass raid upon homes of welfare recipients is not unknown. See *Parish v. Civil Service Comm'n,* 66 Cal.2d 260, 425 P.2d 223 (1967); Reich, Midnight Welfare Searches and the Social Security Act, 72 Yale L. J. 1347 (1963). But that is not this case. Facts of that kind present another case for another day.
>
> "We therefore conclude that the home visitation as structured by the New York statutes and regulations is a reasonable administrative tool; that it serves a valid and proper administrative purpose for the dispensation of the AFDC program; that it is not an unwarranted invasion of personal privacy; and that it violates no right guaranteed by the Fourth Amendment." *Wyman v. James,* 400 US at 326.

New York has followed the decisions in *Camara, supra,* and *See, supra,* in *Finn's Liquor Shop v. State Liquor Authority,* 24 NY2d 647, 249 NE2d 440, cert. den. 396 US 840.

In passing on the validity of searches and seizures conducted by the New York State Liquor Authority (SLA), the court stated that the exclusionary rule enunciated in *Mapp v. Ohio,* 367 US 643, applies to administrative proceedings before the SLA as well as in criminal proceedings.

In *Finn's Liquor Shop, supra,* an SLA inspector obtained permission from the manager of a liquor store to inspect it. The inspector entered a rear room of the store and searched a coat that was hanging there and found some slips indicating a sale of liquor on credit. He had no search warrant. At an SLA hearing, the licensee refused to answer certain questions on Fifth Amendment grounds; his license was suspended and a fine was imposed.

In holding this warrantless search unlawful, the court said: "No State may require, as a condition of doing business, a blanket submission to warrantless searches at any time and for any purpose." 24 NY2d at 658. Such a blanket authority would be unconstitutional. *Cf. Colonnade Catering Corp. v. U.S.*, 410 F2d 197.

In companion cases the court applied the rule in *Mapp v. Ohio, supra,* to a case involving a search under a warrant based on an illegal wire tap order. The SLA annulled petitioner's license. This determination was also annulled. It was noted that in a prior criminal prosecution the evidence seized was ordered suppressed. *LaPente v. State Liquor Authority,* 24 NY2d 647. *Accord: Malik v. State Liquor Authority,* 24 NY2d 647, 661, 249 NE2d 440, cert. den. 396 US 840.

**§ 245.01. Contempt of Court Proceedings as Result of Administrative Search.** In a contempt of court proceeding arising out of an alleged administrative search, the court held in *Village of Laurel Hollow v. Laverne,* 24 AD2d 616, 262 NYS2d 625, affd 17 NY2d 900, 218 NE2d 703, that Fourth Amendment guarantees were applicable. In this case the Village had obtained an injunction against the defendant in a civil proceeding. By sending a building inspector into defendant's premises to search, without a search warrant, they obtained evidence that he had violated the injunction.

> "The entry and search were not intended to lead to summary administrative corrections for the purpose of abating a hazard. . . . There was no immedate major crisis affording neither the time nor opportunity to seek a search warrant. . . . The situation did not involve evidence wrongfully obtained by a private person, . . . (cf. *Sackler* v. *Sackler,* 16 AD2d 423, [229 N.Y.S.2d 61]; *Sackler v. Sackler,* 15 NY2d 40). Here, the Government obtained the evidence by a governmental official acting in his public capacity." *Laverne,* 24 AD2d at 617.

Although this proceeding was technically a civil case "in substance and effect the proceedings were quasi criminal in nature." Their objects were to punish the defendants for violating the injunction. Such punishment could entail a fine or imprisonment. Such unlawfully seized evidence could not be utilized in either a criminal proceeding nor in the instant contempt proceedings. *See also: Boyd v. U.S.*, 116 US 616; *One 1958 Plymouth Sedan v. Pennsylvania,* 380 US 693.

§ 245.02. **Quasi Criminal Proceedings as Result of Administrative Search.** The same theory followed in *One 1958 Plymounth Sedan v. Pennsylvania, supra,* and *Laverne, supra,* was adopted in a proceeding brought by the State Liquor Authority to cancel a restaurant liquor license. In that case a search under a search warrant produced evidence involving the licensee in professional gambling activities on and off the licensed premises. The search warrant was subsequently vacated for want of probable cause in a collateral criminal court action.

In a criminal court prosecution the evidence seized under an unlawful warrant, on an appropriate application, would be excluded from evidence. The same exclusionary rule, the court held, was equally applicable in an administrative proceeding involving penalties, forfeitures and other sanctions for violations of laws or regulations. *Leogrande, Jr. v. S.L.A.,* 25 AD2d 225, 268 NYS2d 433. In affirming *Laverne,* (17 NY2d 900, 218 NE2d 703), the New York Court of Appeals approved the *Leogrande* ruling. "Since the punishment imposed in this contempt proceeding is penal in nature (a fine with imprisonment as an alternative), although the proceeding is civil in form, evidence upon which the punishment was based must be deemed improperly received as the product of an unlawful search (*One 1958 Plymouth* v. *Penn.,* 380 U.S. 693; *Boyd* v. *United States,* 116 US 616; *Mtr. of Leogrande* v. *State Liq. Auth.,* 25 AD2d 225)." *Village etc. v. Laverne,* 17 NY2d at 901, 218 NE2d 703. The New York Court of Appeals affirmed, based on *People v. Friola,* 11 NY2d 157, 182 NE2d 100.

The rule applicable in criminal actions, that a constitutional issue must be preserved by objection at the trial, is applicable *a fortiori* in administrative proceedings. In this case, a substantial part of the evidence on which petitioner's restaurant liquor license was cancelled for permitting gambling was obtained by search warrants which were subsequently vacated.

No objection on this ground to receipt of the evidence having been made at the hearings, the cancellation cannot be annulled on this ground.

> "Unless objection is made, the point of admissibility of evidence is lost. The decision in *People* v. *Friola* (11 NY2d 157) has relevance." *Leogrande v. State Liquor Authority,* 19 NY2d 418, 424. *See also: Lederman v. New York City Transit Authority,* 35 AD2d 996, 317 NYS2d 976.

**§ 246. Immigration Searches.** Officers and certain employees of the Immigration and Naturalization Service (INS) may search certain persons and their effects without a warrant.

8 USC § 1357(c) provides:

> "Any officer or employee of the Service authorized and designated under regulations prescribed by the Attorney General, whether individually or as one of a class, shall have power to conduct a search, without warrant, of the person, and of the personal effects in the possession of any person seeking admission to the United States, concerning whom such officer or employee may have reasonable cause to suspect that grounds exist for exclusion from the United States under this chapter which would be disclosed by such search."

Additionally, § 1357(a)(3) authorizes such INS agents:

> "[W]ithout a warrant . . . within a reasonable distance from any external boundary of the United States, to board and search for aliens any vessel within the territorial waters of the United States and any railway car, aircraft, conveyance, or vehicle, and within a distance of twenty-five miles from any such external boundary to have access to private lands, but not dwellings, for the purpose of patrolling the border to prevent illegal entry of aliens into the United States."

In *Roa-Rodriquez v. U.S.,* 410 F2d 1206, the search of an automobile, on a through highway, 90 miles north of the Mexican border was a "reasonable distance," under this section.

However, the right to search a conveyance to determine if aliens are attempting to enter the country illegally does not authorize a search of the vehicle for contraband without a warrant. *U.S. v. Hortze,* 179 F Supp 913; *U.S. v. Winer,* 294 F Supp 731.

But where INS officers make a lawful arrest, they may conduct a search incidental thereto, and with or without a warrant, seize contraband that the search may reveal. *Abel v. U.S.,* 362 US 217; *Taylor v. Fine,* 115 F Supp 68.

§ 247. **Border Searches.** "The search which customs agents are authorized to conduct upon entry [into this country] is of the broadest possible character." *Landau v. United States Attorney,* 82 F2d 285, 286.

"Unsupported or 'mere' suspicion alone is sufficient to justify such a [border] search for purposes of Customs law enforcement." *Alexander v. U.S.,* 362 F2d 379, 382.

"There is no requirement, as there is in the ordinary search and seizure case, that the searching officers have 'probable cause' for making the search, as that term is used in the Fourth Amendment. . . ." *People v. Furey,* 42 Misc2d 579, 580.

The federal statute (19 USC § 1581(a)) authorizes customs officers to "go on board any vessel or vehicle at any place in the United States" to investigate any violations of customs laws therein. Section 1582 authorizes the Secretary of the Treasury to issue regulations with respect to searching persons or baggage coming into this country (*see* 19 CFR § 23.1). If this search discloses merchandise subject to the payment of duties, 19 CFR § 23.11 authorizes its seizure.

If a vehicle is suspected of carrying merchandise subject to duty, or which is being smuggled into the United States, the vehicle may be stopped and searched. 19 USC § 482.

In *Alexander v. U.S.,* 362 F2d 379, the court said:

> "In conferring upon Customs Officers such broad authority, circumscribed only by Constitutional limitations of the Fourth Amendment, the Congress has in effect declared that a search which would be 'unreasonable' within the meaning of the Fourth Amendment, if conducted by

police officers in the ordinary case, would be a reasonable search if conducted by Customs officials in lawful pursuit of unlawful imports. Judicial recognition of this distinction has given rise to the term 'border search,' in order to distinguish official searches which are reasonable because made solely in the enforcement of Customs laws from other official searches made in connection with general law enforcement.

"Validity for this distinction is found in the fact that the primordial purpose of a search by Customs officers is not to apprehend persons, but to seize contraband property unlawfully imported or brought into the United States. [See The Atlantic 68 F.2d 8 (2d Cir. 1933).] Accordingly, it is well settled that a search by Customs officials of a vehicle, at the time and place of entering the jurisdiction of the United States, need not be based on probable cause; that 'unsupported' or 'mere' suspicion alone is sufficient to justify such a search for purposes of Customs law enforcement." *Alexander, supra,* 362 F2d at 381–382.

The effect of these powers conferred upon customs officers by the statutes mentioned above is to authorize the search first and, if contraband is found which appears to be in violation of Federal law, then the person engaged in the breach of the law shall be arrested and the contraband shall be seized. This is the reverse of the general rule applicable to police officers under which the lawful arrest must, in the ordinary "police" case, precede the search. *See also: People v. Serabie,* 51 Misc2d 914, 273 NYS2d 956; *Henderson v. U.S.,* 390 F2d 805.

**§ 247.01. Border Defined.** The Statute (19 USC § 482) authorizes customs searches at a reasonable distance inland from the border. *Thomas v. U.S.,* 372 F2d 252; *Alexander v. U.S.,* 362 F2d 379, cert. den. 385 US 977; *King v. U.S.,* 348 F2d 814, cert. den. 382 US 926. These cases hold that what constitutes such reasonable distance depends on the facts and circumstances of the particular case. This includes the time and space factors. By this is meant, the elapsed time and distance between the point of entry into the United States and the point and time of the actual search.

In *Thomas v. U.S.,* 372 F2d 252, 254 the court said: "[A] border search is in a separate category from searches generally because it may be predicated upon suspicion. . . . We note [however] there must come a time when a traveler's entry into this country is complete so that the protection of the Fourth Amendment attaches to him." *See also: Glaziou v. U.S.,* 402 F2d 8, cert. den. 393 US 1121.

In such cases, a search warrant should be obtained, and they are obtainable by customs officers, when based on probable cause. *Russo v. U.S.,* 391 F2d 1004.

Thus, in a case where the point of entry into the United States of suspect goods is not clearly defined, a search warrant should be obtained prior to seizure. This is necessary since section 482 limits the power of customs officers to border searches. Accordingly, a non-border search by customs officers without a warrant is unlawful when "there is nothing in the record to suggest that the search of appellant's packages occurred in the course of entry into this country." *Corngold v. U.S.,* 367 F2d 1, 3. In *Corngold,* the suspect packages were received by air in Los Angeles from New York. There were strong indications that they had been shipped to New York from Switzerland without prior customs clearance. Nevertheless, the search therein without a warrant was invalid.

In other cases, a lawful border search may be conducted without a warrant.

In defining the term "border," it is to be noted that the border area is elastic. *U.S. v. Glaziou,* 402 F2d 8, cert. den. 393 US 1121.

When the courts speak of a "reasonable distance" from the border, they indicate four factors to be considered in making this determination: (1) time of entry into this country; (2) time of the actual search; (3) distance travelled from the point of entry to the point where the actual search was made; and (4) was the suspect under surveillance from the point of entry to the point of search.

In many cases, there is little difficulty in deciding that a search was actually a border search.

In *People v. Furey,* 42 Misc2d 579, the defendant was

searched in the area at the John F. Kennedy International Airport between the customs clearance area and the barrier which leads to the area open to the general public. The area was within the jurisdiction of United States Customs, *i.e.,* the "border" (*Furey* at 580) and constituted a valid border search.

In *People v. Luna,* NYLJ, 4/9/65, p. 18, col. 8, the defendant was standing on line in the International Arrival Building at Kennedy Airport awaiting clearance from customs, after his arrival from Mexico. He was taken to the customs room by a customs officer and searched on mere suspicion. Three guns and 150 rounds of ammunition were found on his person. The court held that this was a lawful "border" search.

In *Thomas v. U.S., supra,* the petitioner was stopped and searched six blocks from the border—a point from which the border was in plain view. This was a lawful "border" search.

In *Castello-Garcia v. U.S.,* 424 F2d 482, the search was conducted 105 miles from the border several hours after his entry. However, petitioner had been kept under constant surveillance from the time of his entry until the time and point of the search. The court held this to be a valid border search.

So, too, in *Rodriguez-Gonzalez v. U.S.,* 378 F2d 256, a search conducted 20 miles from the border and 15 hours later, was sustained as a good border search. *See also: Walker v. U.S.,* 404 F2d 900, involving a search 45 miles inland, and eight hours after entry.

On the other hand, in *Valenzuela-Garcia v. U.S.,* 425 F2d 1170, the search took place 48 miles from the point of entry, but petitioner was not under constant surveillance at the time. The court held that this search did not constitute a border search.

Since it is important to detect and apprehend smugglers, it is not always advisable to make the search in the immediate vicinity of the point of border crossing. A later search is lawful if the evidence "discloses no reason to believe that there [was] any 'change of condition of the [vehicle] from the time it crossed the border until it was stopped' [*King v. United States,* 348 F.2d at 816]." *Alexander v. U.S.,* 362 F2d 379, 382.

To summarize the border search rule, in this area, customs searches conducted away from the border pursuant to 19 USC

§ 482, are constitutional. *Murgia v. U.S.,* 285 F2d 14. Accordingly, it is not necessary that the border search be conducted at or in the immediate vicinity of the international border for such search to be legal.

"[T]he legality of the search must be tested by a determination whether the totality of the surrounding circumstances, including the time and distance elapsed as well as the manner and extent of surveillance, are such as to convince the fact finder with reasonable certainty that any contraband which might be found in or on the vehicle at the time of such search was aboard the vehicle at the time of the entry into the jurisdiction of the United States. Any search by Customs officials which meets this test is properly called a 'border search'." *Alexander v. U.S.,* 362 F2d 379, 382.

**§ 247.02. Extent of the Search.** In spite of the broad language of the federal statutes (19 USC § 1581(a); 19 CFR § 23.1), the trend of decisional law seems to be to limit border searches on "mere suspicion," without a warrant, to vehicles, baggage, purses, wallets, and similar items of personalty. *Henderson v. U.S.,* 390 F2d 805.

Though it would seem at first blush that the customs official is at great liberty to search and seize with impunity, the Supreme Court of the United States has set up certain guidelines as to body searches which have been held to be applicable to border searches. Circuit Courts of Appeal have followed and amplified these Supreme Court guidelines.

The first case of some importance pertaining to a "body search" to reach the Supreme Court is *Rochin v. California,* 342 US 165. In that case, based on police information that Rochin was selling narcotics, the police forced their way into his apartment without a warrant. Two capsules, suspected of containing narcotics, were lying on his bedside table. When questioned about them, he swallowed the capsules and the police were unable to retrieve them. The police then took him to a hospital and at their direction a doctor forced an emetic solution through a tube into Rochin's stomach, against his will. Rochin regurgitated and in the vomit two capsules were retrieved. They contained morphine and were introduced at his trial which resulted in a conviction.

The Supreme Court reversed, citing the Due Process Clause of the Fourteenth Amendment. *See also: Malinski v. New York,* 342 US 401.

On the other hand, a federal court, in *Blefare v. U.S.,* 362 F2d 870, 880, has ruled that the method employed, in the course of a border search, to discover packets of heroin in the stomach of defendants suspected of smuggling, whereby vomiting was induced by allowing fluid to flow into the stomach through a tube inserted through the nose and stomach, did not violate defendant's rights, and the packets so discovered were admissible over the objection that they constituted illegally acquired evidence. In arriving at this conclusion, the court pointed out that this was a border search and that *Rochin, supra,* was not; additionally, "there was no feasible alternative procedure to enable the officers to search appellant's stomach."

In *Blefare,* the customs officers had more than mere suspicion that Blefare had narcotics on him. He was an addict with recent puncture marks on his arms and the codefendant stated that he had swallowed narcotics and that Blefare feigned regurgitation to help the codefendant stash some. A doctor had seen Blefare vomit and re-swallow something. The agents also knew that Blefare had crossed the border five weeks earlier and had had narcotics in his stomach at that time and was suspected of narcotics smuggling.

Before a body search for narcotics may be made in a border search, some knowledge of the presence of the narcotics in the body of the suspect is necessary, in spite of the broad language of the statute.

The use of an emetic to retrieve narcotics which have been swallowed, the court noted in *Blefare,* has been approved in *U.S. v. Michel,* 158 F Supp 34, affd sub nom, *King v. U.S.,* 258 F2d 754, cert. den. 359 US 939; *see also: U.S. v. Willis,* 85 F Supp 745 (in which a stomach pump was used and the evidence was held inadmissible); *Lane v. U.S.,* 321 F2d 573, cert. den. 377 US 936; *Barrera v. U.S.,* 276 F2d 654. *Blefare, supra,* 362 F2d at 875.

A significant statement made in the concurring opinion is to be noted: "Because it is a border search cannot make any conduct reasonable, but it probably makes searches lawful that would not be such within the United States (as for example, a search without probable cause, but based on mere suspicion)." 362 F2d at 880.

It is a well known fact that body cavities are used to secrete contraband, especially narcotics, for the purpose of smuggling them into this country. Rectal and vaginal areas, as well as the mouth and stomach are employed. Many cases involving this type of smuggling have appeared in our courts, especially in the Ninth Circuit which includes California.

In the body search cases, one can discern a trend in the decisions away from literally equating the terms "vehicle" and "person" in 19 USC § 1581(a) and 19 CFR § 23.1. This trend indicates a requirement that the customs officer have a little more than "mere suspicion" before he may lawfully embark on a body search, although there is no such requirement for the search of a vehicle or other personal property of the suspect in a border search.

Two recent cases, *Rivas v. U.S.*, 368 F2d 703, and *Henderson v. U.S.*, 390 F2d 805, indicate that in border body searches more than mere suspicion must be present. These cases are obviously the culmination of the trend noted above.

In *Rivas,* a man previously convicted for narcotics violations and a registered user of narcotics was apprehended while crossing the border from Mexico. His appearance indicated that he was under the influence of a narcotic drug at the time. This was noted by the appearance of his eyes, his nervous manner and recent needle marks on his arms. A search of his rectum by a physician, over his protests, disclosed narcotics present.

Although the court noted (*Rivas, supra,* at 709), irrelevantly, that "this *was* a border search. Border searches are unique . . ." (emphasis is the court's), and also stated: "mere suspicion is enough—probable cause is not required," his conviction was sustained on the ground that there were facts present "creating a clear indication or plain suggestion of smuggling." 368 F2d at 710.

In *Henderson,* the court reversed a conviction of a woman charged with smuggling narcotics, where the narcotics were seized as a result of a search of her vagina. Here, unlike *Rivas,* the woman had no record of prior convictions, no needle marks on her person and no reasonable cause to believe that she had narcotics secreted in her vagina.

The importance of the *Henderson* decision lies in the fact that the sole issue before the court was the validity of the border search involving a search of a body cavity, the vagina. The search which was conducted by a physician, over her violent objection, disclosed two packets of heroin.

This decision is also important since it clarifies the rule authorizing border searches of personal property as distinguished from one's body and distinguishes *Rivas*.

Although this court (Ninth Circuit) "has repeatedly upheld border searches of body cavities, including such searches carried out in spite of the violent resistance of the person searched" (*Henderson* at 806 and cases cited), it declined to do so in this case, holding this search to be unlawful.

This decision is based primarily on the holding in *Schmerber v. California,* 384 US at 767–770, in which the court said:

> "The overriding function of the Fourth Amendment is to protect personal privacy and dignity against unwarranted intrusion by the State.
>
> . . . .
>
> "We begin with the assumption that once the privilege against self-incrimination has been found not to bar compelled intrusions into the body . . . the Fourth Amendment's proper function is to constrain, not against all intrusions as such, but against intrusions which are not justified in the circumstances, or which are made in an improper manner. In other words, the questions we must decide in this case are whether the police were justified in requiring petitioner to submit to the blood test, and whether the means and procedures employed in taking his blood respected relevant Fourth Amendment standards of reasonableness.
>
> . . . .
>
> "The interests in human dignity and privacy which the Fourth Amendment protects forbid any such intrusions on the mere chance that desired evidence might be obtained. In the absence of a clear indication that in fact such evidence will be found, these fundamental human in-

terests require law officers to suffer the risk that such evidence may disappear unless there is an immediate search."

Equating an invasion into one's body with an examination thereof, the court, in *Henderson,* at 807 stated:

> "[*Schmerber*] emphasizes that the purpose of the Fourth Amendment is 'to protect personal privacy and dignity against unwarranted intrusion by the state.' To us, this means that every search must be examined in the light of the Amendment's requirement that it not be 'unreasonable.' And we think that this requirement applies to border searches."

Conceding that border searches are unique and that the mere fact that a person is crossing the border is sufficient cause for a search, the rule for such broad searches applies to the contents of baggage, one's vehicle, purse, wallet and similar items. "The mere crossing of the border is sufficient cause for such a search. Even 'mere suspicion' is not required. . . . If, however, the search of the person is to go further, if the party, male or female, is to be required to strip, we think that something more, at least a real suspicion, directed specifically at that person, should be required. . . . Surely, in such a case, to be warranted, the official's action should be backed by at least the 'clear indication,' the 'plain suggestion' required in *Schmerber,* and in *Rivas."* 390 F2d at 808.

It is apparent that these border search cases reflect an awareness of due process requirements as well as an awareness of the right of our society to be free from contraband.

This means that there must be a balancing of the rights of the individual to his privacy and inherent dignity which our society places on the human body, as against the right of our society—a need—to maintain an environment free from pervasive evil influences, *e.g.,* the danger implicit in the indiscriminate distribution and use of dangerous drugs.

Thus far, this balance is achieved by requiring something more than "mere suspicion" to be present to validate a body search. Apparently, that "something more" need not be of such a nature as would be required for a lawful search warrant. That "something more" must lie somewhere in between the two, as indicated in *Rivas* and in *Henderson.*

The case of *Huquez v. U.S.,* 406 F2d 366, is the capstone to *Rivas* and *Henderson.* This was also a border search involving an examination of the rectal area. "Neither Huquez nor his companion was a known, convicted and registered user of narcotics, as the defendants were in . . . *Rivas;* neither of them did or said anything to arouse suspicion." *Huquez* at 378. Under these facts, the court found that the forceful rectal examination in this case "exceeds the constitutional limitations of the fourth amendment on border searches without a warrant, because there was no 'clear indication' that the cavity contained narcotics." *Huquez* at 374.

Additionally, "The 'force process' exerted on appellant exceeds the constitutional limitations of the fifth amendment." *Huquez* at 379.

*Huquez* correlates the *Rivas* and *Henderson* decisions in the light of *Rochin v. California,* 342 US 165, and *Schmerber v. California,* 384 US 757. It also applies the balancing-of-interests test mentioned above in holding this search unlawful.

"Applying what we may call the *Rochin-Breithaupt-Schmerber-Rivas* test of reasonableness of place, methods and conduct to the intrusive body cavity invasion here in *Huquez,* we cannot help but find that appellant has been deprived of his due process rights under the Fifth Amendment." 406 F2d at 381.

It is obvious from a reading of these decisions that each case must be decided on its own set of facts. Accordingly, no hard and fast rule pertaining to the balancing of interests of society against the rights of the individual can be set forth. Nor can any definitive guide lines be set forth to show when, in a particular case, the facts of concealment in a body cavity rise above mere suspicion.

The United States Supreme Court has not as yet spoken on this subject.

(*Note:* The discussion of body searches must not be confused with searches of the person held valid under the Stop and Frisk statutes and case law. *See: Terry v. Ohio,* 392 US 1; *Peters v. New York,* 397 US 40; *People v. Rivera,* 14 NY2d 441, 201 NE2d 32; *cf. Sibron v. New York,* 397 US 40.)

*See also: Body Searches: Examples, § 248, infra.*

**§ 248. Body Searches: Examples.** In *U.S. v. Mont.,* 306 F2d 412, 414, federal officers seized the defendant, suspected of dealing in narcotics after he had placed three glassine envelopes into his mouth. In the ensuing scuffle, Mont kneed the federal officer in the groin. The officer then put his hand into Mont's mouth, and Mont bit it. After further struggle, the officer hit Mont in the solar plexus, and as a result of this blow 25 glassine envelopes containing heroin fell from Mont's mouth. It took another 15 minutes to subdue him. The officers also found another 135 glassine envelopes on Mont's person and in his apartment.

The question of forcible removal of the contraband from Mont's mouth was raised on appeal but, as the court noted, "The Government stresses that the envelopes were not withdrawn from Mont's mouth by Bailey but were exploded by Carrozo's blow to the solar plexus. . . . The distinction between extraction and explosion seems dubious. . . ." The court did not pass on this question.

In *State v. Height,* 117 Iowa 650, 91 NW 935, 938, it was held that a compulsory examination of a person accused of rape conducted for the purpose of showing that at the time of the crime he was suffering from a venereal disease alleged to have been communicated to the prosecutrix, violates the due process clause of the Constitution. All evidence secured as a result of this examination was inadmissible. This was a 1902 decision based to a large extent on the compelled self-incrimination theory of the Fifth Amendment as condemned in *Boyd v. U.S.,* 116 US 616.

On the other hand, a rule requiring a physical examination of a public employee to determine his fitness to continue his position does not constitute an unreasonable search. *People ex rel Wayman v. Seward,* 249 Ill 311, 94 NE 511.

In *State v. Turner,* 101 Ariz 85, 416 P2d 409, the defendant was convicted of assault with intent to murder. In an unprovoked shooting affray, complainant returned defendant's fire, and apparently defendant was hit. Early the next day, defendant entered a hospital for treatment of a wound. The police and sheriff were notified and they arrived at the hospital. A doctor removed a bullet from the defendant's head and handed it to the police who were present with a small group of others.

A ballistics test identified the bullet as coming from the gun of the intended assault victim, the complainant.

Defendant's contention that the bullet was obtained as a result of an unlawful search and seizure was rejected by the court: "In order to constitute such a violation of constitutional rights there must first be a search." *Turner, supra,* 416 P2d at 411.

In *Brent v. White,* 398 F2d 503, 505, petitioner was convicted of rape. Penis scrapings, which revealed menstrual blood of the victim's type, were received in evidence against him. He alleged error in that the taking of these scrapings violated his Fourth Amendment rights.

In disposing of this contention, the court stated:

> "This, too, is devoid of merit, as the scraping constituted a permissible search of the person incident to a lawful arrest and involved no intrusion of the body surface. Additionally, there was threat of imminent destruction of the evidence of menstrual bood. See Application of Woods, N.D.Cal., 1957, 154 F.Supp. 932, cert. denied, Woods v. Heinze, 1958, 356 U.S. 921, 78 S. Ct. 705, 2 L. Ed 2d 716."

This decision follows the rationale of *Schmerber v. California,* 384 US 757.

*See also: § 247.02, supra.*

§ 248.01. **Fingerprints.** In a broad sense, taking of fingerprints does not constitute an invasion of one's person although it is a type of body search. This question was before the Court in *Davis v. Mississippi,* 394 US 721.

There, Davis was detained at police headquarters on suspicion. There was no probable cause for his arrest and no warrant had been issued. He was detained for the sole purpose of taking his fingerprints to see if they matched those found on a window sill by the police who were investigating a rape case. This action by the police violated petitioner's Fourth Amendment rights. Additionally, the Court held that this action in a state criminal prosecution violated due process under the Fourteenth Amendment. The conviction was reversed.

Fingerprint evidence is no exception to the rule that all evidence obtained by searches and seizures in violation of the Constitution is inadmissible in a state court.

§ 248.02. **Hair Clippings.** In *U.S. v. Cox,* 428 F2d 683, 687, 688, hairs found in a get-away car used in a bank robbery were compared with samples of defendant's hair, and used at his trial, resulting in a conviction.

> "The hair samples in question were obtained as the result of a haircut given Cox while he was in Waukesha County Jail in the custody of state officials. Such haircuts are regularly given inmates by prison officials in connection with the regulation of the personal hygiene of prisoners . . . [Cox's haircut] was administered pursuant to jail procedures . . . over a month after defendant's arrest. . . . During the course of the haircut and at the request of the FBI the 'barber' preserved clippings which he had cut from Cox's head in an envelope which he subsequently transmitted to the FBI for analysis."

Defendant at no time objected to the haircut, nor did he ever claim that the haircut was illegally or improperly given. He urged, however, that a search warrant should have been obtained. Cox never claimed the shorn hair and it was left in the barber shop—abandoned—after being cut. This hair, having been abandoned, "Cox may not object to its appropriation by the Government. *Abel v. United States,* 362 US 217, 241. . . ."

In *U.S. v. D'Amico,* 408 F2d 331, 333, which also involved the taking of hair clippings, the court said,

> "[T]he clipping by the officer of the few strands of hair from appellant's head was so minor an imposition that appellant suffered no true humiliation or affront to his dignity. We hold that a search warrant was not required to justify the officer's act.
>
> "We fail to see how the taking of several strands of appellant's hair from his head while the appellant was in

custody was in any way more prejudicial or offensive than the taking of his fingerprints or his photograph. The seizure which occurred in this case was not an unreasonable one or one violative of the Fourth Amendment."

*See also: Schmerber v. California,* 384 US 757, and *U.S. v. Richardson,* 388 F2d 842, 845.

§ **248.03. Mouth.** A slightly similar question arose in *Stewart v. State,* 229 A2d 727, involving narcotics. In that case, after a two-minute kiss between a prison inmate and her visitor, an assistant superintendent of the prison removed from the inmate's mouth a package of narcotics. The Maryland Court of Special Appeals held that a search of inmates of penal institutions which does not amount to harassment or oppression to the extent that it constitutes cruel and unusual punishment is an exception to the general rule that the search of a person without a warrant and the seizure of things which are evidence of a commission of a crime are unreasonable and therefore unlawful. *Cf. People v. Randazzo,* 37 Misc2d 80, affd 15 NY2d 526.

§ **248.04. Blood Tests.** *Schmerber v. California,* 384 US 757, 771, is a drunken driving-blood test case. Schmerber was convicted of drunken driving based on a blood test taken after his arrest, without a warrant, and over his protest.

The blood was taken by a physician from his arm in a hospital where he was a patient as a result of an automobile accident which triggered the drunken driving charge.

The Supreme Court held that "the test was performed in a reasonable manner . . . by a physician in a hospital environment according to accepted medical practice." The Court also sustained the taking of the blood sample as an incident to a lawful arrest, noting that the alcohol in his blood, if any, would disappear within two hours after the arrest, by reason of normal body metabolism. The Court also rejected the claim that this test violated defendant's rights against self-incrimination under the Fifth Amendment, citing *Breithaupt v. Abram,* 352 US 432; *Holt v. U.S.,* 218 US 245, 252–253.

However, the Court in *Schmerber* cautioned that this case

is not to be interpreted as authorizing wholesale intrusions into the body: "It bears repeating, however, that we reach this judgment only on the facts of the present record. The integrity of an individual's person is a cherished value of our society. That we today hold that the Constitution does not forbid the States minor intrusions into an individual's body under stringently limited conditions in no way indicates that it permits more substantial intrusions, or intrusions under other conditions." 384 US at 772.

Blood types are classified generally as types AB, A, B, and O. Schatkin, *"Disputed Paternity Proceedings,"* p. 164 (3rd ed.). Group O is the most common, (45.6% for whites, and 45.8% for blacks). Group A is almost equally common, (40.8%, white; blacks, 27.2%). Wintrobe, *"Clinical Hematology,"* pp. 370–372 (3rd ed.).

Accordingly, in *People v. Robinson,* 27 NY2d 864, 865, 265 NE2d 543, the Court held:

> "Proof that defendant had type 'A' blood and that the semen found in and on the body of decedent was derived from a man with type 'A' blood was of no probative value in the case against defendant in view of the large proportion of the general population having blood of this type and, therefore, should not have been admitted."

In *Holt v. U.S., supra,* the Court said: "[T]he prohibition of compelling a man in a criminal court to be a witness against himself is a prohibition of the use of physical or moral compulsion to extort communications from him, not an exclusion of his body as evidence when it may be material. The objection in principle would forbid a jury to look at a prisoner and compare his features with a photograph in proof." *Holt, supra,* 218 US at 252–253.

Where blood-test samples were taken in criminal prosecution cases from unconscious defendants, the results have been held inadmissible. In *People v. Young,* 42 Misc2d 540, 248 NYS2d 287, the defendant was charged with vehicular homicide. He was unconscious when his blood sample was taken. He was not under arrest at the time, although probable cause to arrest him was established at the time the police requested the blood test to be taken.

*State v. Kroening,* 274 Wis 266, 272–273, 79 NW2d 810, 814–17, was a case identical with *Young, supra.* In *Kroening,* the court said:

> "We do not concede that the right of security of person specified by section 11, art. I, Wis. Constitution, does not extend to portions of the body as well as to its entirety. Surely that security is impaired if public officials may, without consent and without arrest, stick needles into human bodies and draw off and carry away such of the bodies' contents as the officials deem expedient. . . . It is thoroughly recognized that property on the person is not to be seized by zealous officers who have no search warrant and who have not made a valid arrest. . . . We do not understand that the constitutional provisions in question forbids officers to go through one's pockets but permits them to go through his veins."

The pronouncement was made by the court despite the fact that it could not be determined whether, at the time in question, the defendant was unconscious or in a semi-conscious condition.

Further, the court said, the taking of Kroening's blood sample could not be deemed an incident search, since he was not under arrest at the time. *Cf. Schmerber v. California, supra.*

A similar factual situation was presented in *State v. Weltha,* 228 Iowa 519, 292 NW 148. Weltha was convicted of manslaughter in a drunken driving case. While unconscious, and not under arrest, the coroner took a blood sample from him. This action was also deemed unlawful and constituted an illegal invasion of his personal rights. The court ruled that the results of the test should not have been received in evidence.

In the case of *Lebel v. Swinicki,* 354 Mich 427, 93 NW2d 281, a civil suit for damages for the death of a motorist, it was likewise held to be error to admit into evidence the results of the tests of defendant's blood taken from him while he was unconscious, which tests indicated intoxication.

Comparisons of these decisions must be made with *Breithaupt v. Abram,* 352 US 432, 404, which sustained the taking of the blood sample from an unconscious defendant and without a warrant. *Breithaupt* raised the defenses of violation of due process under the Fourth and Fifth Amendments—a defense which the court rejected under *Wolf v. Colorado,* 338 US 25. Three justices dissented in *Breithaupt,* holding that the rule of *Rochin v. California,* 342 US 165 was applicable. *Note: Breithaupt* was a pre-*Mapp* case (*Mapp v. Ohio,* 367 US 643).

In *Breithaupt v. Abram,* 352 US 432, 436, 437, we find some parallels with *Rochin. Breithaupt* involved a drunken driving accident in which three people were killed. Breithaupt was the driver of a truck involved in this fatal accident. A nearly empty whiskey bottle was found in the glove compartment of the truck. When taken to the hospital where he lay unconscious, a strong odor of alcohol was noticed on his breath, and the police asked a doctor to take a sample of Breithaupt's blood to test its alcoholic content. The blood test showed that he was intoxicated at the time of the accident. The results of the test were introduced at his prosecution, and he was convicted of involuntary manslaughter.

The conviction was affirmed, the court holding that in a prosecution in a state court for a state crime, the Fourteenth Amendment does not forbid the use of evidence obtained by an unreasonable search and seizure in violation of the Fourth Amendment (*note:* this is a pre-*Mapp* case), and that *Rochin* was not comparable. The right to be immune from invasion of privacy—as in this case the drawing of blood for proof of intoxication—by use of a hypodermic needle, was far outweighed by the need to protect society from drunken drivers. The taking of blood by a qualified person in a purely routine manner was not "conduct which shocks the conscience."

In effect, the court said that national community standards found this method of extracting blood from defendants in drunken driving cases as morally acceptable and, accordingly, there was no violation of due process. "The blood test procedure has become routine in our everyday life. It is a ritual for those going into the military service as well as those applying for marriage licenses."

However, where a sample of defendant's blood was obtained from him voluntarily but by misrepresentation as to the purpose for which it was sought, such actions were held to be a violation of his Fourth Amendment rights.

Thus, in *Graves v. Beto,* 424 F2d 524, the police, seeking to corroborate a rape victim's complaint, obtained a blood sample from the suspect upon his consent when they informed him it was necessary for an intoxication test. Actually, the police wanted a blood sample to match it with the type found on the victim's mattress. The evidence established that both samples were the same and defendant was convicted.

In reversing the judgment, the Fifth Circuit Court of Appeals held that police violated the Fourth Amendment rights of a rape suspect by obtaining a blood sample from him by a misrepresentation. The consent here did not constitute consent for the type-matching. Further, it was said that *Schmerber v. California,* 384 US 757, does not apply, as that case approved the taking of blood for an intoxication test without a warrant or consent because of the danger that the evidence—the content of alcohol in the blood—would shortly be destroyed. Here, the taking of blood was to determine blood type, and the suspect's blood type would have remained the same no matter how long it took to secure a warrant.

In a slightly parallel case, *Kyhl v. Commonwealth,* 205 Va 240, 135 SE2d 768, the results of a blood test obtained by consent invalidated the consent where an unsterilized needle was used, to extract the blood, in violation of the Virginia statute. The results of the blood test were excluded.

In *Irvine v. California,* 347 US 128, the Court followed the rule of *Wolf v. Colorado,* 338 US 25, which held that there was no violation of due process in a criminal prosecution by a state that did not follow the federal exclusionary rule. *Note: Wolf* was overruled in part by *Mapp v. Ohio,* 367 US 643, 653–655, and *Malloy v. Hogan,* 378 US 1.

The decisive factor in the reversals of both *Rochin v. California,* 342 US 165, and *Irvine, supra,* was not simply the search question but the additional aggravating conduct of the police, whose conduct went beyond search and seizure.

In all search and seizure cases, including body searches, one basic tenet must be borne in mind: "The Fourth Amendment forbids every search that is unreasonable and is construed liberally to safeguard the right of privacy." *U.S. v. Lefkowitz,* 285 US 452, 464.

§ 249. **U.S. Mails.** An examination and recordation of the external markings on first class mail, limited to the notations of the name and address of a sender and his addressee, is known as a "mail cover" or "mail watch." The federal courts have held that such a "mail cover" does not violate federal postal laws or regulations. *U.S. v. Cohen,* 241 F Supp 269; *U.S. v. Schwartz,* 283 F 107; *U.S. v. Costello,* 255 F 876.

Such "mail cover" does not violate the constitution or the postal laws. In *United States v. Cohen, supra,* the court held:

> "In any event, it is clear that the Constitutional guarantees do not extend to prohibit the practice of examining the external markings on first class mail and it has been held that this kind of 'mail watch' does not violate the Postal Laws. . . .
>
> "There is manifestly no violation of constitutional mandate nor stautory guaranty that precludes the *exterior* inspection of a first-class letter or package." *Cohen* at 271–272.

However, a different rule prevails as to the right of postal inspectors to *open* first class mail. To seize and open first class mail, a warrant is required. *Ex parte Jackson,* 96 US 727. *See also: Oliver v. U.S.,* 239 F2d 818, which held that sealed mail enjoys Fourth Amendment protection. Only first class mail bears the prohibition against opening. *People v. Garcia,* 62 Misc2d 666, 669; 39 USC §§ 4057–4058(a).

Packages mailed as air parcel post are classified as first class mail. As such, they may not be opened and examined by postal employees without a warrant, unless that employee is opening dead mail in his official capacity. *People v. Moraitis,* 312 NYS2d 175, 178; 39 USC § 4057; Postal Manual, § 331.11.

Parcel post and non-first class mail may be opened and inspected. "Having deposited a parcel in the mail pursuant to the law, rules and regulations which permit its inspection at any time, neither the sender nor, to the extent of his interest therein, the defendant, as parcel claimant, can complain of its lawful inspection. They have voluntarily submitted to the risk of the procedure which they adopted." *Garcia, supra,* at 670. *See also: Santana v. U.S.,* 329 F2d 854, cert. den. 377 US 990; Postal Manual, §§ 135.7, 331.11.

Additionally, 39 USC § 904 authorizes the postal authorities to seize and impound mail which is posted contrary to law. This power is extended to include the right to search vehicles and their contents as well as offices or stores occupied by a common carrier other than a dwelling for the same type of matter without a warrant. 39 USC § 903.

These statutes read:

> "Section 903. Searches authorized.
>
> "The Postmaster General, by letter of authority, filed in the Department, may authorize any postal inspector or other officer of the Department to make searches for mailable matter transported in violation of law. When the authorized officer has reason to believe that mailable matter transported contrary to law may be found therein, he may open and search any—
>
> "(1) vehicle passing, or having lately passed, from a place at which there is a post office of the United States;
>
> "(2) articles being, or having lately been, in the vehicle;
>
> "(3) store or office, other than a dwelling house, used or occupied by a common carrier or transportation company, in which an article may be contained.
>
> [The terms "other than a dwelling house" used in paragraph 3, *supra,* means just what it says, *i.e.,* that postal inspectors have no right to enter a private home and search for letters without a warrant, *Kelly v. Dunne,* 344 F2d 129.]
>
> "Section 904. Seizing and detaining letters.
>
> "A postal inspector, customs officer, or United States marshal or his deputy, may seize at any time, letters and bags, packets or parcels containing letters which are being carried contrary to law on board any vessel or on any post road. The officer who makes the seizure shall convey the articles seized to the nearest post office; . . ."

The broad powers that postal inspectors have to search and open mail is limited to the public areas of government buildings to enable them to retrieve mail packages and their contents. This power carries with it the authority to open incoming mail in a proper case. *U.S. v. Collins,* 349 F2d 863.

In *U.S. v. Swede,* 326 F Supp 533, a letter mailed from Switzerland arrived in the sorting room in a border area. It aroused the suspicions of customs officers. They opened it and found LSD powder in it. The court denied suppression holding that the envelope was subject to a search without a warrant while within the border area.

39 USC §§ 4057–4058 read:

> "§ 4057. Opening first class mail
>
> "Only an employee opening dead mail by authority of the Postmaster General, or a person holding a search warrant authorized by law may open any letter or parcel of the first class which is in the custody of the Department.
>
> "§ 4058. Wrapping matter not charged with first class postage
>
> "(a) The Postmaster General may prescribe the manner of wrapping and securing mail not charged with first class postage so that the contents of the mail may be easily examined. He shall charge the first class rate of postage on all matter which cannot be examined easily.
>
> "(b) To ascertain whether the proper rate of postage has been paid, postmasters may examine second class mail and remove the wrappers and envelopes from other mail not bearing first class postage if it can be done without destroying them."

With reference to seizure of obscene material by customs and post office officials, *see: Chapter 22, infra.*

The contents of a private letter, sent through the United States mails, may be disclosed by the addressee. If the letter contains matter which is obscene according to current tests of obscenity, the sender may be prosecuted therefor. *U.S. v. Chapman,* 333 F2d 969; *U.S. v. Darnell,* 316 F2d 813.

Similarly, a letter written voluntarily by a prisoner which comes into the hands of prison officials without threats or coercion, in the normal course of prison administration and discipline, and retained by them for use as evidence, is not violative of the prisoner's Fourth Amendment rights. *Stroud v. U.S.,* 251 US 15, 21.

Goods subject to duty can not lawfully be imported by way of foreign mail. Such goods are subject to seizure by customs officers from the person receiving them at the post office. Intent on the part of the sender or receiver not to defraud the government of customs duties if immaterial. *Von Cotzhausen v. Nazro,* 107 US 215.

# Chapter 17

# ABANDONED PROPERTY AND OPEN FIELDS



---

**§ 255. Abandoned Property.** Obtaining possession of contraband or other property by the police after it has been discarded or abandoned may well constitute a seizure, but it does not constitute a "search and seizure."

Property abandoned or discarded by a defendant is no longer in his posssesion. (*See: Distinction Between Search and Seizure, Chapter 9, supra.*)

> "It is well settled that property abandoned by a defendant may be lawfully seized and an arrest may be based on the former possession of the property (*People* v. *Pittman,* 14 NY2d 885; People v. Lopez, 22 A.D. 2d 813; *United States* v. *Zimple,* 318 F. 2d 676, cert. den. 375 U.S. 868." *People v. D'Ambrosio,* 28 AD2d 1130, 284 NYS2d 336–337.

There is no search when the police obtain possession of contraband after the defendant discards it. Under such circumstances, the contraband is no longer in the defendant's possession. *People v. Lopez* 22 AD2d 813; *Abel v. U.S.,* 362 US 217; *Hester v. U.S.,* 265 US 57; *People v. Speller,* 14 NY2d 514, 197 NE2d 625; *U.S. v. Dzialak,* 441 F2d 212.

Whether property has been abandoned is a question of fact. Dropping contraband on the floor of a taxicab or automobile is not an abandonment. *Rios v. U.S.,* 364 US 253; *People v. Adorno,* 37 Misc2d 36.

As the Court noted in *Rios,* "A passenger who lets a package drop to the floor of a taxicab in which he is riding can hardly be said to have 'abandoned' it. An occupied taxicab is not to be compared to an open field, *Hester v. United States,*

265 U.S. 57, or a vacated hotel room, *Abel v. United States,* 362 U.S. 217." 364 US at 262.

Dropping a package on the street, without more, does not constitute an abandonment. In *People v. Anderson,* 24 NY2d 12, 246 NE2d 508, the police approached the defendant without any probable cause to arrest. At this point the defendant dropped a tin box to the ground and the officer retrieved it. It contained heroin. A motion to suppress was denied.

The Court of Appeals reversed, stating that this is not a case of "abandoned" property warranting seizure by the police. There is no proof "that the defendant threw it [the heroin] away or attempted to dispose of it in any manner which might have manifested the requisite intention to abandon. Moreover, the police officer's testimony reveals that he picked up the box so soon after it had been dropped that it is impossible to determine whether or not the defendant, if given the opportunity, would have picked up the box himself." *Anderson* at 14. Additionally, the defendant made no move away from the spot where the box dropped, nor made any move to flee. The court held proof insufficient, as a matter of law, to constitute abandonment.

The leading cases in this area are *Hester v. U.S.,* 265 US 57, and *Abel v. U.S.,* 362 US 217.

In *Hester,* the Court stated that examination by revenue officers, of abandoned property, without a warrant, did not constitute a seizure.

The officers, while concealed, saw one Henderson, drive up to Hester's house in an automobile. They observed Hester give Henderson a quart bottle. The officers, at a given signal, approached the car, whereupon Hester removed a jug from the car and he and Henderson fled across an open field, pursued by the officers, one of whom fired a shot.

During the flight, Hester dropped the jug, which broke, and Henderson threw away his quart bottle. Later, the officers found a broken jar outside of Hester's house.

All of these items contained some liquid which the officers readily recognized as moonshine whiskey. Motions to suppress them at Hester's criminal prosecution were denied.

In sustaining the denial of the suppressal motions the Court stated:

> "It is obvious that even if there had been a trespass, the above testimony was not obtained by an illegal search or seizure. The defendant's own acts, and those of his associates, disclosed the jug, the jar and the bottle—and there was no seizure in the sense of the law when the officers examined the contents of each after it had been abandoned." *Hester, supra,* 265 US at 58.

In effect *Hester* states that privately owned open fields do not enjoy the protection of the Fourth Amendment even though there is no probable cause to search.

*Abel v. U.S., supra,* reaffirmed the rule laid down in *Hester* as to abandoned property.

Colonel Abel was a notorious Russian spy who lived in this country for about 10 years under several aliases. On information supplied by the F.B.I., the Immigration and Naturalization Service obtained an administrative arrest warrant for Abel's deportation.

After a fruitless interrogation in Abel's hotel room, he was taken away under arrest by the I.N.S., charged with being illegally in this country.

Before being escorted out of his room, he was permitted to pack his personal belongings. The Court found that, "A few things petitioner deliberately left on a window sill, indicating that he did not want to take them, and several other things which he chose not to pack up into his luggage he put into the room's wastepaper basket." *Abel, supra,* 362 US at 224.

As soon as Abel left the room, an F.B.I. Agent, Kehoe, who had been in an adjoining room during this time without a search warrant but with the consent of the hotel management, entered Abel's room and proceeded to search it.

Kehoe retrieved from the wastepaper basket the items which were received in evidence at Abel's prosecution for espionage, as items #6 and #7,—a hollowed-out pencil and a block of wood containing a "cipher pad."

In sustaining the admissibility of these exhibits over Abel's claim of violation of his Fourth Amendment rights, the Court said:

> "We have left to the last the admissibility of items (6) and (7), the hollowed-out pencil and the block of wood con-

> taining a 'cipher pad,' because their admissibility is founded upon an entirely different set of considerations. These two items were found by an agent of the F.B.I. in the course of a search he undertook of petitioner's hotel room, immediately after petitioner had paid his bill and vacated the room. They were found in the room's wastepaper basket, where petitioner had put them while packing his belongings and preparing to leave. No pretense is made that this search by the F.B.I. was for any purpose other than to gather evidence of crime, that is, evidence of petitioner's espionage. As such, however, it was entirely lawful, although undertaken without a warrant. This is so for the reason that at the time of the search petitioner had vacated the room. The hotel then had the exclusive right to its possession, and the hotel management freely gave its consent that the search be made. Nor was it unlawful to seize the entire contents of the wastepaper basket, even though some of its contents had no connection with crime. So far as the record shows, petitioner had abandoned these articles. He had thrown them away. There can be nothing unlawful in the Government's appropriation of such abandoned property. See *Hester* v. *United States,* 265 U.S. 57, 58. The two items which were eventually introduced in evidence were assertedly means for the commission of espionage, and were themselves seizable as such. These two items having been lawfully seized by the Government in connection with an investigation of crime, we encounter no basis for discussing their admissibility as evidence." 362 US at 240–241.

In *People v. Sorise,* 58 Misc2d 557, failure to pay motel room rent was held to have terminated Sorise's possessory interest in the room. Accordingly, the motel owner had authority to enter the room and seize the contents. Although *Sorise* is a "standing" case on a motion to suppress, the parallel with *Abel* is obvious. Here too, where the tenant failed to call for the property or even contact the motel owner for it, the property-luggage and toilet articles were deemed abandoned.

In *U.S. v. Manning,* 440 F2d 1105, the Court was also faced with the question of abandoned property similar to *Abel* and *Sorise.*

In *Manning* the defendant on April 5th rented a house for one month. This was undisputed. On May 5th, the police entered with the landlord's consent. They entered through an open door, searched a car parked in the carport and found items which were received in evidence.

The facts indicated that the defendant had remained in the rented house for only a few days. All of his clothing and possessions had been removed, the lawn was unattended, stagnant dishwater was in the sink and some food was on the table.

On these facts the Court found that both the house and the car had been abandoned.

Moreover, if the abandonment had occurred prior to the expiration period, a search of the premises with the landlord's consent would not constitute an unlawful act. *Feguer v. U.S.,* 302 F2d 214.

**§ 256. Open Fields.** The Fourth Amendment mentions the protection of privacy as to "persons, *houses,* papers and effects." The term "houses" in the Amendment does not include an open field. *Hester v. U.S.,* 265 US 57. The two terms are not to be equated, even though, in a strictly legal sense, an open field may be private property. Thus, in *Hester,* the search and seizure of contraband found in an open field was not interdicted.

A man's home is his castle. There he can expect that his privacy will be protected. But an open field is another matter. As the term signifies, it is open and anyone can normally wander across it. One can hardly expect privacy. *Cf. Katz v. U.S.,* 389 US 347, in which the Court stated that the Fourth Amendment protects people, not places. *See also: Wattenburg v. U.S.,* 388 F2d 853, 857.

In *People v. LaRosa,* 25 AD2d 587, the New York Court followed the same rule. In this case, the police, after a complaint about a shooting incident, arrested the defendant, who disclosed that he had secreted some weapons on his property on the day of the shooting incident. Thereupon the police and the defendant went to the hiding place which was located on a vacant wooded lot, the property of the defendant. The lot was about a mile and a half from the complainant's home, "remote from human habitation."

The police dug up and seized the weapons without a search warrant. Although this search and seizure was held not to be incident to the defendant's lawful arrest "and therefore constituted an illegal search to which defendant had not knowingly and voluntarily consented," yet the court said: "It has long been the Federal case law that the protection accorded to the People 'in their persons, houses, papers, and effects, against unreasonable searches and seizures' by the Fourth Amendment of the United States Constitution (see, also, N.Y. Const., art. I, § 12), enforcible against the States through its due process clause . . . does not extend to an open field such as that involved here and that the search of such a place without a warrant is not constitutionally unreasonable. (*Hester v. United States,* 265 U.S. 57. . . ." *LaRosa, supra,* 25 AD2d at 587–588.

In *Katz v. U.S.,* 389 US 347, the Supreme Court said that the Fourth Amendment protects people not places. Does this mean that *Hester* has been overruled or modified? It is conceivable that *Katz* and *Hester* could in certain fact situations run into each other. Would the rule of the "totality of the surrounding circumstances," *Stovall v. Denno,* 388 US 293, 301–302, then come into play? Obviously, the answer to this question would be in the affirmative.

# Chapter 18

## EXIGENT CIRCUMSTANCES AND HOT PURSUIT



§ 260. **Exigent Circumstances.** Where there is danger to life and property, entry into private premises to abate the hazard does not constitute an invasion of privacy such as is proscribed by the Fourth Amendment. Under such exigent circumstances, contraband found in the premises may be seized and the seizure is not unlawful. Exigent circumstances require police to perform many functions unrelated to criminal law enforcement such as assisting persons in distress.

So in *People v. Gallmon,* 19 NY2d 389, 227 NE2d 284, where the police got a radio run to the effect that there was a disorderly man and then proceeded to those premises, a rooming house, where they heard shouting, screaming, clapping of hands which the night manager told them had been going on for several evenings, there was a duty on the police to make appropriate inquiry in the premises.

The police gained entry into the room after the officer had knocked on the door at which time the shouting stopped and a male voice said three times. "Wait a minute, I'm not dressed." The door was opened with a pass key by the night manager at the direction of the police officer who did not announce his office and purpose as required by statute (where entry is for the purpose of arrest).

Under these circumstances, the Court of Appeals held that the statute was not applicable since they did not enter the premises to make an arrest, but their entry was merely investigatory. The same rule prevails under the common law. *Miller v. U.S.,* 357 US 301, 305–310; *Gallmon, supra,* 19 NY2d at 392, 227 NE2d 284.

Furthermore, the court drew a distinction between rooming houses, inns and demised premises, with respect to the authority of the inn keeper to enter.

"It is critically significant that a rooming house is involved rather than demised premises to which the tenant is entitled to exclusive and undisturbed possession. Rooming houses and inns are equivalent for purposes of determining the legality of entry by the landlord or his agents." *Gallmon, supra,* 19 NY2d at 392.

Quoting from the leading case of *deWolf v. Ford,* 193 NY 397, 403, the court noted:

> "[T]he general rule was expressed as follows: 'If the guest is assigned to a room upon the express or implied understanding that he is to be the sole occupant thereof during the time that it is set apart for his use, the innkeeper retains a right of access thereto only at such proper times and for such reasonable purposes as may be necessary in the general conduct of the inn or in attending to the needs of the particular guest. If, for instance, there should be an outbreak of fire, a leakage of water or gas, or any other emergency calling for immediate action in a room assigned to a guest, the innkeeper and his servants must necessarily have the right to enter without regard to the time of day or night and without consulting the wish or convenience of the guest.'" *Gallmon, supra,* 19 NY2d at 392–393.

Again, in *Gallmon,* the court said, "Moreover, even a private individual might make such an entry if it reasonably appears that his intrusion and presence would avert injury to the occupant or his chattels (1 Restatement, Torts 2d, § 197, comment *e,* illus. 8). The point is that no one would have objected to the entry of the policeman in this case if the defendant had been ill or some other emergency had existed, *People* v. *Roberts,* 47 Cal.2d 374." 19 NY2d at 393. *See also: Ker v. California,* 374 US 23; *cf. Stoner v. California,* 376 US 483, 489.

It is also significant that in *Gallmon* the court noted that, "the manager was not acting as the cat's paw of the police; rather, he had made a call for assistance to which the officers had responded. As such, they were acting in aid of the manager in performance of his duty to the occupants of the building including defendant. There is no evidence that he or they knew what was occurring in the room. Indeed, the officers were called to find out." 19 NY2d at 393.

Accordingly, the motion to suppress contraband observed by the police upon their entry and the defendants' conviction therefor were affirmed. *See also: U.S. v. Kuntz,* 265 F Supp 543.

In *People v. Johnson,* 48 Misc2d 907, officers of a Fire Department detected a strong odor of gasoline emanating from an apartment in the early morning hours when the occupants were asleep. They knocked on the door of the apartment in question and, receiving no reply, gained access through a window next to a fire escape. On entering the apartment, they found the premises soaked in gasoline, including the bedding on which the defendant was asleep. Paper currency was scattered about the bed and gasoline was running on the floor. The danger of an imminent explosion, fire and destruction in such a situation is obvious to the layman. The Fire Battalion Chief in charge, as an expert, was of the same opinion and requested police assistance. When the police arrived, he ordered them to arrest the defendant for attempted arson. The incidental search revealed two pistols and narcotics. The arrest and search were held to be lawful.

> "This court holds that an entry into private premises by a public officer [the Battalion Fire Chief], without a search warrant, in pursuance of the authority of law to protect life and property and for the purpose of eliminating a hazard immediately dangerous to health and public safety is constitutionally valid if the purpose be summary and necessary under the exigencies of the circumstances. Hence, if upon such entry, contraband is revealed, the arrest is lawful and proper, and a search of the premises following such arrest, is incidental to the arrest." *Johnson, supra,* 48 Misc2d at 911.

A similar ruling has been made by the Supreme Court of Iowa. There it was held that entry of investigators onto burned premises under a state statute requiring and authorizing investigation into the causes of fire, did not become unlawful, nor did the search become unreasonable merely because evidence of arson was found. *State v. Rees,* 139 NW2d 406.

The New Jersey Superior Court has held to the same effect in *State v. Puryear,* 227 A2d 139. This case also involved entry by the police without a warrant, after the odor of gas fumes was noticed coming out of a second-floor apartment. Upon their entry by force, gambling paraphernalia was seen in the premises.

In *U.S. v. Barone,* 330 F2d 543, the police heard screams in the dead of night emanating from a rooming house. They entered the building and the screams persisted coming from room #7. They knocked on the door, announced they were "police" and then were permitted to enter. The two female occupants of the room denied all knowledge of the screaming. The officers then heard a toilet flush in the bathroom, and the defendant was seen exiting in his undershorts. One officer entered the bathroom and saw currency floating in the commode. He flushed the toilet, and torn pieces of counterfeit currency appeared in the bowl. The officer retrieved all of these items.

The right of the police to enter the apartment under these circumstances and to seize the currency without a warrant was sustained.

> "The police, hearing loud screams in the dead of night, acted, as was their duty, to investigate the source. Police are peace officers and are charged with the duty of the prevention of crime. New York City Charter, § 435. They had every reason to fear that assault or mayhem was being committed.
>
> . . . .
>
> "The right of the police to enter and investigate in an emergency without the accompanying intent to either search or arrest is inherent in the very nature of their duties as peace officers, and derives from the Common Law. See generally Reed v. Case, 4 Conn. 166 (1822). Indeed it is obvious that had the patrolman been denied entry to the apartment they would have had the right, if not the duty, to gain entry forcibly. See Wayne v.

United States, [318 F.2d 205, 209–214]." *Barone, supra,* 330 F2d at 544, 545.

A search of the person of a suspect and the seizure of a loaded gun without a warrant was held lawful in *People v. Teams,* 20 AD2d 803, 804, 248 NYS2d 477. Two anonymous telephone calls to the police reported that "Big Jim" was shooting a gun on St. John's Place. The police officer who reported to the scene knew the defendant as "Big Jim," and as one who had been arrested many times and who had a reputation as the enforcer and strong-arm-man of St. John's Place. The police searched him and found a loaded pistol containing three spent and two unspent cartridges. The search and seizure of the pistol was sustained as, inter alia, the complaints by the anonymous informers, if true, "were then directly imperiling the physical welfare of the community at large." *See also: People v. Taggart,* 20 NY2d 335, 283 NYS2d 1, 229 NE2d 581; and *Schmerber v. California,* 384 US 757.

The search and seizure without a warrant was also sustained in an emergency situation in New Jersey in the case of *State v. Gosser,* 236 A2d 377.

Gosser was convicted of killing his wife. Acting on a telephone call from a friend of the wife, the police went to Gosser's home. When the officer arrived, Gosser appeared. He seemed to be groggy and upset. Caked blood appeared on his face and pajamas. When asked what the trouble was, defendant said he had killed his wife.

A police sergeant then appeared on the scene and Gosser told him he had shot his wife and she was "upstairs." The sergeant and another police officer raced upstairs and searched from room to room. During the upstairs search, the police noticed an empty gun sticking out of a closet in one of the bedrooms and an open box of shotgun shells on a dresser in the hall. The body was found on a bed in the last bedroom entered. Thereafter, defendant was placed under arrest. He told the police that there was a shotgun under the bed where his wife lay. Those items and certain bloody clothing, all of which were in plain view, were seized. Motions to suppress them on constitutional grounds were denied. Defendant contended that a warrantless search of the bedroom area of the house preceded the formal arrest and handcuffing of the defendant and so was not incident to the arrest. Defendant suggests that had he been arrested prior to the search, the search would have been valid. In rejecting this contention the court noted that the Constitution proscribes only unreasonable searches and the common sense of the situation must be weighed in measuring what is "unreasonable." "To dash upstairs to see if the victim was not beyond aid was certainly called for. The gun case, box of shells and the bloody clothing and linen were in plain view. . . . The whole episode was essentially a single continuous event." 236 A2d at 381.

A more dramatic situation appears in *Alonzo v. U.S.,* 439 F2d 991, where, the police, fearing for the safety of an undercover agent who was in the premises with the defendant, entered forcibly. *See also: People v. Maddox,* 46 Cal2d 301, 294 P2d 6, cert. den. 352 US 858.

Likewise, in *U.S. v. Garcia Mendez,* 437 F2d 85, the police looking through a window, observed an automatic pistol inches away from the defendant's hand, and entered forcibly. The rule in *Sabbath v. U.S.,* 391 US 585, was held not applicable in a fact situation such as this (*see: § 194, supra*).

*Cf.: Taylor v. U.S.,* 286 US 1, where officers broke into a garage without a warrant and seized whiskey after they noticed a strong odor of alcohol; *Johnson v. U.S.,* 333 US 10, where officers, without a warrant broke into a hotel room after detecting the odor of burning opium emanating therefrom. The search and seizure in each case was held to be unlawful. Both of these cases involved sumptuary offenses.

**§ 261. Hot Pursuit.** Evidence seized without a warrant during a search conducted while in hot pursuit of a felon is a lawful search and seizure.

This rule has been enunciated in *Warden v. Hayden,* 387 US 294. In *Hayden,* an armed robber entered a taxicab office, took $363 and ran away. Two taxi drivers, hearing the shouts "hold-up," followed the robber to a certain building. One of the cab drivers notified the taxicab dispatcher of this fact and described the robber. The dispatcher immediately notified the police who arrived at the address given in less than five minutes. The police had no warrant. A police officer knocked on the door and was given permission to search the house for the robber by the defendant's wife. Different officers spread out through the building searching the cellar, first and second floors. The defendant was found in an upstairs bedroom, feigning sleep. The defendant was placed under arrest when the police officer in the cellar announced that there was no other man in the house. Meanwhile, one of the officers was attracted by the sound of running water in an adjoining bathroom, investigated and discovered a shotgun and pistol in the toilet flush tank. Another officer " 'was searching the cellar for a man or the money' found in a washing machine a jacket and trousers of the type the fleeing man was said to have worn. A clip of ammunition for the pistol and a cap were found under the mattress of Hayden's bed, and ammunition for the shotgun was found in a bureau drawer in Hayden's room. All these items were introduced against respondent at his trial." *Hayden, supra,* 387 US at 298.

A motion to suppress these items was denied by the trial court. In sustaining this denial, the court held:

> "[N]either the entry without a warrant to search for the robber, nor the search for him without warrant was invalid. Under the circumstances of this case, 'the exigencies of the situation made that course imperative.' *McDonald* v. *United States,* 335 U.S. 451, 456. The police were informed that an armed robbery had taken place, and that the suspect had entered 2111 Cocoa Lane less than five minutes before they reached it. They acted reasonably when they entered the house and began to search for a man of the description they had been given and for weapons which he had used in the robbery or might use against them. The Fourth Amendment does not require police officers to delay in the course of an investigation if to do so would gravely endanger their lives or the lives of others. Speed here was essential, and only a thorough search of the house for persons or weapons could have insured that Hayden was the only man present and that the police had control of all weapons which could be used against them or to effect an escape." *Hayden, supra,* 387 US at 298–299.

And this is a valid search and seizure, the court held, even though "the seizures occurred prior to or immediately contemporaneous with Hayden's arrest, as part of an effort to find a suspected felon, armed, within the house into which he had run only minutes before the police arrived. The permissible scope of search must, therefore, at the least, be as broad as may reasonably be necessary to prevent the dangers that the suspect at large in the house may resist or escape." 387 US at 299.

The former rule that a search for "mere evidence" is an unreasonable search was rejected by the court, overruling *Gouled v. U.S.*, 255 US 298. In doing so, the court authorized such a seizure as incident to a lawful arrest if there is "a nexus—automatically provided in the case of fruits, instrumentalities or contraband—between the item to be seized and criminal behavior. Thus in the case of 'mere evidence,' probable cause must be examined in terms of cause to believe that the evidence sought will aid in a particular apprehension or conviction." 387 US at 307.

The Federal Omnibus Crime Control and Safe Streets Act of 1968 (Pub. L. No. 90–351) has now given this new rule statutory approval in 18 USC § 3103a.

# Chapter 19

## STOP AND FRISK



---

**§ 265. In General.** Under the common law the right of the police to stop and make inquiries of persons abroad in public places concerning suspicious circumstances carries with it the right to frisk such persons for weapons and other implements which might endanger the life or limb of the police officer. *People v. Rivera,* 14 NY2d 441, 446, 201 NE2d 32, cert. den. 379 US 978. The same rule has been sanctioned by the United States Supreme Court in *Terry v. Ohio,* 392 US 1. New York has given statutory approval to the rule (CPL § 140.50) as have most other states. *See also:* Uniform Arrest Act, § 2.

Under the New York statute: (1) The police officer may only stop and frisk the suspect person within the geographical area of such officer's employment; (2) where he reasonably suspects that such person is committing, has committed or is about to commit either (a) a felony or (b) a class A misdemeanor as defined in the penal law.

Further the police officer is authorized, when he reasonably suspects that he is in danger of physical injury, to search the person for a deadly weapon, or any instrument, article or substance readily capable of causing serious physical injury "and of a sort not ordinarily carried in public places by law abiding citizens."

Frisking a suspect under these circumstances does not constitute a search. *People v. Rivera, supra; People v. Pugach,* 15 NY2d 65, 204 NE2d 176, cert. den. 380 U.S. 936; *People v. Peters,* 18 NY2d 238, 219 NE2d 595, affd 392 US 40; *cf. Sibron v. New York,* 392 US 40.

**§ 266. The Constitutionality of Stop and Frisk.** Although the United States Supreme Court did not specifically pass on the constitutionality of the New York Stop and Frisk statute, the decisions in *Terry v. Ohio,* 392 US 1, *Peters v. New York,* 18 NY2d 238, 219 NE2d 595, affd 392 US 40 and *Sibron v. New York,* 18 NY2d 603, 219 NE2d 196, revd 392 US 40, all indicate that the New York statute's constitutionality has been at least partially upheld. Additionally, the theory underlying stop and frisk statutes has survived attack on constitutional grounds. As the court noted in *People v. Peters, supra,* the doctrine that officers can stop a suspect on reasonable suspicion and search the suspect when he reasonably suspects that he is in physical danger, sets forth an adequate constitutional standard which does not violate the individual's rights under the Fourth Amendment.

**§ 267. The Right to Question and Investigate Without a Frisk.** *People v. Rosemond,* 26 NY2d 101, 105, 257 NE2d 23, carries the stop and frisk doctrine one step further. It justifies stopping persons abroad in a public place, questioning them and investigating further where the circumstances are suspicious, even though there is no frisk or custody.

In *Rosemond,* the defendant and another entered a building empty handed and were seen to emerge carrying a package and a suitcase. When the police officer asked Rosemond what he had in the package he replied that he did not know. The other defendant did not reply. After some questioning at length Rosemond said he got it around the corner and led the police to the vestibule of the building he had been seen to enter and leave. On entry therein, an apartment door was found open, the lock broken and chain removed. Further investigation disclosed that the shopping bag and suitcase had been taken from this apartment.

In sustaining the burglary conviction in this case the court said:

> "The significant fact in this case which distinguishes it from all others which have given trouble to the courts is that here there were only questions asked and no search or detention until the answers themselves gave probable cause.
>
> . . . .
>
> "That uniformed police officers were asking questions does not alone make the interrogation coercive. And, of course, there was no custody (cf. *People* v. *Whitehurst,* 25 NY2d 389).
>
> "Thus the problem in this present case can be divided, as it was in *Rivera,* [*People v. Rivera,* 14 NY2d 441], in two parts: (a) the reasonableness of the street inquiry; (b) the acts in consequence of the inquiry. It is not the danger to police in response to the questions that arises in this case, but the kind of answer given to the question which justifies further action." *People v. Rosemond, supra* at 105. See also *People v. Salerno,* 38 Misc2d 467, 235 NYS2d 879; *People v. Land,* 33 AD2d 798, 307 NYS2d 170.

§ 268. **Duty of Police to Stop and Frisk.** Indeed, under certain circumstances the police are under a duty to make appropriate inquiry including the right to stop and frisk persons abroad in a public place. This duty has been upheld in *People v. Arthurs,* 24 NY2d 688, 249 NE2d 462. In that case the court at 690–691, said:

> "The Supreme Court has recognized, as indeed has this court, the reasonableness of police conduct in effecting a limited search of persons in the absence of probable cause for arrest for a chargeable crime (*Terry* v. *Ohio,* 392 U.S. 1, esp. at pp. 26–27; *People v. Taggart,* 20 NY2d 335, 339–340; see Code Crim. Pro., § 180-a, and comments thereon in *Sibron* v. *New York,* 392 U.S. 40, 59–62, and esp. n. 20 at pp. 60–61). And, of course, if the police conduct is reasonable it does not offend constitutional limitations and the evidence obtained as a result of such conduct is admissible (*Terry* v. *Ohio, supra*). . . ."

So too, *U.S. v. Thomas,* 250 F Supp 771, affd 396 F2d 310, held that the mere stopping of a person abroad in a public place, by a policeman does not ipso facto constitute an arrest as contemplated by the Fourth Amendment's probable cause requirement. And this is true under the common law as well as the modern definition of arrest. The test, the court stated, was whether the period of questioning was reasonable under the circumstances.

In determining the question of a "reasonable period of time," the expertise of the officer involved is a relevant factor. Additionally, each case stands or falls on its own particular facts and circumstances. Flight would be one factor (*see: People v. Yazum,* 13 NY2d 302, 196 NE2d 263); untruthful answers would be another (*see: People v. Brady,* 16 NY2d 186, 211 NE2d 815).

§ 269. **The Frisk Incident to the Stop: Time Element.** Once reasonable suspicion and reasonable cause to stop and frisk arise, the right to frisk attaches. It is a right born of an emergency situation and accordingly the frisk should be immediate. *People v. Mack,* 26 NY2d 311, 318, 258 NE2d 703, cert. den. 400 US 960.

As Mr. Justice Harlan said in his concurring opinion in *Terry v. Ohio,* 392 US at 33:

> "Where such a stop is reasonable, however, the right to frisk must be immediate and automatic if the reason for the stop is, as here, articulable suspicion of a crime of violence. Just as a full search incident to a lawful arrest requires no additional justification, a limited frisk incident to a lawful stop must often be rapid and routine. There is no reason why an officer rightfully but forcibly confronting a person suspected of a serious crime, should have to ask one question and take the risk that the answer might be a bullet."

§ 270. **The Area of the Frisk.** Absent emergency circumstances, the frisk is limited to a patting down of the exterior clothing of the suspect. *Terry v. Ohio,* 392 US 1; *Peters v. New York,* 18 NY2d 238, 219 NE2d 595, affd 392 US 40; *Peo-*

*ple v. Rivera,* 14 NY2d 441, 201 NE2d 32, cert. den. 379 US 978. There are situations, however, where the frisk has been sustained beyond the person of the suspect.

In *People v. Pugach,* 15 NY2d 65, 69, 204 NE2d 176, cert. den. 380 US 936, the court held that, within the ambit of an authorized frisk, "The loaded firearm concealed in the brief case carried in the hands of the defendant was in the language of the statute 'concealed upon his person' ([former N.Y.] Penal Law, § 1897)."

> "The fact that the loaded gun was found concealed in the brief case [which he was carrying], rather than in a pocket of defendant's clothing, affords no ground for saying that this 'frisk' was in reality a constitutionally protected search." *Ibid.*

Thus, where defendant had been under surveillance by the police for several months with respect to his complicity and participation in another matter and was taken to the police station for further questioning in regard to that other matter, the police had the right to frisk the defendant. Such a frisk is justified as an incident to an inquiry upon grounds of safety and precaution. *People v. Rivera, supra.*

Citing *People v. Pugach, supra,* the court in *People v. Cassesse,* 47 Misc2d 1031, 263 NYS2d 734, extended the right to frisk to a parked automobile in which defendants were found at 2:30 A.M., after the police, based on a radio run and information given them by unknown informants that a shot had been fired by someone in the vehicle, took the defendants into custody.

In *People v. Bowles,* 29 AD2d 996, 289 NYS2d 526, a frisk of defendant's trousers which he was not wearing at the time but which were on the floor near the bed on which he was lying, was likewise sustained. The court stated, in affirming, that police officers need not wait until the defendant put his trousers on before frisking them, where, as in this case, police had reason to believe defendant is in possession of a weapon (razor).

**§ 271. Informant's Tip.** Tips supplied by informants may give rise to a duty on the part of the police to stop and frisk suspects. Such a frisk was also upheld where police frisked the defendant, acting on tips from various passersby that the defendant, whom they described, had discharged either a pistol or firecrackers. *People v. Arthurs,* 24 NY2d 688, 249 NE2d 462.

In some situations a police officer would be derelict in his duties if he failed to do so. *People v. Taggart,* 20 NY2d 335, 229 NE2d 581.

Similarly in *U.S. v. Lewis,* 362 F2d 759, the right of the police to stop and question a suspect based on information supplied by an express company employee who had observed him carrying a brown carton which apparently came from the express company, was justified. The situation was sufficient to create a reasonable suspicion under the stop and frisk law to justify the police officer's action.

Additionally, suspicious actions by a suspect in an automobile while being questioned by a police officer, authorized the officer to search under the driver's seat, where he found a loaded pistol. Here, in *People v. McKnight,* 26 NY2d 1034, 260 NE2d 552, the court held that the furtive actions of the defendant toward the bottom of the driver's seat warranted the police in reaching under the seat and seizing the loaded pistol found there. Such seizure it would seem, is equated with the frisk in *People v. Pugach* (*§ 270, supra*).

**§ 272. Stop and Frisk: When Not Justified.** Absent suspicious circumstances calling for inquiry, or reasonable cause to believe that a crime has been or is being committed, a stop and frisk is not justified.

Usually the right to stop and frisk is not authorized in petty offenses and traffic infraction cases absent special circumstances. *Rivera, infra,* however, imposes no such limitations. It authorizes the police to act when they observe suspicious or unusual street action. Implicit in the language of that decision is that they make prompt inquiry of a suspect where the suspicious or unusual street action presents reasonable grounds for the belief that the suspect "is committing, has committed or is about to commit a crime," *i.e.,* any crime.

The right to stop and frisk is not authorized in cases involving mere sumptuary offenses. In such situations there is no reasonable cause to believe that the officer is in physical danger. *Sibron v. New York,* 18 NY2d 603, 219 NE2d 196, revd 392 US 40; *People v. Taggart,* 20 NY2d 335, 283 NYS2d 1, 229 NE2d 581.

The same rule applies to mere traffic infractions. *People v. Marsh,* 20 NY2d 98, 228 NE2d 783.

Absent suspicious circumstances calling for inquiry, or reasonable cause to believe that a crime has been or is being committed, the mere fact that a patrolman observed a boy carrying a box of books, does not rise to the dignity of the right to stop the boy for questioning and inquiry. *People v. Anonymous,* 48 Misc2d 713, 265 NYS2d 705.

But the right to question a juvenile in the absence of his parents and absent *Miranda* warnings, is authorized in appropriate circumstances. *In re Nelson,* 58 Misc2d 748, 296 NYS2d 472. *See: § 41.02, supra.*

**§ 273. People v. Rivera.** The leading New York Stop and Frisk case is *People v. Rivera.* On July 10, 1964, the New York Court of Appeals handed down its decision in *People v. Rivera,* 14 NY2d 441, 252 NYS2d 458, 201 NE2d 32, cert. den. 379 US 978. The events in the *Rivera* case occurred in May, 1962. The Court of Appeals decision in that case is based on the law as it existed in 1962.

> "Although similar general principles underlie both the new statute and the validity of police action involved in this case, the prescribed standards of initial action and the grounds and scope of the invasion of the person questioned are somewhat different as laid down in the statute and as posed by the record before us." *Rivera, supra,* 14 NY2d at 443.

These similarities and differences should be noted. The facts in *Rivera* reveal that Rivera and a companion were observed walking up and down in front of a bar for about five minutes, stopping and then looking into the bar, and then repeating these actions. This occurred at 1:25 A.M. in an area that has a high incidence of crime. When the police approached them, Rivera and his companion spoke to each other and then both of them started to walk away rapidly. The police identified themselves, stopped the defendant and one of the officers patted the outside of Rivera's clothing and in the rear felt a hard object that felt like a weapon or gun which he removed and found to be a .22 caliber gun fully loaded.

In its decision the Court of Appeals sustained the seizure of the gun. In doing so, it distinguished a frisk from a search. It held that though a search is constitutionally protected against, a frisk, on the other hand, is a reasonable and constitutionally permissible precaution to minimize the danger to a policeman who is trying to determine whether a crime has been or is about to be committed.

"The frisk is less such invasion . . . than an initial full search . . ." and ought to be distinguished "from the degree of constitutional protection that would surround a full-blown search of the person." 14 NY2d at 446.

Both *Rivera* and the statute authorize the police to stop any person abroad in a public place whom they reasonably suspect is committing or has committed or is about to commit a crime. Both are bottomed on the duty of the police to prevent crime if they can. *People v. Marendi,* 213 NY 600, 609; *People v. Entrialgo,* 14 NY2d 733, 199 NE2d 384; *U.S. v. Vita,* 294 F2d 524, cert. den. 369 US 823. *Rivera* also cites the common law as authority (at 445–446). Both aver a right in the police to invade the person of the suspect to some degree as a measure of self-protection to be exercised by the police. Both recognize the authority of the police to question a suspect who is abroad in a public place.

*Rivera,* however, only authorizes a frisk as distinguished from a full-blown search. The right to conduct a full-blown search would depend on the commission of a crime or as an incident to a lawful arrest. *Harris v. U.S.,* 331 US 145.

The N.Y. Criminal Procedure Law, on the other hand, authorizes a search, in *haec verba.* It likewise limits the authority of the police to stop and question a suspect only when he reasonably suspects the person "is committing, has committed, or is about to commit" a felony or any class A misdemeanor. The statute contains no authority to exercise dominion over the defendant or his possessions during the interrogation. This authority, however, is implicit in its language. The period of time during which the suspect may be detained must also be brief. To allow a longer period might constitute an unlawful arrest. *People v. Jones,* 38 Misc2d 125, 238 NYS2d 49; *U.S. v. Vita,* 294 F2d 524; *Henry v. U.S.,* 361 US 98.

*Rivera* is not without its critics. As Judge Fuld noted in his dissent in *Rivera* at p. 541, quoting Mr. J. Douglas, "There is no crime known as 'suspicion'." Judge Van Voorhis in his dissent in *People v. Sibron,* 18 NY2d 603, 605, 219 NE2d 196, is of a like mind. He quotes from *Malloy v. U.S.,* 354 US 449, 454, "The police may not arrest on mere suspicion," as authority for his position and cites Judge Fuld's dissent in *Rivera* with approval.

Judge Van Voorhis goes further. He argues that if the right to frisk is based on a reasonable fear that the suspect is armed, then, if the frisk discloses a weapon, that alone should be seized and the suspect prosecuted for its unlawful possession.

> "If we go beyond that, then frisking a suspect, which can be done in practice (though not in theory) at the officer's whim, will become a pretext for a general search of the person, without probable cause, which the Fourteenth Amendment was designed to prevent. The power to frisk is an exception to the probable cause rule in search and seizure, and is not a search at all except for the discovery of a dangerous weapon concealed upon the person. There it should end, for all purposes." Van Voorhis dissenting in *People v. Sibron, supra* at 606.

To go further than this by permitting the use in evidence against a defendant, other discovered contraband of a sumptuary nature would "subtly . . . subvert an important part of the Fourth Amendment." *Sibron* at 606. *Cf. Johnson v. U.S.,* 293 F2d 539, cert. den. 375 US 888, wherein the Court did not limit the search under a warrant precisely to the articles of property enumerated in the warrant, especially if they constituted instrumentalities of crime.

Be that as it may, subsequent United States Supreme Court decisions upheld the constitutionality of the stop and frisk doctrine in *Rivera. Terry v. Ohio,* 392 US 1; *Peters v. New York,* 18 NY2d 238, 219 NE2d 595, affd 392 US 40; *cf. Sibron v. New York,* 18 NY2d 603, 219 NE2d 196, revd 392 US 40.

(These cases are discussed *infra.*) The decisions therein were foreshadowed when the Supreme Court denied certiorari in *Rivera,* 379 US 978.

New Jersey has also followed the *Rivera* doctrine. *State v. Dilley,* 49 NJ 460, 231 A2d 353.

New York has also continued to follow *Rivera* in *People v. Taggart,* 20 NY2d 335, 283 NYS2d 1, 229 NE2d 581, app dism 392 US 667 (discussed *infra*), and in *People v. Rosemond,* 26 NY2d 101, 257 NE2d 23.

**§ 274. Terry v. Ohio.** The United States Supreme Court in *Terry v. Ohio,* 392 US 1, has sustained the basic tenents set forth in *People v. Rivera, supra.* That Court has held that where on-the-spot observations of the police officer support a finding of questionable conduct that will justify further investigation, including limited questioning, the policeman has a right to stop a suspect to conduct that questioning. Further, where the policeman's observations justify reasonable belief that the suspect is armed, the policeman has a right to frisk the suspect for weapons.

The Court, however, did not reach the question of the constitutionality of the statute. *See also: Peters v. New York, supra; cf. Sibron v. New York, supra.*

In *Terry, supra,* the petitioner was convicted of carrying a concealed weapon. At the suppression hearing it was disclosed that Officer McFadden, an experienced detective, observed Terry and two codefendants walking with measured pace up and down in front of a store, 10 or 12 times, peering into the store and conferring with each other. McFadden stated " 'Now, in this case . . . they didn't look right to me at the time,' " and he became "thoroughly suspicious," after noting additionally the defendants' "elaborately casual and oft-repeated reconnaissance of the store window." This led him to believe that they were " 'casing a job, a stick-up.' " He felt it his duty to investigate further and feared " 'they may have a gun.' " Deciding that further action was necessary, he approached them and asked them their names. When they " 'mumbled something,' " he spun Terry around, patted Terry down "on the outside of his clothing" and felt a pistol in his left breast pocket. A gun was subsequently removed from Terry and another defendant. *Terry v. Ohio* at 6–7.

Although the court acknowledged that "the Fourth Amendment protects people, not places" (*Katz v. United States,* 389 US 347, 351), and also "wherever an individual may harbor a reasonable 'expectation of privacy,' . . . he is entitled to be free from unreasonable governmental intrusion. Of course, the specific content and incidents of this right must be shaped by the context in which it is asserted. For 'what the Constitution forbids is not all searches and seizures, but unreasonable searches and seizures.' Elkins v. United States, 364 U.S. 206, 222, . . ." *Terry v. Ohio,* 392 US 1, 9. Under the facts and circumstances here established, it was held that where an experienced officer reasonably concludes that criminal activity was in the making, and that where the person with whom he was dealing might be armed and dangerous, the officer, without violating the Fourth Amendment, has a right to stop and frisk that person as a self-protective measure and as a protection to others—such "stop and frisk" being less than a full-blown search. The test to be employed to sustain such a "stop and frisk" is, "would the facts available to the officer at the moment of the seizure 'warrant a man of reasonable caution in the belief' that the action taken was appropriate? *Cf. Carroll* v. *United States,* 267 U.S. 132 (1925); *Beck* v. *Ohio,* 379 U.S. 89, 96–97 (1964)." 392 US at 21–22.

In *Sibron v. New York, supra,* the conviction was reversed because in that case the police in searching Sibron were not looking for weapons but for narcotics. *Terry, supra,* is not applicable to sumptuary offenses—those offenses which deal with private conduct vis-à-vis moral or religious grounds.

*Peters v. New York, supra,* was affirmed on probable cause grounds. In this case the validity of the New York Stop and Frisk Law was not passed on.

§ 275. **People v. Taggart.** In what appears to be an extreme application of the New York Stop and Frisk Law, but seemingly anticipating the *Terry* doctrine, *supra,* the Court of Appeals affirmed defendant's determination as a Youthful Offender.

In *People v. Taggart,* 20 NY2d 335, 283 NYS2d 1, 229 NE2d 581, app dism 392 US 667, an anonymous person telephoned the police and said that on a certain street corner a certain youth had a loaded .32 caliber revolver in his left hand jacket pocket. There was no way of determining the reliability of this informer. A detective went to the street corner and saw defendant, who matched the description given, standing in the midst of a group of children. This, the court held, was an exigency that required immediate police action. The safety of the children and of the police officer would not allow any preliminary questioning or frisking. The detective seized the youth, put him up against a building, and took the revolver out of his left hand jacket pocket. There was no noticeable bulge in the jacket.

The court based its conclusion squarely on the statute, that this was a case where a police officer reasonably suspected that a person in a public place was committing a crime and that he, the police officer, was in danger of life or limb; thus, he may search that person for a dangerous weapon, and if he finds it, he may take it and arrest that person.

> "The detective had at least a reasonably based suspicion that the defendant was committing a crime and was, therefore, entitled to 'stop' him. Moreover, the detective was also warranted in suspecting that the defendant possessed a dangerous weapon which theratened the life of the detective as well as others in the immediate vicinity of defendant. Consequently, the seizure of the weapon was proper. . . ." 20 NY2d at 337.

Concededly, the police did not have probable cause to arrest the defendant based on the information received and the observations that the detective had made. *People v. Malinsky,* 15 NY2d 86, 93–94, 258 NE2d 703; *People v. Coffey,* 12 NY2d 443, 452, 191 NE2d 263, cert. den. 376 US 916. But this was an "emergency" situation.

> "There are exigencies affecting life, limb, or grave property damage in which the police receive information of crime, not sufficient to establish probable cause for arrest and incidental search, and yet which, to any reasonable man, demand the taking of police action to prevent serious harm. In such cases it is not enough to say

> that nothing should be done, or that if something is done, the resultant evidence should be suppressed. . . . [T]he test for action is supposed to be what a reasonable man would do under the circumstances (see *Ker* v. *California,* 374 U.S. 23, 34–35; *Johnson* v. *United States,* 333 U.S. 10, 13–14)." *Taggart,* 20 NY2d at 339.

The rule herein enunciated should be limited to cases "involving serious personal injury or grave irreparable property damage [bomb on an airplane, etc.] and not by the problems associated with the enforcement of sumptuary laws, such as gambling, and laws of limited public consequences, such as narcotics violations, prostitution, larcenies of the ordinary kind, and the like. In this case a loaded pistol was involved. . . . For the police to have ignored the information received is not an acceptable thesis, despite the anonymity and, therefore, the undetermined reliability of the source." *Taggart,* 20 NY2d at 340.

Concededly, in this case the police conducted a "search" rather than a "frisk." The frisk was authorized both at common law, *People v. Rivera,* 14 NY2d 441, and by statute. In this respect, the officer exceeded the limitations of *People v. Peters,* 18 NY2d 238, affd 392 US 40, and *People v. Rivera, supra.* However, a search was sustained in *People v. Pugach,* 15 NY2d 65, cert. den. 380 US 936. *Cf. People v. Sibron,* 18 NY2d 603, revd 392 US 40.

> "In either instance [*Pugach* and *Sibron*] it is suspicion engendered by some circumstance short of constituting probable cause to make an arrest that justifies the invasion of a defendant's person for the discovery of a dangerous weapon. It does not matter whether the suspicion is created by an anonymous telephone call from an unknown informer or the suspicious presence of the defendant in the hall of an apartment house, his behaviour in front of a store on the street, or the protrusion of some concealed object in his clothing which proves to be a knife or a revolver." *Taggart,* 20 NY2d at 344.

It is recognized, however, that using anonymous information as a basis for intensive police action is highly dangerous.

> "To limit its use [the 'search' as opposed to a 'frisk'] to exigent circumstances the police action must relate to matters gravely affecting personal or public safety or irreparable harm to property of extraordinary value. As noted earlier, it should not extend to all contraband or criminal violations." *Taggart,* 20 NY2d at 343.

In *Terry v. Ohio, supra,* the Court equated a "stop" and "frisk" with the terms "seizure" and "search" within the meaning of the Fourth Amendment.

However, a search, within the terms of the stop and frisk laws, is not lawful in cases involving sumptuary offenses. Sumptuary offenses, as noted above, are non-violent crimes—cases associated "with the enforcement of sumptuary laws, such as gambling, and laws of limited public consequence, such as narcotics violations, prostitution, larceny of the ordinary kind, and the like." *Taggart, supra,* 20 NY2d at 340.

Thus, in *People v. Sibron,* 18 NY2d 603, revd 392 US 40, the reversal was based on the fact that the officers's search was not based on any facts that would justify a belief that the defendant was armed and dangerous. Sibron was observed talking with various narcotic addicts and was suspected of having narcotics on his person. The officer was looking for narcotics, a sumptuary offense, and put his hand in Sibron's pocket for that purpose. *Cf. People v. Peters,* 392 US 40, involving a reasonable suspicion of attempted burglary.

Sibron's search was not preceded by any frisk for weapons and it was not "reasonably limited in scope to the accomplishment of the only goal which might conceivably have justified its inception—the protection of the officer by disarming a potentially dangerous man." *Sibron,* 392 US at 65.

As the court noted in *Taggart, supra,* situations may arise requiring prompt police action—entry into constitutionally protected areas—for the purpose of protecting life and property. 20 NY2d at 339. (*See also: Exigent Circumstances and Hot Pursuit, Chapter 18, supra.*)

# Chapter 20

# CURTILAGE



---

§ 280. **Defined.** Curtilage is defined as:

> "The open space situated within a common enclosure belonging to the dwelling house. . . . Such space as is necessary and convenient, and is habitually used, for family purposes, including a yard, garden, or even a field which is near and used in connection with the dwelling." Ballentine, *Law Dictionary* (2d ed. 1948).

The area immediately adjacent to the home—curtilage—is entitled to the same Fourth Amendment protection against unreasonable searches and seizures as is the home. The cases and other authorities prescribe certain basic elements which must be established before a certain area can be labeled "curtilage." There must first of all be a dwelling house—a place where people actually reside or a building intended for that purpose. The area surrounding the dwelling house and structures must be used for the use of the occupants of the dwelling. *Italian-American Building v. Russo,* 132 NJ Eq 319, 28 A2d 196; *In re Burgoon's Estate,* 80 Ohio App 465, 76 NE2d 310; *Fugate v. Commonwealth,* 294 Ky 410, 171 SW2d 1020; *Union Free School v. Baumgartner,* 91 NYS2d 351; *Brock v. U.S.,* 223 F2d 681. The area and its buildings may be fenced or unfenced. *Turknett v. State,* 254 P 985; *Graves v. State,* 283 P 795; *Bruner v. State,* 288 P 369; *Hicks v. State,* 21 Ala App 335, 108 So 612.

The meaning of the word must not be so distorted as to defeat the purpose of the Fourth Amendment which was designed to protect against unreasonable searches and seizures. Nor must it be so broadened so as to serve as refuge for criminals. *Worth v. State,* 12 SW2d 582.

What constitutes curtilage is usually a mixed question of law and fact. The jury decides what constitutes the curtilage, where the facts are in dispute. *Cook v. State,* 83 Ala 62, 3 So 849; *McNutt v. State,* 23 Ala App 43, 120 So 432; *Hutchins v. State,* 3 Ga App 300, 59 SE 848; *Bowen v. State,* 217 Ala 574, 117 So 204.

§ 280.01. **Examples of Curtilage.** The following are examples of areas held to lie within the curtilage as a matter of law.

A house located 36 feet from the defendant's dwelling used for housing defendant's nets and as sleeping quarters for two of the defendant's servants. *Pond v. People,* 8 Mich 150.

The area within one yard of the back steps of defendant's home. *State v. Brooks,* 79 So Car 144, 60 SE 518.

The edge of defendant's yard, 30 feet from his front door. *State v. Frizzelle,* 243 NC 49, 89 SE2d 725.

The garden of the defendant's house. *Doswell v. State,* 34 Ala App 546, 42 So2d 480.

The front and back yard, fenced or unfenced. *Hicks v. State,* 21 Ala App 335, 108 So 612.

Garage, barn, smokehouse, chicken house, and similar property. *Care v. U.S.,* 231 F2d 22; *Walker v. U.S.,* 225 F2d 447; *Kroska v. U.S.,* 51 F2d 330.

A 2½ acre tract on which a large apartment house was erected. *Riverside Apt. Corp. v. Capitol Const.,* 152 A 763, 107 NJ Eq 405. This case involved a mechanics lien.

A barn 80 feet from a dwelling house in a yard or lane. *People v. Taylor,* 2 Mich 250.

A smokehouse having its front and door in the yard of the dwelling house, even though part of the building was not in the yard. *Fisher v. State,* 43 Ala 17; *Roberson v. U.S.,* 165 F2d 752.

A partly constructed residence, in which the owner resided, but from which he was absent at the time. *Morrison v. U.S.,* 262 F2d 449.

The enclosed backyard of a residence where a package

landed after it had been thrown. *Hobson v. U.S.,* 226 F2d 890.

A Finnish bath house adjacent to a dwelling on a small farm. *Wakkuri v. U.S.,* 67 F2d 844.

A garage under a two-story building in which defendant lived, albeit on the upper story. *Temperani v. U.S.,* 299 F 365.

A trash can under the stone stoop of a house. *Work v. U.S.,* 243 F2d 660.

A locked cupboard in a common hallway of an apartment building in which the defendant had an apartment and which was reached by going through the hallway. *U.S. v. Lumia,* 36 F Supp 552.

§ 280.02. **Examples of No Curtilage.** The following are examples of areas found not to lie within the curtilage.

The vicinity of a house which was not used as a dwelling house. *U.S. v. Potts,* 297 F2d 68.

A barn and corncrib separately enclosed by a high fence and located about fifty yards from the dwelling which had an uninclosed yard. *Hutchings v. State,* 3 Ga App 300, 59 SE 848.

The basement of an adjoining building connected with a dwelling house by a covered passageway. *Commonwealth v. Intoxicating Liquors,* 140 Mass 287, 3 NE 4.

A building or other structure used primarily for the manufacture of liquor and not for any domestic purpose. *Hoppe v. State,* 122 Tex Cr R 440, 55 SW2d 1053; *State v. Lee,* 120 Oreg 643, 253 P 533.

A vacant store and a grocery store in which liquor was stored, and which buildings were connected by a hallway across an alley to a store, above which defendant lived. *Pettus v. Commonwealth,* 123 Va. 806, 96 SE 161.

A barn separated from a dwelling by a public highway and a yard, some 100 feet from the dwelling. *Curkendall v. People,* 36 Mich 309.

A store 20 feet distant from a dwelling and not connected with it by a fence or enclosure. *People v. Parker,* 4 Johns 424.

A distillery leased to a third party though near the dwelling house. *U.S. v. Vlahos,* 19 F Supp 166.

An open field. *Hester v. U.S.,* 265 US 57; *Lee v. U.S.,* 221 F2d 29; *Hodges v. U.S.,* 243 F2d 281; *People v. Montes,*

146 Cal App2d 530, 303 P2d 1064; *People v. Grundies,* 413 Ill 145, 108 NE2d 483.

A detached garage leased to a third party by the owner of the residence. *Carney v. U.S.,* 163 F2d 784; *U.S. v. Thomas,* 216 F Supp 942; *People v. Swanberg,* 22 AD2d 902, affd as mod 16 NY2d 649.

A stone outhouse rented out by petitioner "was not his home" under the Fourth Amendment. *Schnitzer v. U.S.,* 77 F2d 233.

A public road located an appreciable distance from the accused's dwelling house. *Nunn v. State,* 19 Ala App 619, 99 So 738.

The area between the dwelling house and the middle of the street. *State v. Boyd,* 126 So Car 300, 119 SE 839.

An open space in front of a stable where the defendant was employed. *Perry v. State,* 94 Ala 25, 10 So 650.

A distillery located on premises. *Hill v. State,* 194 Ala 11, 69 So 941.

As to property included within the curtilage with respect to burglary cases, *see* 43 ALR2d 831 *et seq.;* with respect to homicide cases, *see* 52 ALR2d 458 *et seq.*

**§ 280.03. Apartment Houses.** Usually any area which is not under the domain of any particular occupant of a multiple dwelling is not considered a part of the curtilage area. However, it is not always a simple matter to determine when a particular area is or is not under the necessary domain to make it a part of the curtilage.

Under the Multiple Dwelling Law of New York, it was held that a fire escape is an integral part of each apartment to be used by the occupant thereof as a secondary means of egress, and as such, is a part of the curtilage of the apartment. *People v. Terrell,* 277 NYS2d 926.

A contrary determination was made in *People v. Hailstick,* 283 NYS2d 492. In that case, the landlord of the building had notified the police that he thought the tenants in one of the apartments were dealing in narcotic instruments. A policeman climbed the fire escape, looked into one of the apartments, and on the basis of his observation arrested the occupants.

The court held that since the fire escape is for the use of

other tenants also and is partly under the control of the landlord, the landlord's inferential permission, as part of the information he gave the police, was sufficient to permit the police to use the fire escape platform.

With the advent of high-rise apartment dwellings in urban areas, the concept of curtilage must perforce undergo modification in its application.

The shrinkage of curtilage has continued as urban life has spread. Whereas the front porch of the farmhouse is still part of the curtilage, the same cannot be said of the entrance lobbies and public halls of the modern apartment houses with respect to the apartments of tenants residing in them. *U.S. v. Miguel,* 340 F2d 812; *U.S. v. Conti,* 361 F2d 153.

As the court said in *Conti, supra,* "This court has recently held that a lobby of an apartment house, guarded by a door usually kept locked, is not within the curtilage of a tenant's apartment, and so is not a protected area within which the individual tenants have Fourth Amendment rights. United States v. Miguel, 340 F.2d 812 (2d Cir.), cert. denied 382 U.S. 859, . . . (1965)." 361 F2d at 157.

Following the rationale of *Conti,* the court in *Commonwealth v. Thomas,* 267 NE2d 489, held that the cellar of an apartment house, containing washing machines, dryers, barrels, a hot water heater and other similar and related objects, used in common by the tenants of the building, did not constitute a part of the curtilage of the apartment of the defendant who also resided in the building. *See also: U.S. v. Buchner,* 164 F Supp 836, affd 268 F2d 891, cert. den. 359 US 908.

**§ 280.04. Curtilage Trespass Exception.** There is an exception to the general rule relating to a search and seizure accompanied by curtilage trespass. This occurs when the search and seizure are not unreasonable under the facts and circumstances, bearing in mind that the Fourth Amendment proscription is aimed only at "unreasonable" searches and seizures. This exception to the general rule will probably come into play most frequently in cases involving vehicles.

Thus, a search and seizure of a truck parked on the driveway of defendant's home, concededly involving a trespass on the curtilage, was sustained as reasonable under the circumstances.

In *U.S. v. Taylor,* 428 F2d 515, the court had before it a case involving the possession of stolen tires defendant was loading on his dump truck. The police entered the driveway, searched the truck and seized the tires.

> "While this court has recognized the curtilage doctrine and has held that the area immediately adjacent to the home is entitled to the same protection against unreasonable search and seizures as is the home, Hobson v. United States, 226 F.2d 890 (8th Cir. 1955), this doctrine is subject to the same exception as the Fourth Amendment requirement of search warrants in general; that is, if the circumstances of the individual case make it impracticable to obtain a search warrant, a warrantless search and seizure is valid if it meets the test of reasonableness. Here, we are not dealing with the search of defendant's home or its immediate premises but with the search of a dump truck parked on the defendant's driveway. The truck was obviously being loaded for the purpose of transporting the new tires to some unknown destination and was capable of being driven from the area at any time. Hence, the exception to the Fourth Amendment's search warrant requirement is applicable here.
>
> "Niro v. United States, 388 F.2d 535 (1st Cir. 1968), cited by defendant, is distinguishable because in *Niro* the truck had been parked in the garage some 12 hours after the officers had probable cause to make the search and the subsequent need for haste in making the seizure was brought about, according to the court, by the deliberate and unreasonable delay of the government. Here, Officer Choate's information that new tires were in Taylor's home was not confirmed until he saw the new tires in the process of being loaded into the truck. Wattenburg v. United States, 388 F.2d 853 (9th Cir. 1968), also relied on by Taylor, is not in point as there the search for illegally cut Christmas trees was conducted in the yard and there was no threat of immediately transporting the evidence or the contraband from the area, and no vehicle was involved." *U.S. v. Taylor,* 428 F2d 515, 518.

# Chapter 21

## SEARCH OF MOTOR VEHICLES



---

**§ 285. In General.** Automobiles come within the ambit of the Fourth Amendment with respect to the prohibition against unreasonable searches. They are no more vulnerable to searches than a private residence. *Preston v. U.S.,* 376 US 364; *Henry v. U.S.,* 361 US 98; *Rios v. U.S.,* 364 US 253; *Carroll v. U.S.,* 267 US 132; *Brinegar v. U.S.,* 338 US 160; *People v. Mangino,* 236 NYS2d 439; *People v. Adorno,* 37 Misc2d 36, 234 NYS2d 674; *Harris v. U.S.,* 390 US 234; *People v. Zeigler,* 100 NW2d 456.

Thus, as the court stated in *Rios v. U.S.,* 364 US at 262, fn. 6, a package dropped to the floor of a taxicab by a passenger does not constitute an "abandonment," for an occupied taxicab is not comparable to an open field (*Hester v. U.S.,* 265 US 57), nor to a vacated hotel room (*Abel v. U.S.,* 362 US 217). The same prohibition is equally applicable to cases involving a forfeiture of an automobile used for an illegal purpose. *One 1958 Plymouth Sedan v. Penn.,* 380 US 693.

The general rule is that for the purpose of arrest without a warrant pursuant to statute, a traffic infraction is deemed an offense. Nevertheless, where an arrest is made for a mere traffic infraction, absent special circumstances, such as a reasonable belief that the defendant is armed, a search incident to such an arrest is unreasonable. *People v. Marsh,* 20 NY2d 98, 102, 228 NE2d 783; *U.S. v. Davis,* 441 F2d 28.

For example, where in *U.S. v. Frye,* 271 A2d 788, the police received a tip from an unidentified citizen, that a certain car bearing a given license plate number, was being loaded with shotguns and rifles, and the officer received radio information that the car bore improper plates, the officer was justified in arresting the defendant and frisking him at the time. Here the court found that the aggregate of the information received warranted the police in stopping the car, arresting the defendant and frisking the occupants, even though, as was subsequently discovered, the license plates on the car were the proper plates for it.

In *U.S. v. Capp,* 435 F2d 637, where police were informed that a machine gun, secreted in a red bowling ball bag was in a certain automobile, upon seeing the bag in open view, its search and seizure were lawful, under the circumstances. *See also: People v. Taggart,* 20 NY2d 335, 283 NYS2d 1, 229 NE2d 581.

**§ 286. The Incident Search.** Where a lawful arrest has been made, other than for a mere traffic infraction, a search of the automobile is deemed reasonable, if it is conducted incident to the arrest. The search must be contemporaneous with time and place, and provided that the automobile is within the immediate control of the defendant at the time of arrest. *Preston v. U.S.,* 376 US 364; *People v. Lombardi,* 18 AD2d 177, affd 13 NY2d 1014, 195 NE2d 306; *People v. Beaman,* 44 Misc2d 336, 253 NYS2d 674.

The theory behind the lawfulness of an incident search is that it must be truly incident to the reason for the arrest. In *Preston v. U.S.,* 376 US 364, Preston was arrested on a charge of vagrancy. Search of his automobile was held to be unlawful as not truly incident to the arrest. Nothing that could be revealed by a search of the car would have had any bearing on the issue of vagrancy.

One of the elements in *Beaman, supra,* that made the search of the automobile unreasonable was the fact that at the time of the search, the automobile was not under the defendant's immediate control. Beaman had been arrested on a charge of driving while intoxicated. The police took him to the police station, locked his car and retained possession of the key. He was booked and subjected to tests for intoxication. After completion of the tests, he was incarcerated. The police then unlocked the car, searched it without a warrant and found weapons in it. *Cf. People v. Moschitta,* 25 AD2d 686, 269 NYS2d 70.

**§ 287. Contemporaneous Search.** A search and seizure to be reasonable must be contemporaneous with the time and place of the arrest.

In *U.S. v. Kapatos,* 255 F Supp 332, defendant moved for suppression and return of articles found in his automobile. The court held that the search was reasonable in view of the following facts:

(1) Three years earlier, the defendant had dressed as a policeman and, with a revolver, had stolen an interstate shipment of jewelry from a vehicle.
(2) Six F.B.I. agents, armed with an arrest warrant, observed defendant drive into a service station and arrested him as he started to alight from his automobile.
(3) The search of the automobile commenced simultaneously with the arrest.
(4) The seizure, *inter alia,* of gold buttons and police insignia, found in the trunk of the car, took place within minutes of the arrest.

In *Coolidge v. New Hampshire,* 403 US 443, a search of defendant's automobile which was outside of his house at the time that the defendant was arrested inside of his house, did not constitute a lawful search incident to his arrest. *See also: U.S. v. Doyle,* 373 F2d 875; *Cooper v. Calif.,* 386 US 58; *People v. Webb,* 56 Cal Rptr 902, 424 P2d 342.

**§ 288. Immediate Control.** The vehicle searched must be in the immediate control of the defendant at the time of the arrest. One can be in immediate control of a vehicle without actually being in it.

In *People v. Daily,* 157 Cal App2d 649, 321 P2d 469, Daily was arrested on probable cause without a warrant in the home of the prosecutrix for abortion and conspiracy to commit an abortion. He was searched and his automobile key was found. He told the police that his car was parked some 50–60 feet away. The police, without a warrant, opened his car, searched it and seized certain medicines, materials and instruments used or useful in the commission of abortions, which they found in the trunk. The automobile was held to be within the immediate control of the defendant at the time of his arrest, even though it was some 60 feet away, and the search of the vehicle without a warrant was found to be reasonable as incident to a lawful arrest. With respect to the necessity for obtaining a warrant, the court stated: "A man's automobile, unlike his house, is a mobile object and the need for immediate search is deemed that much greater. See *Carroll v. U.S.,* 267 U.S. 132, 153; *U.S. v. Cefaratti,* 91 U.S. App. D.C. 297, 202 F.2d 13." *Daily* at 471.

In *U.S. v. Cefaratti, supra,* the Court sustained the validity of a search of a motor vehicle, without a warrant, that was more distant from the defendant than in the *Daily* case. The vehicle was held to be within the immediate control of the defendant, and the search authorized as incident to a lawful arrest made without a warrant, but based on probable cause.

In *Cefaratti,* a police officer observed him selling narcotics to one Hallams, but was unable to effect an arrest at that time. At the officer's request, Hallams agreed to meet Cefaratti at a subsequent time and place and buy from him 100 capsules of cocaine and 100 of heroin. Cefaratti appeared at the agreed time and place, was arrested and searched, but no narcotics were found on his person. He gave the police officer the license number of a cab which he just parked. The police officer located the cab, searched it without a warrant, and seized narcotics found concealed therein. In reversing the lower court, the appellate court held:

"We think the search and seizure were legal and the evidence should not have been suppressed. The 'Fourth Amendment has been construed * * * as recognizing a necessary difference between a search of a store, dwelling house, or other structure in respect of which a proper official warrant readily may be obtained and a search of a ship, motor boat, wagon, or automobile for contraband goods, where it is not practicable to secure a warrant, because the vehicle can be quickly moved * * * if the search and seizure without a warrant are made upon probable cause, that is, upon a belief, reasonably arising out of circumstances known to the seizing officer, that an automobile or other vehicle contains that which by law is subject to seizure and destruction, the search and seizure are valid.' *Carroll v. United States,* 267 U.S. 132, 153, 159 . . . ; *Scher v. United States,* 305 U.S. 251 . . . ; *Brinegar v. United States,* 338 U.S. 160. . . . There was nothing unreasonable in the belief of Gabrys, [the police officer] that appellee [Cefaratti] was keeping an appointment to sell drugs and that since the drugs were not on his person they were in the cab." 202 F2d at 14–15. *Cf. Chimel v. California,* 395 US 752.

**§ 289. Seeing and Searching.** Looking into an automobile by natural or artificial light does not constitute a search. A search implies a prying into something. *People v. West,* 12 NY2d 1090, 190 NE2d 532; *People v. Anthony,* 21 AD2d 666, 249 NYS2d 997; *People v. Jordan,* 37 Misc2d 33; *People v. Russo,* 38 Misc2d 957. The distinction between "seeing" and "searching" is illustrated in the case cited below.

In *Harris v. U.S.,* 390 US 234, petitioner's car was seized at the scene of a robbery and towed to the police precinct pursuant to police regulations requiring that the auto be secured against theft. There the police searched the car to remove all valuables. Upon opening a door to secure the window, an officer observed an automobile registration card—the property of the robbery victim. Defendant's motion to suppress this evidence was denied.

The Supreme Court held that this evidence was not obtained

by an illegal search but resulted from measures taken to protect the car while it was in police custody. "Nothing in the Fourth Amendment requires the police to obtain a warrant in these narrow circumstances." Once the door was lawfully opened, the card that was "plainly visible" was lawfully seized as evidence. This was not a general search but an act performed to protect the car. The Court noted, however, that the "admissibility of evidence as a result of search under the police regulation is not presented in this case." 390 US at 236.

§ 290. **Inventory of Cars' Contents and Search.** That items of evidence found in searches of vehicles, lawfully in police custody, when such searches are not made for the purpose of seeking evidence of crime, may not be suppressed is becoming the increasingly accepted view.

In *Heffley v. State,* 433 P2d 666, 668, the court concisely stated the reason for upholding a seizure of articles in such cases. It said:

> "The police officer, when there is just cause, has a duty not only to impound a car from the public highway for its own protection, but also to inventory the contents so that they may be safeguarded for the owner. Such practice is deemed necessary to defeat claims of theft of the car's contents and to protect the temporary storage bailee against false charges."

Where a motor vehicle is lawfully in the custody of the police as bailee for the owner, an *examination* of the vehicle for inventory purposes is a reasonable procedure for the protection of the owner as well as for the police. Such examination does not constitute an "unreasonable" search, but by any standard is reasonable within the Fourth Amendment.

A distinction is made between an examination and a search. It seems obvious that the examination could deteriorate into a search depending on its extent, and absent special circumstances. For example, removing hubcaps and deflating automobile tires and examining the interior of the hubcap space and the interior of the tires, would not under normal circumstances constitute an "examination." On the contrary, the intent to search would be patent. *See: People v. Robinson,* 36 AD2d 375, 320 NYS2d 665.

§ 291. **Search Without a Warrant.** A search of motor vehicles without a warrant has been sustained in two classes of cases: (1) where probable cause exists to believe that the vehicle contains contraband, (2) where the vehicle has been impounded or subject to forfeiture. Likewise other property which is subject to forfeiture, by statute, may also be searched lawfully without a warrant.

In *Trupiano v. U.S.,* 334 US 699, the Supreme Court has held that where it is practicable to obtain a search warrant, one should be obtained, otherwise, a search without a warrant will be held to be unlawful. However, *Trupiano* was overruled in *U.S. v. Rabinowitz,* 339 US 56. A search warrant is no legal fetish, nor is it "a sine qua non to the reasonableness of a search," nor the sole test for a lawful search without a warrant. *U.S. v. Rabinowitz, supra* at 65. But, *Rabinowitz* has in turn been overruled as to the permissible area of a search incident to a lawful arrest in *Chimel v. California,* 395 US 752.

If the vehicle is searched lawfully as incident to a lawful arrest, contemporaneous therewith as to time and place and truly incident to the arrest (*cf.: Preston v. U.S.,* 376 US 364; *State v. Miller,* 206 A2d 835; *Cooper v. California,* 386 US 58; *People v. Marsh,* 20 NY2d 98), and if the vehicle is under the immediate control of the defendant at the time, the search without a warrant is reasonable. *See also: U.S. v. O'Leary,* 201 F Supp 926.

The cases in this area of searches refer to special knowledge of the officer based on reasonable grounds to believe that the vehicles contained contraband. *U.S. v. Cefaratti,* 202 F2d 13; *People v. Lombardi,* 18 AD2d 177, affd 13 NY2d 1014, 195 NE2d 306; *Carroll v. U.S.,* 267 US 132. Basically, however, the searches are valid as incident to lawful arrest.

Other than these two exceptions, "a search cannot be regarded as an incident to lawful arrest where it is remote from it in time and place." *Preston v. U.S., supra. See also: State v. Miller, supra.*

In *People v. Granese,* 32 AD2d 568, 300 NYS2d 215, after the arrest for traffic infractions, a thorough search of the vehicle was made, and stolen property was found under the front seat. This was a search and, absent a warrant, was unlawful.

The court distinguished *Harris v. U.S.,* 390 US 234, where incriminating evidence was found accidentally when the police opened a door to roll up a window. This did not constitute a search. *See also: Coolidge v. New Hampshire,* 403 US at 469–470.

Looking at an automobile identification number does not constitute an unlawful search and seizure. *U.S. v. Hull,* 437 F2d 1, 4.

§ 291.01. **Probable Cause.** Where a vehicle is suspected of transporting contraband, it may be stopped and searched without a warrant. This is not to say that government agents have the right to stop and search any vehicle travelling on the highway. Such a situation would be intolerable. The right to stop and search must be based on probable cause, that is, upon a belief, reasonably arising out of circumstances known to the arresting officer, that an automobile or other vehicle contains contraband.

The leading case on the subject is *Carroll v. U.S.,* 267 US 132. Carroll was convicted for transporting liquor in an automobile. He attacked the conviction on the ground that the search and seizure of his car violated his rights under the Fourth Amendment. Prior to trial he had unsuccessfully moved to suppress the liquor found in his car.

The search and seizure was made without a warrant by some federal prohibition agents as the car was going westward on the road between Detroit and Grand Rapids.

Three months prior to this search and seizure, one of the agents met the petitioner and some others in an apartment in Grand Rapids, and under an assumed name and occupation told them he wanted to buy three cases of liquor. The price was fixed and Carroll and two others said they would get the liquor in about three-quarters of an hour.

One of these men returned and said they could not get the liquor until the next day. These purported vendors were using an Oldsmobile roadster. However, they did not return the next day.

A month later the prohibition agents saw Carroll and the others in the same car driving toward Detroit, but lost them. Two months later the agents, on routine patrol, met Carroll and the others driving in the same auto, coming from Detroit. They followed, stopped them and searched the car and found the liquor. "The officers were not anticipating that the defendants would be coming through on the highway at that particular time, but when they met them there they believed they were carrying liquor; and hence the search, seizure and arrest." *Carroll v. U.S.,* 267 US at 136.

In holding that the search and seizure without a warrant was lawful, the Supreme Court said:

> "The intent of Congress to make a distinction between the necesssity for a search warrant in the searching of private dwellings and in that of automobiles and other road vehicles is the enforcement of the Prohibition Act is thus clearly established by the legislative history of the Stanley Amendment. Is such a distinction consistent with the Fourth Amendment? We think that it is. The Fourth Amendment does not denounce all searches or seizures, but only such as are unreasonable." *Carroll, supra,* 267 US at 147.

The court then reviewed some of the leading search and seizure cases: *Boyd v. U.S.,* 116 US 616; *Weeks v. U.S.,* 232 U.S. 383; *Silverthorne Lumber Company v. U.S.,* 251 US 385; *Gouled v. U.S.,* 255 US 298; and *Amos v. U.S.,* 255 US 313, and noted, that unlike *Carroll,* "In none of the cases cited is there any ruling as to the validity under the Fourth Amendment of a seizure without a warrant of contraband goods in the course of transportation and subject to forfeiture or destruction." *Carroll, supra,* 267 US at 149.

> "On reason and authority the true rule is that if the search and seizure without a warrant are made upon probable cause, that is, upon a belief, reasonably arising out of circumstances known to the seizing officer, that an automobile or other vehicle contains that which by law is subject to seizure and destruction, the search and seizure are vaild. The Fourth Amendment is to be construed

in the light of what was deemed an unreasonable search and seizure when it was adopted, and in a manner which will conserve public interests as well as the interests and rights of individual citizens.

. . . .

"We have made a somewhat extended reference to these [specific] statutes to show that the guaranty of freedom from unreasonable searches and seizures by the Fourth Amendment has been construed, practically since the beginning of the Government, as recognizing a necessary difference between a search of a store, dwelling house or other structure in respect of which a proper official warrant readily may be obtained, and a search of a ship, motor boat, wagon or automobile, for contraband goods, where it is not practicable to secure a warrant because the vehicle can be quickly moved out of the locality or jurisdiction in which the warrant must be sought." *Carroll, supra,* 267 US at 149, 153.

The court then concluded that contraband goods concealed and illegally transported in an automobile or other vehicle may be searched for without a warrant under certain circumstances, *i.e.,* where probable cause is shown to exist for such a search. Where such probable cause exists, the government should have the opportunity "to make the investigation necessary to trace reasonably suspected contraband goods and to seize them." *Carroll, supra,* 267 US at 156.

Such probable cause was demonstrated in this case by the following facts: (1) the petitioner was observed by revenue agents on a road frequently used by bootleggers for the illegal transportation of liquor near Detroit, located on the Canadian border; (2) that this area was one of the most active centers for introducing liquor into this country; (3) they knew or had convincing evidence to make them believe that the Carroll boys were bootleggers; (4) they were in company of others who had offered to sell liquor to the revenue agents and were seen in the same automobile when the offer was made; (5) they were seen coming from the Detroit area when the agents were on routine patrol; (6) they had been observed in the same car driving on the same road several times before. Under these facts the court concluded:

> "In the light of these authorities, and what is shown by this record, it is clear the officers here had justification for the search and seizure. This is to say that the facts and circumstances within their knowledge and of which they had reasonably trustworthy information were sufficient in themselves to warrant a man of reasonable caution in the belief that intoxicating liquors were being transported in the automobile which they stopped and searched." *Carroll, supra,* 267 US at 162.

*Carroll* was decided in 1925. In 1949 the court, in *Brinegar v. U.S.,* 338 US 160, another "bootlegger" case, adhered to the *Carroll* rule. In *Brinegar* the court further defined probable cause.

"In dealing with probable cause, however, as the very name implies, we deal with probabilities. These are not technical; they are the factual and practical considerations of every-day life on which reasonable and prudent men, not legal technicians, act." 338 US at 175.

While *Carroll* involved transporting liquor based on the federal prohibition statutes which authorized searches of vehicles without a warrant, *Brinegar* involved transporting liquor from a "wet" state, Missouri, to a "dry" state, Oklahoma, also in violation of a federal statute.

Citing *Carroll,* the court sustained the warrantless search in *Brinegar,* based on probable cause. Probable cause was held to have been established because one of the agents had arrested Brinegar five months prior for illegally transporting liquor; Brinegar had a reputation as a "bootlegger"; Brinegar's car at the time in question was heavily laden; the car was on a road going toward Oklahoma; Brinegar, on a previous occasion was seen loading liquor into his car in Joplin, Missouri, a rum-running center.

It is interesting to note Mr. Justice Jackson's dissent in *Brinegar.* He would permit warrantless searches only in serious crimes—non-sumptuary offenses. *Brinegar* at 180, 183; *cf. Sibron v. New York,* 392 US 40.

In cases involving the transportation of obscene material in vehicles, a different rule prevails as to the existence of probable cause. This is by virtue of the First Amendment which protects freedom of expression. That freedom includes the right of the public to view non-obscene material. *Butler v. Michigan,* 352 US 380. It is also based on the rule that it is for the court alone to decide what is obscene. *Jacobellis v. Ohio,* 378 US 184; *U.S. v. I Am Curious-Yellow,* 404 F2d 196. If the police were to make that determination, it would make them censors of the community. *Marcus v. Search Warrant,* 367 US 717.

Accordingly, a warrantless search of a car based on the belief that the vehicle contained obscene material absent evidence to that effect, supplied by someone in a position to know, is an unreasonable search. *U.S. v. Peisner,* 311 F2d 94. In *Peisner,* the police halted his automobile after receiving information from the FBI that the defendant was contemplating shipping obscene literature across state lines. The FBI had Peisner under surveillance for some time and also had copies of obscene literature which they had obtained from his premises some five months previously. Obviously they had ample opportunity to obtain a search warrant. Accordingly when a state trooper stopped Peisner's car and saw packages and cartons wrapped in brown paper, as well as some loose books inside, no probable cause existed to search the vehicle without a warrant. There was no showing by anyone in a position to know who could state with reasonable certainty (*e.g.,* prior judicial scrutiny) that the packages and books contained obscene material. Mere suspicion or even belief is insufficient to validate such a search and seizure.

On the other hand, where a car on a turnpike contained hardcore pornographic publications, the seizure was sustained in *State v. Bongiorno,* 103 NJ Super, 515, 247 A2d 893.

In *Bongiorno,* a state trooper stopped defendant's car on the turnpike because it was "riding low." In order to convince the trooper that he was a legitimate businessman, he showed the trooper copies of some "art" magazines that he had in the car. The trooper thought they were hardcore and showed them to the police chief, who agreed with him. The arrest and subsequent seizure without a warrant were sustained. Ordinarily, judicial scrutiny is required prior to seizure and arrest for obscene material. *Marcus v. Search Warrant,* 367 US 717. And it is to be noted that hardcore pornography is obscene by any standard. *Womack v. U.S.,* 294 F2d 204, cert. den. 365 US 859. However, since the trooper was dealing with a moving vehicle, the arrest, search and seizure were held to be valid.

Whether *Chimel,* 385 US 752, and *Vale,* 399 US 30, are applicable to cases involving moving vehicles is moot. *Katz v. U.S.,* 389 US 347, 357, stated "that searches conducted outside the judicial process, without prior judicial approval by judge or magistrate, are *per se* unreasonable under the Fourth Amendment—subject only to a few specifically established and well-delineated exceptions." A search of a vehicle, the court noted, is one of those exceptions. *See, e.g., Carroll v. U.S.,* 267 US 132; *Brinegar v. U.S.,* 338 US 160; *Cooper v. California,* 386 US 58.

Both *People v. Daily,* 321 P2d 469, and *U.S. v. Cefaratti,* 202 F2d 13, involved motor vehicles. *Daily* involved the arrest of a doctor charged with abortion and conspiracy to commit abortion. He was arrested in the apartment of the woman to be aborted and his car, parked some 60 feet away from the woman's house, was searched without a warrant and abortion instruments and medicines were found in the trunk of the car.

*Cefaratti* involved a sale of narcotics. No narcotics were found on his person when he was arrested on a public street. However, it was reasonable to suppose under those facts that the narcotics to be sold would be found in his taxicab, parked a few streets away.

Both searches and seizures, without warrants, were sustained undoubtedly under the theory, enunciated in *Carroll,* and *Brinegar, supra,* that the evidence could readily be spirited away.

Not all searches of a motor vehicle without a warrant not conducted contemporaneously with the arrest of a defendant for a specific crime are unlawful. Such searches are lawful where there is a reasonable belief that the search will produce the fruits, instrumentalities, contraband or evidence of the crime. *People v. Lewis,* 26 NY2d 547, 552; *Chambers v. Maro-*

*ney,* 399 US 42; *Carroll v. U.S.,* 267 US 132; *cf. Preston v. U.S.,* 376 US 364.

This rule has been extended in a robbery case, *People v. Brown,* 28 NY2d 282, 270 NE2d 302, where the court sustained a search of a vehicle not based on defendant's arrest but based on its finding that there was probable cause to make the search independent of the fact of the defendant's arrest. The victim had described the assailant and the car he used in committing the robbery. Shortly thereafter, a police officer observed the defendant driving the car and his description and that of the car matched the information previously communicated to the police. After the defendant's arrest, and at a later time the car was thoroughly searched at the police station where personal property belonging to another victim of a previously committed robbery was discovered in the trunk of the car. It is these latter items which the defendant sought to have suppressed. The court held that where probable cause for searching the car arose from the facts relating to the second robbery, that did not bar the use of evidence relating to the first robbery uncovered in the course of a properly initiated search. In addition, the court stated that the limitations of time and place that related to the search of vehicles incident to a lawful arrest (*Preston v. U.S.,* 376 US 364) did not apply in these circumstances. The court sustained the search of the vehicle, at a later time and after the accused had been arrested, where there was probable cause to search the vehicle itself.

**§ 291.02. Vehicles Seized as Evidence of a Crime.** Although in *Harris v. U.S.,* 390 US 234, the Supreme Court did not reach the issue as to whether a vehicle seized as evidence of or as an instrumentality of a crime may be searched without a warrant, there is authority for such a warrantless search. And this is true even though there is no applicable forfeiture statute. *Abrams v. State,* 223 Ga 216, 154 SE2d 443; *State v. McCoy,* 437 P2d 734; *People v. Chapman,* 67 Cal Rptr 601. Logic commends such authority. *Harris* involved the police seizure of a car to be used as evidence in a robbery case after it had been removed to the police station for tagging. Harris was already in custody. (*Discussed, § 289, supra.*)

*See also: § 293, infra.*

§ 291.03. **Stolen Car.** The driver of a stolen car, *e.g.*, the thief, has no standing to complain of a warrantless search. A person in wrongful possession of property is not an "aggrieved party." *Jones v. U.S.*, 362 US 257, does not hold to the contrary. *Kaufman v. U.S.*, 323 F Supp 623, 628.

§ 291.04. **Consent.** The owner of an automobile, premises or other property, may consent to a search and a third party may not object even where the search discloses property for possession of which the third party is subsequently prosecuted. *People v. Lane,* 10 NY2d 347, 179 NE2d 339; *People v. Kortwright,* 236 NYS2d 385; *People v. Angevine,* 47 Miscd 374, 262 NYS2d 784.

Consent to a search freely given by one in authority destroys any claim of illegal search and seizure. *Amos v. U.S.*, 255 US 313.

> "It has consistently been held that consent to a search may be operably given by a person other than the defendant, if that person occupies the premises or vehicle searched or has possession of the property seized, and the evidence thus obtained is admissible against the defendant (*People* v. *Matthews,* 21 AD2d 883; *People* v. *Kortwright,* 236 N.Y.S.2d 385)." *People v. Mosley,* 26 AD2d 668, 669, 272 NYS2d 493.

This rule applies where a car, registered in a wife's name, was searched on consent of her husband. The wife had been indicted for grand larceny and the alleged fruits of that crime ($20,000) were found in the automobile. In denying the motion to suppress this evidence, the court held that even though the car was registered in the wife's name, it had been bought with her husband's money; each of them drove the car; each of them had keys to the car; each had an operator's license; and each had half of the registration certificate, and thus they owned and possessed the car jointly. Under these circumstances, the husband had the power to consent to a search of the family car. Furthermore, the court said, "the certificate of registration is not conclusive proof of title but presumptive evidence of ownership. (*Paglia v. State of New York,* 278 App. Div. 281, affd. 303 N.Y. 821.)" *People v. Sapienza,* 51 Misc2d

786, 789, 274 NYS2d 32, 35. *See also: People v. Helmus,* 50 Misc2d 47.

The immunity from unreasonable search and seizure is a personal one. *People v. Mosley,* 26 AD2d 668, 272 NYS2d 493. *See also: People v. Lane,* 10 NY2d 347, 179 NE2d 339; *cf.: People v. Coffey,* 12 NY2d 443, 191 NE2d 263; *U.S. ex rel Coffey v. Fay,* 344 F2d 625.

In view of this rule it has been held that where the owner of an automobile had voluntarily consented to a search of his automobile in which a firearm was found, the firearm would be admissible against the co-defendants who were passengers in his car.

> "The immunity from unreasonable search and seizure being personal, one cannot object to the searching of another's premises or property if the latter consents to the search, even though property is found, for the possession of which defendant is subsequently prosecuted." *People v. Mosley,* 26 AD2d 668, 669.

§ 292. **Blood Tests.** Many states have statutes providing that a person operating a motor vehicle is deemed to have consented to certain chemical tests when he is charged with driving while intoxicated. *Kyhl v. Commonwealth,* 135 SE2d 768; *Breithaupt v. Abram,* 352 US 432.

For example, New York has a similar statute (Vehicle and Traffic Law, § 1194, (1)). It provides, in part, that the operator of a motor vehicle shall be deemed to have consented to a chemical test of his breath, blood, urine or saliva for the purpose of determining the alcoholic content of his blood, provided the test is administered at the direction of a police officer having reasonable grounds to believe that the person was operating a motor vehicle in an intoxicated condition, or while his ability to do so was impaired by alcohol.

Implicit in this statute is the requirement that the defendant shall have been arrested for drunken driving or driving while impaired, and that the arrest was based on probable cause. *People v. Young,* 42 Misc2d 540, 248 NYS2d 287.

Thus, where a jury found a defendant guilty of driving while intoxicated, the determination carried with it a finding that the arrest was lawful. Accordingly, the defendant was deemed to have consented to the taking of the blood sample. *People v. Biester,* 24 AD2d 1021, 266 NYS2d 46; *cf. People v. Young, supra,* and cases cited.

As noted above in § 248.04, the U.S. Supreme Court, in *Schmerber v. California,* 384 US 757, has sustained the lawfulness of forcible taking of a blood sample as a search incident to lawful arrest. It also held that it did not constitute compulsory self-incrimination, nor violate due process. *See: Breithaupt v. Abram,* 352 US 432.

It is reversible error to permit testimony that the defendant refused to take a drunkometer test. *People v. Paddock,* 29 NY2d 504; *People v. Stratton,* 286 AD 323, affd 1 NY2d 664, 133 NE2d 516; *cf. Schmerber v. California,* 384 US 757.

**§ 292.01. Drunkometer Tests.** Where a defendant is refused his constitutional right to consultation with an attorney before submitting to a drunkometer test, his conviction will be reversed and the drunkometer reading excluded. But, this right to consult with counsel may not be used as an excuse to delay and thus vitiate a meaningful drunkometer reading. In *People v. Gursey,* 22 NY2d 224, 228, 239 NE2d 351, the defendant wanted to consult by telephone with a particular attorney. He sought no delay. Granting his request would not have interfered substantially with the effectiveness of a drunkometer test. Denial of his request violated his right of access to counsel.

In *People v. Fogerty,* 18 NY2d 664, 666, 219 NE2d 801, defendant agreed to submit to a chemical test for intoxication. Thereafter, his attorney learned that there were no rules or regulations on file with the Department of State governing the tests. Accordingly, he argued that the results of the test must be suppressed. The court held that the failure to file rules governing the tests did not affect the admissibility of the test results if found to be intrinsically accurate and reliable.

**§ 293. Impounded Vehicles.** By statute, certain property, especially vehicles, are subject to forfeiture, when used in connection with the commission of a crime. These statutes authorize actions *in rem* against the vehicle and the vehicles may be impounded.

When impounded under these circumstances, a search of the vehicle by an officer, without a warrant, is lawful. *Lockett v. U.S.*, 390 F2d 168; *One Chevrolet etc. v. Commonwealth,* 158 SE2d 755; *U.S. v. Lewis,* 303 F Supp 1394; *U.S. v. Francolino,* 367 F2d 1013, cert. den. 386 US 960; 49 USC § 782.

A stolen vehicle may be impounded when recovered by the police. Certainly as the "fruits" of a crime, it could be searched lawfully without a warrant. Impounding a stolen vehicle would normally be done to hold it for the lawful owner. *U.S. v. Graham,* 391 F2d 439; *Kaufman v. U.S.*, 323 F Supp 623.

Property found in a car may also be impounded to safeguard it for its lawful owner and for its use as evidence against the would-be thieves. *People v. Manzi,* 21 AD2d 57; *People v. Sullivan,* 29 NY2d 69; *Kaufman v. U.S., supra.*

In *Manzi, supra,* some police officers observed three men peering into parked cars. One of them was then observed kicking in the door window of a parked station wagon and then, leaning into the car, he began to examine certain property in the back of the vehicle. The police immediately arrested these three, examined the interior of the car and discovered two brass stands on wheels, a case of liquor, two portable TV sets and some canned foods. A uniformed police officer was left to guard the vehicle with instructions to tell the owner to call for his property at the police station. One of the arresting officers, a detective, testified that the property was then removed to the police station "to safeguard it, to use as evidence against the three men who were charged with attempted grand larceny, and to insure that the owner would be available as complainant in court the next day." The owner of the vehicle appeared early that morning, and it was disclosed that the property in question had been stolen by him and some others. A motion to suppress was denied by the trial court.

In sustaining this decision, the Appellate Division said:

> "Since the police were privileged to remove the articles from the vehicle, now unsecured, in order to safeguard them both for the owner and for use as evidence against

the would-be thieves, there was no illegal search and seizure.

"The described activity of the police constitutes no trespass or illegal invasion of privacy. The vehicle had become unsecured and the articles now physically as well as visually exposed to still another attempted theft. Failure to protect the property would have subjected the police to ridicule, and properly so. They should and did act to safeguard the articles for their owner, whoever that might be. . . . [P]olicemen . . . are expected to protect property as well as the citizenry. . . ." *Manzi, supra,* 21 AD2d at 58, 59.

Where there is probable cause to believe that an automobile was subject to seizure and forfeiture as a carrier of contraband, it may be lawfully searched even though the owner or driver is not present at the time of the search. In *U.S. v. Lewis,* 303 F Supp 1394, the defendants were observed using the automobile under circumstances that gave the federal officers probable cause to believe that the vehicle was being used in narcotics traffic. Accordingly, it was subject to seizure and forfeiture, and a search was lawful. *See:* Contraband Seizure Act, 49 USC § 782; *cf.: Chimel v. California,* 395 US 752; *U.S. v. Francolino,* 367 F2d 1013, cert. den. 386 US 960; *Coolidge v. New Hampshire,* 403 US 443.

Reason would seem to dictate that such a practice would be lawful. *See: Abrams v. State,* 223 Ga 216, 154 SE2d 443.

Forfeiture proceedings, though technically denominated as civil proceedings, are actually quasi-criminal in that, if successful, they effect a penalty. *Boyd v. U.S.,* 116 US 616; *Village of Laurel Hollow v. Laverne,* 17 NY2d 900, 901, 218 NE2d 703.

In such cases the protection of the Fourth Amendment exclusionary rule is applicable. Thus, the forfeiture action, if instituted, will be unsuccessful if it has been tainted by an unlawful search and seizure, even though the vehicle has been used for an illegal purpose. *One 1958 Plymouth v. Pennsylvania,* 380 US 693; *Berkowitz v. U.S.,* 340 F2d 168.

In *Cooper v. California,* 386 US 58, Cooper's car was seized by the police when he was arrested in it on a charge of trafficking in narcotics. His vehicle was not searched until one week later, and without a warrant. Under California law, the vehicle was subject to seizure pending a forfeiture proceeding (Cal. Health and Safety Code, § 11610 [West 1964]). Accordingly, narcotics found in the car during this search without a warrant were lawfully seized. The vehicle was lawfully impounded and thus it was not necessary for the police to obtain a search warrant. *Cf. Preston v. U.S.,* 376 US 364, where Preston's car was searched, without a warrant, after he had been arrested on a vagrancy charge.

**§ 294. Traffic Violations as Pretext to Search.** A traffic offense may not be used as a pretext to justify a search for evidence of a different offense or crime. *U.S. v. Lefkowitz,* 285 US 452; *Taglavore v. U.S.,* 291 F2d 262; *U.S. v. Tate,* 209 F Supp 762; *People v. Sapp,* 43 Misc2d 81, 249 NYS2d 1020; *cf.: People v. Isaac,* 38 Misc2d 1018; *People v. Marsh,* 20 NY2d 98, 288 NE2d 783.

As the court pointed out in *People v. James,* 46 Misc2d 138, there must be a causal relationship between the traffic offense and the search. In *James,* a vehicle was found illegally parked in the same location for two days. This in and of itself authorized the police officer to tag it for the parking violation, but nothing more. There was no right to search it. The search, which followed, disclosed a gun and the motion to suppress was granted. The People argued that the presence of the automobile in the same location, for a period of two days, constitutes an abandonment. The court rejected this argument. Even if the vehicle had been actually abandoned, such a "motor vehicle does not have the same sanctity as a defendant's dwelling house in the constitutional field of 'search and seizure.' *People v. Harper,* 26 Ill. 2d 85." *Cf. People v. Sullivan,* 29 NY2d 69.

The search must be related to the crime, unless the search is made for a weapon that could be used to escape or for some other unlawful purpose. *Agnello v. U.S.,* 269 US 70; *People v. Sapp,* 43 Misc2d 81, 249 NYS2d 1020; *People v. Beaman,* 44 Misc2d 336, 253 NYS2d 674. *See also: U.S. v. Nygard,* 324 F Supp 864, where search of defendant's car was made after police received information that defendant was armed and enroute to kill his father.

Thus, following an arrest for a traffic violation (leaving the scene of an accident), the vehicle was searched for the registration certificate. A credit card and gas sales slip were found. The search was unlawful as the traffic violation was found to be a pretext to conduct a general search. *U.S. v. Lefkowitz,* 285 US 452. The motion to suppress was granted.

The following are types of cases involving minor traffic offenses used as an excuse to unlawfully search an automobile without a warrant: taxi double parked, *People v. Blodgett,* 46 Cal2d 114, 293 P2d 57; passing a stop sign, *People v. Zeigler,* 100 NW2d 456; passing a stop sign, *Burley v. State,* 59 So2d 744; one headlight burning, *People v. Gonzalez,* 356 Mich 247, 97 NW2d 16.

**§ 294.01. Traffic Violations as Authority to Arrest.** Other violations of traffic regulations may constitute cause for arrest, and searches incident thereto. *People v. Scianno,* 20 AD2d 919; *People v. Isaac,* 38 Misc2d 1018, 239 NYS2d 624; *cf. People v. Marsh,* 20 NY2d 98, 228 NE2d 783. Taking New York statutes as an example, the following is to be noted:

Failure to register a motor vehicle constitutes a traffic infraction under certain circumstances. Vehicle and Traffic Law § 401(1) (18).

Failure to produce a certificate of registration for the vehicle is presumptive evidence of operating an unregistered motor vehicle. V.T.L., § 401(1).

A search of an automobile on mere suspicion, absent a warrant, is impermissible. *U.S. v. O'Connell,* 43 F2d 1005; *People v. Jordan,* 37 Misc2d 33.

Operating a motor vehicle without being licensed is a traffic infraction. V.T.L., § 501(10).

Failure of the operator to produce an operator's license on demand is presumptive evidence that he is not duly licensed. V.T.L., § 501(1e),(4a).

The police are authorized to stop a motor vehicle in order to check the driver's operator's license and certificate of registration. *People v. Battle,* 12 NY2d 866, 187 NE2d 793.

This authority does not carry with it the right, in and of itself, to search the defendant's automobile. *U.S. v. Murray,* 51 F2d 516; *People v. Jordan, supra; People v. Hoffman,* 24 AD2d 497.

§ 294.02. **Illegally Parked Vehicles.** In *People v. Sullivan* 57 Misc2d 208, 292 NYS2d 37, revd 29 NY2d 69, defendant's automobile was towed to a police auto pound for illegal parking in a 'towaway" zone. There, his car was searched and a loaded hand gun was found. He moved to dismiss his indictment on the ground that the grand jury had received "illegal evidence," seized during an illegal search of the automobile. The lower court in dismissing the indictment, (reversed in the Court of Appeals, 29 NY2d 69) held that when the police impound a vehicle for violation of any traffic ordinance, they may *not* search the vehicle without a warrant, under the guise of "inventory regulation," which violates the owner's rights under the Fourth Amendment. This rule, the court held, does not preclude seizure of contraband in open view in the vehicle or a search where the vehicle is seized as evidence of a crime and is forfeit. *See also: Cooper v. California,* 386 US 58; *People v. Jordan, supra; cf.: People v. Manzi,* 21 AD2d 57, 248 NYS2d 306; *People v. James,* 46 Misc2d 138; *People v. Marsh,* 20 NY2d 98, 100–102, 228 NE2d 783. The "open view" doctrine of *Harris v. U.S., supra,* is not applicable here.

Note the distinction in *People v. Manzi, supra,* where certain articles were removed from a motor vehicle after the window of the car had been kicked in by three men who explored its interior. The police had removed these articles subsequently proved to have been stolen by the owner of the car. The police had no search warrant but the Appellate Division held that the articles were not seized from Manzi but were lawfully being safeguarded in the possession of the police. The police, the court said, "are expected to protect property."

*See also: § 290, supra.*

§ 294.03. **Traffic Violations—Exceptions.** In *People v. Marsh,* 20 NY2d 98, 101, 228 NE2d 783, the court struck down a search made incident to an arrest on a warrant for failure to answer a summons for a traffic infraction. There the court held that there are no "fruits or implements" of traffic infractions.

*People v. Marsh* was reaffirmed in *People v. Coleman,* 24 NY2d 1005, 250 NE2d 237. Coleman was arrested for hitchhiking on the public highway—a traffic infraction. Unless the officer is in danger of assault or has probable cause for belief that the defendant is committing a crime, a search is unauthorized.

The same reasoning was sustained in *People v. Phinney,* 22 NY2d 288, 239 NE2d 515, where the court also indicated that a minor traffic infraction "is not a crime" and that most of the constitutional safeguards afforded criminal defendants are not applicable to such a minor offense. It may be, however, that in traffic cases involving serious consequences, including a loss of an operator's license and a fine, that the rule may be modified. However, the court did not reach that question in *Phinney.*

**§ 295. Self-Incrimination: Accident Reports.** All states require that the operator of a motor vehicle involved in an accident which results in personal injury or property damage must identify himself to the victim or to a police officer who may be present at the scene. If this is not possible, the operator of the vehicle must identify himself as soon as physically able to a police or judicial officer. This rule applies regardless of fault and failure to do so is a misdemeanor. Violation of this statute may also entail revocation or suspension of the drivers license and vehicle registration.

In such a California hit-and-run case, *California v. Byers,* 71 Cal2d 1039, 458 P2d 465, 402 US 424, the defendant asserted that this statute infringed on his Fifth Amendment privilege against self-incrimination. Four United States Supreme Court Justices held there is no constitutional right to refuse to file an income tax or to flee the scene of an accident in order to avoid the possibility of legal involvement. 402 US at 427–428.

Byers's claim was rejected by the Supreme Court when Mr. Justice Harlan also voted to reject Byers's contention, albeit for different reasons. Harlan stated that the hit-and-run statute can be enforced only if the state does not use the information so obtained from the operator of the vehicle in connection with any criminal proceedings.

Thus, the Supreme Court, in this closely divided case, refused to strike down state laws requiring the driver of a car involved in an accident to stop and identify himself. *California v. Byers, supra. See also: State v. Sawyer,* 230 A2d 781, a pre-*Byers* case.

**§ 296. Licensing and Registration.** Most states have regulations requiring that operators of vehicles be licensed and that motor vehicles be registered. In New York, as well as in other jurisdictions, a police officer may stop a motor vehicle to check the certificate of registration and license of the operator. *People v. Russo,* 38 Misc2d 957.

If, while doing so, he observes a crime being committed in his presence or has reasonable grounds for so believing, he may make an arrest. In *People v. Russo, supra,* the officer, while stopping the vehicle to check its registration certificate and the operator's license, observed a sawed-off shotgun on the car seat. This did not constitute a search. The presence of the driver in the car gave the officer probable cause to believe that the vehicle's operator was in possession of that weapon. The arrest which followed was lawful.

In *Lipton v. U.S.,* 348 F2d 591, a California officer stopped a minor who was driving an automobile with out-of-state license plates, for the sole purpose of ascertaining whether he was a licensed operator. The young man was unable to produce a license. The court held that this constituted probable cause to arrest the minor for driving without a license. Upon learning via radio that the car was stolen, it was held that the officer also had probable cause to arrest him on the charge of driving a stolen vehicle.

**§ 297. What Constitutes Operating a Motor Vehicle.** To constitute "operating a motor vehicle," the vehicle need not be moving at the time. Thus, where defendant was behind the steering wheel of a parked truck with the engine not running, and where he admitted being the operator, these facts constituted authorization for the police to ask for the certificate of registration. *People v. Barth,* NYLJ, 4/14/65, p. 18, col. 8.

An admission by the registered owner standing near his vehicle that he was the driver involved in an accident, was held to be a valid admission sufficient to establish, prima facie, the element of "operating a motor vehicle." *People v. Belcher,* 302 NY 529.

Starting the motor constitutes operation of the automobile in a case where the defendant was charged with driving while intoxicated even though the motor stalled before the car actually moved. *People v. Domagala,* 123 Misc 757, 206 NYS 288.

The words "operating a motor vehicle" include not only the motion of a vehicle but also acts which engage the machinery of the vehicle, which alone, or in sequence, will set in motion the motive power of the vehicle. *Flournoy v. State,* 106 Ga App 756, 128 SE2d 528.

Even though there is no direct proof that defendant drove the car, circumstantial evidence may nevertheless establish that fact. Thus, when defendant was "found by the police officers, . . . seated *alone* in a drunken state in his automobile which was *damaged* and halted against a guardrail, while the engine was running," it was sufficient to conclude that he drove the car. *People v. Blake,* 5 NY2d 118, 154 NE2d 390.

It was held in *People v. Klepper,* 25 NY2d 46, 250 NE2d 51, that in a traffic violation case, identity of the offender may be established prima facie by the official entries and contemporaneous memoranda made by the arresting officer. It is not essential that the officer be able to pick out the offender in the courtroom when the case is called for trial. Detailed memoranda of the information contained in the offender's driver's license and automobile registration is valid proof under the circumstances.

**§ 298. Summary.** A motor vehicle enjoys the same constitutional protection under the Fourth Amendment as houses, homes and places of business. However, the ease with which motor vehicles may be moved has resulted in liberalizing the rule governing searches. (*See:* § *285, supra.*)

Minor traffic infractions are not crimes. Therefore, there

can be no truly incident search to an arrest for a traffic infraction without a warrant. (*See: §§ 294–294.03, supra.*)

Where an arrest is made for a crime while defendant is in, or in control of a motor vehicle, a search of the vehicle without a warrant must be contemporaneous in time and area and truly incident to the purpose of the arrest. (*See: § 287, supra.*)

A person may be in control of a motor vehicle without actually being in it. (*See: § 288, supra.*)

A consent to search a vehicle may be given by the owner or person in control. Passengers in the vehicle at the time may not be heard to complain. They have standing to move to suppress if the search and seizure were unlawful and the items seized are sought to be used against them in a criminal prosecution. (*See: § 191.04, supra.*)

In many states, including New York, a licensed motor vehicle operator shall be deemed to have consented in advance to a chemical test of his breath, blood, urine or saliva for the purpose of determining the alcoholic content of his blood when he is arrested for driving while intoxicated. However, it is reversible error to permit testimony that defendant refused to take such test. (*See: §§ 292–292.01, supra.*)

A defendant is entitled to the presence of his attorney when a drunkometer test is administered, providing the request for the aid and presence of counsel is not used as an excuse to delay the test and thus vitiate any meaningful drunkometer reading. (*See: § 292.01, supra.*)

A vehicle, subject to seizure and forfeiture, may be searched without a warrant. (*See: § 291, supra.*)

But a traffic infraction charge may not be used as an excuse to search. (*See: § 294, supra.*)

Motor vehicles may be stopped by the police for the purpose of checking the registration and the operator's license. Contraband, in open view, observed in the vehicle at the time, may be seized without a warrant. (*See: § 296, supra.*)

Looking into an automobile by natural or artificial light and observing its contents does not constitute a search. (*See: § 289, supra.*) An abandoned motor vehicle may be searched.

A "radio run," designated by the police department as an "All Point Bulletin" (APB), is sufficient probable cause for an arrest and incident search without a warrant. And this is true even though the information relayed by the "radio run" proves to be false. (*See: § 291.01, supra.*)

Requiring the operator of a motor vehicle involved in an accident to identify himself, does not violate his privilege against self-incrimination. ( *See: § 295, supra.*)

A motor vehicle impounded for a traffic infraction may be examined by the police. Such examination if it does not deteriorate into a search, does not constitute an unreasonable search under the Fourth Amendment. (*See: § 293, supra.*)

# Chapter 22

# SEARCH AND SEIZURE OF OBSCENE MATERIAL



---

**§ 305. In General.** In the search and seizure area, obscene material enjoys a special status even though it is contraband. *Roth v. U.S.*, 354 US 476. The reasons for this peculiarly favored position are based on the free-speech and free-press provisions of the First Amendment, which have been absorbed into the Fourteenth Amendment's Due Process Clause. *Gitlow v. New York,* 268 US 652; *Fiske v. Kansas,* 274 US 380; *Cantwell v. Connecticut,* 310 US 296; *Beauharnais v. Illinois,* 343 US 250.

**§ 306. Definition of Obscene Material.** Sex and the portrayal of sex are not synonymous with obscenity, "but only material dealing with sex in a manner appealing to prurient interest is obscene." *U.S. v. Peisner,* 311 F2d 94. Nudity is not synonymous with obscenity. *Roth v. U.S., supra; People v. Gonzales,* 107 NYS2d 968.

Whether material is obscene is a question of law. *Jacobellis v. Ohio,* 378 US 184; *U.S. v. I Am Curious-Yellow,* 404 F2d 196; *People v. Noroff,* 63 Cal Rptr 575, 433 P2d 479.

The present accepted test for determining obscenity evolved from *Roth v. U.S., supra,* and is set forth in *Memoirs v. Massachusetts,* 383 US 413. *Roth* fixes the minimum standards a *state* may employ in judging publications to be obscene. *People v. Stabile,* 58 Misc2d 905, 296 NYS2d 815.

*Memoirs v. Massachusetts, supra,* holds that a work is obscene if three elements coalesce: (1) the dominant theme of the material taken as a whole appeals to prurient interest in sex; (2) the material is patently offensive because it affronts contemporary community standards relating to the description or representation of sexual matters; and (3) the material is "utterly without redeeming social value." 383 US at 418.

This test was amended by three cases. In *Ginzburg v. U.S.,* 383 US 463, the Court held that when objective examination of the material fails to establish obscenity, the Court may examine into the publisher's intent and consider the advertising material issued in connection with the material. If the publisher attempted by the advertising to "titilate" the sexual interests of the public, it may accept his advertising at face value and declare the publication obscene. This is known as the "pandering" test.

In *Mishkin v. New York,* 383 US 502, the Court held that a publication aimed at deviant sexual groups is obscene if it appeals to the prurient interest of those groups.

In *Redrup v. New York,* 386 US 767, the Court further amended the *Memoirs* rule by holding that material is obscene if it is hardcore pornography, and in borderline cases it may be proscribed if it is sold to minors in violation of some local statute, or if it is foisted upon an unwilling public, or if it is pandered.

Hardcore pornography is material depicting sexual intercourse, sodomy, or masturbation. However, in *Pinkus v. Sheriff,* 429 F2d 416, affd sub nom *California v. Pinkus,* 400 US 922, by an equally divided court, Mr. Justice Douglas abstaining, involving a "stag" motion picture in which a naked woman feigned masturbation, the circuit court noted at p. 417, "In the state court trial, the prosecution introduced no persuasive testimony that the material was offensive to contemporary notions of free expression." In *U.S. v. 35* MM. *Motion Picture Film,* 432 F2d 705, fn.2 at 707, the court held that the overall "redeeming social value" test redeemed the film from the condemnation of obscenity even though it depicted female masturbation and cunnilingus. Such material is held obscene by any standard, absent "social justification or excuse." *People v. G.I. Distributors,* 20 NY2d 104, 228 NE2d 787; *People v.*

*Richmond County News,* 9 NY2d 578, 175 NE2d 681; *People v. Noroff,* 63 Cal Rptr 575, 433 P2d 479; *Womack v. United States,* 294 F2d 204, cert. den. 365 US 859; *U.S. v. Wild,* 422 F2d 34, affd 397 US 98.

The New York and Federal tests for obscenity are identical. *People v. Stabile,* 58 Misc2d 905, 296 NYS2d 815.

In *New York Feed Company v. Leary,* 397 US 98, and in *Milky Way Production v. Leary,* 397 US 98, the United States Supreme Court held that the New York statute which defines obscenity and prohibits its sale, is not unconstitutional.

**§ 307. What the First Amendment Covers.** The First Amendment covers the spoken and written word. Its protection is not limited to published material alone, such as books, newspapers and magazines, but included are drawings, pictures (still and motion pictures), theatrical productions, the dance, phonograph records, the graphic arts and the fine arts. In short, it affords protection to all forms of communication, all means and methods by which someone is attempting to convey some thought or message to someone else. *Joseph Burstyn, Inc. v. Wilson,* 343 US 495; *Winters v. New York,* 333 US 507; *In re Giannini,* 72 Cal Rptr 655, 446 P2d 535; *Jacobellis v. Ohio,* 378 US 184; *Weaver v. Jordan,* 64 Cal2d 235, 49 Cal Rptr 537, 411 P2d 289.

**§ 307.01. Obscene Material Distinguished from Contraband.** Obscene material is contraband and enjoys no special constitutional protection, *i.e.,* it is not protected by the First and Fourteenth Amendments.

However, by virtue of the free speech and free press provisions of the First Amendment, obscene material is not equated with contraband, such as hand guns and narcotics. Accordingly, it may not be seized out-of-hand. The reason for this rule is to protect the right to publish non-obscene material, *Marcus v. Search Warrant,* 367 US 717, and the right of the public to read and view it. The First Amendment protects both rights, the right to publish and the right of the public to have access to published material. *Marcus v. Search Warrant, supra; U.S. v. 18 Packages of Magazines,* 238 F Supp 846;

*Butler v. Michigan,* 352 US 380; *Stanley v. Georgia,* 394 US 557.

Another reason for the rule is to prevent the police from acting as censors, *Marcus v. Search Warrant, supra.*

**§ 308. Search Warrants: Specificity.** Search warrants issued for the seizure of alleged obscene material must be specific. Thus, a warrant authorizing a search of the defendant's home and seizure of property described as obscene photographs, negatives, prints, and equipment used to reproduce any lewd or obscene material, or any and all records used to conduct this type of operation was held to be invalid because the description of the property to be seized was defective in that to much was left to the discretion of the officer to determine what was lewd and obscene. *People v. Rothenberg,* 20 NY2d 35, 228 NE2d 379.

Supplemental oral instructions given to the officer by the issuing magistrate can not save such a warrant, where the instructions were not recorded. *People v. Hughes,* 31 AD2d 235, 237–238. In *Hughes,* the court noted that in such instances it is the better practice for the issuing magistrate to attach to the search warrant copies of the pictures to be seized or to describe them in detail on the record. *See also: Stanford v. Texas,* 379 US 476, 478–479, 485.

In order to prevent a search under a valid warrant from deteriorating into an exploratory or general search—long condemned—courts have vitiated an otherwise lawful search, where books not mentioned in the search warrant have been seized, in addition to those mentioned. In those cases, all of the books have been ordered suppressed, *People v. Kimmel,* 34 Ill2d 579, 217 NE2d 785; *cf. Weeks v. U.S.,* 232 US 383.

**§ 309. Seizure of Obscene Material.** Inasmuch as the First Amendment has been absorbed into the Fourteenth, *Gitlow v. New York,* 268 US 652, the courts have held that the Due Process Clause of the Fourteenth requires that obscene material may not be seized by governmental agents without prior examination by a judicial officer for his determination that the material sought to be seized is obscene. This is a necessary caveat to protect freedom of speech and of the press. The leading case in this area is *Marcus v. Search Warrant,* 367 US 717, which held: "The discretion to seize allegedly obscene materials cannot be confided to law enforcement officials." This is the essence of the "prior judicial scrutiny" rule. *See also: A Quantity of Books v. Kansas,* 378 US 205; *Bantam Books v. Sullivan,* 372 US 58.

There are strong indications that hardcore pornography is an exception to the rule. *Womack v. U.S., supra; Jacobellis v. Ohio, supra,* concurring opinion of Stewart, J. at p. 197; *Ginzburg v. U.S.,* 383 US 463, dissenting opinion, Stewart, J.

Another exception pertains to seizures of alleged obscene materials where the police officer, prior to seizure, has knowledge that the material in question had been judicially found to be obscene. *People v. Matherson,* 16 NY2d 509, 208 NE2d 180; *People v. Reshes,* 39 Misc2d 723.

The better rule seems to be, however, that even in the exceptions noted, prior judicial scrutiny is the safer practice.

As to seizure of obscene material in a motor vehicle based upon probable cause, *see: § 291.01, supra.*

**§ 310. The Incident Search.** The rule of prior judicial scrutiny cannot be evaded by seizure of alleged obscene material as incident to a lawful arrest.

"This result cannot be avoided by the rubric of a search incident to a lawful arrest. . . . [T]he Supreme Court has apparently determined that borderline speech must be protected by the application of relatively elaborate procedures prior to suppression via seizure. Such procedures are impossible to follow in a seizure incident to arrest." *U.S. v. Brown,* 274 F Supp 561, 565. *See also: People v. Peskin,* 16 NY2d 511, 208 NE2d 180; *People v. Kozak,* 56 Misc2d 337; *Von Cleef v. New Jersey,* 395 US 814.

It is to be carefully noted, however, that where obscene materials seized are the very "instrumentalities and evidence of the crime for which appellants were indicted and lawfully arrested," then the seizure is lawful. In *U.S. v. Wild,* 422 F2d 34, which cites *Milky Way Productions v. Leary, supra,* and *New York Feed Company v. Leary, supra,* the defendant was indicted for mailing hardcore pornographic color slides through the mails. He was arrested under a warrant issued based on the indictment. At the time of the arrest and incident thereto, additional slides of the same kind were seized. The seizure was held lawful. These slides were held to be the very "instrumentalities and evidence" of the crime for which he was indicted.

In effect, the United States Supreme Court affirmed *Wild,* by its affirmance in *New York Feed Company v. Leary,* and *Milky Way Productions v. Leary, supra.*

**§ 311. Seizure by United States Customs.** United States Customs officers may seize without a warrant obscene material imported for commercial distribution, 19 USC § 1305(a), provided that a judicial determination as to the obscenity allegation is promptly resolved by a court of competent jurisdiction, *i.e.,* not more than 60 days after the seizure. *U.S. v. Reidel,* 402 US 351. *See also: Freedman v. Maryland,* 380 US 1; *U.S. v. One Book Entitled etc.,* 249 F Supp 911; *U.S. v. Reliable Sales Co.,* 376 F2d 803.

When forfeiture of alleged obscene material is sought by the U.S. Customs, the action is by way of a libel under the Admiralty rules (Title 28 USC). These actions are civil and in rem—not criminal. *U.S. v. One Carton Positive Film,* 247 F Supp 450. The burden of proving obscenity is on Customs (*U.S. v. One Book Entitled etc.,* 249 F Supp 911), by a preponderance of the evidence rule. *U.S. v. One Carton Positive Film,* 247 F Supp 450.

The guidelines in these cases, in testing for obscenity, are the same as those laid down in *Memoirs v. Massachusetts,* 383 US 413. *See also:* 19 USC § 1305.

A libel filed by Customs does not constitute a seizure unless the Court so decides. *U.S. v. One Carton Positive Film, supra.*

**§ 312. Post Office Cases.** Federal statutes prohibit sending obscene material through the mails. 18 USC § 1461. The Federal Government may prohibit the use of the mails for commercial distribution of obscene material. 18 USC § 1461. This ruling made in *U.S. v. Reidel,* 402 US 352, reaffirms the rule in *Roth v. U.S.* 354 US 476, 485, which stated that obscene material is not constitutionally protected.

In *Reidel, supra,* the Court further held that Section 1461 is not unconstitutional as applied to the distribution of obscene materials to willing recipients. Although recognizing that the mere private possession of obscene matter cannot be made a crime (*Stanley v. Georgia,* 394 US 557), the Court declares that *Stanley* "compels no different result" since it "neither overruled nor disturbed the holding in *Roth.*" Stanley's right to have and peruse obscene material in the privacy of his own home, the Court continued, does not protect the seller of such material. Whatever the scope of the "right to receive" referred to in *Stanley,* it is not so broad as to immunize the dealings in obscenity—"dealings that *Roth* held unprotected by the First Amendment." *U.S. v. Reidel, supra,* 354–355. Consequently, the seller, unlike the private citizen who has a right to prohibit unwanted governmental intrusion into the privacy of his home, has no right to do business in obscenity and use the mails in the process in violation of the statute. Congress may constitutionally prevent the mails from being used for distributing pornography.

The Supreme Court does take note of the argument that adults should have complete freedom to possess, deal in, and produce what communicative materials may appeal to them so long as children are not involved or there is no imposition upon unwilling recipients. Such a rule, the Court observed, "may prove to be the desirable and eventual legislative course. But if it is, the task of restructuring the obscenity laws lies with those who pass, repeal, and amend statutes and ordinances. *Roth* and like cases pose no obstacle to such developments." *U.S. v. Reidel, supra* at 357.

Nevertheless, it is doubtful if *Reidel* authorizes the seizure of such material out of hand by postal authorities. A necessary predicate for sustaining such seizures by the Postmaster is a judicial determination that the material in question is obscene. *Glanzman v. Christenberry,* 175 F Supp 485. The Postmaster himself has been given no authority by the Congress to make such a determination. *Hannegan v. Esquire Inc.,* 327 US 146. *See also: Manual Enterprises v. Day,* 370 US 478.

The standards in determining obscenity laid down in *Memoirs v. Massachusetts, supra,* also apply to material sent through the mails. *U.S. v. Davis,* 353 F2d 614; *U.S. v. Klaw,* 350 F2d 155.

However, where the mails were being used to defraud, the action by the Postmaster in barring the material was sustained. *Donaldson v. Read Magazine,* 333 US 178.

*See also: § 249, supra.*

**§ 313. Prior Adversary Proceedings.** In New York, there must be a prior adversary proceeding to obtain an injunction to restrain the sale and distribution of material alleged to be obscene. This is a civil proceeding, in effect, a trial to determine if the suspect material is obscene. A true copy of the matter sought to be enjoined is attached to the moving papers, or, in any event, is presented to the court on the hearing. (*See, e.g.,* N.Y. CPLR § 6330.)

Theatrical productions and motion picture films are not mentioned in the statute. Nevertheless, in cases involving ex parte warrants for the search and seizure of alleged obscene motion picture films, where there was no prior judicial scrutiny of the film, many federal courts have vacated the warrants and voided the searches, in the absence of prior adversary proceedings on the question of the films' obscenity. *208 Cinema, Inc. v. Vergari,* 298 F Supp 1175, affd in part, revd in part; *U.S. v. Marti,* 421 F2d at 1271, cert. den. 397 US 934; *Tyrone, Inc. v. Wilkinson,* 410 F2d 639; *Metzger v. Pearcy,* 393 F2d 202; *Bethview Amusement Corp. v. Cahn,* 416 F2d 410; *Cambist Films v. Illinois,* 292 F Supp 185; *Dombrowski v. Pfister,* 380 US 479.

This does not immunize defendant from criminal prosecution for alleged violation of obscenity statutes even though the seized film is ordered returned to him. He is still required to make the film available to the prosecution for his trial on the criminal charge. *Kingsley Books, Inc. v. Brown,* 354 US 436; *Bethview Amusement Corp. v. Cahn, supra; Tyrone, Inc. v. Wilkinson, supra; cf. Boyd v. U.S.,* 116 US 616.

Additionally, New York State courts, in which criminal proceedings are pending, have declined to order suppression of the seized films.

"It seems clear that the burden of the current decisions

is to give effect to the right of the prosecutor to seize, preserve and introduce the allegedly obscene materials and, at the same time, so limit the seizure that the law enforcement officers cannot, in effect, restrict the dissemination, or promotion, of the materials by means of the seizure." *People v. Hall,* 60 Misc2d 850, 853.

The thrust of the federal decisions, as noted in *People v. Hall, supra,* is to prevent suppression of non-obscene material (*A Quantity of Books v. Kansas,* 378 US 205) and thus avoid the evils of governmental censorship (*Marcus v. Search Warrant,* 367 US 717).

*A Quantity of Books* and *Marcus* involved massive seizures of books under state statutes authorizing warrants for the seizure of obscene material as a first step in civil proceedings seeking their destruction. It is the "massive seizures" that are condemned since they result in suppression in violation of the First Amendment.

The United States Supreme Court in *New York Feed Company v. Leary,* 397 US 98, and in *Milky Way Productions v. Leary* 397 US 98, held that the First Amendment does not require an adversary hearing on the question of obscenity before allegedly obscene material can be seized. However, these two cases involved color slides, not motion picture films and therein may lie the difference.

To seize a motion picture film deprives the public of viewing what may be non-obscene. This would constitute suppression under the First Amendment. *People v. Hall,* 60 Misc2d at 853. To seize color slides, on the other hand, does not constitute a "massive seizure" condemned in *A Quantity of Books,* and *Marcus, supra.*

In *People v. Hall,* 60 Misc2d at 851, the court held that the search warrant issued by the judge who had viewed the film was valid and sufficient to establish "reasonable and probable cause." This language compels the conclusion that a lawful search warrant may issue for a motion picture film based on prior judicial scrutiny, even in the absence of a prior adversary proceeding required in *Tyrone Inc. v. Wilkinson,* 410 F2d 639, and the cases which followed it.

*Hall* was a lower court decision. However, in affirming a motion picture obscenity conviction, the New York Court of

Appeals in *People v. Heller,* 29 NY2d 319, 277 NE2d 651, decided December 1, 1971, came to the same conclusion.

In *Heller,* the motion picture was seized and the defendant arrested under warrant issued by a judge after he had viewed the film at the theater. Appellant argued that the film's seizure was invalid since he was entitled to an adversary proceeding on the question of the film's obscenity before the judge who issued the warrant.

In rejecting this contention, the court sustained the issuance of the warrant based upon the viewing of the film by a judge in a public theater.

As to the more specific question whether this judicial scrutiny should have been followed by an adversary hearing, the court stated:

> "The additional question is whether the scrutiny should have been followed by an adversary hearing. The Supreme Court has not held that; in its most recent comment on the problem suggests it is not moving in that direction (*Lee Art Theatre* v. *Virginia,* 392 U.S. 636 [1968]).
>
> "There a Virginia conviction was reversed on authority of *Marcus* (*supra*). Not only was there no judicial scrutiny in advance, but the policeman's affidavit, used as a basis for the warrant, was both subjective and general. There was an absence of 'any inquiry by the justice of the peace into the factual basis for the officer's conclusions' (p. 637). Of course, that was not enough under *Marcus.*
>
> "But what is of relevancy for the present case is the observation by the Supreme Court that 'we need not decide in this case whether the justice of the peace should have viewed the motion picture before issuing the warrant' (p. 637). This implies that had the Justice done so, as the Judge in the present case did, it would have been sufficient. There is no suggestion that an adversary hearing, an extreme departure from standard American practice on warrants, would also have been required.
>
> "Thus the decisions of the Second Circuit in *Astro Cinema Corp.* v. *Mackell* (422 F.2d 292 [1970]) and *Bethview Amusement Corp.* v. *Cahn* (416 F.2d 410 [1969], cert.

den. 397 U.S. 920), requiring adversary hearings before warrants are issued, go beyond any requirement imposed on State courts by the Supreme Court." 29 NY2d at 322–323.

The logic of the *Heller* opinion, destroys the rationale behind the decisions in *Tyrone, Inc. v. Wilkinson, supra,* and the federal decisions which followed in its wake.

Generally, federal injunctive relief against state prosecutions in this area has been denied. *Studebaker v. Gitlin,* 360 F2d 692, 697; *Carmichael v. Allen,* 267 F Supp 985; *New York Feed Company v. Leary, supra; Milky Way Productions v. Leary, supra.*

**§ 314. Pretrial Motions to Suppress and to Dismiss Criminal Prosecution.** The determination of obscenity is a question of law. Accordingly, material may be attacked pretrial by a motion to dismiss the information or indictment which charges a violation of an obscenity statute. *People v. Noroff,* 63 Cal Rptr 575, 433 P2d 479; *People v. Stabile,* 58 Misc2d 905, 296 NYS2d 815.

Likewise, in a proper case, the courts will entertain a motion to suppress where, as a matter of law, the material is not obscene. *People v. Noroff, supra; People v. Stabile, supra.*

# Chapter 23

## EAVESDROPPING



---

**§ 320. In General.** Today modern sophisticated electronic devices have made it very difficult to detect the eavesdropper. These devices, the wiretap and the electronic "bug" have come to the attention of the courts with increasing frequency particularly in the area of prohibitions of the Fourth Amendment.

Section 605, Title 47, U.S. Code, prohibits wiretapping. Based on the theory that this statute was not one of constitutional dimension, the prohibition had been held for some time not applicable to criminal prosecutions in state courts. *Schwartz v. Texas,* 344 US 199; *Benanti v. U.S.,* 355 US 96; *Nardone v. U.S.,* 302 US 379.

Subsequently, in *Lee v. Florida,* 392 US 378, *Schwartz, supra,* was overruled under the rationale of *Mapp v. Ohio,* 367 US 643. But it was held in *Lee* that the rule was not retroactive.

This decision was superseded three days later by the enactment of the Federal Omnibus Crime Control and Safe Streets Act of 1968 (Pub. L. No. 90–351). This act also supersedes § 605 of Title 47. It reaffirms the common law prohibition against eavesdropping and, with certain exceptions, establishes control over eavesdropping devices, 18 USC §§ 2512–2513, and provides remedies against unlawful eavesdropping, 18 USC § 2520. In effect, it directs the states to follow the same federal procedures in authorizing eavesdropping under state law in order to avoid the constitutional infirmities present in some state statutes. 18 USC §§ 2516(2), 2518. *See, e.g., Berger v. New York,* 388 US 41.

A federal court order permitting wiretapping and "bugging" is authorized when the interception may provide or has provided evidence involving the following offenses: any offense punishable by death, or imprisonment for more than one year under 42 USC §§ 2274–2277 (relating to the enforcement of the Atomic Energy Act of 1954); or under offenses relating to espionage, sabotage, treason, riots; offenses dealing with restrictions on payments and loans to labor organizations; certain offenses involving murder, kidnapping, robbery, or extortion; certain offenses involving bribery of public officials and witnesses, bribery in sporting events, transmission of wagering information, influencing or injuring an officer, juror or witness generally, obstruction of criminal investigations; Presidential assassinations, kidnapping and assault; interference with commerce by threats or violence; interstate and foreign travel or transportation in aid of racketeering enterprises; offer, acceptance or solicitation to influence operations of employee benefit plans; theft from interstate shipment; embezzlement from pension and welfare funds; interstate transportation of stolen property; certain offenses involving counterfeiting; certain offenses involving bankruptcy fraud; offenses dealing with narcotics, marihuana and other dangerous drugs; certain usurious transactions; conspiracy to commit any of the foregoing offenses. 18 USC § 2516(1).

The intercept order must be based on an affidavit establishing probable cause and specificity is required similar to that required in affidavits for a search warrant. The affidavit must detail the offense involved as well as the nature and location of the facilities involved in the intercept requested, a description of the type of communications sought to be intercepted, and the identity of the persons involved, if known. Additionally, the affidavit must contain a statement as to whether or not other investigative procedures have been tried and failed or why they reasonably appear to be unlikely to succeed if tried or to be too dangerous. A time limit for the life of the order must be stated, which cannot exceed 30 days. An extension period may not exceed 30 days. A "return" is also required. The order may be issued *ex parte,* and must be specific as to what intercept is authorized.

Only the Attorney General, or an assistant Attorney General specially designated by the Attorney General, may authorize an application to a Federal judge of competent jurisdiction for an intercept order. Such order may only be executed by the Federal Bureau of Investigation or the Federal Agency having responsibility for the investigation of the offense as to which the application is made. 18 USC § 2516(1). Emergency intercepts are authorized providing application for a court order is made within 48 hours. 18 USC § 2518.

In effect, the federal statute, 18 USC § 2516(2) directs the states to follow the federal statute in state prosecutions for the offenses of murder, kidnapping, gambling, robbery, bribery, extortion or dealing in narcotic drugs, marihuana or other dangerous drugs, or other crimes dangerous to life, limb, or property, and punishable by imprisonment for more than one year, or any conspiracy to commit any of the foregoing offenses.

Only the principal prosecuting officer of any state, or the principal prosecuting officer of any political subdivision thereof may apply to a state judge for a state intercept order. 18 USC § 2516(2).

The rationale behind the enactment of this section is to avoid any conflict between the states and the federal government as to whether or not the offense of eavesdropping has been preempted by the latter, thus precluding the states from enacting legislation in this field. It must be noted, in this regard, that it is usually difficult to determine in advance whether communications sought to be intercepted will be interstate or intrastate. Only the federal government would have jurisdiction over the former.

Any "aggrieved" person may move to suppress the contents of an intercepted communication or evidence derived therefrom on the ground that "(i) the communication was unlawfully intercepted; (ii) the order of authorization or approval under which it was intercepted is insufficient on its face; or (iii) the interception was not made in conformity with the order of authorization or approval." 18 USC § 2518(10).

The judge issuing or denying an intercept order, shall within 90 days cause to be served on the parties named therein an inventory of the history of the order or its denial including a statement as to whether or not communications were intercepted. 18 USC § 2518(8). A copy of material intercepted must be served on each party not less than ten days before trial, hearing or proceeding, otherwise the material may not be received in evidence. 18 USC 2518(9). Evidence obtained by wiretapping or "bugging" in violation of the provisions of the Federal Omnibus Crime Control and Safe Streets Act are inadmissible in evidence. 18 USC § 2515.

Basically the federal and New York intercept statutes are the same. They are both based on the rule that the Fourth Amendment extends not only to persons, papers, houses and effects, but also to verbal evidence. *Hoffa v. U.S.*, 385 US 293. *Also see:* N.Y. CPL art. 700.

The principal difference between the two statutes lies in the types and number of offenses in which intercept warrants may be issued. Whereas the federal statute, 18 USC § 2516, as noted above, limits interception to certain specified offenses, the New York statute is much broader. Under the New York Criminal Procedure Law, intercept warrants may be authorized in most malum per se felony and conspiracy cases, and additionally in cases involving gambling, narcotics, weapons, bribery, prostitution and eavesdropping.

§ 321. **Methods Employed in Eavesdropping.** Eavesdropping is accomplished with the naked ear as well as by sophisticated electronic devices and the more commonly used method of simply cutting into a telephone wire or the use of an induction coil. All of these methods have come to the attention of various courts.

§ 321.01. **Naked Ear.** It is, unfortunately, common to overhear the conversation of others. Such casual acts can hardly come within the category of eavesdropping. But where the act is deliberate and is perpetrated by government agents in an area "wherever an individual may harbor a reasonable 'expectation of privacy' . . . , he is entitled to be free from unreasonable governmental intrusion." *Terry v. Ohio,* 392 US 1, 9; *see also: Katz v. U.S.,* 389 US 347.

*Katz* was a "bugging" case. It raised questions involving curtilage among others. Thus, if a police officer put his ear to a closed door leading to a private office or apartment, and in this manner overheard conversations pertaining to the commission of a crime, his act under *Katz* might constitute an invasion of privacy vitiating the arrest. *Wong Sun v. U.S.,* 371 US 471; *People v. Rodriguez,* 11 NY2d 279, 286, 183 NE2d 651. On the other hand, if the overheard conversations were in a voice loud enough to be heard outside of the closed door and without putting an ear to the door, there would be no "expectation of privacy" and no violation of the rule in *Katz. See: Lopez v. U.S.,* 373 US 427; *U.S. v. Llanes,* 398 F2d 880. Thus, when a person knowingly exposes his activities to public view and hearing, he is not entitled to have those activities protected against search and seizure.

In *Ponce v. Craven,* 409 F2d 621, police, summoned by a motel manager, arrived and made observations of a man and woman through their open bathroom window. The police could clearly see into the motel unit as well as understand the conversation. They made their observations from the motel parking area and obtained entry into the motel unit by a ruse. Both occupants were arrested and convicted for the illegal possession of narcotics.

Rejecting the argument that the police were trespassers, the Circuit Court held that, unlike a home owner or tenant (*see: Stoner v. California,* 376 US 483), a motel transient does not have exclusive use of the area, as he must share corridors, sidewalks, yards, parking lots, and trees with other occupants. The parking lot from which the police made their observations was an area in which defendants, at best, had a "shared property" right, with others, including the police. Observing what was in plain sight (*Harris v. U.S.,* 390 US 234) and listening in on the conversation were not violative of any "right to privacy" under these facts.

Similarly, the New York Courts held that a "wired" informer who, by means of a radio device concealed on his person, transmitted contemporaneously to the police incriminating conversations with the defendant, did not violate the law. The court noted that the eavesdropping statute expressly exempted all conversations overheard with consent of "a party to" or "of at least one party" to the conversation. *People v. Gibson,* 23 NY2d 618, 246 NE2d 349. *See also: Lopez v. U.S.,* 373 US 427; *cf.: Katz v. U.S.,* 389 US 347; *U.S. v. Hoffa,* 436 F2d 1243; *U.S. v. Hoffa,* 437 F2d 11.

It is apparent that the "invasion of privacy" rule in *Katz* requires a close study and reevaluation of its import and meaning as measured against the provisions of the Fourth Amendment. *Cf. Lopez v. U.S.,* 373 US 427.

### § 321.02. Mechanical and Electronic Devices.

(1) *Alligator Clip.* This is a device clipped to a telephone wire, which, in effect, becomes a telephone extension when attached to a listening device. No signal is emitted to indicate its presence. The use of alligator clips does not involve the interception of a telephone message within the purview of 47 USC § 605. *Rathbun v. U.S.,* 355 US 107. Conversations overheard by use of that device, with the consent of one of the persons to the conversations, would not be rendered inadmissible. *See:* 18 USC § 2511(2)(a),(d).

However, the Pennsylvania Supreme Court has held that a telephone extension is a "device for overhearing" a telephone conversation within the purview of the statute. Thus, where a detective testified to communications that he overheard by use of an extension telephone in his office with the consent of one of the parties to the conversation, there was no violation of the Pennsylvania statute. However, had this been an *interception* on consent of only one of the parties, a different result would obtain under the Pennsylvania statute. *Commonwealth v. Murray,* 206 Pa Super 298, 213 A2d 162. The use of the alligator clips would not seem to be affected by either *Katz* or *Kaiser, infra.*

(2) *Pen Register.* The pen register is a device which merely records the telephone number dialed by the sender's telephone. It does not overhear or record any conversations. Some federal courts have condemned its use, holding that the fruits of its use are inadmissible. *U.S. v. Gugliemo,* 245 F Supp 534,

affd 371 F2d 176; *U.S. v. Dote,* 371 F2d 176; *U.S. v. Caplan,* 255 F Supp 805, 808.

However, local and federal courts in the New York area have held to the contrary. In *People v. Green,* 63 Misc2d 435, the court held that the use of a pen register, installed by the telephone company at the request of a subscriber harassed by telephone calls, was lawful, and a motion to suppress information as to the source of the telephone calls was denied.

In arriving at this conclusion, the court held that the consent of the receiver of the telephone calls to the recordation of the calls logged on the pen register, absent a court order, "did not constitute an unlawful 'interception' of the calls placed to him." *People v. Green, supra* at 438, citing *Rathbun v. U.S.,* 355 US 107. The court also noted that the United States Court of Appeals (2d Circuit) approved the logic of the *Rathbun* case in *U.S. v. Kaufer,* 406 F2d 550 when it "reasoned that 'each party to a telephone conversation * * * may allow another to overhear the conversation'." *People v. Green, supra* at 438 citing *U.S. v. Kaufer,* 406 F2d 550. To this effect the court also cited *Harmon v. Commonwealth,* 209 Va 574, 166 SE2d 232, as follows:

> " 'In the case before us * * * the pen register was attached * * * with the knowledge and consent of * * * the intended recipient of the calls. If, under the *Rathbun* case the listening by a third party to a telephone conversation with the consent of one of the parties to the conversation, was not an interception of communication forbidden by the statute, then surely the showing made with the consent of Miss Reed, the intended recipient of the messages, that certain calls had been made from the telephone of the defendant to her telephone was not a violation of the federal statute'." *People v. Green, supra* at 438, citing *Harmon v. Commonwealth, supra. See also: People v. Schneider,* 45 Misc2d 680, 257 NYS2d 876; *cf.: Katz v. U.S.,* 389 US 347; *People v. Kaiser,* 21 NY2d 86, 233 NE2d 818, affd 394 US 280, rhrg den 394 US 1025.

(3) *Electronic Eavesdropping.* Prior to *Katz v. U.S.,* 389 US 347, evidence obtained by eavesdropping (bugging), which

involved a physical trespass on the bugged premises, was held to be illegally obtained. *Clinton v. Virginia,* 377 US 158; *Silverman v. U.S.,* 365 US 505.

For example, *Clinton v. Virginia, supra,* involved a "spike" mike which was driven through a party wall to pick up conversations in an adjoining room. In *Silverman,* an electronic device was intruded to connect with a metal duct in an adjoining room. These physical intrusions were deemed to be trespasses rendering the conversations overheard illegal evidence and inadmissible.

On the other hand, the use of an electronic device affixed to a party wall, without intrusion and which acted as a stethoscope, by which conversations were overheard, was held to be legal eavesdropping and evidence so obtained was admissible. *Goldman v. U.S.,* 316 US 129; *cf. On Lee v. U.S.,* 343 US 747.

The theory behind these decisions was that the Fourth Amendment's ban against unreasonable searches and seizures related to physical intrusion into constitutionally protected areas, such as one's home or place of business.

In *Katz v. U.S., supra,* this theory was abandoned. The *Katz* case involved the bugging of a public telephone booth which federal agents had probable cause to believe was being used in gambling activities. The "bug" was placed on top of the phone booth and only the caller's conversation was recorded. There was no physical intrusion or trespass into the phone booth itself.

Undoubtedly influenced by the development of highly refined electronic eavesdropping devices (the "mike" in the martini olive, for example), which enables one to overhear private conversations without trespass, the court held in *Katz* that the Fourth Amendment protects people, not places. "[W]hat he [Katz] sought to exclude when he entered the booth was not the intruding eye—it was the uninvited ear." Equating the use of a phone booth, where the toll has been paid, with one's home, office or taxi, the Court said that the caller, "is surely entitled to assume that the words he utters into the mouthpiece will not be broadcast to the world." The fact that the phone used by Katz was a public phone for use by anyone, was irrelevant under this new theory. "To read the

Constitution more narrowly is to ignore the vital role that the public telephone has come to play in private communication." *Katz* at 352.

(4) *Other Electronic Devices.* Devices such as miniphones, wire recorders and Fargo devices are used primarily to corroborate a witness' testimony as to certain conversations or oral statements of the defendant. They are secondary evidence. Even without these devices, the witness may testify as to the oral statements made. *See: On Lee v. U.S.,* 343 US 747.

In *Holt v. U.S.,* 404 F2d, 914, the 10th Circuit held that the *Katz* rule does not prohibit the use of an electronic device concealed on an informer to record his conversations with other persons, as approved in *Lopez v. U.S.,* 373 US 427, since his eavesdropping, as in *Lopez,* was merely to corroborate a conversation to which the informer could testify in any event. The introduction of the corroborative testimony, however, will often depend basically on whether the government's witness was exploiting some illegal act of a governmental agent in obtaining the recording. *Wong Sun v. U.S.,* 371 US 471. Violation of the *Wong Sun* rule would render the recorded statements inadmissible.

(5) *The Miniphone.* This is an electronic device used for recording conversations. It is small in size, strapped to a person's body and readily concealed. Evidence obtained by this device is not "wiretap" evidence and has been held admissible in *Benson v. California,* 336 F2d 791 cert. den. 380 US 951, and in *People v. Ryan,* 13 NY2d 1105, 196 NE2d 269. The court held that admissibility of this evidence was not violative of the Fifth or Fourteenth Amendments.

(6) *Wire Recorder.* This is a device similar in use and character to the miniphone. In *Lopez v. U.S.,* 373 US 427, the Court held admissible, conversations recorded on this device in a revenue agent's pocket when he was lawfully on the petitioner's premises.

(7) *Fargo Device.* This is also similar to a wire recorder and miniphone, except that it transmits what it "hears" to a recorder, some distance away. Conversations recorded by this device were held to be admissible. *Todisco v. U.S.,* 298 F2d 208.

The *Lopez* case, *supra,* is a "wired informer" case; the device is also known as a "kel set." The Second and Seventh Circuits have differed as to the admissibility of evidence received and transmitted by these devices.

The Seventh Circuit, in *U.S. v. White,* 405 F2d 838, 843, sitting *en banc,* held that:

> "[T]he surreptitious placing of the kel set on informer Jackson was for all conceptual purposes the same as the surreptitious wiring of the telephone booth in *Katz* [*Katz v. United States,* supra]. Each act was part of the 'bugging' technique by which a conversation was transmitted to an 'uninvited ear'—government agents. The crucial fact in each case is that the respective speakers did not consent to the overhearing of their statements and that the conversations were overheard by third persons uninvited by the speaker."

Also, the court noted that the police failed to follow the example set in *Osborn v. U.S.,* 385 US 323, where a warrant had been issued authorizing the "bugging."

In *White,* the court also stated that *Katz v. U.S., supra,* overruled *On Lee v. U.S.,* 343 US 747.

One week later, the Second Circuit, in *U.S. v. Kaufer,* 406 F2d 550, a case similar to *White, supra,* involving a transmitter-recording device and a telephone extension, came to a contrary decision. The defendant sought to overturn his conviction by virtue of *Katz v. United States, supra.* The court held that *Katz* "has no application to this case." Observing that *Katz* "involved electronic surveillance performed without the knowledge of any of the participants in the intercepted conversations," whereas here the conversation was recorded with the consent of one of the parties to the conversation, a procedure upheld in *Lopez v. U.S.,* 373 US 427. *Lopez,* the court concluded, has not been overruled by *Katz.* Generally speaking, *Katz* holds that: (1) conversations and oral statements are "things" that may be "seized," just as tangibles, within the purview of the Fourth Amendment; (2) the Fourth Amendment's ban against unreasonable searches and seizures is to protect people not places; (3) the Fourth Amendment may be violated by the use of electronic eavesdropping devices without physical intrusion or trespass; (4) eavesdropping is constitutionally acceptable if a lawful warrant issues based on probable cause setting forth precise limits outlined by the court and providing for its "return."

**§ 322. Tape Recordings as Evidence.** Some jurisdictions, notably Pureto Rico, record all oral trial testimony with tape recorders. The efficacy of this practice is doubtful. Often the tape recorder fails to function. In one case, *People v. Ruggiero,* 16 NY2d 550, 208 NE2d 465, a new trial was required.

In another case, *People v. Columbo,* 24 AD2d 505, the tape recordings, untranscribed, were offered as the minutes of the trial and as part of the record on appeal. The court rejected this practice.

Tape recordings are frequently not clear. They must be played back at the same speed (r.p.m.) employed in the original recording.

In *Columbo, supra,* the court made the following suggestions regarding the use of the tape recordings in a trial: (1) transcripts should be prepared and distributed to counsel in advance of trial; and (2) the tapes should be played back in the presence of counsel but in the absence of the jury for the purpose of comparison and to obtain rulings on alleged inadmissible material.

**§ 323. Disclosure by Government of Contents of "Bugged" Conversations.** Where the government admits that a defendant's conversations were overheard by an illegal electronic device, he must be given an opportunity to prove at a hearing before a judge whether any evidence presented against him at his trial was tainted by the use of the illegal bug or tap.

In *Kolod v. U.S.*, 390 US 136, rejecting the policy used by the Department of Justice in this area, that it alone decides what tapes of the "bug" or tap were relevant to the issue, the Court said that *ex parte* determination was unacceptable as a substitute for "such determination in an adversary proceeding in the District Court." Furthermore, this ruling requires that *all* recordings taken by the government must be disclosed and the Court alone would decide whether any evidence used in obtaining petitioner's conviction was tainted by the use of any unlawful eavesdropping. *See also: People v. Miller,* 28 AD2d 1205, 285 NYS2d 495.

Where an intercept order has been approved or an application therefor has been denied, notice thereof must be served on the persons concerned not more than 90 days after the approval or denial, together with a statement as to whether there was an actual intercept. 18 USC § 2518(8)(d)(3).

If a motion is made, the court may permit inspection of the material intercepted. 18 USC § 2518.

In any event, the contents of the intercepted material or evidence derived therefrom shall not be received in evidence or otherwise disclosed in any trial, hearing, or other proceeding in a Federal *or* State court unless each party has been served at least 10 days in advance, with a copy of the material intercepted, the court intercept order and the application upon which it was based. 18 USC § 2518(9).

**§ 324. Disclosure of Witnesses Through Illegal Intercept.** Where the identity of witnesses had been obtained by use of an illegal wiretap, can the causal connection between this information and the People's proof become so attenuated as to dissipate the taint and thus render the evidence admissible?

The court in *People v. Scharfstein,* 52 Misc2d 976, 277 NYS2d 516, 517, 520, was faced with this question in a case of first impression. The defendants were indicted for the crimes of abortion. The names of women aborted were obtained by use of a wiretap order, subsequently held to be invalid. Without being apprised that their identities had been obtained by reason of this invalid wiretap order, the women made statements and testified voluntarily before the grand jury which returned the indictments.

In this circumstance, the court held that the evidence thus obtained was not subject to suppression, since there was no exploitation of the primary taint. In other words, the aborted women were not told, in words or substance, "We got your name from the wiretap, so you had better talk." In effect, these women had been told they had been followed to the doctor's office and that the district attorney wanted to speak to them in connection with an investigation he was conducting (*cf. U.S. v. Tane,* 329 F2d 848, in which the witness refused to make any statements incriminating Tane until the Assistant District Attorney revealed that he had in his possession conversations obtained from an unlawful wiretap).

In reviewing the leading federal cases in this area, the court in *Scharfstein* said:

"Despite general statements to the contrary, not all leads to evidence which come to light because of some antecedent illegal act by law enforcement officials is legally suppressible under the poisonous tree doctrine." (p. 520). If, for instance, causal connection between information obtained through illicit wiretapping and the government's proof becomes so attenuated as to dissipate the taint, the evidence is admissible. *Silverthorne Lumber Co. v. U.S.,* 251 US 385; *Nardone v. U.S.,* 308 US 338; *Nardone v. U.S.,* 302 US 379.

Quoting from *Wong Sun v. U.S.,* 371 US 471, 487, 488, the court in *Scharfstein* noted: "We need not hold that all evidence is 'fruit of the poisonous tree' simply because it would not have come to light but for the illegal action of the police." 277 NYS2d at 522.

For the reasons set forth, the court in *Scharfstein* denied suppression, "Though the intercepted information here was used to learn the identity of the witnesses, the information, in a legal sense, was not 'exploited' for the witnesses [the women aborted] gave their statements and subsequent testimony voluntarily. The wiretaps were not used to coerce them into testifying. Under such circumstances, the testimony of a witness may not be equated with a tangible object.

"It is the same as if by a trespass the police saw a defendant committing a crime in his home, and at the same time saw someone else therein witnessing its commission. Would it be held to be an invasion of the defendant's constitutional rights, warranting a suppression, if the witness were followed and asked and told what he witnessed in the home? The answer seems obvious. The situation here, legally, would seem to be on all fours." 277 NYS2d at 524–525.

In an analagous case, *Smith v. U.S.,* 324 F2d 879, the identity of an eyewitness was disclosed by the defendants themselves while they were being detained illegally in that they were denied prompt arraignment in violation of the *McNabb-Mallory* rule and Fed R Crim P 5(a). Nevertheless, the court allowed the eyewitness' testimony since the connection between the identification and his subsequent testimony was too attenuated.

**§ 325. Attacking the Eavesdropping Order.** In *People v. McDonnell,* 18 NY2d 509, 510, 223 NE2d 785, a defendant was charged with bookmaking and conspiracy by conspiring with one Urbinati and his wife to use their telephone as an answering service for bookmaking in Nassau County. Although the phone was not listed in the defendant's name, it would follow that the phone was actually being used and maintained for his benefit, if the charges against him were true. Accordingly, it was held that he had "standing" to question the validity of the wiretap order for Urbinati's telephone. *See: Jones v. U.S.,* 362 US 257.

*See also: § 320, supra,* and *§ 326, infra.*

**§ 326. Motion to Suppress Evidence Obtained by Unlawful Electronic Surveillance.** In cases involving eavesdropping, the burden is on the defendant to establish that an intercept was in existence. The burden then shifts to the government to prove that the evidence proffered was not tainted by the tap. *U.S. v. Agueci,* 310 F2d 817, cert. den. 372 US 959; *U.S. v. Casanova,* 213 F Supp 654.

There is some authority for the proposition that not only has the defendant the burden in the first instance of proving the existence of a wire-tap, but that he also has the burden of establishing that the evidence offered against him was tainted by the tap. *U.S. v. Weinberg,* 108 F Supp 567.

In *Alderman v. U.S.,* 394 US 165, the Court reviewed the rules as to who has standing to move to suppress evidence obtained by means of alleged unlawful eavesdropping (electronic surveillance).

The rules enunciated are: (1) Fourth Amendment violations can only be urged by those whose rights were violated by the search itself; (2) these rights cannot be urged by those who are aggrieved solely by the introduction of damaging evidence itself; (3) co-conspirators and co-defendants do not have any special standing to object to the evidence; (4) any petitioner is entitled to the suppression of government evidence originating in electronic surveillance violating *his own* Fourth Amendment right to be free of unreasonable searches and seizures; and (5) violations would occur if the government agents unlawfully overheard conversations of the petitioner himself or conversations occurring on his premises, whether or not he was present or participated in those conversations.

Should it be determined that petitioner had standing to object, the surveillance records should be turned over to him without prior screening by the trial court. *See also: U.S. v. Hoffa,* 436 F2d 1243; *cf. Kolod v. U.S.,* 390 US 136.

Should the government elect not to reveal any facts because of national security, (*Alderman, supra,* involved sending of information to Russia), the dismissal of the case would result.

*Alderman* was remanded to determine if (1) any evidence was illegally obtained by the government, and (2) which of the petitioners has standing to object to its introduction.

Thus, evidence obtained by means of electronic surveillance is now deemed to be evidence obtained by a search and sizure within the ambit of the Fourth Amendment and in this respect is equated with tangibles. *Katz v. U.S.,* 389 US 347; *People v. Grossman,* 45 Misc2d 557, 257 NYS2d 266; revd other grds 27 AD2d 572. This evidence accordingly is subject to a motion to suppress under Fed R Crim P 41(e). *See also:* 18 USC § 2518(10).

An illegal wiretap may be the subject of a civil suit based in tort. Such a wiretap was held to be an intrusion into one's "solitude of seclusion—an invasion of one's right to privacy." Publication of the tapped conversation is not an element of the tort committed, but publication might aggravate the damages suffered. *Fowler v. Southern Bell Tel.,* 343 F2d 150.

*See also: The Motion to Suppress, Chapter 25, infra.*

# Chapter 24

## THE INFORMER



---

§ 332. **Definition.** The generally accepted use of the term "informer" in search and seizure cases is "one who was a witness to a crime, one who was an accomplice to a crime, or one who actually observed the fruits or instrumentalities of a crime in the possession of the accused," and who gave such information to the authorities. *People v. Mitchell,* 30 AD2d 845, 847.

§ 333. **Use of Informers and Constitutional Guarantees.** The use of informers is not violative of a defendant's rights under the Fourth Amendment guarantee against unreasonable searches and seizures. *Hoffa v. U.S.,* 385 US 293.

In *Hoffa,* a "friend" of Hoffa's turned "state's evidence." The Court stated in that case that the Fourth Amendment was not meant to protect a wrongdoer's misplaced belief in a confidant.

> "Neither this Court, nor any member of it has ever expressed the view that the Fourth Amendment protects a wrongdoer's misplaced belief that a person to whom he voluntarily confides his wrongdoing will not reveal it. Indeed, the Court unanimously rejected that very contention . . . in Lopez v. United States, 373 U.S. 427, 83 S. Ct. 1381, 10 L. Ed.2d 462." 385 US at 302.

The Court also held that Hoffa's rights under the Fifth and Sixth Amendments were not violated by the use of an informer, citing *U.S. v. Dennis,* 183 F2d 201, 224, which said,

> "Courts have countenanced the use of informers from time immemorial; in cases of conspiracy, or in other cases when the crime consists of preparing for another crime, it is usually necessary to rely upon them or upon accomplices because the criminals will almost certainly proceed covertly."

§ 334. **When the Informer Must Be Identified.** Public policy generally forbids the disclosure of an informer's identity. *Scher v. U.S.,* 305 US 251; *Miller v. U.S.,* 273 F2d 279, cert. den. 362 US 928; *Roviaro v. U.S.,* 353 US 53; *People v. Malinsky,* 15 NY2d 86, 255 NYS2d 850, 204 NE2d 188. But there is no hard and fast rule relating to disclosure of identity of an informer. The problem calls for a balancing of the public interest as against a defendant's right to prepare his defense. Where the informer is a mere transmitter of information and is not in any sense a competent witness to the crime itself, and where there is strong and dependable proof of the accuracy of his information, proper balance makes nondisclosure appropriate. *People v. Coffey,* 191 NE2d 263, 12 NY2d 443, 453, citing *People v. McShann,* 50 Cal2d 802. Where the informant's information was tested by independent observations, the informant's name is properly withheld. *People v. Marshall,* 13 NY2d 28, 34.

Carrying the rationale of *People v. Valentine,* 17 NY2d 128, 216 NE2d 321, *People v. White,* 16 NY2d 270, 213 NE2d 438, and *People v. Malinsky, supra,* into the area of the requirement for the disclosure of the informant's name, the New York Court of Appeals has held that there is no need to disclose his identity where a search warrant was obtained based (1) on information supplied by a reliable informant, (2) personal observations of the police officer, or (3) the officer's expertise in the particular crime involved. *People v. Pena,* 18 NY2d 837.

This rule was reaffirmed in *People v. Cerrato,* 24 NY2d 1, where the court held that probable cause for the issuance of the search warrant was established since it was based on information supplied by a reliable informant, and where the officer's independent observations verified the reliability of the informer by a police stake-out. Where "a showing of probable cause did not depend solely upon the officer's testimony of the communications from the avowed informer," disclosure is not required. *Malinsky, supra* at 94.

Disclosure may be called for in order to establish the informer's reliability and the resultant probable cause for the arrest. *Cochran v. U.S.,* 291 F2d 633, 636. *See also: People v. Cerrato, supra.* Where disclosure of the informer's identity or the contents of his communication is relevant and helpful to the defense of the accused, or is essential to a fair trial, the privilege to withhold disclosure must give way. *Roviaro v. U.S.,* 353 US 53; *Miller v. U.S.,* 273 F2d 279, cert. den. 362 US 928; *Wilson v. U.S.,* 59 F2d 390; *People v. Malinsky, supra; People v. Coffey,* 12 NY2d 443, cert. den. 376 US 916.

Where the identity of the informer is essential to the defense as, where this turns upon an officer's good faith, the rule forbidding disclosure will be waived. *Scher v. U.S., supra; People v. Cerrato, supra; People v. Malinsky, supra.*

Where the informer was the sole participant in the transaction charged, the prosecution would be required to disclose his identity unless there was sufficient evidence apart from his confidential communication to establish the legality of a search without a warrant, or an arrest without a warrant. In that instance, the defendant would probably be entitled to a bill of particulars. *Roviaro v. U.S., supra; People v. Pena, supra; cf.: People v. Taylor,* 59 Misc2d 597; *People v. Malinsky, supra.* But a defendant is not entitled to a bill of particulars to determine whether or not an informer was employed, and what dealings, if any, he had with law enforcement officers. *People v. Taylor, supra. See also: People v. Gatti,* 167 Misc 545, 547. Where the informant was not an active participant in the crime, nor was the person with whom the accused dealt, the prosecution need not divulge the informant's identity. *People v. Cerrato, supra.*

*Roviaro v. U.S.,* 353 US 53, has largely been followed in cases where the defense is fraud and entrapment, (*U.S. v. Russ,* dissent Smith, J., 362 F2d 843, 846), but the question arose as to whether it should be followed in instances of alleged mistaken identity. *See: People v. Williams,* 51 Cal2d 355, 359–60; *People v. Lollis,* 177 Cal App2d 665, 669, 2 Cal Reptr 420 (dictum); *cf.: U.S. v. Coke,* 339 F2d 183; *Brady v. Maryland,* 373 US 83, 87; *Rugendorf v. U.S.,* 376 US 528, 534–5; *U.S. ex rel Meers v. Wilkins,* 326 F2d 135.

In *U.S. v. Russ, supra,* the defendant challenged the sufficiency of his identification as the person who allegedly sold narcotics to a government agent named Paschal. Russ did not testify nor did he present any witnesses in his behalf. Nevertheless, he challenged his identification through the cross examination of Paschal and of another witness who was also a government agent. The cross examination disclosed inconsistencies. It was argued that the informer, who it was claimed had introduced Paschal to the defendant, was the only unbiased witness who could bolster defendant's claim that he was not the person who had made the sale. The defendant did not urge that the informer be produced, but did urge the disclosure of his identity so that he could produce him if he wished. This denial of disclosure, defendant asserted, deprived him of a fair trial. The informer played no central role in the transaction. Defendant's challenge was rejected. All the informer did was introduce Paschal to the defendant. The sale took place out of the sight and hearing of the informer, and his role was limited.

In *Roviaro v. U.S.,* 353 US 53, 60–61, the Court said: "Where the disclosure of an informer's identity . . . is relevant and helpful to the defense of an accused, or is essential to a fair determination of a cause, the privilege [to withhold identity] must give way." In *Roviaro,* the Court required disclosure, but in that case, unlike *Russ,* the informer played a central role in the transaction.

As the Court also observed in *Roviaro,* there is no hard and fast rule or doctrinaire approach to the question of disclosure. Each case must turn on its own peculiar circumstances.

In a similar situation, *U.S. v. Coke,* 339 F2d 183, 184, disclosure was not required where the informant was merely a tip-off man. In neither *Russ* nor *Coke* was there any claim of entrapment or fraud, nor did counsel indicate why disclosure of the informant was desired.

On all of the facts in *U.S. v. Russ, supra,* and balancing the government's interest in not revealing the identities of informers and the right of a defendant to a fair trial, the Court held that disclosure was not required. But the Court was careful to point out that this decision "is not to be interpreted as affording the government a basis for smug adherence to nondisclosure in all cases." 362 F2d at 845.

Disclosure was not ordered where the informer told government agents he had seen petitioner's car drive into the garage of a known narcotics dealer in Tiajuana. The petitioner was arrested at the border driving a similar car. Disclosure of his identity would have put his life in danger. *Lamenca v. U.S.*, 381 F2d 993.

It was held in *U.S. v. D'Angiolillo,* 340 F2d 453, that when an informer's testimony may be relevant to the defense, the defendant is entitled to his name and to such information as the government may have concerning his whereabouts and to a reasonable amount of cooperation in securing his appearance. However, the government is not required to call him as a witness, nor guarantee his appearance.

> "[T]he government is not the guarantor of its informant's presence at trial, United States v. Holiday, 319 F.2d 775 (2d Cir. 1963); United States v. Cimino, 321 F.2d 509 (2d Cir. 1963), cert. denied sub nom. D'Ercole v. United States, 375 U.S. 967, 84 S. Ct. 486, 11 L. Ed.2d 416 (1964); Cimino v. United States, 375 U.S. 974, 84 S. Ct. 491, 11 L. Ed.2d 418 (1964); United States v. D'Angiolillo, 340 F.2d 453 (2d Cir.), cert. denied, 380 U.S. 955, 85 S. Ct. 1090, 13 L. Ed.2d 972 (1965); cf., United States v. White, 324 F.2d 814 (2d Cir. 1963), . . . ." *U.S. v. Russ,* 362 F2d 843, 844.

**§ 334.01. Informer as a Witness.** A police informer who testifies against a defendant in a state trial must give his true name and address when requested on cross examination. *Smith v. Illinois,* 390 US 129. The Sixth Amendment bars a state prosecution witness, to whom defendant allegedly sold heroin, from refusing to reveal his real name and address upon cross examination, since an accused has a fundamental right to confront witnesses against him. *Smith v. Illinois, supra,* citing *Pointer v. Texas,* 380 US 400, 407–408.

In *Smith v. Illinois,* it was held that failure to permit the defendant to elicit the true name and address of a government witness "is effectively to emasculate the right of cross-examination itself," and violates the defendant's rights to be confronted with witnesses against him. But, where revealing true identity would endanger the life of the informer, nondisclosure of his true identity may be proper. *See* concurring opinion, White, J., *id* at 133–34; *see also: Lamenca v. U.S.,* 381 F2d 993. Questions which tend merely to harass, annoy or humiliate a witness may go beyond the bounds of proper cross examination. *Smith v. Illinois, supra* at 133.

Where an informer is produced at the trial and refuses to answer any questions about the case, he should be declared a hostile witness if defendant requests it. In *Clingan v. U.S.*, 400 F2d 849, petitioner was on trial for a liquor tax violation and the informer was called as a witness. He refused to answer any questions. The defense asked that he be declared a hostile witness, and the request was denied. This was error. The appellate court ruled that, where substantial doubt exists that the informer is telling the entire story, a defendant is entitled to have him ruled an adverse or hostile witness and to question him as such.

**§ 334.02. Disclosure on Hearing to Test Warrant or Arrest.** In determining whether probable cause existed for the issuance of a warrant or for arrest without a warrant, the disclosure of the informer is not required. *State v. Burnett,* 42 NJ 377, 201 A2d 39; *Miller v. U.S.,* 273 F2d 279, cert. den. 362 US 928; *U.S. ex rel Coffey v. Fay,* 344 F2d 625. *See also: U.S. v. Freeman* 358 F2d 459.

In *U.S. ex rel Coffey v. Fay, supra,* the Second Circuit made a similar ruling, holding that in a state hearing to determine if probable cause existed to arrest a defendant without a warrant, failure to disclose the identity of the informer did not deprive defendant of his right to a fair hearing under the Fourteenth Amendment. *Cf. Jencks v. U.S.,* 353 U.S. 657.

The state is not required to disclose the identity of the

informer in order to afford the defendant an opportunity to make use of information obtained from sources wholly independent of the informer, even though the informer may have provided clues which set the investigation in motion. *U.S. ex rel Coffey v. Fay, supra.*

Where the informant's information had turned out to be accurate as to appellant's selling narcotics activities, and the federal narcotics agents' personal observations gave sufficient confirmation that appellant was selling narcotics, the name of the informers need not be disclosed when the issue is probable cause. *U.S. v. Tucker,* 380 F2d 206. *See also: U.S. v. Shyvers,* 385 F2d 837, 839; *McCray v. Illinois,* 386 US 300.

**§ 334.03. Independent Corroboration.** The Court of Appeals in *People v. Malinsky,* 15 NY2d 86, 255 NYS2d 850, 204 NE2d 188, would permit corroboration of a police officer's testimony by independent proof, other than by disclosure of the informer. Judge Fuld in his opinion cites *People v. Coffey,* 12 NY2d 443, 191 NE2d 263, cert. den. 376 US 916, which involved an informer whose non-disclosure was upheld on the ground that a showing of probable cause did not depend solely upon the officer's testimony of the communications from the avowed informer, but on the presence of strong and reliable proof of the accuracy of the informer's information, which was checked prior to the arrest.

In *Malinsky,* Judge Fuld contrasted those facts with *Coffey.* In effect, he held that corroboration of the police officer's testimony may be effected by independent proof of the informer's existence, his informing and his reliability. Where this proof is made, the informer's identity need not be disclosed. A district attorney's testimony could be the independent corroborative proof of the credibility of the officer if he (the district attorney) could testify that he met the informer who told him what the police officer testified he was told. *People v. Malinsky,* 15 NY2d at 94–95.

On the other hand, a district attorney's testimony that after the defendant's arrest he spoke to the informer, established the informer's existence but not his reliability. For this testimony to have had any probative value, it must have related to a conversation the district attorney had with the informer before the arrest and not after. Additionally interviewing the informer in the presence of the arresting officer is undesirable and ill advised. *People v. Dong,* 47 Misc2d 726, 263 NYS2d 102, affd 50 Misc2d 120.

As in *Coffey, supra,* the United States Supreme Court has held to the same effect in *McCray v. Illinois,* 386 US 300. *McCray* involved an arrest by Illinois state officers. Under Illinois law (and that of other states), the judge presiding at a preliminary hearing may order disclosure of the identity of an informer where an arrest and search were made without a warrant, when the police acted in reliance upon facts supplied by an informer of known reliability. Disclosure is not mandatory but discretionary. This rule of the "informer's privilege" is an evidentiary rule, "a well-established testimonial privilege long familiar in the law of evidence." 8 Wigmore, *Evidence,* § 2374 (McNaughton ed. 1961); *cf.: Roviaro v. U.S.,* 353 US 53; *Rugendorf v. U.S.,* 376 US 528.

At the preliminary suppression hearing, the trial court, on objection by the People, refused to direct disclosure of the identity of the informant whose tip to the police that McCray had narcotics in his possession led to his warrantless arrest and search.

This disclosure, the Supreme Court held, was not required either by the due process clause of the Fourteenth Amendment or by the confrontation clause of the Sixth Amendment. The Court pointed out that in its supervisory role over the federal courts it has been unwilling to impose any absolute rule requiring disclosure of an informer's identity, even in formulating evidentiary rules for criminal trials, particularly where the issue is a preliminary one such as the existence of probable cause and where guilt or innocence is not at stake. It also refused to impose such a rule on the states. *McCray,* 386 US at 311–312. *See also: U.S. ex rel Coffey v. Fay,* 344 F2d 625; *U.S. v. Freeman,* 358 F2d 459; *People v. Coffey,* 12 NY2d 443; *State v. Burnett,* 42 NJ 377, 201 A2d 39.

Following the rationale of *Malinsky,* the court held in *People v. Boniface,* 37 AD2d 728, 323 NYS2d 876, 879, that disclosure of the informer was required where the showing of probable cause depended solely upon the testimony of a law enforcement officer as to the communications received from an avowed informer. In this case the officer on cross-examination refused to answer questions about the names of the prior cases in which the informant's reliability was established. Thus, there was no basis for the validity of the assertion that the informer was credible or reliable. *Cf. U.S. v. Marti,* 321 F Supp 59.

**§ 335. The Informer and Probable Cause.** *Draper v. U.S.,* 358 US 307, is often cited as authority that probable cause may be established if based on information supplied by an informant, who from past experience, the officer had found to be reliable and accurate. Actually, there was more to the probable cause issue in *Draper* than a mere communication by a reliable informer. As the Supreme Court said in *Ker v. California,* 374 US 23, 36:

> "In *Draper v. United States,* 358 U.S. 307 . . . (1959), we held that information from a reliable informer, corroborated by the agents' observations as to the accuracy of the informer's description of the accused and of his presence at a particular place, was sufficient to establish probable cause for an arrest without warrant."

That description was detailed down to the "zippered briefcase" and the defendant's habitual "fast pace" all of which the agent observed before the arrest. It must be borne in mind that in *Draper* the informer was disclosed by name. His existence and reliability were not questioned although he died before the trial.

In any event, *Draper* is as far as the Court has ever gone in finding probable cause. Later cases decided by the Supreme Court pose the question whether the Court would go that far again. Does not the issue of probable cause require some additional personal observations in addition to what "an informant of known reliability" may have conveyed to an officer? Must there not be some showing that the informant who relayed the information was "credible" or that his information was indeed "reliable"? Must there not be more than a detailed description from a tested informant, which leads directly to the defendant? *Aguilar v. Texas,* 378 US 108; *Rugendorf v. U.S.,* 376 US 528; *Wong Sun v. U.S.,* 371 US 471; *cf.: People v. Martin,* 13 NY2d 332; *People v. Santiago,* 13 NY2d 326, 196 NE2d 881.

In *Smith v. U.S.,* 358 F2d 833, 837, a majority held that *Aguilar v. Texas, supra,* did not modify *Draper,* "when we observe that the Supreme Court continues to cite *Draper* without intimating that it has been modified. In light of this we can only conclude that *Aguilar's* 'specific' rules were not intended to exhaust all the possible ways of using hearsay information as part of the basis for probable cause and indeed were not aimed at situations like those in *Draper* and the present case." *But see* dissent by Chief Judge Bazelon, at 838.

In *U.S. v. Pitt,* 382 F2d 322, a case analgous to *Draper,* the following facts were disclosed: A reliable informant told a government agent that a black man accompanied a white man called Topper in a red Plymouth station wagon with a Maryland license plate bound for Washington from New York and carrying a large amount of heroin. The agent knew that Topper (an alias) had been twice convicted for narcotics violations and was suspected of continued narcotics activities. A car fitting this description was stopped by the police in Baltimore. A white man and a black man were in it. A search of the car disclosed narcotics. Citing *Draper,* the court held that probable cause to arrest without a warrant was present. The officer, as in *Rugendorf v. U.S., supra,* was not required to have personal knowledge of all the facts establishing probable cause. This could rest on the collective knowledge of all the officers concerned with the case.

Both *Draper* and *Coffey* have been followed by the United States Supreme Court in *McCray v. Illinois,* 386 US 300. There the Court held a tip by an informant of known reliability, that defendant was on a certain street with narcotics in his possession, gave Illinois police probable cause to arrest and search him without a warrant. *Cf. Beck v. Ohio,* 379 US 89.

In *McCray,* the issue of probable cause arose out of a preliminary suppression hearing at which (1) each officer described with specificity what the informer actually said and why it was thought the information was credible; (2) each officer informed the court of the underlying circumstances from which the informant concluded that the narcotics were where he claimed they were, and some of the underlying circumstances from which the officer concluded that the informant was credible or his information reliable; and (3) there were certain personal observations by the police to the effect that the defendant was seen in an alley with two different persons at separate intervals. Based on the foregoing, a finding that the officers had probable cause to believe that the defendant had committed or was committing a crime in the presence of the officers, was justified. *See also: Brinegar v. U.S.,* 338 US 160, 175–176; *Henry v. U.S.,* 361 US 98, 102; *Beck v. Ohio,* 379 US 89, 91; *People v. Marshall,* 13 NY2d 28, 191 NE2d 798; *People v. Hook,* 15 NY2d 776, 205 NE2d 536; *People v. Santiago,* 13 NY2d 326, 196 NE2d 881.

In this type of preliminary hearing, the court is not dealing with the criminal charge itself. "The Fourth Amendment is served if a judicial mind passes upon the existence of probable cause." *McCray,* 386 US at 307. This, under Illinois and other state laws, occurs when the judge listening to the police officer's testimony decides whether to accept or reject it, just as he does on an ex parte application for a warrant. In both situations, the judge is concerned, not with whether the informant lied, but whether the officer (or affiant, as the case may be) is truthful in relating what he was told by the informant. It is for the court then to decide whether, on the basis of the circumstances related by the officer, probable cause to make the warrantless arrest and search or to issue a warrant has been established. *See also: People v. Solomine,* 18 NY2d 477, 223 NE2d 24; *State v. Burnett,* 42 NJ 377, 201 A2d 39; *Draper v. U.S., supra.* Under these circumstances, there is no violation of the Fourth Amendment.

Following the rationale of *Draper, Coffey,* and *McCray,* it would seem that the accurate description of the defendant, supplied by an anonymous informer, without more, does not of itself establish probable cause to search and arrest a defendant without a warrant.

As all these cases indicate, it is incumbent upon the People to establish that the police had other information, not derived from the informer, sufficient in itself to constitute probable cause. This other information could consist of personal observations by a police officer (*People v. Rogers,* 15 NY2d 422,

208 NE2d 168; *People v. Santiago, supra; People v. White,* 16 NY2d 270, 213 NE2d 438), independent corroboration by others of known reliability as to the information supplied by the informer (*People v. Coffey,* 12 NY2d 443, 191 NE2d 263, cert. den. 376 US 916), observations of fellow officers of the government engaged in a common investigation (*U.S. v. Ventresca,* 380 US 102; *Rugendorf v. U.S.,* 376 US 528), or police broadcasts (*People v. Wilson,* 16 AD2d 207).

> "The controlling principle seems to be that it is not necessary for the officer making the arrest to know of the reliability of the informer or to be, himself, in possession of information sufficient to constitute probable cause provided that he acts upon the direction of or as a result of communication with a superior or brother officer or another police department provided that the department as a whole was in possession of information sufficient to constitute probable cause to make an arrest. This record does not show that any of the law enforcement officers had facts before them sufficient to indicate that this anonymous informer was reliable, or that the police had other information, not derived from the informer, which was sufficient in itself, to constitute probable cause." *People v. Horowitz,* 21 NY2d 55, 60, 286 NYS2d 473, 476–477, 233 NE2d 453. *See also: People v. Wilson, supra.*

It is to be noted that in *Draper* and *McCray, supra,* the informers were reliable informers. In *People v. Taggart,* 20 NY2d 335, 283 NYS2d 1, 229 NE2d 581, the police were faced with an emergency situation—a man with a loaded gun among school children. In *Horowitz, supra,* the contraband involved was stolen bonds and obscene prints—sumptuary offenses.

In New York, disclosure of the identity of an informer is required to sustain a finding of probable cause, where the legality of a search without a warrant is in issue and the communications of an informer are claimed to establish probable cause, unless there is sufficient evidence apart from his confidential communication. *Roviaro v. U.S.,* 353 US 53, 61. *See also: People v. Malinsky,* 15 NY2d 86, 92, 255 NYS2d 850, 204 NE2d 188.

Where a hotel manager informed the police that defendant

had paid his hotel bill with a stolen credit card, probable cause to enter defendant's room without a warrant and to arrest him under Mississippi law was found to exist. *U.S. v. Lowery,* 436 F2d 1171.

In certain situations the fact that an informer is unknown is not controlling. In *U.S. v. Sullivan,* 321 F Supp 597, the police received an anonymous telephone tip that the defendant who was wanted in connection with an armed bank robbery could be found at a specified address. The defendant's picture had been taken in the bank by a hidden camera. It had been published in the newspapers and the police knew his name and address. When they called at the address they recognized the defendant from the photo and arrested him. Probable cause to make this arrest without a warrant was present the court held, because (1) the police knew of the bank robbery, and (2) they had a photo of the defendant taken at the scene from which they could recognize him.

Where the record discloses no probable cause to arrest without a warrant except for information conveyed by an informer, disclosure of his identity will be required. Otherwise, probable cause may be established on the acceptance of a police officer's testimony that he obtained a communication from a reliable, unnamed informer. Failure to produce an informer would deprive the defendant of any opportunity to rebut the police officer's crucial testimony. The defendant, in such a situation, would be unable to prove that the informer did not in fact exist, or that, if he did exist, the police knew him to be unreliable, or that the information he gave to the police was different from that testified to. *People v. Malinsky, supra; cf.: State v. Burnett,* 42 NJ 377, 201 A2d 39; *U.S. ex rel Coffey v. Fay,* 344 F2d 625.

**§ 335.01. Search Warrants.** *Aguilar v. Texas,* 378 US 108, involved a search warrant based on police officers' affidavit in support of a warrant application in which they stated they had received reliable information from a credible person and believed that heroin and other narcotics were being kept at the described premises.

The affidavit was silent as to further information concerning the undisclosed informant or the reliability of his information.

In vacating the warrant, the court stated that an affidavit for a search warrant may indeed be based on hearsay and need not reflect the personal observations of the affiant. However, in such a situation, the magistrate issuing the warrant must be informed of the underlying circumstances relied on by the informant from which the affiant concludes that the undisclosed informant was creditable or that his information was reliable. *See also: Giordenello v. U.S.,* 357 US 480; *U.S. v. Harris,* 403 US 573.

In *Rugendorf v. U.S.,* 376 US 528, a search warrant was issued based on an affidavit which was factually inaccurate in two respects and which was also based in part on hearsay statements of a confidential informant of known reliability. The Court held the warrant valid because there was a substantial basis for crediting the hearsay. The Court ruled that hearsay, if it provides sufficient evidence of probable cause, justifies the issuance of a search warrant. *Jones v. U.S.,* 362 US 257.

*Rugendorf* involved stolen furs of considerable value. The "reliable informant" said he saw furs of a certain type and number in petitioner's basement. An F.B.I. agent told the affiant that certain furs of the same general description and number had been stolen in Alabama. A check of records disclosed that the only robbery in the United States involving furs of the same number and description were those stolen in Alabama. The furs were reported stolen in February. The informant told the affiant about them in March of the same year. In effect, the Court held that probable cause was established in spite of the hearsay information, where there was a substantial basis, as here, for crediting the hearsay.

*Wong Sun v. U.S.,* 371 US 471, did not involve a search warrant, but an arrest without a warrant bottomed on alleged probable cause, and an informant. The Court held that the informant was too untested, and that his information was too vague. Although the informant in *Wong Sun* gave the name of the seller of the narcotics involved, the police were not given an address where he could be found. All they were told was that the seller had a laundry on a street thirty blocks long. The police picked out one laundry on that street, entered it by a ruse and at a time when they did not have sufficient evidence to enter any premises or arrest and search any individual. The Court ruled that the basis for an arrest without a warrant could not be any less stringent than the basis for an arrest with a warrant. To hold otherwise would make it more expedient for the police to make warrantless arrests. Flight in this case did not constitute evidence of probable cause. *Cf.: People v. Jackson,* 23 AD2d 635, 257 NYS2d 72; *People v. Yazum,* 13 NY2d 302, 196 NE2d 263.

§ 336. **The Informer and Exigent Circumstances.** Although, as a general rule, information obtained from an anonymous informant of unknown reliability, without more, is no valid basis for an arrest, search or frisk by the police, exigent or emergency circumstances may be present to justify police action.

In *People v. Taggart,* 20 NY2d 335, 283 NYS2d 1, 229 NE2d 581, an anonymous informant telephoned the police that a persons answering Taggart's description was on a certain street with a loaded revolver in his left hand coat pocket. A detective saw the defendant at the named street standing among a group of children. He placed defendant against a wall, put his hand in the left hand pocket, and took out a loaded revolver. The detective had not noticed any bulge in the pocket. "For the police to have ignored the information received is not an acceptable thesis, despite the anonymity and, therefore, the undetermined reliability of the source."

> "The point is that the Constitution forbids 'unreasonable' searches and what is reasonable is determined by the circumstances and the exigencies are not to be ignored (see *Camara, v. Municipal Ct.,* 387 U.S. 523, 538–539)."
>
> . . . .
>
> "It is recognized, however, that using anonymous information as a basis for intrusive police action is highly dangerous. To limit its use to exigent circumstances the police action must relate to matters gravely affecting personal or public safety or irreparable harm to property of extraordinary value. As noted earlier, it should not extend to all contraband or criminal violations." *Taggart,* 20 NY2d at 340, 343.

This is not the rule in cases associated with the enforcement of sumptuary laws, such as gambling, and laws of limited public consequences as narcotics violations, prostitution, larcenies of the ordinary kind and the like. Since the credibility of the officers, in anonymous tip cases, should be carefully scrutinized, the police should be required to make contemporaneous or reasonably prompt detailed records of any such communications which should be subject to inspection and examination on a suppression hearing on the issue of credibility. *People v. Taggart,* 20 NY2d at 243.

In *People v. Arthur,* 24 NY2d 688, 301 NYS2d 614, 249 NE2d 462, a passerby told a police officer that defendant had a pistol. Some bar patrons told him that a man answering defendant's description "had discharged a pistol or firecrackers." Another passerby told the officer that the defendant had a pistol. All of these informants were unconnected with each other. Defendant was apprehended and a pistol was found on his belt. In affirming the conviction the court observed: "Of course, the absence of the patrolman's informants makes it impossible to verify the fact that there were such informants or that they gave the information ascribed to them. But it would be requiring the impossible that in all street encounters, however brief and evanescent, the police officer must obtain documentation or witnesses to verify his every act. . . . [T]his case does not present the same problem as that considered in *People* v. *Malinsky* (15 NY2d 86) in which the otherwise unsupported testimony of a police officer depended upon an unnamed confidential informant whose identity the police were unwilling to disclose, an unwillingness not present in this case. Generally, the rules as to undisclosed confidential informants involve different and special considerations and applications (see *McCray* v. *Illinois,* 386 U.S. 300; *People* v. *Coffey,* 12 NY2d 443, cert. den. 376 U.S. 916). The further difference in this case is that the aggregate of coincidental information given by the two passersby and the bar patrons constituted a circumstantial basis, providing probable cause and about which the police officer could testify from his own knowledge and be cross-examined." Both the officer and defendant knew the bar patron informers by first and nicknames, although neither could obtain their presence at the trial. *People v. Arthur,* 24 NY2d at 692–693.

**§ 337. "Tested" Informers.** For the purpose of establishing probable cause for the issuance of a search warrant based in part on information supplied by an informant, the reliability or credibility of the informant should not be established by the sole fact that he supplied information to the officer on a prior occasion which led to the arrest of another. The past information must have resulted in arrest and conviction. *People v. Burnham,* 30 AD2d 813.

Where a "tested" informant is relied on, his reliability is in effect endorsed by the officer who uses him. In assisting the court in its evaluation of the worth of this informant, certain inquiries are pertinent.

1. Is he a paid informant?
2. Does the officer know his real name, address, marital status, occupation and criminal record, if any?
3. Does the officer know where the informant can be contacted; where and under what circumstances does he establish this contact; is it by accident or by appointment; how was contact established in the case on trial?
4. How often has the officer seen the informant over a given period of time?
5. If the informant is paid, how much is he paid, and does the officer keep a record of these payments, and has he submitted vouchers to the police department for reimbursement?
6. In what specific cases has the informant supplied information to the police officers, and the dates of the trials of those cases?

**§ 337.01. "Untested" Informers.** Information received from a reliable informer, which is corroborated by the personal observations of the police as to the accuracy of the informer's description of the accused and of his presence at a particular place, is sufficient to establish probable cause for an arrest without a warrant. This is the reliable informer rule. *Draper v. U.S.,* 358 US 307.

Untested informers may be used providing their information can be substantiated by a reasonable standard of testing against other known facts. *People v. Santiago,* 13 NY2d 326, 196 NE2d 881; *People v. Marshall,* 13 NY2d 28, 191 NE2d 798; *People v. Chiagles,* 237 NY 193.

Although an informer may be untested and unreliable in a technical sense in that the police have never used his services, the story he relates may be credible. Technical rules cannot be applied in determining reasonableness or unreasonableness. The total circumstances of the case must be examined in determining if probable cause exists. *State v. Miller,* 47 NJ 273, 220 A2d 409; *People v. Denerstein,* 26 AD2d 334, 274 NYS2d 473.

"Substantiation of information can come either from the informer's own character and reputation or from objective checking of the tale he tells." *People v. Coffey,* 12 NY2d 443, 191 NE2d 263; *Rodgers v. U.S.,* 267 F2d 79.

Statements made by an informer against his own penal interests, even by an untested informant, may be considered as one factor as a basis for the accuracy of the information he gives, since such an assertion is not likely to be deliberately false or heedlessly incorrect. *U.S. ex rel Coffey v. Fay,* 344 F2d 625; 5 Wigmore, *Evidence,* § 1457, pp. 262–3, (3rd ed. 1940).

Flight may constitute some evidence of probable cause. *People v. Yazum,* 13 NY2d 302, 196 NE2d 263.

Personal observations by the police and knowledge of the suspect's reputation may constitute substantiation of the informer's information. *People v. Martin,* 13 NY2d 332; *People v. Santiago,* 13 NY2d 326, 196 NE2d 881; *People v. Teams,* 20 AD2d 803, 248 NYS2d 477.

Known facts may result from the personal observations of the officer. *People v. Santiago, supra; People v. Martin, supra.*

Police broadcasts may constitute sufficient probable cause. *People v. Wilson,* 16 AD2d 207.

*See also: U.S. ex rel Wilson v. LaVallee,* 367 F2d 351, habeas corpus denied; and *People v. Horowitz,* 27 AD2d 367, 279 NYS2d 536, dissent by Stevens, J., remitted and determination withheld, 21 NY2d 55. The facts in *Horowitz* differ materially from those in *People v. Wilson, supra. Horowitz* is analagous to a "hearsay upon hearsay" situation. The dissent in *Horowitz* was in effect sustained by remitting the case back to the trial court for a further hearing on the motion to suppress.

Observations of fellow officers of the government engaged in a common investigation are a reliable basis upon which probable cause can be founded. *U.S. v. Ventresca,* 380 US 102; *Rugendorf v. U.S.,* 376 US 528; *People v. Rogers,* 15 NY2d 422, 208 NE2d 168.

Vague and general information given by an untested informant may not be used as an excuse to commit a trespass even though probable cause might be thus obtained. *Wong Sun v. U.S.,* 371 US 471.

The basic test to be applied in determining the existence of probable cause is whether, at the point of arrest, a prudent man would be warranted in believing that the offense has been committed or that there is reasonable ground for belief of guilt. *Henry v. U.S.,* 361 US 98; *Brinegar v. U.S.,* 338 US 160; *People v. Dong,* 47 Misc2d 726, affd 50 Misc2d 120; *also see: U.S. v. Harris,* 403 US 573.

**§ 337.02. Undercover Informers.** In *Osborn v. U.S.,* 385 US 323, Osborn, a lawyer, was convicted for attempting to bribe a member of a jury panel in a prospective federal criminal trial. An informer, under a federal court order, recorded a conversation with the attorney as the court desired verification of the charge that the attorney was attempting to bribe jurors in the pending case (*Hoffa v. U.S.,* 385 US 293). There could hardly be a clearer example of "the procedure of antecedent justification before a magistrate that is central to the Fourth Amendment," as "a precondition of lawful electronic surveillance." *Osborn,* 385 US at 330. The Court held that Hoffa was not denied his rights under *Miranda v. Arizona,* 384 US 436, or *Massiah v. U.S.,* 377 US 201, or *Escobedo v. Illinois,* 378 US 478, by the government's failure to arrest him after having compiled sufficient evidence, since there is no constitutional right to be arrested. 385 US at 303–304, 310.

In *Lewis v. U.S.,* 385 US 206, the Court ruled that the Fourth Amendment was not violated when a federal narcotics agent, by misrepresenting his identity and stating his willingness to purchase narcotics, was invited into petitioner's home where a narcotics transaction was consummated and the narcotics were thereafter introduced at petitioner's criminal trial over his objection. The Court noted that at no time did the agent see, hear, or take anything that was not contemplated, and in fact, intended by the defendant as a necessary part of his illegal narcotics business.

# Chapter 25

## THE MOTION TO SUPPRESS



---

**§ 342. In General.** An aggrieved person may move to suppress evidence obtained by an unlawful search and seizure in violation of the Fourth Amendment, *Mapp v. Ohio,* 367 US 643; evidence obtained by means of unlawful eavesdropping, *Berger v. New York,* 388 US 41; coerced admissions or confessions or statements obtained in violation of the *Miranda* warnings, *Miranda v. Arizona,* 384 US 436; *Jackson v. Denno,* 378 US 368; *People v. Huntley,* 15 NY2d 72, 255 NYS2d 838, 204 NE2d 179; evidence whose source is tainted as "fruit of the poisoned tree," *Wong Sun v. U.S.,* 371 US 471; and tainted in-court identification, *Wade v. U.S.,* 388 US 219; *Gilbert v. U.S.,* 388 US 263; *People v. Ballot,* 20 NY2d 600, 286 NYS2d 1, 233 NE2d 103.

**§ 343. The Federal Rule.** The Federal Rules of Criminal Procedure contain no provision for a motion to controvert a warrant. Where the warrant suffers from the proscribed infirmities or where certain evidence sought to be introduced in a criminal case is alleged to have been unlawfully obtained, the remedy in the federal courts is to suppress under Rule 41(e), and for a return of the property.

Rule 41(e) reads: "A person aggrieved by an unlawful search and seizure may move the [appropriate] district court . . . for the return of the property and to suppress for the use as evidence anything so obtained on the ground (1) the property was illegally seized without warrant, or (2) the warrant is insufficient on its face, or (3) the property seized is not that described in the warrant, or (4) there was not probable cause for believing the existence of the grounds on which the warrant was issued, or (5) the warrant was illegally executed. . . . If the motion is granted, the property shall be restored unless otherwise subject to lawful detention and it shall not be admissible in evidence at any hearing or trial. . . ."

The mere fact that the defendant denies what the officer alleges as a fact in his supporting affidavit does not require a vacatur of the search warrant. *U.S. v. Nagle,* 34 F2d 952.

Where it was alleged that agents of the Internal Revenue Service unlawfully seized records or information obtained therefrom, a motion to enjoin the agents from instituting any criminal, civil or administrative action against the petitioners based thereon was held premature. The District Court held that such motion might be made when the file is referred to the United States Attorney for presentation to a grand jury. *Plato v. Katzenbach,* 253 F Supp 1021; *cf.: Kohatsu v. U.S.,* 351 F2d 898; *U.S. v. Blue,* 384 US 251. *See also: West v. U.S.,* 359 F2d 50, cert. den. 385 US 867, which held that the introduction of allegedly illegally seized evidence before a federal grand jury does not invalidate the indictment.

A defendant in a criminal prosecution, who claims that his Fourth Amendment rights have been violated by the seizure of certain evidence sought to be introduced against him at his trial, may move to exclude that evidence. Fed R Crim P 41(e); N.Y. CPL art. 710. The exclusion is not automatic. If suppression is desired, it must be sought by motion.

The *Weeks* Exclusionary Rule (*Weeks v. U.S.,* 232 US 383)

which was applicable only to federal prosecutions required that the motion to suppress be "timely," *i.e.,* before trial. In *Gouled v. U.S.,* 255 US 298, the court modified the "timeliness" concept, by permitting the motion to be made during trial where defendant learns for the first time that there appears to have been an unlawful search and seizure.

**§ 343.01. Statute of Limitations.** Title VII, Part B of the Organized Crime Control Act of 1970 (Pub. L. No. 91–452) places a five year statute of limitations on the claim of an aggrieved party against whom evidence is sought to be introduced which it is claimed was the result of a "primary taint."

18 USC § 3504 states in part:

> "(2) disclosure of information for a determination of evidence is inadmissible because it is the primary product of an unlawful act occurring prior to June 19, 1968, or because it was obtained by the exploitation of an unlawful act occurring prior to June 19, 1968, shall not be required unless such information may be relevant to a pending claim of such inadmissibility; and
>
> "(3) no claim shall be considered that evidence of an event is inadmissible on the ground that such evidence was obtained by the exploitation of an unlawful act occurring prior to June 19, 1968, if such event occurred more than five years after such allegedly unlawful act."

18 USC § 3504(b) includes in the term "unlawful act" the use of electronic surveillance instruments.

The statute, of course, applies to Federal Courts only. The validity of the statute of limitations raises the questions as to whether Congress may lawfully impose any statute of limitations on the exercise of basic rights afforded to an individual by the Constitution.

This new statute of limitations tends to erode Fourth Amendment protections. If a five-year statute may be enacted, why not a one-year or a one-day statute? This provision of the new law is still to be tested.

No such statute of limitations is prescribed in most states including New York. However, the N.Y. CPL § 710.40 prescribes the time when suppressal motions must be made.

**§ 344. The New York Rule.** The decision of *Mapp v. Ohio,* 367 US 643, which extended the exclusionary rule to the states by virtue of the Fourth and Fourteenth Amendments, did not disturb the rule laid down in *Weeks* or *Gouled.* Nor did *Mapp* deprive the states of the power to prescribe procedural requirements with respect to preserving the question of alleged violations of Fourth Amendment rights. *People v. Friola,* 11 NY2d 157, 227 NYS2d 423, 182 NE2d 100. By enacting the Criminal Procedure Law Article 710, New York has adopted the federal practice as set forth in Fed R Crim P 41(e).

Article 710, by § 710.20, authorizes an omnibus motion by an aggrieved person to suppress illegally obtained evidence.

Where there is an issue of voluntariness of defendant's admission or confession before the court, failure to move before trial to suppress is not deemed a waiver. That issue may still be raised during trial. CPL § 710.70(3). Thus, despite a determination by the court that the statements attributed to the defendant were made voluntarily, that question must nevertheless be submitted to the jury for its final determination under the new statute. CPL §§ 60.45, 710.70(3); *Jackson v. Denno,* 378 US 368; *People v. Huntley,* 15 NY2d 72, 255 NYS2d 838, 204 NE2d 179. *Cf. Lego v. Twomey,* 30 L Ed2d 618, 92 SC 619.

Whenever the people intend to offer at a trial evidence of a statement made to a public servant, which, if involuntarily made, would render it suppressable on motion under CPL § 710.20, notice must be served upon the defendant specifying the particular evidence. CPL § 710.30(1). The federal rule is the same. *Reed v. Follette,* 268 F Supp 936; *Rogers v. Warden,* 381 F2d 209.

In violation and misdemeanor cases, pretrial suppression motions must be heard during trial if the People so request. CPL § 710.40(3). An intermediate appellate court, regardless of objections or exceptions, may reverse in the interest of justice, where illegal evidence was received and without that evidence, the judgment of conviction was against the weight of the evidence. *People v. West,* 12 NY2d 1090, 240 NYS2d 159, 190 NE2d 532.

Generally, the motion to suppress must be made in the court having trial jurisdiction of the offense or violation.

The decision in *People v. Gatti,* 16 NY2d 251, 265 NYS2d 641, 212 NE2d 882, has in effect been codified in CPL § 710.50. The statute provides: (a) that if an indictment is pending in a superior court, or if the defendant has been held by a local criminal court for action of a grand jury, the motion must be made in the superior court; (b) if an undetermined felony complaint is pending in a local criminal court, the motion must be made in the superior court which would have jurisdiction of the offense charged, were an indictment to be found; (c) if an information, misdemeanor or traffic infraction is pending in a local criminal court, the motion must be made in that court.

§ 345. **The Purpose of a Suppression Hearing.** The purpose of a suppression hearing is not to determine guilt or innocence but to determine whether the police had lawful cause to take the action leading to the arrest and seizure. *Brinegar v. U.S.,* 338 US 160; *People v. Zimbardo,* 21 NY2d 15, 286 NYS2d 237, 233 NE2d 263; *People v. Coffey,* 12 NY2d 443, 240 NYS2d 721, 191 NE2d 263; *People v. Merola,* 30 AD2d 963.

The basic principle of the criminal law that the People must establish the guilt of a defendant beyond a reasonable doubt as to every element of the crime charged, (*People v. Schryver,* 42 NY 1; *People ex rel Bushnell v. Midland Terrace,* 45 NYS2d 642; *People v. Winig,* 7 Misc2d 803, 163 NYS2d 995; *U.S. v. Secondino,* 347 F2d 725), does not obtain on motions to suppress.

§ 346. **Burden of Proof.** The burden of proof at a hearing on a motion to suppress must not be confused with the burden of proof required in making the motion itself. As to the motion, there is a presumption of regularity of the conduct of the government's officers. Where the government has filed a memorandum in opposition to the defendant's motion and indicated its intention to adduce evidence to contradict some of the material allegations in the motion papers, the burden is then on the defendant to make a prima facie showing in support of the motion. Defendant's supporting affidavit may be insufficient to cast upon the government the burden of going forward. *U.S. v. Okawa,* 26 FRD 384, citing *U.S. v. Warrington,* 17 FRD 25.

Under the Federal practice, it would seem that the defendant is required in his moving papers to come forward with facts that create an issue. A mere general denial is insufficient. As stated above, the reason for the rule is based on the theory that the police are presumed to have acted lawfully. *U.S. v. Warrington,* 17 FRD 25; *Eaker v. U.S.,* 76 F2d 267; *U.S. v. Vatune,* 292 F 497.

A motion to suppress requires a supporting affidavit by one who has personal knowledge of the facts. Affidavits based upon information and belief may be submitted, providing the sources of knowledge and the basis of belief are stated. *People v. Vasquez,* 50 Misc2d 12, 269 NYS2d 229; *People v. Leonard,* 33 AD2d 1010, 308 NYS2d 77; N.Y. CPL § 710.60(1).

There are three elements of proof required.

(1) Defendant must establish that he is a "person aggrieved" and has standing to make the motion. *Ker v. California,* 374 US 23; *Jones v. U.S.,* 362 US 257; *U.S. v. Friedman,* 166 F Supp 786; *U.S. v. Nirenberg,* 19 FRD 421; *Brandon v. U.S.,* 270 F2d 311; *People v. Smith,* 35 Misc2d 533, 230 NYS2d 894; *Wilson v. U.S.,* 218 F2d 754.

(2) The evidence obtained must have been by an unlawful search and seizure. *Nardone v. U.S.,* 308 US 338; *White v. U.S.,* 194 F2d 215; *U.S. v. Lustig,* 163 F2d 85; *U.S. v. Lipshitz,* 132 F Supp 519; *cf. Wilson v. U.S.,* 221 US 361.

(3) If a search warrant is attacked, defendant must show absence of probable cause for its issuance. *Batten v. U.S.,* 188 F2d 75; *U.S. v. Rellie,* 39 F Supp 21; *People v. Alfinito,* 16 NY2d 181.

The rules applicable to a hearing on a motion to suppress are:

(1) The People are under the necessity of going forward in the first instance with evidence to show that probable cause existed both in obtaining a search warrant (if a search warrant has issued), and in sustaining the legality of a search made without a warrant as incident to an arrest. *People v. Malinsky,* 204 NE2d 188, 15 NY2d 86, 91, fn. 2 and cases cited. (2) Thereafter the burden devolves upon the defendant to show by a preponderance of the credible evidence, the absence of probable cause. *People v. Whitehurst,* 254 NE2d 905, 25 NY2d 389, 391; *People v. Baldwin,* 250 NE2d 62, 25 NY2d

66, 71 (dissenting opinion); *People v. Merola,* 30 AD2d 963, 964.

It is error to place the onus of showing the legality of the search on the People. *People v. Merola,* 30 AD2d 963. The sole exception to the rule requiring the defendant to establish the illegality of the search and seizure is found in those cases where it is contended that the search was made on consent. In such an instance, the burden is on the People, *Channel v. U.S.,* 285 F2d 217; *U.S. v. Rutheiser,* 203 F Supp 891, and the burden rests heavily upon the People to establish the waiver of a constitutional right. *Bumper v. North Carolina,* 391 US 543; *People v. Whitehurst,* 25 NY2d 389, 254 NE2d 905.

Respecting searches under a warrant, it would seem that the People would be required at the hearing to introduce the warrant and the supporting affidavits to establish, prima facie, probable cause. The burden of going forward to establish the illegality of the warrant then devolves upon the person attacking the warrant. Moreover, should any fair doubt arise from the testimony taken at the hearing to suppress based on the attack on the warrant, the doubt should be resolved in favor of sustaining the warrant. *People v. Alfinito,* 16 NY2d 181, 186, 211 NE2d 644; *People v. Rogers,* 15 NY2d 422, 208 NE2d 168; *U.S. v. Ventresca,* 380 US 102.

The federal courts have likewise held that the burden is on the defendant who seeks to suppress evidence obtained under a regularly issued warrant, to show want of probable cause. *Batten v. U.S.,* 188 F2d 75; *U.S. v. Rellie,* 39 F Supp 21; *Chin Kay v. U.S.,* 311 F2d 317; *Irby v. U.S.,* 314 F2d 251, cert. den. 374 US 842; *U.S. v. Nagle,* 34 F2d 952.

This theory, that the moving party, *i.e.,* the defendant, has the burden of sustaining his position, on a motion to suppress has resulted in federal decisions to the same effect. *Wilson v. U.S.,* 218 F2d 754; *U.S. v. Lipshitz,* 132 F Supp 519; *Addison v. U.S.,* 317 F2d 808, cert. den. 376 US 905, stay den. 376 US 936, rehrg den. 376 US 966; *U.S. v. Poppitt,* 227 F Supp 73; *U.S. v. Thomas,* 216 F Supp 942; *Hardin v. U.S.,* 324 F2d 553.

A search warrant is not a *sine qua non* to an incident search where a lawful arrest has been made. However, if the defendant contends that the Government had ample opportunity to obtain a search warrant, the burden of establishing that fact is on the defendant, as well as the necessity for the warrant. *Carrol v. U.S.*, 267 US 132.

Where a search was conducted under a search warrant, the burden of proving want of probable cause for its issuance is on the defendant. In a doubtful or marginal case, a search under a warrant may be sustained, where, without one, it would fall. *U.S. v. Ventresca,* 380 US 102.

Where defendant produces substantial evidence that letters or other documents have been illegally seized, the burden then shifts to the Government to demonstrate that the evidence it offers has an independent origin similar to wiretap cases. *U.S. v. Paroutian,* 299 F2d 486.

Where a defendant moves to suppress, the burden to show a prima facie issue of unlawful search and seizure is his, the movant's. *Nardone v. U.S.*, 308 US 338.

Hearsay evidence is admissible on the issue of probable cause. *Draper v. United States,* 358 US 307; *People v. Coffey,* 12 NY2d 443, 191 NE2d 263; *People v. Helmus,* 50 Misc2d 47, 48–49, 269 NYS2d 613; CPL § 710.60(4).

**§ 347. Standing to Move to Suppress: Aggrieved Person.** Under the so-called "standing" cases, the federal courts are in agreement that the burden of proof is on the movant to establish that he is a person "aggrieved" within the purview of the Fourth Amendment and Rule 41(e), *i.e.*, that his right of privacy has been invaded. *Jones v. U.S.*, 362 US 257; *Brandon v. U.S.*, 270 F2d 311, cert. den. 362 US 943; *Murray v. U.S.*, 333 F2d 409; *U.S. v. Culver,* 224 F Supp 419; *Schnitzer v. U.S.*, 77 F2d 233.

The rule does not change where the items illegally seized from a third party are not items of contraband. *U.S. v. Granello,* 243 F Supp 325, affd 365 F2d 990.

There is a trend to broaden the rule as to who may challenge the legality of a search. The Fourth Amendment is applicable to one's place of business. *U.S. ex rel DeForte v. Mancusi,* 379 F2d 897, affd sub nom *Mancusi v. DeForte,* 392 US 364; *cf. U.S. v. Bozza,* 365 F2d 206.

The person aggrieved by an unlawful search and seizure

includes anyone legitimately on the premises where a search occurs. This means that a guest or invitee has "standing" to move to suppress if he is the victim of the search and seizure. That is to say, that if the search was directed against him as distinguished from one who claims prejudice only through the use of evidence gathered as a consequence of a search and seizure directed at someone else, he has "standing" under the federal rule to move to suppress.

Where the property seized constitutes contraband (*e.g.*, narcotics) which it is unlawful to possess, a person has no *legal* property right therein. For the purpose of the motion to exclude, however, the contraband must nevertheless be considered private property. Accordingly, the defendant need not assert a proprietary interest in the articles seized in order to move for its exclusion. *Jones v. U.S.*, 362 US 257; *U.S. v. Jeffers,* 342 US 48; *McDonald v. U.S.*, 335 US 451; *People v. Ibarra,* 386 P2d 487, 490–491.

An outline of the facts in some of these cases will illustrate the "standing" rule.

In *Jeffers, supra,* narcotics were found in a hotel room occupied by Jeffers' aunts who permitted him to use the room ignorant of the fact that he stored narcotics there. The narcotics were discovered as a result of an unlawful search and seizure of the hotel room in which no one was present at the time. Jeffers claimed the narcotics were his when he was arrested on the day following the search. The Government contended that it was not Jeffers' privacy that had been invaded, but if there was any invasion of privacy, it was his aunts'. Therefore, they argued that Jeffers had no standing to move to suppress and the narcotics seized were admissible in evidence against him.

The Court rejected the contention that the seizure and the search were two distinct acts. On the contrary, they were bound together and were not isolable (*Jeffers* at p. 52). As contraband, the narcotics were not Jeffers' legal private property and need not be returned to him. Nevertheless, they were deemed private property within the ambit of the motion to exclude.

In *McDonald, supra,* there was a gambling conviction of McDonald and his house guest. Evidence was illegally seized from McDonald. The Court held that since the evidence was unlawfully seized from McDonald, it could not be used against his guest. The majority did not go further than this, but Mr. Justice Jackson, joined by Mr. Justice Frankfurter, in a concurring opinion stated "even a guest may expect the shelter of the rooftree he is under against criminal intrusion." (*McDonald* at p. 461).

In *Jones, supra,* which is still considered the leading "standing" case, the status of a guest in the search and seizure area was again before the Court. Jones was a guest in an apartment when an unlawful search disclosed narcotics, possession of which is a crime. Although he denied any connection with the narcotics, the Court, nevertheless, held that the exclusionary rule protected him also since Federal Rule of Criminal Procedure 41(e), as redefined, covered "anyone legitimately on the premises where a search occurs." Jones, it was held, was "a person aggrieved by an unlawful search and seizure" under 41(e) and thus had standing to move to suppress. *Cf.: Walder v. U.S.,* 347 US 62; *People v. Rawluck,* 14 NY2d 609, 198 NE2d 266.

Conversely, in *U.S. v. Humphrey,* 409 F2d 1005, the court held that the illegal search of the driver of an automobile gave his passenger no standing to move to suppress contraband found on the passenger who was arrested and searched, based on probable cause. Originally the driver had been stopped for a traffic violation and his search was held unlawful. The court reiterated the rule that suppression can only be urged by those whose rights were violated by the search itself and "not by those who are aggrieved solely by the introduction of damaging evidence," citing *Alderman v. U.S.,* 394 US 165.

In *Mancusi v. DeForte,* 379 F2d 897, affd 392 US 364, following refusal of certain union officials to obey a subpoena duces tecum, the union office was searched unlawfully. (A subpoena duces tecum does not qualify as a valid search warrant. *Mancusi v. DeForte, supra; People v. DeGrandis,* 12 NY2d 812, 187 NE2d 130.) The petitioner was a union official who had a desk in the union office, which was also occupied by other union officials. Having permission from the owner to maintain a desk in the office, he had "standing" to object to an unauthorized search. He too was protected from an unreasonable search and seizure as to evidence thus seized and sought to be used against him in a conspiracy charge. He had a right to be secure in his home, office and any part thereof that was used by him by virtue of the Fourth Amendment.

To recapitulate, in *U.S. v. Jeffers, supra,* an unlawful search was made of an apartment which Jeffers had permission to use. But no one was present at the time of the search.

In *Jones v. U.S., supra,* Jones also had permission to use the apartment in question which was unlawfully searched while he was a guest there.

In *People v. Cefaro,* 21 NY2d 252, 234 NE2d 423, the New York court adopted the rule that a stranger has no standing to assert that evidence in another's house or premises has been seized unlawfully against the owner or tenant of the premises. Here if the defendant had been present in the apartment when the search was made and the evidence sought to be suppressed was taken from the possession of one of the defendants, he might well have had standing to apply to have its use suppressed in support of criminal charges against him.

Standing to make the motion to suppress is a right accorded to the victim of the alleged unlawful search and seizure, or one sought to be charged with the evidence seized who was present in the premises at the time of the execution of the unlawful search and seizure. *Jones v. U.S.,* 362 US 257, 261; *People v. Swiontuk,* 20 NY2d 840, 231 NE2d 773; *People v. DeVivo,* 23 AD2d 753, 258 NYS2d 1013; *cf. People v. McDonnell,* 18 NY2d 509, 223 NE2d 785.

In *Cefaro, supra,* a stolen camera was found in the apartment of one Barth as a result of an unlawful search and seizure. Cefaro was charged with a burglary and it was contended that the camera taken from Barth's apartment was one of the fruits of the burglary. Cefaro moved to suppress the use of the camera in the case against him (the burglary charge) on the ground that it was unlawfully seized from Barth. This the court declined to do, stating: "The camera could not, of course, have been utilized as evidence against Barth on a charge of receiving stolen property. That is a different matter, however, from using it as evidence in support of the burglary and larceny charges against Cefaro,

Josephs and Russo [co-defendants]. It was not found in their apartments, and they were not persons aggrieved by the search and seizure in somebody else's premises. . . . If Cefaro, Josephs or Russo had been present in Barth's apartment when the search was made and the camera taken from the possession of one of them, he might well have standing to apply to have its use suppressed in support of the criminal charges against him." *Cefaro,* 21 NY2d at p. 257.

It would, therefore, also follow that a defendant would have no standing to move to suppress evidence offered as against him, which had been unlawfully seized from the person of a third party.

The search of an apartment without a warrant where defendant slept occasionally, but had his home elsewhere, and who was not in the apartment at the time of the search, and whose right to privacy was not invaded by the search, was held to be legal. In effect, the court held that this defendant was not an "aggrieved" person. *Murray v. U.S.,* 333 F2d 409.

Thus, it can be concluded that the "standing" rule has been modified in search and seizure cases to include those persons who are lawfully on the premises at the time of the unlawful search, as well as those who used the premises lawfully, such as guests and invitees, and against whom the items seized by an unlawful search are sought to be used in a criminal prosecution.

Defendants charged with failing to file income tax returns did not have standing to avail themselves of any illegality in government's seizure of a third party's records. There, the court in affirming stated:

"We need not reiterate what we have recently said as to standing in United States v. Bozza, 365 F.2d 206, 222–223 (2 Cir 1966), or repeat the citation of the authorities there assembled. Granello and Levine have not shown that any of the papers held to have been unlawfully seized from Birrell were theirs; he stood toward them not as a partner but as a buyer." *U.S. v. Granello,* 243 F Supp 325, affd 365 F2d 990.

Defendant, who was in New York at the time of the search of the Florida apartment of a woman to whom defendant allegedly mailed narcotics, who made no allegation that he owned, rented, used, lived in or controlled the apartment, had no standing to raise the issue of legality of a search. *U.S. v. Liguori,* 373 F2d 304.

Illinois defendants charged with thefts and burglary have sufficient "possessory interest" in the items involved to move for suppression of unlawfully seized evidence if "possession provides basis on which their convictions could be obtained and enhanced." *People v. DeFilippis,* 34 Ill2d 129, 214 NE2d 897.

In *People v. Ibarra,* 386 P2d 487, 490–491, the court held that a defendant may challenge the legality of a search even though he denies that the contraband was taken from him and even though he asserts no proprietary interest in the premises that were entered. *See also: Jones v. U.S.,* 362 US 257; *U.S. v. Jeffers,* 342 US 48.

> "In order to qualify as a 'person aggrieved by an unlawful search and seizure,' one must have been the victim of a search and seizure, one against whom the search was directed, as distinguished from one who claims prejudice only through the use of evidence gathered as a consequence of a search or seizure directed at someone else." *Jones v. U.S.,* 362 US 257, 261. The person making the suppressal motion must allege and prove "that he, himself, was the victim of an invasion of privacy." *Jones* at p. 261.

Another test for "aggrieved person" is whether he is entitled to a restoration of the property sought to be suppressed in the event the motion is granted. *Cf. People v. Rawluck,* 14 NY2d 609, 198 NE2d 266.

§ 348. **The New Jersey Rule.** The owner of a barber shop was held to have standing to move to suppress evidence seized from a third party in the barber shop. A fruitless search of the barber shop also was conducted under an invalid warrant on the theory that the search was aimed at the owner. It was his privacy which was invaded and his barber shop that was designated in the warrant. As the unlawful search took place in premises in which the defendant had proprietary, possessory or participatory interest, he was held to have standing to move to suppress. The court was apparently reluctant to disavow the federal "standing to suppress" rule enunciated in *Jones v. U.S.,* 362 US 257, which limits the right to move to suppress to those persons whose privacy was invaded. This may account for what appears to be a strained interpretation of the factual situation. The same result could have been obtained had the court followed the New York rule laid down in *People v. Coffey,* 12 NY2d 443, 191 NE2d 263, but now disavowed by *People v. Cefaro, supra,* and *People v. Swiontuk,* 20 NY2d 840, 231 NE2d 773, which permits a defendant to move to suppress in unlawful "third party" search and seizure cases, or if the court had decided the case under the *Wong Sun* rule (*Wong Sun v. U.S.,* 371 US 471) which precludes the government from exploiting a primary illegal act committed by its agents, *i.e.,* "the fruits of official illegality." *State v. LaDuca,* 89 NJ Super 159, 214 A2d 423.

**§ 349. The California Rule.** California follows a rule slightly different from New York's. When the question of legality of an arrest or search and seizure is raised, either at the preliminary hearing or at the trial, the defendant establishes a prima facie case when he establishes that an arrest was made without a warrant, or that private premises were entered or searched without a warrant. If he shows any one of these elements, California holds that the burden then devolves on the People to show proper justification. If there is no evidence that the arrest was made without a warrant, or that private premises were entered or searched without a warrant, then the entry is presumed to be lawful. *People v. Boyles,* 45 Cal2d 652, 290 P2d 535; *People v. Gorg,* 45 Cal2d 776, 291 P2d 469; *People v. Jennings,* 142 Cal App2d 160, 298 P2d 56; *People v. Mace,* 38 Misc2d 533, 237 NYS2d 769.

**§ 350. Preserving Fourth Amendment Rights.** Where prior to *Mapp,* a conviction was obtained based on unlawfully seized evidence, appellate courts will review the convictions in the light of *Mapp,* where appeals from those convictions are still before the appellate courts. *People v. Stokes,* 15 NY2d 534, 202 NE2d 567; *People v. Yarmosh,* 11 NY2d 397, 184 NE2d 165; *People v. Britton,* 26 AD2d 586.

The constitutional issue involved will be deemed to have been preserved for appellate review, if that issue was raised, somehow, during the trial, even though no specific objection on constitutional grounds had been made. *People v. Stokes, supra; People v. Wade,* 12 NY2d 61, 187 NE2d 111; *People v. O'Neill,* 11 NY2d 148, 182 NE2d 95; *People v. Friola,* 11 NY2d 157, 182 NE2d 100; *People v. Yarmosh, supra.*

Such a situation existed in *People v. Ostolaza,* 19 AD2d 871, where the appeal was held in abeyance pending the determination by the trial court whether the search and seizure were incidental to a lawful arrest. This was authorized even though the defendant had not objected to the introduction of the fruits of the search and seizure into evidence during the trial but where "he did preserve his right to review of the constitutional issue on appeal by cross-examining the police officers extensively as to the absence of a search warrant, the manner of entry into the room where the contraband was first found, the extent of the search, the role played by an informer prior to the arrest and other related circumstances upon the legality of the search, seizure and arrest (*People v. O'Neill,* 11 N.Y.2d 148; *People v. Friola,* 11 N.Y.2d 157)."

**§ 351. Waiver of Motion to Suppress.** Unless a defendant has moved to suppress either before or during trial, the constitutional issue has not been preserved and he will have been deemed to have waived his rights to move. *People v. Peterson,* 25 AD2d 437, 266 NYS2d 884.

**§ 351.01. Waiver by Plea of Guilty.** A defendant who knowingly and voluntarily pleads guilty waives his right to move to suppress. After entering such a plea he may not thereafter attack the judgment of conviction by *coram nobis* or other post-conviction remedy on the ground that he had a valid constitutional basis for making a motion to suppress or to exclude certain evidence. *People v. La Barth,* 19 NY2d 649, 225 NE2d 213; *People v. Dash,* 16 NY2d 493, 208 NE2d 171; *People v. Nicholson,* 11 NY2d 1067, 184 NE2d 190.

**§ 351.02. Presence of Defendant at the Suppression Hearing: Waiver.** A defendant has a constitutional and statutory right to be present at all stages of the proceedings. The right "may be waived in a non-capital case by an absent defendant whose counsel voluntarily proceeds without him in the apparent belief that his absence will not prejudice his position or his defense." *People v. Colombani,* 22 AD2d 956, affd 16 NY2d 1055, 213 NE2d 460.

A defendant may thus voluntarily waive his right to be present at a hearing held on a motion to suppress. This waiver does not constitute a denial of due process. *People v. Brighenti,* 22 AD2d 956, affd 16 NY2d 753, 209 NE2d 733; *People v. Colombani, supra.*

In *People v. Anderson,* 16 NY2d 282, the court held that the statutory hearing on a motion to suppress is part of the "trial," even though held prior to trial. Although the defendant does not have the right to be present at the hearing of a motion to decide a pure question of law, he does have an absolute right to be present at the suppression hearing, since, for the purposes of the due process requirement, the suppression hearing is deemed a part of the "trial." The word "trial," at which a defendant charged with a felony has a right to be present, includes an examination of the case by the court in all stages where questions of fact are to be determined. Thus, the unexplained absence of a defendant from the hearing on his motion to suppress required reversal of his conviction. It also required the reversal of the conviction of his codefendant where the evidence, not suppressed, might have been improperly before the jury to the prejudice of the codefendant.

A request to exclude the public from a suppression hearing, made by the defendant, may be granted, if prejudice to a fair trial may be reasonably anticipated by reason of publication of the testimony and findings adduced at the hearing.

However, a request by defendant to exclude the press alone, is not a request for a closed hearing.

Any prejudice resulting from publication of the trial court's determination on the ground of prejudice would permit defendant to move for a change of venue. *People v. Higgins,* 28 AD2d 1016. *See also: Stroble v. California,* 343 US 181; *People v. Fein,* 18 NY2d 162, 219 NE2d 274; *cf. People v. Pratt,* 27 AD2d 199.

**§ 352. Habeas Corpus and Coram Nobis.** By a sharply divided court, the New York Court of Appeals has held that where defendant was convicted, and while appeal was pending, the United States Supreme Court rendered its decision in *Mapp v. Ohio* 367 US 643, and thereafter judgment of conviction was affirmed by the Court of Appeals and by the United States Supreme Court, which stated that constitutional questions under *Mapp* were not presented by the record with sufficient clarity, writ of error coram nobis was not thereafter available to the defendant who claimed that evidence against him was obtained by unlawful searches and seizures. *People v. Mishkin,* 20 NY2d 716, 229 NE2d 454; *cf.: People v. Friola,* 11 NY2d 157, 182 NE2d 100; *People v. Stokes,* 15 NY2d 534, 202 NE2d 567.

However, defendant's claim that evidence obtained by an illegal search and seizure was used against him could not serve as a basis for coram nobis relief, where the contention was raised on appeal from the judgment of conviction and was rejected by the Appellate Division as being without merit. *People v. Speilman,* 26 AD2d 574, 271 NYS2d 441.

If a defendant was induced to refrain from moving to suppress certain evidence and to plead guilty because of fraud and perjury alleged to have been committed by a police officer, he was held entitled to coram nobis relief to establish that contention. In that case, the officer swore that he had searched defendant's premises pursuant to a search warrant and found narcotics. Defendant was indicted and pleaded guilty. Another attorney, subsequently assigned to represent the defendant, produced evidence that no search warrant had been issued. Although the district attorney had no knowledge of the perjury, the court granted the coram nobis application. *People v. Calero,* 23 AD2d 698, 258 NYS2d 207; *cf. People v. Malinsky,* 15 NY2d 86, 204 NE2d 188.

The federal courts had adopted a rule that failure to object at a criminal trial did not preclude raising the issue of illegal search and seizure at subsequent post-conviction proceedings. However, it is now the federal rule that a state prisoner who seeks federal habeas corpus relief on the ground that he was the victim of an unlawful search and seizure must first exhaust his remedies in the state courts (including appellate courts) before his petition in the federal courts will be entertained. *Reed v. Follette,* 268 F Supp 936.

The Second Circuit Court of Appeals has ruled that such review may also be had by federal habeas corpus, but the court should be "'wary of blindly applying this doctrine to every case involving such a plea'." *Rogers v. Warden,* 381 F2d 209.

§ 353. **Consent to Suppress Based on Error of Law.** Where the District Attorney has consented to a motion to suppress on a mistaken view of the law, the court granting the motion may, on motion by the district attorney, vacate its previous order of suppression, and decide the motion *de novo,* even during trial. Resulting prejudice to the defendant would entitle him to a mistrial, but can not deter the court from rehearing the suppression motion.

In *People v. Cefaro,* 45 Misc2d 990, 991–992, affd 28 AD2d 694, 21 NY2d 252, after some testimony had been taken before trial on a motion to suppress, the district attorney consented to an order of suppression in the mistaken belief that the defendant had "standing" to make the motion. During trial, before a judge other than the one who granted the motion, the district attorney asked to be relieved of his consent and for a denial of the defendant's motion to suppress. Both motions were granted by the judge who had heard the original suppression motion, while the trial was held in suspense.

§ 354. **Finding of Facts Discretionary.** In deciding a motion to suppress, the court hearing the motion may state the facts upon which it relies, in either granting or denying the motion. *People v. Lombardi,* 18 AD2d 177, affd 13 NY2d 1014; *People v. Lopez,* 19 AD2d 809, 243 NYS2d 333.

The rule in *Lombardi* and *Lopez* that appears to require a judge to state his findings of fact is explained in *People v. Alfinito,* 16 NY2d 181, 211 NE2d 644. In that case, the officer who had applied for a search warrant stated, in his supporting affidavit, among other things, that on two separate dates he had seen the defendant in his apartment. At the hearing on the motion to suppress, the officer again swore to the same facts. However, the defendant's wife and another testified that the defendant was not at the apartment at any of the times testified to by the police officer. In granting defendant's motion to suppress, the trial court made no specific findings of fact. The Court of Appeals held:

> "[T]here is no strict rule of law that a decision on such a motion must always be accompanied by express findings. In many instances such as the present one, the issue is so narrow that granting or denying the motion sufficiently implies the findings. Of course, in any appropriate situation, the appellate court may remit for additional findings, and that is the meaning of *People v. Lombardi,* 18 A.D. 2d 177, affd. 13 N.Y.2d 1014, and *People v. Lopez,* 19 A.D. 2d 809." 16 NY2d at 186.

Thus, where the issues on the hearing are so narrow that findings are implicit in the court's decision, separate findings of fact are not required. In *People v. Zimbardo,* 21 NY2d 15, 233 NE2d 263, the court said that in the absence of an opinion, the order suppressing evidence, issued after a hearing on a motion to suppress, must be deemed to be based either on lack of probable cause, or, if the facts testified to by the officer would constitute probable cause if credible, that the hearing judge did not, in fact, think the officer was telling the truth.

§ 355. **Change of Venue.** Publication in the press of the basis for denying a defendant's motion to suppress may require a change of venue. "The release and publication of the decision of . . . county court denying defendant's motion to suppress (1) certain statements alleged to have been made by him and (2) alleged evidentiary leads [articles of clothing] obtained at the time of such questioning may well have prejudiced defendant's right to a fair trial in the county of venue. Therein the court made detailed findings in favor of the People and against the defendant upon testimony of witnesses called by the respective parties that presented sharp factual issues. It would have been preferable to follow the procedure outlined in *People v. LaBelle,* 44 Misc2d 324, 327, 330, 253 NYS2d 897, 901, 903–904." *People v. Marturano,* 24 AD2d 733, 263 NYS2d 469, 470.

**§ 356. Appeal of Suppression Order.** An order denying a motion to suppress is an intermediate order, and no separate appeal lies from an order of denial. It may be reviewed on appeal from the judgment of conviction. *People v. Gibbs,* 21 AD2d 980; *People v. Merz,* 20 AD2d 918, 249 NYS2d 475; CPL § 710.70(2).

If defendant's motion to suppress is denied, the order denying the motion may be reviewed on appeal from the judgment of conviction notwithstanding the fact that such conviction is predicated upon a plea of guilty. *U.S. ex rel Molloy v. Follette,* 391 F2d 231, cert. den. 391 US 917; *People v. Winslow,* 31 AD2d 561, 294 NYS2d 451; CPL § 710.70(2).

Where defendant pleaded guilty to one count in an indictment to cover all counts and a judgment of conviction was entered only on the count to which he pleaded, there was no basis to review the order denying the motion to suppress. *People v. Koposesky,* 25 AD2d 777.

**§ 357. Federal Rule: Appeals by the Government.** The right of the Government to appeal from the district courts directly to the United States Supreme Court, in criminal cases, is authorized by 18 USC § 3731. As to cases involving orders granting suppression, the statute gives the Government the right to appeal from an order, granting a motion for return of seized property or a motion to suppress evidence, made before trial of a person charged with a violation of any law of the United States, if the United States attorney certifies to the judge who granted such motion that the appeal is not taken for the purpose of delay and that the evidence is substantial proof of the charge pending against the defendant.

Section 3731 does not authorize piecemeal appeals, *i.e.,* appeals from interlocutory orders. The appeals authorized are only those based on a final order or disposition of the case other than an acquittal. *Sisson v. U.S.,* 399 US 267, 299.

The New York rule, CPL § 450.20(8), and the federal rule, 18 USC § 3731, are similar.

**§ 358. Where Motion Is Granted: Effect on Indictment.** When a motion to suppress evidence has been granted, that does not mean that the indictment must ipso facto be dismissed.

Where, for example, a defendant has been indicted for burglary, suppression of the alleged fruits of the crime does not preclude the People from attempting to establish its commission by circumstantial evidence. Where an indictment has been secured in such a case, based on circumstantial evidence, the indictment must be dismissed unless the evidence presented to the grand jury points to the defendant's guilt, *i.e.*, that all the established circumstances are consistent with guilt and inconsistent with innocence. *People v. Bearden,* 290 NY 478; *People v. Gogarty,* 5 AD2d 413, 172 NYS2d 734.

An indictment based upon circumstantial evidence that does not possess the degree of certitude which the law requires as to those facts bearing upon the accused's guilt must be dismissed. *People v. Lewis,* 275 NY 33.

**§ 359. Evidence Considered at Suppression Hearing.** A decision on a suppression motion must be based solely on testimony at the hearing and an appeal court may not consider other evidence adduced at the trial held later. *See: People v. Matera,* 45 Misc2d 864, 258 NYS2d 2.

Where a pretrial motion to suppress has been denied and the facts disclose that the contraband evidence had been the subject of a "seizure" (*i.e.,* abandoned or lost property as distinguished from a "search and seizure") the question is no longer a constitutional one, but an evidentiary one. It is for the trial court to determine its admissibility.

**§ 360. Admissibility of Defendant's Suppression Hearing Testimony at His Trial.** Some courts have permitted evidence of a defendant's testimony on his suppression motion to be put in evidence at his trial on the ground that it was voluntary and relevant to the issues.

However, the United States Supreme Court has now held that such a rule is likely to inhibit a defendant from asserting his Fourth Amendment rights as to illegally seized evidence and that, by his testimony upon the motion, a defendant should not be required in legal effect to waive his Fifth Amendment privilege against self-incrimination. In other words, a defendant should not be compelled to waive one constitutional right (Fifth Amendment) in order to exercise another constitutional right (Fourth Amendment).

Accordingly, the Court held that the defendant's testimony, given by him on his suppressal motion hearing, is inadmissible against him at the trial on the issue of guilt unless he made no objection. It would seem, therefore, that his testimony given at the suppression hearing would not be admissible against him as part of the People's case. *Simmons v. U.S.,* 390 US 377. Apparently, as in *People v. Kulis,* 18 NY2d 318, 221 NE2d 541, it can be used to attack his credibility on cross-examination.

# TABLE OF CASES

References are to sections

## TABLE OF CASES

**References are to sections**

References are to sections



—D—

References are to sections

# TABLE OF CASES

References are to sections

References are to sections

References are to sections

# TABLE OF CASES

**References are to sections**

References are to sections

References are to sections

# TABLE OF CASES

**References are to sections**

References are to sections

References are to sections

## TABLE OF CASES

References are to sections

References are to sections

## TABLE OF CASES

References are to sections

References are to sections

References are to sections



—Q—



—R—

References are to sections

References are to sections

References are to sections

## TABLE OF CASES

References are to sections

References are to sections

# TABLE OF CASES

**References are to sections**

References are to sections

References are to sections

# GENERAL INDEX

References are to sections

References are to sections

# GENERAL INDEX

References are to sections



—B—

References are to sections

References are to sections

References are to sections

## GENERAL INDEX

**References are to sections**

References are to sections

References are to sections

# GENERAL INDEX

References are to sections